AF876618

PUSHING THE BOUNDARIES: NEW FRONTIERS IN CONFLICT RESOLUTION AND COLLABORATION

RESEARCH IN SOCIAL MOVEMENTS, CONFLICTS AND CHANGE

Series Editors: Patrick G. Coy and Isidor Wallimann

Recent Volumes:

Volume 22:	Edited by Patrick G. Coy
Volume 23:	Political Opportunities, Social Movements and Democratization, Edited by Patrick G. Coy
Volume 24:	Consensus Decision Making, Northern Ireland and Indigenous Movements, Edited by Patrick G. Coy
Volume 25:	Authority in Contention, Edited by Daniel J. Myers and Daniel M. Cress
Volume 26:	Edited by Patrick G. Coy
Volume 27:	Edited by Patrick G. Coy
Volume 28:	Edited by Patrick G. Coy

RESEARCH IN SOCIAL MOVEMENTS, CONFLICTS AND CHANGE VOLUME 29

PUSHING THE BOUNDARIES: NEW FRONTIERS IN CONFLICT RESOLUTION AND COLLABORATION

EDITED BY

RACHEL FLEISHMAN

Program on the Analysis and Resolution of Conflicts
Syracuse University, Syracuse, NY, USA

CATHERINE GERARD

Program on the Analysis and Resolution of Conflicts
Syracuse University, Syracuse, NY, USA

ROSEMARY O'LEARY

Program on the Analysis and Resolution of Conflicts
Syracuse University, Syracuse, NY, USA

Emerald

JAI

United Kingdom – North America – Japan
India – Malaysia – China

JAI Press is an imprint of Emerald Group Publishing Limited
Howard House, Wagon Lane, Bingley BD16 1WA, UK

First edition 2008

Copyright © 2008 Emerald Group Publishing Limited

Reprints and permission service
Contact: booksandseries@emeraldinsight.com

No part of this book may be reproduced, stored in a retrieval system, transmitted in any form or by any means electronic, mechanical, photocopying, recording or otherwise without either the prior written permission of the publisher or a licence permitting restricted copying issued in the UK by The Copyright Licensing Agency and in the USA by The Copyright Clearance Center. No responsibility is accepted for the accuracy of information contained in the text, illustrations or advertisements. The opinions expressed in these chapters are not necessarily those of the Editor or the publisher.

British Library Cataloguing in Publication Data
A catalogue record for this book is available from the British Library

ISBN: 978-1-84855-290-6
ISSN: 0163-786X (Series)

ISOQAR QUALITY ASSURED ISO 9001
UKAS QUALITY MANAGEMENT 026
Certificate number 1985

Awarded in recognition of Emerald's production department's adherence to quality systems and processes when preparing scholarly journals for print

INVESTOR IN PEOPLE

CONTENTS

LIST OF CONTRIBUTORS

Thomas E. Boudreau	Department of Political Science, Maxwell School of Syracuse University, Syracuse, NY, USA
Patrick G. Coy	Center for Applied Conflict Management and Department of Political Science, Kent State University, OH, USA
Neil Funk-Unrau	Menno Simons College, University of Winnipeg, Winnipeg, Canada
Heather Getha-Taylor	Department of Political Science, University of South Carolina, Columbia, SC, USA
Bruce Hemmer	Department of Political Science, University of California, Irvine, CA, USA
Fethi Keles	Department of Anthropology, Maxwell School of Syracuse University, Syracuse, NY, USA
Darren Kew	Program in Dispute Resolution, University of Massachusetts Boston, Boston, MA, USA
Louis Kriesberg	Department of Sociology, Syracuse University, Syracuse, NY, USA
Haleigh La Chance	Center for Conflict Resolution (CCR), Salisbury University, Salisbury, MD, USA
Robert La Chance	Center for Conflict Resolution (CCR), Salisbury University, Salisbury, MD, USA
Gregory M. Maney	Department of Sociology, Hofstra University, Hempstead, NY, USA

Marie Pace	Program Officer, Center for Mediation and Conflict Resolution, U.S. Institute of Peace, Washington, DC, USA
Heather Pincock	Department of Political Science and Program on the Analysis and Resolution of Conflicts, Maxwell School of Syracuse University, Syracuse, NY, USA
Brian D. Polkinghorn	Center for Conflict Resolution (CCR), Salisbury University, Salisbury, MD, USA
Robert A. Rubinstein	Department of Anthropology, Program on the Analysis and Resolution of Conflicts, The Maxwell School of Syracuse University, Syracuse, NY, USA
Lynne M. Woehrle	Behavioral Science Department, Mount Mary College, Milwaukee, WI, USA

PREFACE

The Program on the Analysis and Resolution of Conflicts (PARC) at Syracuse University's Maxwell School of Citizenship and Public Affairs is widely and rightly regarded as a leading center in the theory and practice of conflict analysis and its resolution. In a fitting tribute to its 20th anniversary, many researchers, academics, and practitioners who once studied there returned in 2007 to present their current research and work in the field. This wonderfully edited collection of peer-reviewed papers is the welcome result, and is yet another example of the cutting-edge work that has long been associated with PARC.

It is especially fitting that some of the best of the papers presented at that conference should appear as a volume of the *Research in Social Movements, Conflicts and Change* series.

Research in Social Movements, Conflicts and Change (RSMCC) was launched by Louis Kriesberg at Syracuse University about a decade before he also founded the Program on the Analysis and Resolution of Conflicts at Syracuse. Thus, for many years PARC provided a fertile and congenial home for the RSMCC series, helping it fill a unique niche at the intersection of research on social movements and conflicts. This present collection continues that tradition in splendid style. I am not sure who is welcoming who home, but it is a grand homecoming nonetheless.

Patrick G. Coy
Series Editor

INTRODUCTION

The research articles in this volume were initially presented at a conference, entitled "Cutting Edge Theories and Recent Developments in Conflict Resolution," which celebrated the 20th anniversary of the Program on the Analysis and Resolution of Conflicts (PARC) at Syracuse University's Maxwell School of Citizenship and Public Affairs. Presenters were encouraged to submit their papers for consideration, and following a rigorous peer review and revision process, nine articles were accepted. The volume explores some of the major themes of conflict analysis, including how powerful dominant discourses can both soothe and exacerbate conflict, the roles of civic organizations in promoting peace and incubating democratic principles, the ways in which different forms of dialogue are used to heal historically dysfunctional intergroup relations, and the importance of a deeply institutional, structural understanding of ethnocentrism and racism. The authors conducted their research in several different countries – the US, Canada, Bosnia, and Northern Ireland – and used a wide range of analytical techniques including in-depth interviews, surveys, and document analysis. What holds them together is the rigorous tie they make between theory and empirical data. Some authors have built conflict theory inductively, based on their own research and/or secondary sources, while others have tested existing models with empirical data. These articles collectively make a solid contribution to theoretical development in the conflict analysis field.

In "Renegotiation of Social Relations through Public Apologies to Canadian Aboriginal Peoples," Neil Funk-Unrau analyzes public apology statements as a renegotiation of dysfunctional social relations and a potential remedy for interparty power imbalances. The author conducts a comparative analysis of public apologies by Canadian churches that seek to pave the way for a renewed relationship with Canadian Aboriginal communities. He highlights broad apologies acknowledging and expressing regret for colonial injustices, as well as apologies for specific instances of physical or sexual abuse within the residential school system. Funk-Unrau finds that the success of an apology in renegotiating a historically problematic relationship depends on the extent to which it succeeds in four tasks: creation of a mutually acceptable narrative of historic wrongs, articulation of a mutually acceptable moral norm, deliberate public acceptance of responsibility by the more powerful party, and offering of mutually acceptable amends through a process of restitution and reparation. This fascinating analysis demonstrates how the public apology statement may serve a complex dialogical function in repairing relationships between perpetrators and victims in a conflict situation.

In "Teaching through Talk? The Impact of Intergroup Dialogue on Conceptualizations of Racism." Heather Pincock presents original research on the effects of an intergroup racial dialogue on high school students in Syracuse, NY. The author investigates whether bringing students of different backgrounds together for an extended dialogue about racism will improve participants' understanding of two complex concepts: white privilege and institutional racism. After conducting in-depth interviews with participants from both urban and suburban school districts, Pincock developed a coding framework designed to assess respondents' understanding of these concepts. She finds that participants' understanding of both concepts is very limited to begin with and that most do not gain greater understanding through the dialogue. However, there is evidence that the dialogue experience sensitizes participants to previously unnoticed manifestations of racism in their communities. She finds that the main challenge participants face in understanding institutional racism is the capacity to adopt structural thinking, while their main challenge in understanding white privilege is an inability to personalize the concept. In light of the limited effectiveness of the dialogue in teaching complex concepts, Pincock urges dialogue practitioners to consider their prioritization of contact-related goals versus curricular goals.

"Bridging the Macro with the Micro in Conflict Analysis: Structural Simplification as a Heuristic Device," by Fethi Keles is a theory-building article that introduces an original theoretical concept called *structural simplification*, based on the reverse process, *structural amplification*, developed by the anthropologist Marshall Sahlins (2005). Structural simplification is the process by which macropolitical discourses are reconfigured at the local, village level. Keles applies this concept to the ethnonationalist, exclusivist macropolitical discourse prevalent in Bosnia during the 1992–1995 war. Using the ethnographic work of Tone Bringa (1996), Keles demonstrates how this macropolitical discourse manifested itself in a reconfiguration of power relations at the village level, creating ethnic tensions where they had not been before. In supporting structural simplification as the root of village-level ethnic conflicts, Keles argues against the idea that ancient enthnonationalism, or a "clash of civilizations," caused this violence. He also presents structural simplification as a heuristic tool for conflict analysis, one that can be used to enhance our understanding of the linkage between macro- and microlevel conflict.

In "The Democratization of Peacebuilding: Democratic Exposure and Externally Democratic Ideology of Peacebuilding NGOs in Northern Ireland and Bosnia," Bruce Hemmer examines the effects of various "democratic exposure" variables on the development of an ideology of public participation in societies historically plagued by conflict. The author is particularly interested in the role of peacebuilding organizations in democratization: Are peacebuilding organizations "islands of democracy" that help incubate democratic thought, provide a venue for learning democratic procedures, and prepare people to participate politically in external society? Using data collected from 65 peacebuilding nongovernmental organizations (28 in Northern Ireland and 37 in Bosnia), Hemmer examines the relationships between three democratic exposure variables (level of societal democratization, democratic procedures internal to the NGO, and mentorship from outside democracies) on what he calls "externally democratic ideology," which is the ideology of participating politically in the larger society. He finds evidence that democratic procedures internal to the NGO strengthen the ideology of political participation, particularly where levels of societal democracy are low. Mentorship by outside democracies, on the other hand, had no appreciable effect. Thus, peacebuilding NGOs, by serving as "islands of democracy" within undemocratic societies, may play an important role in promoting societal democratization.

Patrick G. Coy, Gregory M. Maney, and Lynne M. Woehrle in "Blessing War and Blessing Peace: Religious Discourses in the US During Major Conflict Periods, 1990–2005" offer an analysis of the role of religious sentiments and ideas in justifying both war and peace. They argue that the deep embeddedness of religious symbols, beliefs, and language in the US constitutes a hegemonic discourse that can be harnessed by both proponents and detractors of war. Through an in-depth content analysis over five conflict periods, they demonstrate how war proponents (such as US President George W. Bush) and detractors (specifically, 15 peace movement organizations) employ religious discourse to add deeper significance and resonance to their claims. Analyzing statements by Bush in the period immediately after 9/11, the authors found that he employed religious discourse and symbols to justify a binary (good versus evil) vision of the world and a demonization of the enemy. In response, the peace movement both challenged Bush's use of religious discourse and harnessed it to turn the moral demands of religion back onto him. Coy, Maney, and Woehrle also find that peace movement organizations conducted remedial education on Islam and utilized religious appeals to encourage members to participate in nonviolent protests. They conclude that religious discourse is a powerful and resonant tool for motivating and legitimating the US peace movement.

In "Reconsidering Leadership Theory and Practice for Collaborative Governance: Examining the U.S. Coast Guard," Heather Getha-Taylor presents original research on the key elements of public-sector leadership in a collaborative environment, one that increasingly favors boundary-spanning and negotiation skills over directive, hierarchical authority. Data from interviews with superior and average collaborators in the Department of Homeland Security (DHS), as well as federal human resources experts, were analyzed using three collaborative leadership models. Four core competencies were identified: *continual learning*, *external awareness*, *interpersonal skills*, and *oral communication*. In addition, respondents from the US Coast Guard, a DHS agency that is highly praised for its exceptional leadership, reported *creativity/innovation* as a core attribute. The author argues that human resources tools, such as awards and assessments, should reflect these competencies in order to encourage the development of strong collaborative leaders. She also argues for the development of new models of public-sector leadership that stress the supporting or human-relations style of management.

In "Changing an Enemy into a Friend: A Model for Reframing Narratives in Protracted Social Conflict through Identity Affirmation," Thomas E. Boudreau and Brian D. Polkinghorn build the theoretical argument for an original model of conflict reduction through "identity affirmation." This is a process by which one group "rehumanizes" the other by understanding and explicitly affirming the others' identity, including recognition and validation of the others' pain, defeat, and suffering. These theoretical reflections were inspired by a case study in which the Onondaga County Sheriffs' Department repaired relations with a local Indian nation by returning ancestral remains of great spiritual value. Use the concepts of "identity frames" and "characterization frames" developed by Lewicki, Gray, and Elliott (2003), the authors describe the epistemic encounter between parties in conflict, and explain how these parties can adjust their frames to allow for identity affirmation to occur. In outlining a tentative model for conflict resolution through identity affirmation, they highlight four key aspects: leadership, recognition, validation, and the transparency of future time.

Marie Pace and Darren Kew in "Catalysts of Change: Applying New Forms of Practice to the Context of Nigeria's Democratic Development" examine the relationship between conflict resolution workshops/programs and democratic development in Nigeria. They argue that these programs provide a "discursive space" in which people living in a conflict-ridden society can gain democratic experience. As such, they play an important role in catalyzing the social transformation of political cultures, values, and norms that is critical for democratization. The authors stress the importance of a "third wave sensibility" for conflict practitioners – that is, a deep understanding of the socially-constructed worldview of parties to a conflict – as well as the importance of a "multichanneled" approach to conflict transformation. They conclude by calling on conflict resolution practitioners to consider the democratic impacts of their work, as well as highlighting the potential theoretical synergies between conflict resolution theories and democratic theory.

In "Constructing a Baseline Understanding of Developmental Trends in Graduate Conflict Resolution Programs in the United States," Brian Polkinghorn, Haleigh La Chance, and Robert La Chance present an accounting and analysis of the current state of the field of conflict resolution education. The authors begin by providing a history of the development of conflict resolution as a field using the metaphor of four historical "waves." Conflict resolution graduate programs are broken into three categories: conflict resolution, peace studies, and alternative dispute resolution, and the authors describe how these three program types have been intertwined and have diverged over time. In the second part of the article, they provide information on 94 graduate conflict resolution programs in the US including statistics on geographical location, types of institutions housing the programs, curricula, faculty, and program resources. They conclude by speculating on the future directions of the field.

Former PARC directors, Louis Kriesberg and Robert Rubenstein, have the last word by individually commenting on this special issue and its implications for the future of the field.

This special issue contributes to the fields of conflict resolution and collaboration in several areas. Looking at the volume as a whole, we find that the authors have illuminated the following themes:

(1) Civic organizations are important in incubating and providing a forum for both peace activism and democratic experience.

- In Coy, Maney, and Woehrle's work, peace movement organizations are seen as critical to the peace movement, especially in terms of their ability to shape the moral discourse and energize their supporters.
- Hemmer finds that peacebuilding organizations can be "islands of democracy" in conflict-ridden societies, providing a forum for people to gain democratic exposure and experience. Pace and Kew come to a similar conclusion regarding conflict resolution workshops in Nigeria.

(2) Powerful discourses are often harnessed to soothe or to exacerbate conflict.

- Religious discourses as analyzed by Coy, Maney, and Woehrle are used to promote and validate both peace and war.
- In Keles' article, macropolitical discourses on ethnonationalism are transformed at the local level and used to promote ethnic violence.
- In Funk-Unrau's analysis, apology discourses are used to renegotiate and soothe a historically violent relationship between the churches and Aboriginal people.
- In Boudreau's and Polkinghorn's work, in-group "identity" discourses (identity frames) and discourses that characterize out-groups (characterizations frames) can be adjusted to allow each group to "affirm" each other's identity, an important step toward reconciliation.

(3) Conflict resolution requires the renegotiation of social relationships. Part of this process is the recognition and validation of the pain and suffering caused to the "out-group."

- In Funk-Unrau's article, the two historically antagonistic groups had to create a "mutually acceptable narrative of historic wrongs" and "articulate a mutually acceptable moral norm" in order for the apology to be successful in soothing conflict.
- Boudreau and Polkinghorn find a solution to conflict in the "identity affirmation" that can rehumanize the excluded "other."
- Pincock shows how an understanding of white privilege made participants more attuned to racial divisions in everyday life.

(4) Dialogue can be used as a tool in healing relationships between groups that are historically dysfunctional or problematic.

- Funk-Unrau talks about the apology statement as an important form of interaction (a sort of "dialogue") between groups that need to heal their relationship.

- Pincock discusses the potential for intergroup dialogue to change the way people think and talk about racism in the US (although the intergroup dialogue was not very successful at teaching complex concepts, it was able to break down communication barriers).

(5) Understanding of racism and ethnocentrism at the institutional and structural levels is important in analyzing and approaching conflicts.
- Pincock speculates on why students had difficulty getting past an individualist explanation of racism and understanding the structural, institutional aspect – that is, the structures and institutions of our society are racist in themselves.
- Keles explores how ethnocentrism becomes institutionalized at the local level. It manifests itself partly as individual racism (i.e., individuals become "racist"), but also institutionally, for example, in the exchange of greetings and the way people talk about dress.

(6) Effective leaders bring a deep understanding of underlying dynamics to how they manage intergroup conflict.
- Getha-Taylor finds that excellent collaborative leaders remain flexible and innovative, open to ideas outside of the box, and attuned to their surroundings.
- Boudreau and Polkinghorn find that diplomatic leadership is one of the four key aspects of identity affirmation.
- Pincock finds that intergroup dialogue opens up participants' awareness of persistent and structural inequalities that exist in society (especially if they are in the privileged group). It is difficult to take leadership action on racial conflict without this fundamental understanding of its origins.

Taken as a whole, this volume tells us that the study of conflict resolution is flourishing and that the field is becoming even broader. It pushes us to question some of our assumptions about the impact of conflict resolution practices and introduces new ideas for further research in conflict resolution and collaboration.

ACKNOWLEDGMENTS

The editors of this volume thank Lisa Mignacca, Chris Praino, and Carin McAbee for their expert assistance.

REFERENCES

Bringa, T. (1996). *Being Muslim the Bosnian way: Identity and community in a central Bosnian village*. Princeton, NJ: Princeton University Press.

Lewicki, R. J., Gray, B., & Elliott, M. (Eds). (2003). *Making sense of intractable environmental conflicts: Concepts and cases*. Washington, DC: Island Press.

Sahlins, M. (2005). Structural work. *Anthropological Theory*, *5*(1), 5–30.

Rachel Fleishman
Rosemary O'Leary
Catherine Gerard
Editors

RENEGOTIATION OF SOCIAL RELATIONS THROUGH PUBLIC APOLOGIES TO CANADIAN ABORIGINAL PEOPLES

Neil Funk-Unrau

ABSTRACT

The purpose of this chapter is to examine public apology as a socially acceptable means of institutional communication and the renegotiation of social relations that seeks to redress the power imbalance between the parties to this interaction. After presenting a basic definition of an apology as a communicative act and discussing the social relational implication of the public form of such an act, the paper examines one particular grouping of public apologies – those coming from Canadian Christian church denominations or communities seeking a renewed relationship with Canadian Aboriginal communities. A comparative analysis of the text and context of several of these apology interactions can provide some fascinating hints about the role of public apology in creating a new joint social narrative, affirming common moral norms, clarifying accountability for past relations and empowering the marginalized community through some form of compensation.

Pushing the Boundaries: New Frontiers in Conflict Resolution and Collaboration
Research in Social Movements, Conflicts and Change, Volume 29, 1–19
Copyright © 2008 by Emerald Group Publishing Limited
All rights of reproduction in any form reserved
ISSN: 0163-786X/doi:10.1016/S0163-786X(08)29001-4

The public apology, a public expression of remorse and accountability for personal or institutional wrongdoing, has become an almost taken-for-granted aspect of current social discourse. Almost a decade ago, Cunningham (1999) presented an exhaustive listing of public apologies made during the latter part of the 20th century, subdividing these into those made by individuals, professional and commercial organizations, religious organizations, spiritual leaders, governments and heads of state. More recently, Slansky and Sorkin (2006) compiled a collection of North American celebrity apologies uttered over a 25-year period as one more example of the pervasiveness and almost ritualistic quality of this form of public discourse. Alongside these dramatic expressions of contrition and good intentions, a growing body of academic literature seeks to analyze and understand the specific components of these expressions, the contexts that give rise to them and the implications and consequences of the statements publicly made.

While the linguistic study of specific apology texts and the careful analysis of the situations and intentions of the apologizer is important, the wider context of institutional public apologies deserves much more scholarly attention. The purpose of this paper is to present an exploratory analysis of the contexts of institutional public apologies[1] and thereby indicate how such statements can serve as crucial steps within ongoing social interactions. At its most ideal, such statements can represent a socially acceptable means of institutional communication and the renegotiation of social relations intended to redress the power imbalance between the parties to this interaction. The implications of such an analysis can be demonstrated through the examination of one particular grouping of public apologies – those coming from Canadian Christian church denominations or communities (hereafter referred to as Churches) seeking a renewed relationship with Canadian Aboriginal communities. This grouping includes a range of apologies from those expressing a general recognition of the complex and problematic historical relationship with Aboriginal communities to those responding to very specific allegations of physical and sexual abuse. A comparative analysis of several of these apology interactions can provide some fascinating hints about the role of public apology in contemporary public discourse.

BASIC DEFINITION OF APOLOGY

In its simplest and most basic form, an apology is a speech act, a form of oral communication from one party to another designed to carry out several specific simultaneous communicative and moral functions (Tavuchis, 1991; Govier, 1998; Engel, 2001). The power of this particular speech act lies in the extent to which it articulates and enacts several key aspects to create a space for reconciliation and healing.

The apology acknowledges a specific situation as one that violated the listener. A particular event is reframed and given meaning to validate the listener and acknowledge the pain of the listener as legitimate. The recognition and acknowledgment of the painful event according to the terms perceived by the victim can transform the trauma of victimization into a process of mourning which includes both apologizer and listener, thereby beginning the rebuilding of relationships (Barkan, 2000). According to Govier and Verwoerd (2002) and Lazare (2004), this aspect of acknowledgment is the most crucial aspect of the process, providing a basis for moving through the rest of the process and toward potential future reconciliation.

An apology also provides a vehicle for the expression of remorse and the acceptance of responsibility for the wrongdoing that occurred (Alter, 1999). Implicit or explicit in this expression of accountability and remorse is the recognition of the impossibility of undoing the harm that has been done (Minow, 1998). The moral asymmetry between the speaker and listener created by the acknowledgment of the speaker's responsibility for the wrongdoing is further heightened by the recognition that no future action can remove this asymmetry. Herein lie the ambiguity and the power of the apology process. As noted by Tavuchis (1991, p. 34), "We are faced, then, with an apparently enigmatic situation in which the offender asks forgiveness as the necessary and symbolic corrective for a harmful action on the flimsiest of grounds: a speech act that is predicated on the impossibility of restitution".

The expression of accountability and remorse within this type of statement also implicitly or explicitly emphasizes the moral vulnerability of the apologizer. By offering the apology without justification or defense, the speaker deliberately takes on the vulnerability of moving the speech encounter toward an unknown endpoint (Schneider, 2000). The expression of this vulnerability institutionalizes a symbolic exchange whereby the speaker legitimizes the pain of the listener, as well as the social and moral norms they hold, in the hope that the listener will respond in a reciprocal fashion. Some analysts define apology as an "exchange of shame and power" (Schneider, 2000; Lazare, 1995). Roles are reversed as the apologizer deliberately places her/himself at the mercy of the listener who may or may not accept the apology.

Last, but not least, is the requirement of some visible material means of redressing, even if only symbolically, the harm that has been done through some form of reparation or compensation. Alter (1999) also identifies reparation as a specific task or element of the apology process. Govier and Verwoerd (2002) reframe this aspect in their discussion of moral and practical amends – a concept which links reparation to other ways of making amends, such as the assurances of changed behavior and expressions of remorse noted above. According to Schriver (1998), the integrity of the apology is validated by gestures of reparation. However, Schriver distinguishes between imposed demands for reparation versus voluntary offers of reparation, noting the difference between the demands imposed on Germany in 1918 and the reparations offered by Germany to the victims of Nazism after 1949.

In the midst of growing public demands for apologies in response to a variety of contemporary and historical injustices, insufficient attention has been given to the implications of the type of apology demanded or voluntarily offered. Any assessment of the usefulness and the meaningfulness of an apology process must confront the question of whether the type of apology under consideration can bear the weight of the tasks expected of it. Tavuchis (1991) provides a useful typology that categorizes apologies as coming from one to one, from one to many, from many to one and from many to many. Each of these categories of apologies raises unique issues and concerns. The different implications of these types of apology can best be understood in terms of the implications of movements along three continua – private versus public, personal versus institutional, and specific versus general.

Tavuchis (1991) notes that the greatest difference between one-to-one apologies and other types is the movement of this encounter from a partially private to a completely public sphere of discourse. Issues of vulnerability and legal liability loom much larger in the public sphere. The apologizer stands vulnerable and defenseless before a multitude of listeners, instead of just one. The audience responds in judgment, evaluating the degree of perceived sincerity of the apology and the degree of extended punishment or reparation to be attached to it.

An institutional apology is one directed by some institution toward an individual or limited group of individuals or a larger societal grouping perceived to have been harmed by the institution. The apology process may occur within the private or public realm, depending on the extent to which a public apology is volunteered or demanded within the specific circumstances. An appropriate institutional apology can provide a public and visible acknowledgment of wrongdoing that simply cannot be matched by any individual apology (Govier & Verwoerd, 2002). An institutional apology also has significant implications regarding the acknowledgment of institutional responsibility for what happened and the responsibility to ensure that the regrettable situation is not repeated – an aspect particularly significant if the apologizer is a State institution because a State institution is generally perceived as the institution of ultimate accountability in most national contexts (Cunningham, 1999; Gibney & Roxstrom, 2001; Negash, 2006).[2]

An institutional apology also necessitates a degree of separation between the institution making the statement and the individuals most directly implicated by it. Institutional discourse creates communicative and emotional distance simply by the nature of this type of discourse. An institutional statement cannot express remorse and deep emotion, for example, without in some way expressing these feelings at a personal level and thereby making it a more personal response. The Church apologies to be discussed below demonstrate several different attempts to make an institutional statement more personal.

The separation between individuals or groups directly implicated in a specific harmful act and the apologizing institution is even more significant if the recipients of the apology are members of a distinct social grouping, rather than the specific individuals who suffered the harm being addressed, and if the wrongdoing occurred in the distant past, perhaps well before the lifetime of the apology recipients. However, such temporal and generational distance can also be beneficial. Schriver (1998) notes that healing for the victims is only possible through a process of remembering the past, telling the truth about it in a way that brings both sides together. Thus, an apology process has the potential of creating a space for the remembrance of that which others tried hard to forget and a space to reassert a moral claim about the wrongdoing as a basis for the restoration of a healthier relationship between those who represent the victims and those who represent the perpetrators. Given the enormity (in most, if not all, such cases) of the event to be overcome, forgiveness and restoration takes much time, possibly decades or even a century or more.[3] Thus, an apology provided by future generations may begin a process of reconciliation that would have been impossible to consider earlier.

Some of the difficulties noted above are further heightened by any attempt to define the wrongdoing in precise and specific terms. As noted by Bavelas (2004) in her linguistic analysis of several Canadian Church apologies to Aboriginal peoples, several of the later apologies responded to specific cases of physical and sexual abuse for which the institution could be sued rather than general spiritual and cultural colonization. These statements try to minimize legal liability by exhibiting more cautious and evasive language and are thereby more easily labeled as partial or nongenuine apologies. Bavelas' distinctions highlight the tension between responses to general concerns and responses to specific situations for which the apologizer could be held legally liable.

PUBLIC APOLOGY AS A RENEGOTIATION OF SOCIAL RELATIONS

The set of Aboriginal apologies to be discussed in this article have already begun to receive some scholarly attention. Bavelas' (2004) linguistic analysis has already been mentioned. Bergen (2007) analyzes these apologies as expressions of the nature of the Christian Church and the Church's mission of reconciliation. In addition, Durocher (2002) explores the significance of these statements for the acknowledgment and truth-telling of historic injustices.

This article attempts to extend this research to another level by exploring the process of apologizing in the context of a mutual renegotiation of a dysfunctional social relationship. The analysis of the text of specific statements, the nature and motivation of the apologizer and the impact of the apology as a public response to historical injustice are all important. However, it is essential to understand these aspects from within the context of a public discourse. Within this discourse, the demand for an apology or the spontaneous offer of one, along with the varied levels of response to such a statement, all form a complex social interaction reframing the relationship between the apologizer and the offended party.

Several scholars have begun to address the concept of apology as a joint negotiable process rather than a unilateral declaration. One example is Lazare's (2004) discussion of the negotiation of an apology and the creation of a statement jointly by the apologizer and the recipient. Negash (2006) provides several case studies of negotiated partial apologies, statements which do not include all the elements of a full apology but do include sufficient assurances to smooth diplomatic relations.

Particularly useful for the purposes of this paper are the public apology criteria presented by Negash (2006) – truth-telling, public remorse, acknowledgment of (and accountability for) wrongdoing, and restitution – a list roughly analogous to the basic elements of an apology as discussed above. Negash indicates that the relative weight given to each of these criteria depends in part on whether this apology is intended to mend social relations on a surface level or to facilitate a deeper process of societal healing.

Analysis of a public apology as a jointly negotiated process rather than a static statement emphasizes the mutual interaction implicit in each of the apology components discussed by Negash. From this perspective, the element of truth-telling begins the process of jointly creating and affirming a new and more hopeful narrative of the past. Expressions of remorse, as well as the response to such expressions, serve to create and gain joint affirmation of a suitable moral norm about this agreed-upon narrative. Verbal and nonverbal expressions of accountability gain significance as the first concrete steps in a newly defined social relationship. Offers and acceptance of reparations become another way of offering some amends for the wrongdoing as well as affirming and celebrating these new relations.

Following is an examination of several specific public apologies to Canadian Aboriginal peoples from Canadian Church institutions, a set of apologies that provide a potentially rich resource for comparison and analysis because they represent very distinct institutional responses to very similar situations. After summarizing the contexts of the three apology statements, I will analyze them in terms of differing attempts at the renegotiation of a dysfunctional social relationship.

CHURCH APOLOGIES TO CANADIAN ABORIGINAL PEOPLES

The best-known example of a faith-based apology for the church role in the legacy of colonialism is the apology offered by the United Church of Canada (UCC) in 1986. McKay and Silman (1997) describe the events leading up to the apology and the Aboriginal response to it. The idea was first raised at the UCC General Council Executive in 1984 when an Aboriginal representative to the Council demanded an apology for colonial injustices. In the next 18 months, a pamphlet was sent out to all UCC congregations, informing them of the request for an apology and encouraging them to reflect on this. The apology was officially requested in October 1986 at the UCC General Council meeting at Sudbury, Ontario, whereupon Aboriginal council members withdrew to a nearby teepee and a sacred fire to wait and pray for about two hours until UCC leaders arrived with the General Council's apology statement:

> Long before my people journeyed to this land, your people were here, and you received from your elders an understanding of creation, and of the mystery that surrounds us all that was deep and rich and to be treasured.
>
> We did not hear you when you shared your vision. In our zeal to tell you the good news of Jesus Christ we were closed to the value of your spirituality.
>
> We confused Western ways and culture with the depth and length and breadth and height of the gospel of Christ.
>
> We imposed our civilization as a condition of accepting the gospel.
>
> We tried to make you be like us and in so doing we helped to destroy the vision that made you what you were. As a result, you, and we, are poorer, and the image of the Creator in us is twisted, blurred and we are not what we are meant by God to be.
>
> We ask you to forgive us and to walk together with us in the spirit of Christ so that our peoples may be blessed and God's creation healed. (cited in McKay & Silman, 1997, p. 175)

Then Aboriginal elders spoke about the damage done through the imposition of rigid criminal justice and social welfare systems on societies that had no comparable structures and of the families broken or cast aside as a result (Sinclair, 1986). The elders did not immediately accept the apology, promising only to take it back to their people for further deliberation and response. In the following months, the statement was discussed within Aboriginal circles and eventually accepted.[4] In the meantime, regional and national UCC representatives embarked on the major task of communicating the implications of the apology to congregations across the country and promoting the idea that each congregation set aside one Sunday in the next year as a Native Apology Sunday to reflect on these implications further.

While this statement acknowledged the damage done to indigenous peoples in general terms, subsequent church apologies responded to the growing public awareness in the early 1990s of a specific example of the destructiveness of colonial systems. Perhaps the clearest and the most destructive expression of the colonialist drive to civilize and Christianize was the coercive imposition of an educational system designed to isolate Aboriginal youth from their families, communities and lifestyles in order to change them into exemplary Canadian citizens (Miller, 1996; Milloy, 1999). This imposed educational system began with the development of church-run residential and day schools as early as the mid-1600s, but only after 1880 did the Canadian government take control of Aboriginal schooling and begin a concentrated effort to confine Aboriginal children in government-sponsored residential educational facilities. At the height of the residential school system, the Canadian government funded approximately 80 institutions, all administered by church agencies (primarily Catholic, Anglican, Methodist and Presbyterian). Most of these schools continued operations until the 1950s or later, with the last ones closing down in the 1990s.

One layer of hardship was directly related to the poverty experienced by most of the residents. Despite the initial idealism of bringing civilization to cultures considered to be dying, the Canadian government underfunded the schools for most of their existence. Thus, the actual schooling was substandard with inadequate supplies, and much of the average schoolday was spent in the industrial, farming or food production tasks required to keep the institution afloat. In many schools, students became almost a source of slave labor, providing work that was crucial simply for institutional survival. In addition to hardship and overwork, some students faced direct physical and sexual abuse from institutional staff and administrators who used their positions of authority to assert their power over those in their charge. As devastating as this was, perhaps the most extreme form of abuse was the deliberate attempt to tear young impressionable students away from their families and communities and indoctrinate them into a language, a worldview and a culture completely alien to their home experience.

The impact of this hardship and abuse spread far beyond the lives of the individual survivors. Many of these survivors returned home years later, completely alienated from their home community and from the outside world, unable to thrive in either setting. Some communities lost entire generations to these schools – generations unable to pass on the ideals, the parenting skills and the survival skills of their ancestors. The loss of these generations has had a profound impact through the decades in terms of increased alcoholism, drug dependencies, violence, suicide and various patterns of abuse passed on from residential school survivors to their children, their grandchildren and their wider community networks.

By the early 1990s, as survivors of residential schools began to speak out about the abuse and trauma they endured, Church apologies took on a different tone as they attempted to respond to specific situations in specific times and places rather than the former blanket condemnations of the colonialist missionary endeavor. Examples of national Church apologies that make direct reference to residential school abuse include those made by the Oblates of Mary Immaculate (OMI) on behalf of the Roman Catholic Church in 1991, the Primate of the Anglican Church of Canada (ACC) in 1993, and the UCC again in 1998.[5] As noted below, each of these three apologies was offered in a different context (from a large public celebration to a relatively small workshop setting), delivered in a different manner (from very formal to very personal) and received a different response (from skepticism and outrage to wholehearted acceptance). As a set of similar apologies, this grouping can provide useful data for a comparative analysis.

The OMI apology was presented within a text read by the OMI leadership in July 1991 as part of the annual Catholic Aboriginal pilgrimage to Lake St. Anne in Alberta, Canada. The audience was approximately 15,000–25,000 people, mostly individuals who would have attended Catholic residential schools and had traveled great distances to participate in this annual pilgrimage. The document is several pages long, too long to be copied here, and includes first a general apology for culturally imperialist attitudes, then a specific apology for harms committed through the residential school system, followed by an extensive section (approximately one quarter of the entire statement) to honor the hard work, good intentions and dedication of the missionaries who staffed and administered these schools. This qualification was not, however, enough to assuage the wounded feelings of OMI members who had not been consulted about the statement and felt personally attacked by it. Therefore, five months later, the OMI leadership published an apology to those who were hurt or offended by the first apology (Durocher, 2002). In response to the initial apology, many church officials continued to defend the residential school system, claiming that "the schools stimulated cultural resistance, fostered a pan-Indian identity and culture, and laid the groundwork for much of contemporary Indian rights movements" (Furniss, 1995, p. 32).

Durocher (2002) describes the ACC apology as the most personal statement of this whole group. The Primate of the ACC participated in a Anglican Aboriginal gathering which included several days of hearing the survivors of Anglican residential schools recount the abuses they had suffered and continued to suffer – stories of family destruction, loss of language and identity, alcoholism and suicide. On the sixth day of the gathering, the Primate responded with a very personal apology. Excerpts from the two-page document indicate the general tone:

> Together here with you I have listened as you told your stories of the residential schools. I have heard the voices that have spoken of pain and hurt experienced in the schools, and the scars which endure to this day. I have felt shame and humiliation as I have heard of

suffering inflicted by my people, and as I think of the part our church played in that suffering ...

I am sorry, more than I can say, that we were part of a system which took you and your children from home and family. I am sorry, more than I can say, that we tried to remake you in our image, taking from you your language and the signs of your identity. I am sorry, more than I can say, that in our schools so many were abused, physically, sexually, culturally and emotionally .... (cited in Durocher, 2002, p. 165–166)

The UCC responded to specific allegations of residential school abuse in 1997 with a "Statement of Repentance" which acknowledged church participation in the residential school system and reaffirmed the 1986 apology. However, this was insufficient to silence the allegations of abuse by survivors of certain schools. One year later, the Moderator of the UCC offered a personal apology to former residential school students, their families and their communities. The tone of this apology contrasts sharply with the tone of the general United Church apology presented 12 years earlier.[6]

As Moderator of The United Church of Canada, I wish to speak the words that many people have wanted to hear for a very long time. On behalf of The United Church of Canada, I apologize for the pain and suffering that our church's involvement in the Indian Residential School system has caused. We are aware of some of the damage that this cruel and ill-conceived system of assimilation has perpetrated on Canada's First Nations peoples. For this we are truly and most humbly sorry.

To those individuals who were physically, sexually, and mentally abused as students of the Indian Residential Schools in which The United Church of Canada was involved, I offer you our most sincere apology. You did nothing wrong. You were and are the victims of evil acts that cannot under any circumstances be justified or excused.

We know that many within our church will still not understand why each of us must bear the scar, the blame for this horrendous period in Canadian history. But the truth is, we are the bearers of many blessings from our ancestors, and therefore, we must also bear their burdens.

Our burdens include dishonouring the depths of the struggles of First Nations peoples and the richness of your gifts. We seek God's forgiveness and healing grace as we take steps toward building respectful, compassionate, and loving relationships with First Nations peoples.

We are in the midst of a long and painful journey as we reflect on the cries that we did not or would not hear, and how we have behaved as a church. As we travel this difficult road of repentance, reconciliation, and healing, we commit ourselves to work toward ensuring that we will never again use our power as a church to hurt others with attitudes of racial and spiritual superiority. We pray that you will hear the sincerity of our words today and that you will witness the living out of our apology in our actions in the future. (cited in Durocher, 2002, p. 160–161)

ANALYSIS OF SPECIFIC ABORIGINAL APOLOGIES

Each of these apology situations can be viewed as an acknowledgment of a dysfunctional social relationship between a relatively powerful Canadian institution and a social group significantly impacted by this institution throughout several centuries of interaction. The apology situation represents a potential turning point in this relationship – a potential best viewed when this situation is understood in the context of an attempted renegotiation of this relationship. The effectiveness and long-term impact of this renegotiation is dependent on the extent to which the apology situation succeeds in four interrelated tasks – creation of a mutually acceptable narrative of historic wrongs (which includes some form of truth-telling), articulation of a mutually acceptable moral norm (which includes a sincere public expression of remorse), the deliberate public acceptance of responsibility for the wrongs on the part of the more powerful party (i.e., acknowledgment of wrongdoing) and the offering of mutually acceptable amends to affirm the new relationship being created (as done through a process of restitution and reparation). While space does not permit a full analysis of each apology situation, the four apologies will be compared in terms of these tasks.

Truth-Telling as the Creation of a New Social Narrative

All four apology statements introduced above involve a retelling of the history of the Canadian missionary legacy. They change this narrative from the story of faithful missionaries bringing enlightenment to the heathen masses into a narrative that places the missionary endeavor firmly within the context of Euro-Canadian colonization of the indigenous peoples of this continent. While the 1986 United Church statement addresses this in a general way, subsequent apologies respond directly to the growing public and Aboriginal awareness of the harsh legacy of the residential school system. Thus, some very specific actions at some very specific locations are highlighted and described as part of this new narrative.

This articulation of a new understanding of historical wrongdoing raises several important issues when viewed as part of an ongoing social dialogue. For example, the way in which the apology is received by the offended party and by the membership of the apologizing institution can indicate the extent to which both sides articulate and affirm this new historical narrative. The 1986 UCC experience provides insight on both points. Aboriginal elders responded to the statement by affirming the narrative of the harms of colonialism and speaking about the damage done through the imposition of rigid criminal justice and social welfare systems on societies that had no comparable structures (Sinclair, 1986). In the following years, regional and national representatives embarked on the major task of communicating the implications of the apology to congregations across the country and promoting the idea that each congregation set aside one Sunday in the next year as a Native Apology Sunday so as to reflect on these implications further. Thus, the apology situation provided a context for further dialogue about the damage of colonialism as well as the stimulus for a major national education campaign within the UCC constituency.

This experience stands in contrast to the OMI experience of following up the apology to Aboriginal peoples with a second apology to those church workers offended by the implications of the new narrative. The OMI apology was offered in a public setting before thousands of listeners and in a liturgical rather than a dialogical or interactive context – altogether a situation that did not encourage any direct Aboriginal response to the statement. The subsequent vigorous internal debate within the OMI order demonstrated that many church officials disagreed vehemently with the historical narrative presented through the apology statement (Furniss, 1995).[7]

Public Remorse as the Affirmation of Moral Norms

All of the apology statements describe historical relations and specific experiences in a way that inserts a moral judgment into the situation to express sorrow, regret and remorse for breaking the moral norms held by the offended party. The ACC and second UCC statements further emphasize this expression of remorse through the extremely personalized form in which the statement is written; the remorse is not an abstract institutional response but arises from the deep emotions of specific individuals addressing specific situations.

Whether made privately or publicly, or in general or specific terms, the reception of an apology statement is largely dependent on the perceived sincerity of the speaker – something which is partially dependent on the degree and perceived sincerity of remorse expressed. In a recent study of responses to different types of apology for personal injury caused by a traffic infraction, the inclusion of a strong expression of remorse for what happened is a major factor helping to defuse disputes and enhance the possibilities of satisfactory settlements (Ribbennolt, 2003, 2006). A similar point is made by recent interactional justice studies described by Scarlicki, Folger, and Gee (2004). An apology statement lacking in remorse will be perceived as insincere or manipulative and will stimulate a more negative response than the absence of any apology at all.

This public expression of remorse is significant here particularly as a public reinforcement of the moral norms of the injured party and the apologizer's public affirmation of these norms. The recreated historical narrative is told in such a way so as to emphasize these now mutually accepted norms and show how these norms have been broken. This then sets the stage for the next two steps in this social dialogue – taking responsibility for the transgression of these norms and agreeing on some visible means to make amends (even if only symbolically) for the damage that has been done.

Public Accountability and Liability

Acknowledgment of the moral norms of the offended party and expression of remorse for the transgression of these norms moves the whole interaction into risky territory because this leads directly to the public acceptance of responsibility for these transgressions and the risk of being held legally liable for the damages. Schneider (2000) notes that the nature of the North American legal system works against establishing a setting that could allow a sincere acknowledgment of responsibility to be offered and heard. Whereas such an admission implies vulnerability on the part of the apologizer and a willingness to accept the demands and the judgment of the one who has been wronged, adversarial legal processes require both sides of any dispute to defend their interests and state their position in the strongest way possible. Any sign of vulnerability in this context is a weakness to be exploited by the opposing side.

Questions of legal liability loom larger in more recent Church apologies than in the earlier UCC apology. As noted by Bavelas (2004), the earlier more general statement on the impact of colonialist policies affirms the direct role of the Church in assenting to and implementing these policies, whereas later apologies, identifying very specific abuses, adopt a more passive tone as if the Church was somehow caught up in the swirl of attitudes and events. As the events of wrongdoing are identified more specifically and the apology is directed to specific individuals who suffered the harm, statements of taking responsibility become more muted and indirect. The desire for reconciliation and a new, more equal relationship is tempered by the fear that full acceptance of responsibility will leave Church institutions vulnerable to every demand for compensation. The possibility of creating a new social relationship depends on the extent to which such fears are overcome, and the expression of accepting responsibility is perceived by all sides as genuine.[8]

Reparation as Amends and Renewal of Relationship

Should apologies be viewed as something distinct from or integrally connected to offers of reparations and material compensation for wrongdoing? Taft (2000) decries the subversion of a moral expression of apology into something to be traded for personal material benefit within a legal context as occurs, for example, when a defendant in a civil suit offers an apology in the hopes of mitigating demands for compensation. Taft's concern about treating an apology as a moral act or as a marketable commodity highlights the ambiguity of the relationship between apologies and reparations in other public settings outside the local courtroom. Other researchers disagree about the necessity of linking the apology process to reparations. Alter (1999) and Brooks (1999) include some concrete form of reparations as one of the essential elements of an apology process. On the other hand, Cunningham (1999) defines the sincerity of an apology in terms of the rebuilding of relationships, concluding that reparation may follow from this but can occur independently.

In his examination of reparation of historical injustices, Barkan (2000) asks whether the growing public legitimacy of the apology process merely whitewashes specific injustices and cheapens reparation. Barkan views the apology process as part of a growing cultural trend of performative guilt. The public apology acts paradoxically as a ritual of public confession that may mitigate the demand for material compensation, yet by its expression provides the core of restitution by validating victim memories and identities. Minow (1998) goes further to describe an apology as the symbolic dimension of reparation, simultaneously preparing the way for an offer of material reparation and acknowledging that no adequate reparation is possible. For these writers, the prevalence and popularity of appeals for apology both complement and transcend the economic aspects of rectifying injustices.

Rather than viewing the public apology as the symbolic dimension of reparation, this paper suggests that reparation can be also perceived as the symbolic dimension of apology, as the symbolic response to the damage that has been done and as a symbolic affirmation of the renewed relationship the apology process is intended to create. Public apologies such as those introduced above acknowledge the impossibility of undoing the harm and of paying the cost of all damages created. Since the reparation can never fully recompense all victims, it becomes a gift voluntarily provided by the apologizer to the offended party as a concrete marker of changing dynamics and a renewed relationship.

Several of the national churches, most specifically the UCC and the ACC, accompanied their public statements with the establishment of special healing funds designed to disburse resources for the healing of individuals and communities impacted by residential schools. As Durocher (2002) notes, these funds were perceived as credible in the context of the apology statement, whereas the offer of financial compensation on its own would have limited value because the offended party would not feel fundamentally respected without the tangible expression of the ideals articulated in these statements.

CONCLUSION

A wide range of substantive issues surround the articulation and usefulness of a public apology intended to move toward the healing and renewal of a complex relationship such as that existing between Canadian Aboriginal communities and Christian Church denominations. This brief survey of several of these issues indicates some of the research and analysis which may be useful to both sides in this historical and contemporary encounter as well as providing deeper insight into the significance of a public apology process in general.

The series of public apologies presented by the UCC, OMI and the ACC demonstrate several different attempts to begin a dialogical process of acknowledging the harms of the past and envisioning the relationship with Aboriginal peoples in the future. Four important components of the apology process represent aspects that are better understood in the context of this renegotiation of social relations. Truth-telling of past wrongs facilitates the joint affirmation of a common historical narrative. The public expression of remorse emphasizes the joint affirmation of moral norms and acknowledges transgressions of these norms. Acknowledgment of responsibility for these transgressions becomes the first significant step in changing the dynamics and ideals that created the previous situation. The acceptance of some form of reparation then becomes an acceptance of the attempt to make amends and the affirmation of the renewed relationship that both sides have begun to articulate.

Much more research is still required to flesh out the analysis of public apologies in general and these apologies specifically as attempts to renegotiate dysfunctional social relations. For the study of public apologies in general, these case studies and comparisons can point toward a new way of understanding what an apology is and what it can accomplish. Such an apology is more than a static statement; it is a process that can move opposing sides closer to reconciliation or drive them further apart. More richly detailed case studies of a variety of institutional and social apologies are needed to demonstrate the specific factors that can help or hinder the renewal of relationships.

For these specific case studies, more work could be done to elicit and analyze differing aboriginal responses to each of these church apologies, thereby highlighting the problems and the potential of the apology process as a significant step toward social reconciliation. More work also needs to be done to set these specific apology experiences into the wider context of Canadian neocolonialism and aboriginal resistance. This paper is only the first step, one of the initial attempts to explore a few of the many questions that still need to be asked and answered.

NOTES

1. A more precise definition of 'apology' will be provided later in the paper. An apology is 'institutional' if expressed by a group or an institution instead of an individual and 'public' if expressed in a way intended to be heard by a bystander audience.

2. This point is further reinforced by recent indigenous pressure in Canada and in Australia for apologies to indigenous peoples to come from the highest levels of federal authority, not just from the specific institutions most directly implicated in the wrongdoing.

3. Although an apology statement frequently includes a plea for forgiveness, apology and forgiveness should not be viewed as an inevitable part of the same process. I consider an apology to be one step that can create space for forgiveness to occur but the former does not necessarily imply the latter. A full discussion of the relationship between apology and forgiveness is beyond the scope of this paper.

4. Some participants in the 1986 General Council still claim, in personal conversation, that the apology was eventually acknowledged but has still never been officially accepted.

5. The Presbyterian Church of Canada (PCC), the other major administrator of residential schools, is conspicuously missing from this list. PCC presented a statement of confession in the early 1990s – a statement that also identifies the wrongs done, expresses remorse and asks for forgiveness – but some analysts (including Durocher, 2002) do not consider this to be an apology because it does not include specific apology terminology. Bavelas (2004) does include the PCC statement

in her analysis of church apologies. A more extensive contextual comparison of this statement with the case studies discussed here is worth pursing further.

6. Both UCC apologies are cited in full in this paper because both are relatively short. This comparison also highlights the contrast between an institutional statement about a general concern and a personal statement about a very specific act of wrongdoing.

7. One reviewer of this article makes an important point that more information should be provided about this controversy. This topic remains one of the many areas ripe for further research and analysis.

8. The concept of collective responsibility should also be carefully distinguished from collective guilt. Therefore, individuals who have no direct connection to specific acts of wrongdoing can still be held collectively responsible for redressing the wrongdoing due to their voluntary acceptance of membership within the institution held responsible for it.

ACKNOWLEDGMENTS

The author wishes to thank colleagues at Menno Simons College for their support of this research project and the organizers of the 20th anniversary conference of the Program for the Analysis and Resolution of Conflict (PARC), Syracuse University, for providing a forum for further discussion of these ideas. In addition, the author owes a debt of gratitude to Catherine Morris, Trudy Govier, Evita Roche, Neil Sargent and the four anonymous reviewers who critiqued this paper before publication.

REFERENCES

Alter, S. (1999). *Apologizing for serious wrongdoing: Social, psychological and legal considerations*. Ottawa, ON: Law Commission of Canada.

Barkan, E. (2000). *The guilt of nations: Restitution and negotiating historical injustices*. New York, NY: W.W. Norton and Company.

Bavelas, J. (2004). *An analysis of formal apologies by Canadian Churches to First Nations*. Victoria, BC: Centre for Studies in Religion and Society, University of Victoria.

Bergen, J. M. (2007). Church apologies and the politics of reconciliation. *Vision*, *8*(1), 80–87.

Brooks, R. L. (1999). The age of apology. In: R. L. Brooks (Ed.), *When sorry isn't enough: The controversies over apologies and reparations for human injustice* (pp. 3–11). New York, NY: New York University Press.

Cunningham, M. (1999). Saying sorry: The politics of apology. *Political Quarterly*, *70*, 285–293.

Durocher, A. P. (2002). *Between the right to forget and the duty to remember: The politics of memory in Canada's public church apologies*. Ph.D. dissertation, Graduate Theological Union, Berkeley, CA.

Engel, B. (2001). *The power of apology: Healing steps to transform all your relationships*. New York, NY: Wiley.

Furniss, E. (1995). *Victims of benevolence: The dark legacy of the Williams Lake Residential School*. Vancouver, BC: Arsenal Pulp Press.
Gibney, M., & Roxstrom, E. (2001). The status of state apologies. *Human Rights Quarterly*, *23*, 911–939.
Govier, T. (1998). *Dilemmas of trust*. Montreal, QC: McGill – Queen's University Press.
Govier, T., & Verwoerd, W. (2002). The promise and pitfalls of apology. *Journal of Social Philosophy*, *33*, 67–82.
Lazare, A. (1995). Go ahead, say you're sorry. *Psychology Today*, *28*(1), 40–42.
Lazare, A. (2004). *On Apology*. New York, NY: Oxford University Press.
McKay, S., & Silman, J. (1997). A First Nations movement in a Canadian Church. In: G. Baum & H. Wells (Eds), *The reconciliation of peoples: Challenge to the churches* (pp. 172–183). New York, NY: Orbis Books.
Miller, J. R. (1996). *Shingwauk's vision: A history of native residential schools*. Toronto, ON: University of Toronto Press.
Milloy, J. S. (1999). *A national crime: The Canadian government and the residential school system, 1879 to 1986*. Winnipeg, MB: University of Manitoba Press.
Minow, M. (1998). *Between vengeance and forgiveness: Facing history after genocide and mass violence*. Boston, MA: Beacon Press.
Negash, G. (2006). *Apologia politica: States and their apologies by Proxy*. Lanham, MD: Lexington Books.
Ribbennolt, J. K. (2003). Apologies and legal settlement: An empirical examination. *Michigan Law Review*, *102*, 460–516.
Ribbennolt, J. K. (2006). Apologies and settlement levers. *Journal of Empirical Legal Studies*, *3*, 333–373.
Scarlicki, D. P., Folger, R., & Gee, J. (2004). When social accounts backfire: The exacerbating effects of a polite message or an apology on reactions to an unfair outcome. *Journal of Applied Social Psychology*, *34*, 322–341.
Schneider, C. D. (2000). What it means to be sorry: The power of apology in mediation. *Mediation Quarterly*, *17*, 265–280.
Schriver, D. W., Jr. (1998). Is there forgiveness in politics: Germany, Vietnam and America. In: R. D. Enright & J. North (Eds), *Exploring forgiveness* (pp. 131–149). Madison, WI: University of Wisconsin Press.
Sinclair, D. (1986). Of course we forgive you. *United Church Observer*, *50*(October), 10–12.
Slansky, P., & Sorkin, A. (2006). *My Bad: 25 years of public apologies and the public behavior that inspired them*. New York, NY: Bloomsbury Publishing.
Taft, L. (2000). Apology subverted: The commodification of apology. *Yale Law Journal*, *109*, 1135–1160.
Tavuchis, N. (1991). *Mea Culpa: A sociology of apology and reconciliation*. Stanford, CA: Stanford University Press.

TEACHING THROUGH TALK? THE IMPACT OF INTERGROUP DIALOGUE ON CONCEPTUALIZATIONS OF RACISM

Heather Pincock

ABSTRACT

This chapter examines the goals and outcomes of intergroup dialogue through the evaluation of a dialogue program between city and suburban high school students located in Syracuse, NY. The Community Wide Dialogue to End Racism, Improve Race Relations and Begin Racial Healing (CWD) organizers share with a wide range of conflict theorists and practitioners the impulse to bring citizens together to talk about complex social conflicts. Two of the main goals of this program, to build participants' understandings of institutional racism and white privilege, are examined here. Drawing on in-depth interviews with a small sample of dialogue participants, a framework is developed for categorizing participant awareness and understanding of institutional racism and white privilege. The analysis suggests that relatively modest levels of understanding of both concepts should be anticipated from participants both before and after completion of a dialogue of this type. While dramatic changes resulting

Pushing the Boundaries: New Frontiers in Conflict Resolution and Collaboration
Research in Social Movements, Conflicts and Change, Volume 29, 21–53
Copyright © 2008 by Emerald Group Publishing Limited
All rights of reproduction in any form reserved
ISSN: 0163-786X/doi:10.1016/S0163-786X(08)29002-6

from the dialogue are not found, the data indicate that the dialogue does have demonstrable impacts on the ways participants think and talk about institutional racism and white privilege. The central challenges faced by participants in understanding the concepts, specifically ability to personalize white privilege and capacity to adopt structural ways of thinking about institutional racism, are identified and described. This research helps to clarify the range of outcomes we can feasibly expect when bringing citizens together to talk about social conflicts by providing a qualitative framework for measuring awareness and understanding of white privilege and institutional racism.

The impulse to address complex social conflicts by bringing everyday citizens together to talk is shared by a range of conflict theorists and practitioners. Intergroup dialogue finds its origins in social psychology and is based on the contact theory hypothesis, which asserts the potential for face-to-face interaction to ease tensions between identity groups (Allport, 1954; Pettigrew, 1998). In political science as well, a range of theorists have pointed to the potential for discursive forums to address social conflict through what they call deliberative democracy (Bohman & Rehg, 1997). Despite the common impulse to address conflict through dialogue, the goals articulated by proponents vary widely from problem solving (Fung & Wright, 2003), to formation of considered opinion (Fishkin, 1995), to building relationships of trust and understanding (Saunders, 1999) to developing the skill and dispositions required of democratic citizens (Gurin, Nagda, & Lopez, 2004; Merelman, Streich, & Martin, 1998; Nagda, Kim, & Truelove, 2004; Mansbridge, 1983). Discursive processes are often designed with multiple goals in mind and in practice incorporate design features from a wide range of models.

In this paper I consider intergroup dialogue programs focused on domestic US race relations that are appearing in growing numbers in educational and community settings (Walsh, 2006, 2007; Zirkel & Cantor, 2004; Schoem & Hurtado, 2001). These programs aim to reduce intergroup tensions and break down stereotypes by putting the contact theory hypothesis into practice (Pettigrew & Tropp, 2000; Worchel, 1986; Kardia & Sevig, 2001).[1] In many cases, they also aim to build participants' awareness and understanding of specific concepts related to racism (Lopez, Gurin, & Nagda, 1998; Lopez, 2004; Stephan & Vogt, 2004). I focus on these latter goals in an effort to contribute to existing research that explores the advantages and disadvantages of the intergroup dialogue format for conveying complex concepts to participants (Beale & Schoem, 2001; Gurin, Dey, Hurtado, & Gurin, 2002; Hurtado, 2001; Roberts & Kay Inc., 2000).

The case I examine is the *Community Wide Dialogue to End Racism, Improve Race Relations and Begin Racial Healing* (CWD) program in Syracuse, New York. The program, as the title suggests, aims broadly to end individual and institutional forms of racism through honest interpersonal exchange between everyday citizens. This paper draws on evaluation research of a CWD initiative in Syracuse high schools, where they joined suburban and city high school students for six weeks of interaction and discussion on topics relating to racism. Interviews conducted with CWD organizers (staff, volunteers, teachers, and participants) as part of this program evaluation identified multiple indicators of success, which can be separated into two general categories. The first set of indicators relate to the expectation that through processes of direct face-to-face exchange with fellow citizens about racism and race relations, participants acquire a better understanding and acceptance of *each other* as human beings. Goals related to this are to break down stereotypes and reduce animosity between racial and locational (urban versus suburban school) identities, to establish social networks across these identity groups, and to build commitment among participants to behave as racial allies in the future.[2] The second set of indicators relate to the expectation that the dialogue can help participants develop a better understanding of the *concept* of racism, including an understanding of strategies for its redress. Goals related to this are to build understanding and awareness of individual prejudice, institutional racism, white privilege, segregation, and affirmative action.[3]

We may have good reasons, however, to be skeptical of the potential for these interventions to have a dramatic impact on participants, and particularly on their grasp of complex concepts. First, dialogue interventions are short and isolated, lasting approximately 15 to 20 hours over the course of two to three months. As a result they will likely have a difficult time competing with more ubiquitous interactions with family members and peers that play a central role in shaping participants' understandings of race and racism (Tatum, 1997). In addition, organizers of intergroup dialogue face important decisions about how to design their programs to balance their interests in accomplishing both contact and curricular goals. Readings, lectures, and other explicitly didactic strategies must be balanced with group discussion, sharing of personal experiences, and experiential activities. Intergroup dialogue theorists and practitioners refer to this variously as the trade-off between enlightenment and encounter, curriculum and contact, or content and process (Nagda et al., 2004; Lopez, 2004; Beale & Schoem,

2001). Because CWD's high school program is organized as an extra-curricular activity that students participate in voluntarily, there are practical limits on the extent to which curricular programming can be emphasized in the dialogue. Furthermore, while the high school–aged participants come to the dialogue at a stage of life where they are likely susceptible to strong influence, their current cognitive abilities and emotional maturity are also expected to place limits on their capacity to grasp and articulate these complex concepts.

Taking these goals and constraints as departure points, and focusing specifically on institutional racism and white privilege, I examine the way dialogue participants talk about these concepts before and after the dialogue in an effort to identify the impact of the experience on their understanding of racism. In describing their goals, organizers use language of "awareness" and "understanding" of these concepts, but what kind of changes should be expected given the constraints and limitations placed on the dialogue? And how can these changes be captured by empirical research given our expectation that they will be fairly modest? The semi-structured interviews conducted with dialogue participants provide a resource for exploring these questions. The research elaborated upon here, while small in scale and exploratory in nature, provides a framework for conceptualizing different levels of understanding and awareness of white privilege and institutional racism. This is a first step toward systematically measuring the impact of intergroup dialogue on participant understandings of racism-related concepts. I therefore ask: How do participants talk about these concepts? Do they talk about them differently after the dialogue? Why or why not? How might we explain differences in outcomes? Answers to these questions will inform theorizing about the range of outcomes we can feasibly expect when we bring citizens together to talk about social conflicts in general, and racism in particular.

The paper proceeds as follows. First, I provide a brief overview of the CWD dialogue program and introduce its main features. Second, I discuss the study's methodology by introducing details about the participants, semi-structured interviews, and coding frameworks used to analyze participant comments about institutional racism and white privilege. Next, I describe the findings drawn from my analysis of the interview data. The analysis suggests that relatively modest levels of understanding of both concepts should be anticipated from participants both before and after completion of a dialogue of this type. While dramatic changes resulting from the dialogue are not found, the data indicate that the dialogue does have demonstrable impacts on the ways participants think and talk about institutional racism and white privilege. I conclude with a discussion of the main challenges to building understanding of institutional racism and white privilege that are suggested by the findings and propose some directions for future research.

COMMUNITY WIDE DIALOGUE'S HIGH SCHOOL EXCHANGE PROGRAM: AN OVERVIEW

CWD's high school dialogue began in 2003 when it was first piloted with students from one city and one suburban school in the Syracuse, New York area. Since then dialogue groups have been convened every year at the pilot high schools and the program has now been expanded into several other schools in the Syracuse area. The data included here are drawn from study of two dialogue groups that occurred between 2004 and 2005 at the original pilot schools.

As Table 1 indicates, the city school has a very multiracial and multiethnic population. The suburban school in this pairing is ten miles from the center of Syracuse and has an approximately 90% white population. In each cycle,

Table 1. School Statistics 2002–2003.

	Schools			
	City[a]		Suburban[b]	
	n(1329)	%	n(1471)	%
Ethnic/racial composition				
AI, A, A, PI[c]	33	2.5	59	4.0
Non-Hispanic black	621	46.7	27	1.8
Hispanic	85	6.4	15	1.0
Non-Hispanic white	590	44.4	1370	93.1
Other information				
Limited English proficiency[d]	139	10.5	10	0.7
Eligible for free lunch[e]	511	38.5	40	2.7

[a]http://www.emsc.nysed.gov/repcrdfall2003/cir/421800010039.pdf
[b]http://www.emsc.nysed.gov/repcrdfall2003/cir/421001060002.pdf
[c]American Indian, Alaskan, Asian, or Pacific Islander.
[d]Because the ethnic/racial categories are limited, this statistic is included to give a richer picture of the schools' diversity.
[e]This statistic is designed to give a limited indication of the varied socioeconomic profiles of the two schools.

roughly 25 to 30 sophomores, juniors, and seniors from each school are selected to participate in the dialogue.[4] In addition to the student participants, approximately six students from each school who have already completed a dialogue cycle are selected to become group facilitators. Students are arranged in groups of 10 to 12, with equal numbers from each school in each group. Each group is facilitated by two students, one from each school, and supervised by one adult teacher, administrator, or CWD program staff member. The student facilitators participate in a 12 hour training program prior to the beginning of the dialogue session. In this training, they have their own dialogue group and take turns facilitating the sessions.

Modeled on the Study Circles[5] approach (Roberts & Kay inc., 2000), the dialogue is convened over a period of several months, and consists of six to seven sessions that take place alternately at each school[6] and are organized as follows:

Session 1: Participants receive a dialogue handbook[7] which outlines the agenda for each session. They meet in their small groups and establish ground rules for their future discussions and also list the stereotypes they have about each other's schools. They are paired up and the visitors "shadow" their partners for half the school day. They conclude in their small groups by revisiting the list of stereotypes they generated earlier.

Session 2: In the small groups each participant talks about their ethnic and racial background and shares a family portrait with the group. Visitors now shadow their partners for a half day in the other school environment. They reconvene at the end to revisit the list of stereotypes generated during Session 1.

Session 3: Participants meet for two hours and are led by facilitators through a series of discussion questions about the causes and possible solutions for racial tension.

Session 4: Participants take part in an exercise which I refer to here as "Stepping Forward." This exercise is based on the white privilege inventory questionnaire in Peggy McIntosh's article *White Privilege: Unpacking the Invisible Knapsack* (McIntosh, 1989, p. 11). They line up at one end of the cafeteria (where the dialogue is conducted) and a CWD organizer reads out loud a series of nine statements (see Appendix A). Participants are instructed to take a step forward if the statement applies to them. When the activity is complete, white students are standing further ahead than black[8] and other students of color. After some discussion in the large group, discussion of the activity continues in the small groups.

Session 5: Participants enter to find the tables marked with signs such as "African American", "European American", "Foreign Born" etc. and are instructed by organizers to sit at "the table where you belong." Cookies and milk[9] are found at the "European American" table while crackers and water are found at all other tables. CWD organizers observe to see whether the various groups notice the inequity. Discussion of the exercise begins in the larger group and the debrief continues in the smaller groups. For the second half of day five, participants take part in an exercise designed to demonstrate the importance of allies, which is followed by small group discussion of the same topic.

Session 6[10]: CWD organizers present a brief overview of affirmative action policies and student facilitators present several skits portraying different perspectives, followed by small group discussion.

Session 7: On the last day of the dialogue, students meet in their small groups and discuss the scenarios listed in the handbook that call for a response from antiracist activists. They also draw and present a picture that represents their ideal for a planet free from racism and racial injustice.

METHODOLOGY

Participants and Data

Findings are based on interviews with 20 participants in the CWD program. Interviews were conducted in two waves between June 2004 and March 2005. Post-dialogue interviews were conducted with the nine participants who make up "Group 1," one small group from the Dialogue 1 cycle. Pre- and post-dialogue interviews were conducted with the 12 participants who make up "Group 2," a small group from the Dialogue 2 cycle.[11] During the interviews, participants were asked to describe their racial and ethnic background. Group 1 includes two white, two black, and two Asian participants, two participants of mixed racial background,[12] and one Latino participant. Group 2 includes six white, four black, and two Asian participants. The overall distribution across both groups is eight white, three Asian, two mixed, six black, and one Latino. More detailed information about participants is included in Appendix B. All interviews and data analysis were conducted by the author who is a white woman in her mid-twenties. It is possible that this affected the comfort level of different participants during interviews, which in turn may have influenced their ways of talking about race, racism, and their dialogue experience. While I have remained attentive to this possibility throughout, and found no indication of a systematic bias in the results, it is not likely that the effects of this dynamic can be entirely eliminated from the analysis.

Conceptualizing and Coding Racism: Institutional Racism and White Privilege

In interviews conducted prior to the evaluation research, CWD organizers listed among their explicit goals that participants leave the dialogue with increased awareness and understanding of white privilege and institutional racism, and in so doing acquire a way of conceptualizing racism that is broader than individual prejudice. In the best known definition of white privilege, Peggy McIntosh calls it the "invisible package of unearned assets that I can count on cashing in each day, but about which I was 'meant' to remain oblivious" (McIntosh, 1989, p. 10). In other words, white privilege highlights the ways that whites, even when they do not hold any racist beliefs or commit overtly racist actions, benefit from individual and institutional manifestations of racism. The concept has been used in antiracist education to engage whites who believe they have no personal experience with racism, simply because they do not hold racist beliefs. There is less consensus surrounding the precise meaning of institutional racism (Williams, 1985; Bourne, 2001) but it generally refers to the "the anonymous operation of discrimination in organizations, professions, or even whole societies" (Cashmore, 1996, p. 169). Institutional racism highlights the potential for policies and practices to have racist consequences even without having been designed or implemented with racist intentions. Familiarity with the concept of institutional racism provides a greater appreciation of the historical as well as contemporary causes of inequality across racial groups and the forces that create and perpetuate these disparities.

Interview questions probe, among other things, the extent to which participants understand these concepts pre- and post-dialogue and the relationship between that understanding and their experience in the dialogue. Participants were asked to say how they would define racism if they were required to give a definition. Definitions were examined to see how much they emphasized individual prejudice, white privilege, and institutional racism. To further assess the extent to which dialogue participants understand institutional racism I ask the following three questions. First,

Table 2. Individualist and Structural Explanations.

Example 1: Followed in Stores

Individualist explanation: Individual store employees who are racially prejudiced follow racial minorities believing that they are more likely to steal. [individual explanation].

Example 2: Representation in US Congress

Racial minorities are underrepresented in the US Congress because racially prejudiced voters will not vote for them because of their race [individual explanation].

Racial minorities are underrepresented in the US Congress because structural inequalities make them less likely to have the education and wealth to compete fairly with whites [structural explanation].

Example 3: Band-Aids

Band-Aids are made to match lighter skin tones because of market forces and prevailing norms that favor dominant groups [structural explanation].

do they recognize the term? Second, when given a prompt,[13] can participants offer relevant examples of institutional racism? Third, do participants offer relevant examples in other parts of the interview?[14] Examples are considered relevant if they can be explained by structural as opposed to individualist explanations. The differences between individualist and structural explanations are illustrated in Table 2 where I provide brief explanations to three examples included in the "Stepping Forward" exercise (see Appendix A). These explanations are by no means intended to be exhaustive as the examples are clearly far more complicated and nuanced than is suggested here.[15] They are offered in order to illustrate in a simplified form the distinction between individual and structural explanations of racism that is central to the concept of institutional racism. They are intended to match the degree of depth a program the length of the dialogue can realistically reach as well as the capacity of high school students to know, understand, and articulate explanations for these examples.

Participants' descriptions of various examples are taken as indicative of their grasp of institutional racism. In some cases (Example 1) the institutional factors contributing to the phenomena are quite indirect and explanations are likely to emphasize individual prejudice. In cases like Example 2, a fairly simple account of both individual and structural explanations might be offered. In others (Example 3), individual explanations while technically plausible,[16] are not very convincing and persuasive explanations require a structural account. Therefore, having identified the relevant examples, I assess the extent to which participants describe these examples in ways that indicate a grasp of their structural causes. To do so I look for evidence of two key aspects of the concept. First, do participants talk about the examples in ways that acknowledge the anonymous character of institutional racism? More specifically do they understand the structural factors that are at play in these examples and the possibility of racist consequences in the absence of racist intentions? Second, do participants acknowledge both the historical and contemporary forces that produce institutional forms of racism? Based on the results of this analysis I place participants in one of three categories to describe the extent to which they understand institutional racism. The categories are listed in Table 3.

To assess participants' understanding of white privilege I ask the following questions. First, do participants recognize the term "white privilege" and can they provide an accurate definition? Second, do participants acknowledge the advantages enjoyed by whiter people in contemporary society? Third, can participants provide relevant examples of these advantages? The concept of white privilege is more elastic than that of institutional racism and the two in fact overlap because white privilege is a product of both individual and structural forms of racism, depending on the context and example. As a result I consider any example that recounts differing experiences across racial groups, where whites are thought to benefit, as a relevant example of white privilege whether it highlights individual prejudice, structural inequality, or both (Examples 1, 2, and 3 in Table 2 are therefore all considered relevant examples of white privilege). Having identified relevant examples, I assess the level of "personalization" that is indicated by participants' responses. In other words, I look for examples showing awareness of how the participants themselves are personally affected by the operation of white privilege. This notion of personal impact is central to the concept itself, as defined by McIntosh, and takes different forms depending on the racial identity of the individual. Personalization is indicated through examples based on direct personal experience and/or those encountered in one's own local community. Based on the results of this analysis, I place participants in one of three

Table 3. Coding Framework for Institutional Racism.

Low: Participant explains racism solely with reference to the attitudes and actions of racially prejudiced individuals and does not offer relevant examples of racism with structural causes.
Medium: Participant offers relevant examples of racism with structural causes but these explanations are conflicting, partial, or not fully expressed.
High: Participant offers relevant examples of racism with structural causes and these explanations are articulated in ways that acknowledge the contemporary forces that produce institutional racism.

Table 4. Coding Framework for White Privilege.

Low:	Participant does not acknowledge advantages enjoyed by whites in contemporary society and does not offer relevant examples of these advantages.
Medium:	Participant offers relevant examples of white privilege but does not fully acknowledge the advantages enjoyed by whites in contemporary society. Examples may be hypothetical, historical, and/or depersonalized.
High:	Participant offers relevant examples and acknowledges the advantages enjoyed by whites in contemporary society in ways that are personalized.

categories to describe the extent to which they understand white privilege, which I specify in Table 4.

FINDINGS AND ANALYSIS

Defining Racism

Overwhelmingly, and with consistency across pre- and post-dialogue interviews, participants provide definitions that underscore an understanding of racism that is limited to instances of individual prejudice. Definitions refer to individual beliefs, judgments, and acceptance of stereotypes, as well as feelings of dislike or even hatred toward people of different races.[17] While the definitions most often refer to individually held beliefs, occasionally they make reference to individual actions as well. For example, when Jenn, a white participant from the suburban school defines racism in her post-dialogue interview as "Just pretty much anyone like treating someone differently because of like who they are and like what they look like and stuff," she is indicating that racism has something to do with individual behavior as well as individual beliefs.

One of the most complicated post-dialogue responses to the question, where Maya struggles with larger structural and cultural aspects of racism, ultimately concludes with an account of racism that highlights the role played by fear in individual forms of prejudice.

> *How would you define racism if you had to give a definition?*[18]
>
> Um actually I d- I have this thing about racism that like it's not really race it's more economic and more your background um because yeah people see what color your skin is first but it's I don't know we all really come from the same place and like scientific or religiously like we still come from the same place and we just I don't know like my dad, my dad's a scientist and he says you know racism you know race doesn't really exist

> we're all the same race, like whites are actually three quarters black and like but it's more I think the problem is more we invented racism maybe to explain our problems with I think it's we're afraid of what's different it's not different skin color but different lifestyles different backgrounds. (Maya City, Mixed)

Only in a couple of instances do post-dialogue definitions of racism suggest a broader conceptualization of racism. Chantelle, a black city school participant, thinks that racism means "treating one group superior" but her definition is not developed enough to make it clear whether this conceptualization goes beyond individual prejudice to include institutional racism.

With respect to white privilege, only Neena, an Asian suburban school participant, comes close when she says racism has to do with "giving privileges maybe to a different uh skin color race" but again, her awareness of white privilege is not by any means confirmed in her definition of racism. No significant differences appear between responses from city versus suburban or whites versus people of color and overall comparison between the participants' pre- and post-dialogue responses show no tendency toward increased complexity in their definitions of racism. Such a change would be the most obvious indication that the dialogue successfully causes participants to adopt a broader concept of racism. Fortunately the interviews explore other indicators of conceptual understanding, which I examine taking each term, institutional racism and white privilege, in turn below.

An initial analysis of responses to questions about institutional racism and white privilege reveals a fairly simple and straightforward story. Participants do not recognize the term institutional racism and rarely offer a relevant example when prompted. In contrast, participants do recognize the term white privilege and in almost all cases are able to provide a relevant example when asked. There is little variation across interview responses with regard to these findings, suggesting one or both of the following conclusions. First, white privilege may be an easier concept to grasp than institutional racism and second the dialogue may be better designed to teach the former than it is the latter. Yet a broader analysis of the interviews as a whole reveals a more complex picture and suggests alternate ways for thinking about and measuring awareness and understanding of key concepts targeted by the dialogue. Throughout their interviews, participants often recount relevant examples that suggest different (and often better) understandings of institutional racism and white privilege than those articulated in their response to direct questions about the concepts. In light of this, I broadened the analysis to look at all relevant examples mentioned throughout the interview and developed the aforementioned coding framework to characterize participant levels of understanding of the concepts.

Table 5 summarizes each participant's understanding of institutional racism and white privilege as expressed in post-dialogue interviews and, where available, pre-dialogue interviews. Below, I describe the distribution of responses across Low, Medium, and High categories of understanding and provide exemplary responses for each in order to demonstrate the different ways that participants talk about institutional racism and white privilege. Next, I discuss the similarities and differences between pre- and post-dialogue interviews with Group 2 participants, focusing on the impact of the dialogue on participants' ways of talking about these concepts.

Table 5. Responses for Institutional Racism and White Privilege.

Name	Race, School	Institutional Racism		White Privilege	
		Post	Δ	Post	Δ
Group 1					
Chantelle	Black, city	Medium	n/a	High	n/a
Jason	White, city	High	n/a	Medium	n/a
Maya	Mixed, city	Medium	n/a	Medium	n/a
Neena	Asian, suburb	Medium	n/a	Medium	n/a
Jessica[a]	White, suburb	Medium	n/a	High	n/a
Alicia	Mixed, suburb	Medium	n/a	High	n/a
Megan	Asian, suburb	Medium	n/a	High	n/a
Nicole[a]	Black, city	Medium	n/a	High	n/a
Erik	Latino, city	Medium	n/a	High	n/a
Group 2					
Megan[a]	Asian, suburb	Medium	–	High	–
Agnes	White, suburb	Low	–	Medium	–
Jenn	White, suburb	Low	–	Medium	–
Ann	White, suburb	Medium	–	High	Δ
Chris	White, suburb	Medium	Δ	Medium	Δ
Patrick	White, suburb	Low	–	Medium	–
Yvette[a]	Black, city	Low	–	Medium	Δ
Lester	Black, city	Medium	–	High	–
Sophie	Asian, city	Medium	–	High	Δ
Janelle[a]	Black, city	Medium	Δ	High	–
Emily	White, city	High	–	High	–
Andrew	Black, city	Medium	–	High	–

Note: Δ indicates participants whose pre-dialogue responses were coded in a different category from their post-dialogue ones.
[a]Indicates participation in multiple dialogue cycles.

Institutional Racism

The categories of Low, Medium, and High are not intended to capture absolute measures of understanding with respect to institutional racism, but have instead been developed inductively as a way to capture the range of understandings contained within the data. Therefore, the few participants whose responses have been coded as "High" do not offer complete structural accounts of the examples they describe. Nevertheless, their responses stand out in comparison to others who rely entirely on individual explanations. For example, Emily's response is one of few that captures the cumulative nature of institutional racism, though her explanation here does not provide an account for *why* or *how* this cycle of inequality is initiated.

> *Ok, um there's this term institutional racism have you heard that before? How would you explain it?*
>
> Well I would explain that like institutional racism is like um just that people in higher jobs are white and its institutionalized from where I guess like college degrees even you know like there's more white people with college degrees and so your teachers are mostly white and then your administrators are mostly white and then after that like the administration downtown is all white you know like no joke and then like as you go up and up like senators, congressmen, the president, that's like all institutionalized racism, I think, I think anyways. (Emily, White, City)

Emily is also one of the only participants who recognizes and uses the term institutional racism in her response. Though "term recognition" is certainly not the only indicator of conceptual understanding, it suggests a better grasp of concept than those cases where no such recognition, even after a definitional prompt, is indicated.

As Table 5 shows, I locate the majority of participants in the "Medium" category, which is characterized by an ability to describe examples of institutional racism despite a limited ability to explain their structural causes. Sophie's pre-dialogue comments illustrate this well as she combines structural observations on residential segregation with a description of individual level prejudice in her analysis of racial inequality.

> *What do you think could be done in society to improve race relations or eliminate racism?*
>
> Um, I think they could give people more like equal opportunities like if you go to the South Side or like the bad parts of like whatever side you're living on, you see more like black people or Hispanic people living like more like in the ghetto-ish areas, I think that like, but they're, now they're helping to like rebuild people's houses and they're trying to get more like control over those areas just to make them nicer and give people more equal opportunities or I'm sure there's still people that don't want to hire people at jobs because of their race or they think they're just going to do something wrong 'cause

> they're black. I think just making sure everyone gets a fair chance at things. (Sophie, Asian, City)

Alternately, those in the "Medium" group sometimes give structural explanations that are formulated entirely in historical terms. This exhibits what Kluegel and Bobo (1993) have called "soft-structuralism," an understanding that acknowledges the role of the legacy of slavery but does not take note of contemporary forces that continue to perpetuate racial disparities (i.e., "hard-structuralism," see also Lopez et al., 1998). Maya's response is illustrative of this.

> I mean the white privilege is more just because of their economic advantage, like it's just the facts of this country that the whites have more money in general ... I mean it just it seems like it's always been that way it just started like I don't know ever since we had slaves obviously they started off being extremely poor when they were freed and then it just it's getting better but it hasn't. (Maya, Mixed, City)

In contrast, the few participants whose responses are categorized as "Low" understanding do not provide relevant examples of institutional racism when prompted or at any point in their interview. When they do provide examples that might be explained structurally, they are followed by explanations that are unambiguously individualist. An illustrative example is Agnes' explanation for why bandages are made to match lighter skin tones.

> I think it's just, like when did Band-Aids come out or I don't even know, I guess before the people were like racist I guess and they were like oh no black person can't wear our Band-Aids or whatever let's just make it white because it matches our skin so I guess they must have been made a long time ago like the race issue must have been really big back then that they would create that. (Agnes, White, Suburb)

Agnes' reliance on an individualist explanation, even for an example where it seems not to provide an adequate account of the phenomena, indicates a limited awareness of institutional racism.

Although the small number of cases included in the analysis make it difficult to definitively identify or rule out any clear pattern, outcomes for institutional racism do not appear to map strongly onto the racial or locational identities of the participants. Overall for institutional racism, participants cluster in the Medium category, while several exhibit a Low understanding and very few demonstrate a High understanding.

White Privilege

The categories of "Low," "Medium," and "High" for white privilege have also been developed inductively based on the range of responses present in the data. Overall, participants' responses are clustered in the High and Medium categories with just one pre-dialogue interview indicating a Low understanding of white privilege. Chris' response prior to the dialogue is the only time that a participant denies the existence of white privilege, making this the exemplar of "Low" understanding.

> *Ok um do you think that people with uh lighter skin or whiter skin um have an advantage in Central New York or in Syracuse or in America?*
>
> I don't think so. … I don't really think that just 'cause a black, a person has darker skin, that doesn't mean anything so I don't understand why they would be on different playing fields. (Chris, White, Suburb)

What is much more common among the respondents is the acknowledgment of advantages for whites in abstract or detached ways that do not connect such advantages directly to one's own personal experience. Jenn's response provides a good illustrative example of the sort of depersonalized account of white privilege that is categorized here as "Medium" understanding.

> *Ok, um do you think that um, do you think that people of lighter skin color or white people um have any advantages um in Central New York or in the US?*
>
> I've never myself experienced it but I'm sure there are times when that happens.
>
> *Could you um think of any examples where that might happen?*
>
> Probably in jobs or like when you're, I know um, some of the kids in one of the, when we were having a discussion with them they were talking about how sometimes they'll get followed in stores and stuff, like not really followed but they'll be watching them more closely than other people. … Yeah, like I don't know I think there's more like advantages for white people than there are for colored people definitely but I don't know, I've never really experienced it so I don't really know. (Jenn, White, Suburb)

Other respondents describe examples of white privilege in ways that are personalized and therefore demonstrate a relatively "High" understanding of the concept. Andrew's discussion of white privilege is indicative of this as he recounts several personal anecdotes about the ways he has and continues to experience white privilege in his day-to-day life. In the excerpt below, Andrew describes one instance, the college application process, where whites need not consider their racial identity.

> *Ok, um, there's this term white privilege, did you guys use that term at all?*
>
> I think we used it once, and we understand, you know, white is a privilege, being white, just like I said with the jobs you, you become privileged or with schools … for

> example college applications .... It's, I mean it's like hard to realize, you really have to think about it, do I wanna check that box so, I think there is a privilege, when you're white you have, you don't really have to worry about checking that box or not. (Andrew, Black, City)

Though a fairly mundane example, it captures the idea that part of the privilege associated with being white is the luxury of not having to consider one's own racial identity in everyday life. As the results in Table 5 show, people of color are more likely to articulate white privilege in ways that demonstrate "High" levels of understanding. While five out of six black participants demonstrate a "High" understanding of white privilege, three out of eight white participants are categorized in the same way. That whites have a harder time personalizing white privilege is not surprising given McIntosh's claim that they are meant to remain unaware of the way white privilege functions in their everyday lives. Nevertheless, as I will elaborate below in my discussion of the white privilege results, this complicates the task of dialogue organizers seeking to build participant awareness of the concept because it highlights the way personalization is influenced by participants' racial and school identities.

Does the Dialogue Build Understanding of the Concepts?

Pre-dialogue interviews with Group 2 participants make it possible to draw some tentative conclusions about the dialogue's ability to change the way participants understand and talk about institutional racism and white privilege. The "delta" (Δ) column in Table 5 indicates the cases where a Group 2 participant's pre-dialogue interview is coded differently from their post-dialogue interview. As the results indicate, very few participants make notable shifts across categories after participating in the dialogue. Such changes would be the most obvious evidence that the dialogue successfully builds participants' awareness and understanding of the concepts. In the few cases where this does occur, it is notable that the change is related to particular material encountered in the dialogue. The juxtaposition of Ann's comments about white privilege pre- and post-dialogue exemplifies this kind of change.

> *Ok, um do you think that people with uh lighter skin or whiter skin have any advantages in Syracuse or in Central New York or in America?*
>
> I think so because um I don't know just it seems that people tend to see white people in a better sense than like an African American person...
>
> *Like in what kind of situations?*

Like, um… I don't know like if you're like walking on the street in the dark and you look behind you and there's like a white person behind you, you might not be as like afraid as if there was a black person behind you because of stereotypes again. (Pre-dialogue, Ann, White, Suburb)

Uh huh, ok um do you think that people of um lighter skin color or white people have any advantages in Central New York or in the US?

I think they do like I didn't realize this before the dialogue but some people were saying how like when they would go into a store like they, like an employee would like follow them and make sure they didn't steal something I guess, … so, when we were talking about it in the group it seemed like almost all of the black, darker people had had that happen to them and like I've never heard of that happening, like it's never happened to me or like any of my friends. (Post-dialogue, Ann, White, Suburb)

Ann's comments make fairly evident that her tendency to describe white privilege in a more personalized manner than before comes as a direct result of her experience in the dialogue. More specifically, one of the examples included in the "Stepping Forward" exercise and the similar personal experiences of the people of color in her small group are responsible for the change. Ann recognizes that she and her friends, who she describes earlier in the interview as primarily white, have had a different experience than the black students she met in the dialogue. This example appears to have helped her to personalize the concept of white privilege, at least with respect to one example, and recognize the "invisible assets" she carries as a result of being white.

Although Table 5 indicates that cases like Ann's are exceptional, limiting the analysis to instances of change across categories underemphasizes the impacts of the dialogue. While these categories provide a way to systematically map all participants, much of the nuance in individual responses is lost in this presentation of the data. Though not captured as movement between Low, Medium, or High categories of understanding of either concept, comparison of pre-dialogue to post-dialogue interviews indicates that the experience leaves strong impressions on participants which do alter the ways they think and talk about racism. This seems to happen primarily through the introduction of examples, often drawn from the "Stepping Forward" exercise and reinforced by the personal stories of fellow dialogue participants.[19] Where pre-dialogue data are available, the post-dialogue examples of white privilege and institutional racism offered by participants are more elaborate and detailed, even when they are not more personalized (in the case of white privilege) or understood more structurally (in the case of institutional racism).

Ann's comments are not unique in their reference to examples drawn directly from the "Stepping Forward" exercise. Other, though fewer, participants also reference "Cookies and Milk" as an activity designed to teach about white privilege. While almost every example from "Stepping Forward" is given throughout the interviews, the example of people of color being followed in stores is particularly salient for many participants. That example is offered by almost half of the participants, appears consistently across Group1 and Group 2 interviews, and is salient at both Low and High ends of understanding. If the example was concentrated in the interviews from one group in particular, it might be an indication that it stemmed from a particular conversation which became memorable to participants. The fact that this example appears consistently across both dialogue groups suggests that it has an inherent salience for dialogue participants regardless of the direction discussions take.

Similar changes occur with respect to institutional racism. Agnes, for example, while continuing to describe racism individualistically, says that the dialogue experience prompted her to notice residential segregation while driving around Syracuse and its surrounding areas for her driving lessons.

> Yeah, Well I think it was because before I wouldn't really have noticed I would have just been like oh people you know because the people are just like, 'cause when you like it's the second you go into the city you don't really see any white people and like you see all these like African Americans walking out it's sort of like the same thing except I didn't really notice it before, I was just like, no [inaudible], I was just like why are they all living here when they could be living somewhere else in like a white neighborhood if that's what you're going to call it. I guess it raised awareness about it 'cause I didn't really notice it before. (Agnes, White, Suburb)

Although she does not provide an explanation for racial segregation that relates it to institutional factors, she credits new observations in her everyday life to her experience in the dialogue. Though pre-dialogue interviews were not conducted with Group 1 participants, their post-dialogue comments often match these in attributing important impacts to the dialogue. Alicia's comments suggest a Medium-level understanding of institutional racism because she does not articulate structural explanations for the examples she gives. Yet she is remarkably insightful on the subtleties of institutional racism and reports recognizing this subtlety as a result of the dialogue.

> No, I started to because it's really subtle, like there's, with the institutions it's more subtle than someone blatantly saying a racist fact, and it's something you really have to think about ... [the dialogue] made me really more aware and look at things that I would never realize before and say wow you know that really is out there. (Alicia, Mixed, Suburb)

These interviews suggest that the impact of the dialogue with respect to concepts is mainly to attune participants to examples that occur in their everyday lives. While it does not equip them with the historical background, factual information, or analytical tools to explain or fully make sense of these examples, the dialogue experience does equip them to talk about these examples with others in ways that over time, through subsequent pedagogical interventions[20] and life experiences, may help to strengthen conceptual understanding in more measurable ways.

DISCUSSION

Though the coding framework developed here is not effective at capturing change resulting from the dialogue, it does serve to highlight the key challenges that participants experience in trying to grasp the concepts of institutional racism and white privilege. Overall, participants appear to struggle most with the "personalization" of white privilege, and this struggle takes different forms depending on the social identity of the participant in question. With respect to institutional racism, most participants do not demonstrate the structural thinking required to fully grasp this concept. Below I elaborate on each of these challenges in turn and explore their implications for intergroup dialogue design and research.

White Privilege and Personalization

The frequency with which participants talk about white privilege as a phenomenon that exists elsewhere or has not directly affected them clarifies the central challenge in building awareness and understanding of this concept. Not surprisingly given the nature of the concept, the ability to personalize experiences of white privilege is related to an individual's racial identity. As noted above, black participants appear better equipped to understand the concept of white privilege prior to, during, and after the dialogue experience. Theories of racial identity development suggest this is because blacks experience the social world differently from whites, and in ways that make the phenomena of white privilege more obvious to them (Helms, 1990; Tatum, 1992, 1997). Andrew's response supports these expectations by suggesting that his grasp of the concept relates to the preexisting heightened sensitivity to white privilege that comes from being a person of color.

> Nope, I don't think it made it any clearer for me because I've noticed it, you know you always notice it especially when you're the minority, I guess they say the minority, they al- you notice things that aren't correct in your society or your life. (Andrew, Black, City)

While the data clearly support Andrew's insight about the relative ease most black participants have in personalizing white privilege compared to most white participants, it also suggests that ability to personalize white privilege is complicated by the interaction between racial and school identity. School identity (city versus suburban), which overlaps strongly with socioeconomic class, is very salient due to the "exchange" format of the dialogue. The complex interaction between race and class contributes to uncertainty on the part of several participants concerning white privilege.

For example, though the cases are few, the comments of white city students indicate an uncertainty concerning their relationship to white privilege. Jason and Emily both express doubt concerning the extent to which they individually benefit from white privilege; Jason's comments are illustrative of this.

> For me personally I haven't had any like experiences with that I think I'm on like the same page as everybody, like here I notice it like you know everybody's the same you know I'm sure if you take just take it out of context you know look at numbers like more African Americans are here than like at [suburban school] and it's almost like all the money goes to [suburban school] and everything like that and then you look here but is being white in going here, I don't see a major white privilege. I still had to work hard to get into college I still you know had to work hard to get money to pay for college you know and sometimes I almost think that it's a little bit harder being like a white boy you know sometimes I don't get as many scholarships and my parents not being very wealthy or anything like that it's hard. (Jason, White, City)

The prominence of school funding inequities and their relationship to the racial makeup of city versus suburban schools as well as a partial understanding of affirmative action initiatives leaves Jason skeptical that he himself, as a white male, benefits from white privilege. Emily's understanding is categorized as higher, because she describes the way she benefits as a white student from teacher favoritism. But her interview comments overall display a similar uncertainty about her relationship to white privilege. Though she acknowledges examples of her own racial privilege, her interview is dominated by narratives of "reverse racism" and class-based disadvantages. In sum, both Emily and Jason struggle to disentangle the significance of race versus class in their assessments of their own privilege as white people.

Inversely, suburban students of color also experience difficulties with personalization of white privilege. Despite being white, Emily and Jason describe to different degrees the ways they consider themselves as "victims" of white privilege. In contrast, like their white suburban peers, minority suburban students seem more likely to view their relationship to white privilege in neutral terms, as something they neither benefit nor suffer from. While the small number of cases make generalizations inappropriate, both[21] cases exhibit this neutrality, though to different degrees. Like most of her white peers Neena, an Indian-American suburban student, describes white privilege as something she has never thought about or experienced and says "it became clear there is a white privilege some places, and I'm sure there is one here too but I just I don't know." Megan, who is Korean and adopted into a white family does recount personalized examples of white privilege during parts of her interview and her understanding is therefore categorized as "High." In particular she describes her struggle to conform to standards of white beauty and her experience of discrimination at the hands of some of her white peers. At the same time however, she does not identify personally with the description of white privilege offered by black participants.

> It was kind of weird, some people who are minorities here, like complained a lot, there was like some complaining in my group and it was, it got like really old, and I mean I know like, like I feel bad saying that but um, it just, it was annoying after a while.
>
> *What kind of stuff do you mean, like complaining?*
>
> They were just like, actually, I should, I feel so bad saying this because I mean maybe like I don't see it, but I like feel like I would see it because I am, like a minority ... I mean I'm a minority too I don't get treated like that. (Megan, Asian, Suburb)

It is unclear if the challenges Megan and Neena have in personalizing white privilege are more strongly related to their position as nonblack people of color or to their position as people of color at suburban schools. But their comments, like those of Jason and Emily, do suggest that the particularities of their social identities are crucial to their understanding of white privilege.

Therefore not only is personalization the key challenge to grasping white privilege but participants who find themselves located on opposite sides of the race/class divide at the same time (person of color/suburban or white/city) have a challenging time locating themselves in relation to the concept. In addition, not all nonwhite participants relate to the concept in the same way. This suggests that a greater emphasis on the way various social identity groups are advantaged or disadvantaged by white privilege in the dialogue curriculum would help participants understand the concept and its significance to them personally. Although participants overall exhibit a basic understanding of white privilege, the data suggest that increased attention in the dialogue curriculum to the universal reach of white privilege (a concept that all individuals can relate to personally) as well as its particular nature (an experience that is heavily dependent on an individual's social identity) would help to reduce skepticism and uncertainty about the prominence and significance of white privilege among many dialogue participants.

Institutional Racism and Structural Thinking

Despite the fact that they are highly related and introduced simultaneously through the dialogue's "Stepping Forward" activity, participants have an easier time recognizing and describing examples of white privilege. The analysis suggests that this is in large part due to the well-documented barriers individuals encounter to adopting structuralist ways of thinking (Lopez et al., 1998; Kluegel & Bobo, 1993). While white privilege can be partially understood without any appeal to structural thinking, institutional racism cannot, and interviews suggest this distinction accounts for the differences in outcomes.

Though the prominence of the "Followed in Stores" example for dialogue participants is highlighted above, other examples of white privilege offered include teacher favoritism, employment opportunities and hiring practices, customer service in restaurants, on buses, and in grocery stores, and housing discrimination (contacting landlords over the telephone). It is notable that all these examples can be explained through individual prejudice, without reference to structural causes. In fact, when the sources of white privilege are elaborated upon in interviews, they remain situated within this individual level of analysis. Agnes' account of white privilege is representative of this tendency.

> *Uh huh, um why do you think they have, they get those advantages?*
> Well I'm not like saying like everyone gets those advantages it's just like if they do get those advantages it's because like the person who like gave them advantages are like racist like they're not like open minded at all, they still have like that narrow minded view that they're better even though they're not. (Agnes, Suburban, White)

A further illustration of the challenge participants experience with respect to structural thinking is evident through the juxtaposition of participant comments about the "Followed in Stores" example to another highly salient example from "Stepping Forward," the "Band-Aid" example ("I can choose blemish cover or bandages in "flesh" color and have them more or less match my skin"), which is exemplary of both white privilege and institutional racism. As noted in Table 2, unlike the store example, which can be simplistically understood to result exclusively from the prejudice of individual store clerks, the locus of blame is much harder to locate with the Band-Aid example. The latter is more explicitly disconnected from individual-level prejudice and requires structural thinking in order to be associated with racism. Participants struggle a great deal with this example, with some trying to force it into an individualistic lens, and others rejecting it entirely as an example with any racial significance. In addition to Agnes' account of the Band-Aid example excerpted above, comments from Megan, Maya, and Yvette illustrate this difficulty.

> Maybe just the Band-Aid, they didn't know what color to make it so they just made it in between. It's not 'cause they want black people to feel inferior or they don't want it to match someone's skin color. It's just a Band-Aid. (Megan, Asian, Suburb)

> I don't think the Band-Aid makers are racist, it's not you know racism it's I don't know I don't know what it is but it's not racism. (Maya, Mixed, City)

> *And do you think that that's an example of racism?*
> No, I think that's just an example of skin tone, I mean Band-Aids come in all different colors now and so but they were talking about the original Band-Aid. (Yvette, Black, City)

These explanations contrast with Jason's, who is the only participant to offer an explanation for the Band-Aid example that references structural factors.

> And do you think that something like that like Band-Aids or is it just the convenience of being able to have Band-Aids or do you think that it is related to something bigger or?
> I think that's related to something bigger I mean, I don't know, it's just I think everything is all intertwined white flight and that stuff and just the way it is that there's more white people in America than there are black people so you know things are more marketed and then there's a lot of people living in suburbia so it's more you know marketed towards that. (Jason, White, City)

Therefore, while participants exhibit fairly high levels of understanding with respect to white privilege, this understanding is largely confined to examples of the concept based on individual manifestations of prejudice and this does not translate easily into understanding of institutional racism. Though a wide range of examples are mentioned in participant interviews, the most salient are drawn from the "Stepping Forward" exercise, suggesting that this activity is the central mechanism through which participants learn about these concepts. Yet the dialogue activity does not make an explicit distinction between institutional racism and white privilege, nor the different causal logics at play for each example. Unpacking these nuances, though necessary for a better understanding of these concepts, does not appear to be the purpose of the dialogue format, which instead encourages participants to reflect on personal experience and react to those of others. As a result, the activity may not be the most effective way to introduce structural thinking to dialogue participants. This is evident in Emily's strong individualistic reaction to the Stepping Forward exercise, in which she felt personally, and unfairly, blamed.

> Just like stepping forward was really hard and because every step you took you felt like you were blamed for something that you didn't do that you didn't set up, that yeah everybody notices but what are you going to do about it, like I'm a high school student, why should I be you know, I felt like I was being like shamed because I kept taking a step forward and nobody else was. (Emily, White, City)

Emily is not alone in her reaction to the activity and many of her peers recount feelings of discomfort, guilt, and resentment as a result of the Stepping Forward and Cookies and Milk activities. Her comments demonstrate that while dialogue activities leave very powerful impressions on participants about racial inequality, their emotional quality may distract even the most structural thinker from thinking about the problem in structural ways. If structural thinking is a desired goal, and it seems this is needed in order for institutional racism to be understood, adjustments to the format are likely necessary to incorporate more didactic methods of teaching complex concepts in general and encouraging structural thinking in particular.

CONCLUSION

In addition to providing practical insights about strategies that might be employed within dialogue programs to address the challenges participants encounter in understanding complex concepts, this research raises some methodological lessons for researchers hoping to measure the impacts of intergroup dialogue empirically. First, the limited scope of this research must be acknowledged. Focusing on twenty cases across two cycles of one dialogue program has allowed for in-depth analysis of participants' experiences of the dialogue and has yielded useful insights about the kinds of impacts we might realistically expect to follow from interventions of this kind. Yet this approach limits the extent to which these findings can be generalized to other contexts. The applicability of these findings to dialogue programs with a different design and/or a different profile of participants must be explored through further research. While the data presented here are likely to have relevance to a wide range of intergroup dialogue contexts,[22] the age and maturity of participants as well as the balance between curricular and contact elements are important factors to consider when developing expectations about and measuring a dialogue program's impacts. Furthermore, the findings have suggested that future research should explore the impacts of the dialogue over a longer time span. This would make it possible to test the theory, suggested by short-term interviews, that the dialogue serves an awareness-raising function that contributes to more concrete understandings of white privilege and institutional racism later in life.

This analysis of CWD's intergroup dialogue program suggests that participants come into the dialogue with different levels of awareness of white privilege and institutional racism. Identifying all the factors that determine this is far too complex a task to undertake here; however, it is clear that racial and school identity as well as general cognitive sophistication and articulateness are important factors in determining the level at which participants conceptualize racism. While participants leave the dialogue with these abilities largely unchanged, the program does have notable impacts on their capacity to talk about white privilege and institutional racism. The dialogue appears to raise participants' awareness of relevant examples of these two phenomena in their everyday lives, though it does not equip them to articulate complete explanations of these examples. To the extent that dialogue organizers and researchers desire to have more pronounced impacts in these areas, the findings suggest that increased emphasis on personalization of white privilege and structural thinking about institutional racism are strategies that hold promise. Overall, the analysis suggests that while important and measurable impacts on awareness and understanding are possible, dialogue organizers and researchers should have relatively modest expectations about the kind of changes an encounter-based intergroup dialogue program can generate with respect to complex concepts.

NOTES

1. See Walsh (2007, p. 197) for the argument that intergroup dialogue programs depart in important ways from Allport's contact hypothesis.

2. Though not the focus of the analysis here, participant responses in post-dialogue interviews suggest that stereotypes and animosity are reduced, that new *informal* social networks are established *within* schools among dialogue participants, and that individuals leave the dialogue with an increased sense of commitment to behave as racial allies.

3. The two sets of indicators are of course connected since understanding of these concepts contributes directly to understanding of each other's experiences. Still, I believe that the distinction remains analytically useful.

4. The suburban school has an application form, while students were individually invited by teachers and administrators at the city school.

5. This dialogue model was developed by the Study Circles Resource Center (SCRC), now known as Everyday Democracy. See www.everyday-democracy.org

6. Although the basic format of the dialogue program remained the same for both cycles under study here, there are several differences between Dialogue 1 and Dialogue 2 worth noting. First, Dialogue 2 incorporated one extra session for a total of seven sessions, the content of which I elaborate below. Second, there were longer breaks in between sessions during Dialogue 2 than there were for Dialogue 1. As a result Dialogue 1 spanned from March to May 2004 while Dialogue 2 spanned from November 2004 to February 2005. However, as I will discuss further, the data do not suggest that these differences had a significant impact on the outcomes I focus on here, making it possible to consider the two interventions in tandem.

7. The handbook was adapted by CWD organizers from SCRC resource material. See Flavin-McDonald & McCoy 1997.

8. I have chosen to use the term black instead of African American because research shows it to be the preferred self-description and it also serves as a more inclusive term in light of the African diaspora (Cashmore, 1996, pp. 13–14). I recognize that this is by no means a settled debate. In the interest of consistency I will also use the term white instead of European American.

9. Although the dialogue handbook highlights debrief questions about segregation for this exercise, I call it "Cookies and Milk" because that aspect of the activity appears most salient in participant interviews.

10. This session was not included during Dialogue 1 but was subsequently added to Dialogue 2 program in part because the topic of affirmative action evoked so much interest in previous cycles of the dialogue.

11. Group 1 and Group 2 have one participant in common, making the total number of participants 20. Megan participated in the dialogue for the first time with Group 1 and a second time as a facilitator of Group 2.

12. This category describes participants who identify the race or ethnicity of one parent differently from the other. See Appendix B for more information.

13. Interview protocols vary slightly between Group 1 and Group 2 pre- and post-interviews. Prompts consist of either a definition of institutional racism or a question encouraging participants to give a broader articulation of racism as it operates in

society. In post-interviews participants are asked first if they recognize the term "institutional racism" and are subsequently given a prompt if necessary.

14. While the best indication of a participants' grasp of institutional racism pertains to their response to questions about the term, other examples offered through the interview give a broader sense of the participants' grasp of the concept.

15. For example, the stereotyping that produces Example 1 is reinforced by institutional causes such as patterns of media coverage and criminal sentencing. Example 2 is also related to the history of voting rights, composition of electoral districts, as well as the many factors that produce educational and wealth disparities between racial groups. I thank an anonymous reviewer for clarifying this point.

16. For example: "Band-aids are made to match lighter skin tones because the designers and makers of band-aids are racially prejudiced."

17. Interestingly, a number of participants conceptualized racism quite widely to include discrimination on the basis of gender, religion, and sexuality in their definitions (and in one case hair color as well). For these participants racism seems to be synonymous with discrimination against any group.

18. Interviewer comments are in italics and participant comments are in regular font.

19. For confirmation and elaboration of the importance of storytelling to intergroup dialogue programs see Walsh (2007, Ch. 7–8) and Rojas et al. (2005).

20. These would likely need to be more in-depth than the dialogue program and might come in the form of high school or college course content. Table 5 indicates that additional iterations of the dialogue do not have dramatic impacts.

21. Although Alicia is technically a third suburban person of color, she lived in the city and attended city schools for most of her life and therefore identifies more strongly as a city school student.

22. For example, Walsh notes the distinction between programs in civic versus educational contexts (2007, p. 244). The CWD High School Exchange Program shares elements of both contexts because its participants are students and it takes place at their schools but participation is voluntary and it does not take place in a formal classroom setting.

ACKNOWLEDGMENTS

I thank Beth Broadway, Andrea Barnwell, and everyone at Community Wide Dialogue for making this research possible. Bruce Dayton has provided helpful guidance at all stages of the project. Tina Nabatchi provided extremely helpful feedback on an earlier draft of this paper, as did Rachel Fleishman and three anonymous reviewers; I am grateful to each of them. I am also very thankful for the insightful input from Anirban Acharya, Hannah Allerdice, Nadine Georgel, Matt Guardino, Deepa Prakash, and Azamat Sakiev. While I am strongly indebted to all of the Labove, all shortcomings of the paper are mine alone.

REFERENCES

Allport, G. W. (1954). *The nature of prejudice*. Cambridge: Addison-Wesley.

Beale, R. L., & Schoem, D. (2001). The content/process balance in intergroup dialogue. In: D. Schoem & S. Hurtado (Eds), *Dialogue: Deliberative democracy in school, college, community, and workplace*. Ann Arbor: University of Michigan Press.

Bohman, J., & Rehg, W. (Eds). (1997). *Deliberative democracy: Essays on reason and politics*. Cambridge: MIT Press.

Bourne, J. (2001). The life and times of institutional racism. *Race and Class*, *42*(2), 7–22.

Cashmore, E. (1996). *Dictionary of race and ethnic relations*. New York: Routledge.

Fishkin, J. (1995). *The voice of the people: Public opinion and democracy*. New Haven: Yale University Press.

Flavin-McDonald, C., & McCoy, M. L. (1997). *The busy citizen's discussion guide: Facing the challenge of racism and race relations* (3rd ed.). Pomfret: Study Circles Resource Center.

Fung, A., & Wright, E. O. (Eds). (2003). *Deepening democracy*. London: Verso.

Gurin, P., Dey, E. L., Hurtado, S., & Gurin, G. (2002). Diversity in higher education: Theory and impact on educational outcomes. *Harvard Educational Review*, *72*(3), 330–366.

Gurin, P., Nagda, B. A., & Lopez, G. E. (2004). The benefits of diversity education for democratic citizenship. *Journal of Social Issues*, *60*(1), 17–34.

Helms, J. E. (1990). *Black and white racial identity: Theory, research, and practice*. New York: Greenwood Press.

Hurtado, S. (2001). Research and evaluation on intergroup dialogue. In: D. Schoem & S. Hurtado (Eds), *Dialogue: Deliberative democracy in school, college, community, and workplace*. Ann Arbor: University of Michigan Press.

Kardia, D., & Sevig, T. (2001). Embracing the paradox: Dialogue that incorporates both individual and group identities. In: D. Schoem & S. Hurtado (Eds), *Dialogue: Deliberative democracy in school, college, community, and workplace*. Ann Arbor: University of Michigan Press.

Kluegel, J. R., & Bobo, L. (1993). Dimensions of whites' beliefs about the black-white socioeconomic gap. In: P. Sniderman, et al. (Eds), *Prejudice, politics, and the American dilemma*. Stanford: Stanford University Press.

Lopez, G. E. (2004). Interethnic contact, curriculum, and attitudes in the first year of college. *Journal of Social Issues*, *60*(1), 75–94.

Lopez, G. E., Gurin, P., & Nagda, B. A. (1998). Education and understanding structural causes for group inequalities. *Political Psychology*, *19*, 305–329.

Mansbridge, J. (1983). *Beyond adversary democracy*. Chicago: University of Chicago Press.

McIntosh, P. (1989). White privilege: Unpacking the invisible knapsack. *Peace and Freedom*, *July/August*, 10–12.

Merelman, R. M., Streich, G., & Martin, P. (1998). Unity and diversity in American political culture: An exploratory study of the national conversation on American pluralism and identity. *Political Psychology*, *19*, 781–807.

Nagda, B. A., Kim, C. W., & Truelove, Y. (2004). Learning about differences, learning with others, learning to transgress. *Journal of Social Issues*, *60*(1), 195–214.

Pettigrew, T. F. (1998). Contact theory. *Annual Review of Psychology*, *49*, 65–85.

Pettigrew, T. F., & Tropp, L. R. (2000). Does intergroup contact reduce prejudice? Recent meta-analytic findings. In: S. Oskamp (Ed.), *Reducing prejudice and discrimination*. London: Lawrence Erlbaum Associates.

Roberts & Kay Inc.. (2000). *Toward competent communities: Best practices for producing community-wide study circles*. Pomfret: Study Circles Resource Center.
Rojas, H., Shah, D. V., Cho, J., Schmierbach, M., Keum, H., & Gil-De-Zuniga, H. (2005). Media dialogue: Perceiving and addressing community problems. *Mass Communication and Society*, *8*, 93–110.
Saunders, H. S. (1999). *A public peace process: Sustained dialogue to transform racial and ethnic conflicts*. New York: St. Martin's Press.
Schoem, D., & Hurtado, S. (Eds). (2001). *Dialogue: Deliberative democracy in school, college, community, and workplace*. Ann Arbor: University of Michigan Press.
Stephan, W. G., & Vogt, P. W. (2004). *Education programs for improving intergroup relations*. New York: Teachers College Press, Columbia University.
Tatum, B. D. (1992). Talking about race, learning about racism: The application of racial identity development theory in the classroom. *Harvard Educational Review*, *62*(1), 1–24.
Tatum, B. D. (1997). *Why are all the black kids sitting together in the cafeteria?* New York: Basic Books.
Walsh, K. C. (2006). Communities, race, and talk: An analysis of the occurrence of civic intergroup dialogue programs. *Journal of Politics*, *65*(1), 22–33.
Walsh, K. C. (2007). *Talking about race: Community dialogues and the politics of difference*. Chicago: University of Chicago Press.
Williams, J. (1985). Redefining institutional racism. *Ethnic and Racial Studies*, *8*(3), 323–348.
Worchel, S. (1986). The role of cooperation in reducing conflict. In: S. Worchel & W. G. Austin (Eds), *Psychology of Relations*. Chicago: Nelson Hall Publishers.
Zirkel, S., & Cantor, N. (2004). 50 Years after *Brown v. Board of Education*: The promise and challenge of multicultural education. *Journal of Social Issues*, *60*(1), 1–15.

APPENDIX A

"Stepping Forward" Activity

DOES SKIN COLOR MAKE A DIFFERENCE IN CENTRAL NEW YORK?

Read the examples out loud. After each example, take a step forward if the statement is true for you. Look around the room to see who stepped forward and who remained in place.

- I can be sure that my school materials accurately show my people now and in history.
- I can choose blemish cover or bandages in "flesh" color and have them more or less match my skin.
- I can be pretty sure that if I ask to talk to "the person in charge," I will be facing a person whose skin is the same color as mine.
- If a police officer stops me on the street, I can be sure I haven't been singled out because of my skin color.

- I can easily buy posters, postcards, picture books, greeting cards, dolls, toys, and children's magazines featuring people that look like me.
- I can turn on the television or open the front page of the paper and see people that look like me widely represented, or represented positively.
- If dressed nicely, I can go shopping knowing that I will not be followed or harassed in the store.
- Some or most of my teachers are the same skin color as me.
- Most of the people in the US Congress are the same skin color as me.

APPENDIX B

Table B1. Participant Information.

Pseudonym	School	Year	Sex	Role	Racial/Ethnic Background Summary[a]	Racial/Ethnic Background Details[b]
Group 1						
Chantelle	City	Soph	F	P	Black	n/a
Jason	City	Senior	M	P	White	Irish, Polish
Maya	City	Junior	F	P	Mixed (Thai and white[c])	Thai, Canadian (Dutch, English, Scottish, Welsh)
Neena	Suburb	Junior	F	P	Asian	Indian, American (born in USA)
Jessica	Suburb	Junior	F	F	White	Polish, British, Native American, Irish, Scottish, Czech, German
Alicia	Suburb	Soph	F	P	Mixed (white, black, Native American)	English, Scottish, Irish, Seminole Indian, African American
Megan	Suburb	Junior	F	P	Asian	Korean, American (adopted by white parents)
Nicole	City	Junior	F	F	Black	African American
Erik	City	Junior	M	P	Latino	Puerto Rican
Group 2						
Megan[d]	Suburb	Senior	F	F	Asian	Korean, American (adopted by white parents)

Agnes	Suburb	Junior	F	P	White	Armenian
Jenn	Suburb	Junior	F	P	White	Christian, Caucasian
Ann	Suburb	Junior	F	P	White	Italian, Irish, Polish, Caucasian
Chris	Suburb	Soph	M	P	White	Irish, Catholic, Conservative
Patrick	Suburb	Junior	M	P	White	White, Caucasian, Irish, Catholic
Yvette	City	Senior	F	P	Black	Black, little bit Native American way back
Lester	City	Junior	M	P	Black	Latin, black, Indian, White, African American
Sophie	City	Senior	F	P	Asian	Asian, Jewish, South Korea (adopted by white parents)
Janelle	City	Junior	F	F	Black	African American
Emily	City	Junior	F	P	White	White, Welsh, English
Andrew	City	Senior	M	P	Black	Black, African, African American

[a]This column lists simplified descriptions of each respondent's racial and ethnic background.
[b]This column lists all racial and ethnic background categories mentioned by the respondents.
[c]In the cases where participants identify as mixed, I have underlined the racial identity that participants say others are most likely to categorize them as.
[d]Megan participated in Group 1 and again in Group 2 as a facilitator.

BRIDGING THE MACRO WITH THE MICRO IN CONFLICT ANALYSIS: STRUCTURAL SIMPLIFICATION AS A HEURISTIC DEVICE

Fethi Keles

ABSTRACT

This chapter presents a theoretical argument that looking at how some grand matters of politics are simplified for practical use on the street is necessary to adequately understand how ordinary Serbs and Croats (and to a limited extent, Muslims) were transformed into enemies of their neighbors, workmates, and covillagers in the havoc wrought in Bosnia-Herzegovina between 1992 and 1995. Locals' shifting attitudes toward consanguinal identity, expressions of greeting, and dressing patterns are found to be examples of everyday practices through which perceived differences in civilization, competitive ideas of statehood, and macro-constructions of group identity produce ethnic conflict. A broad conclusion is that attention to localized manifestations of the macro-political *will yield more comprehensive understanding in analyses of ethnic conflict.*

Pushing the Boundaries: New Frontiers in Conflict Resolution and Collaboration
Research in Social Movements, Conflicts and Change, Volume 29, 55–69
Copyright © 2008 by Emerald Group Publishing Limited
All rights of reproduction in any form reserved
ISSN: 0163-786X/doi:10.1016/S0163-786X(08)29003-8

Explanations of collective violence based solely on the macro concepts of state, nation, religion, and history tend to remain rigid. They fail to capture the relatively unimpeded processes and mechanisms in and through which such macro concepts are appropriated at the local level to justify symbolic and physical aggression toward one's kinsmen, next-door neighbor, and fellow villager. Blaming collective political violence on differences in civilization, competitive ideas of statehood, and normative constructions of ethnonational group identity falls short of explaining how these differences, competitions, and vying constructions manifest themselves in the everyday practices of victims and perpetrators of destructive political conduct. What, then, is needed is a binocular look: one that is both aware of the defining characteristics of macrostructural phenomena[1] *and* that considers how – through which processes and mechanisms – macrostructural phenomena are embodied, internalized, and instrumentalized for aggressive purposes by real human beings in real locales. In other words, one that is both aware of the intrinsic properties of a given macrocosm and the *simplification* of overarching, conflicting political identities defining that macrocosm to a given microcosm.

In relating, then, a brief account of the havoc wrought in Bosnia-Herzegovina between 1992 and 1995, I will seek in this paper to approximate the kind of look described above. To do so, I will heed the caveat that "In place of global explanations of [collective violence], a more particularistic approach, one that adequately deals with multiple levels – from small scale to large scale – on which collective violence occurs, yields greater understanding" (Rubinstein, 1994, p. 986). To convey a sense of the battles fought to achieve various objectives (keeping demographics in balance, controlling access to territory, the governmental apparatus, and *the* history of the region – in other words, controlling *politics per se*), I will employ an anthropological perspective. This perspective not only looks at the grand picture painted by various social scientific accounts of the 1992–1995 Balkan War, but is also ethnographically informed as to how the macroreligious, macropolitical, and macrohistorical colors of the grand picture are fine-shaded, or localized, on the street, in the village, at the workspace, and so on. Unless we look at how grand matters of politics are or can be simplified for practical use on the street, we will fall short of adequately understanding why ordinary Serbs and Croats (and to a limited extent, Muslims) were transformed into ardent enemies of their long-time neighbors, workmates, and covillagers. In what follows, I will be relying on a limited number of ethnographies of the Balkan War as well as on some key anthropological observations by political anthropologists with view to developing a conceptual tool with which macro- and micro-level factors can be bridged to yield a better understanding of collective violence and its consequences.

In a recent, insightful article, the anthropologist Marshall Sahlins created the phrase "elementary form of structural amplification" (Sahlins, 2005, p. 25) with which he intended to capture the process in which a conflict characterized by its local nature is *inflated* to the supralocal level. Charting the course of Cuban and US governments' and publics' heavy involvement in what was otherwise an oft-repeated and ordinary state of affairs,[2] Sahlins documents how the little Elian Gonzalez became entangled in discussions of communism, freedom, and the Cold War. The fight over Elian's custody, waged initially between Elian's relatives in Miami and Cuba, engaged the larger ideological opposition between American and Cuban governments and publics. Sahlins refers to the process wherein a minor, localized dispute engages a broader set of opposition as "structural *amplification*" which makes a macrohistory out of a microhistory (Sahlins, 2005). In my discussion below, I chart the course of a reverse process – one in which an ethnonationalist and exclusivist discourse gets appropriated in a village whose inhabitants have otherwise been living in relative peace and harmony. In other words, I look at how ethnonationalist macropolitics gets *deflated* only to be reconfigured within the power relations in a rural context. I will thus appropriate Sahlins' term with a slight modification: "Structural *simplification*" of ethnonationalist exclusivism in a central Bosnian village, or the reconfiguration of power relations in a rural context out of macropolitical discourse.

In the first section below, I will provide a brief account of the 1992–1995 war in the Balkans which ended with the peace agreement signed in Dayton, Ohio in 1995 during the Clinton presidency. The second section discusses some macrolevel phenomena whose on-the-ground appropriation will be treated in the third section, where I rely on Bringa's (1996) ethnographic analysis of a village in central Bosnia called Dolina (a pseudonym). In the fourth section, I seek to shed some anthropological light on the subject matter with reference to the work of such political anthropologists as Friedman (1998) and Tambiah (1996). I end the paper with some concluding thoughts, inspired by Lewellen (2003) and Gledhill (2000), on the benefits of anthropological thinking for a better understanding of the processes in which grand concepts such as history, ethnicity, and religion get dissolved and find parochial manifestation. As a result, power relations in a given microcosm may come to be conceptualized rather differently compared to how they were before, with the end result being "collective violence."

A BRIEF HISTORY OF THE 1992–1995 WAR IN BOSNIA[3]

After Josip Broz's (Tito) one-party socialist rule over former Yugoslavia ended in 1980 with Tito's death, a struggle ensued over the federal republic's economic, political, and military resources among representatives of the six republics and two autonomous regions that had constituted the federal Yugoslav Republic. Through his control of the party apparatus which outlived Tito and with his influence over national media, Serbian leader Slobodan Milosevic gained immense political power. He used that power to amend the Serbian constitution to strip Kosovo[4] of its autonomy. Witnessing Milosevic's repressive policies against Kosovars (namely the Albanian Kosovars) and his maneuvers to capture the federal government apparatus, other entities in former Yugoslavia[5] sought to separate themselves entirely from the federal structure by declaring their independence through their governments, which had been recently elected before the onset of the war in 1991. By that time Milosevic had acquired the tools that he thought would help him create the "Greater Serbia": political power and total control of the military. To Croatia's vote for secession from the federal structure, the Milosevic-controlled Yugoslav National Army responded by seizing one-third of Croatian territory and massacring thousands of Croatians. The Bosnian declaration of independence was followed with the siege of Sarajevo – the capital of Bosnia-Herzegovina in early April, 1992. Commanding the heavy and sophisticated artillery of the army of former Yugoslavia, Milosevic and his Bosnian Serb compatriot Radovan Karadzic engaged in systematic ethnic cleansing throughout Bosnia-Herzegovina with the aid of fierce nationalist propaganda emanating mainly from Serbia. The end result of four years of war was the killing of some 200,000 Bosnians,[6] organized use of rape as a military tactic against Muslim and Croatian women, severe instances of torture, and destruction of infrastructure such as power systems, schools, hospitals, transportation networks, etc. The war officially ended with the conclusion of the Dayton Peace Accords in Dayton, Ohio, in December 1995. Serbians were granted 49% of the territory they occupied in Bosnia-Herzegovina, while the remaining 51% is now the Federation of Bosnia-Herzegovina composed of Muslim and Croat rotating leadership, each governing its own territory with a separate government, police force, and military but being subject to a central government's rule in matters of finance and foreign policy.[7]

What should the war in former Yugoslavia be blamed on at a macrophenomenal level? How was the road to genocide paved in Bosnia?

Relying on Norman Cigar's (1995) benchmark study *Genocide in Bosnia*, I would like to emphasize in concise form some of the important overarching factors instrumentalized by the Serbian political decision-making mechanism to induce Serbian public opinion into believing in the legitimacy of Serbian government's dream of achieving a pure "Greater Serbia" at the expense of other ethnic, non-Serb groups populating Bosnia-Herzegovina. These factors pertain to competitive ideas of statehood in the post-Tito era, normative constructions of ethnic superiority and vulnerability, and the supposed threat of escalating radical religious (Islamic) fundamentalism. Two other factors, voiced by some American writers such as Robert Kaplan and Samuel Huntington, include the idea of the ever-presence of historically embedded ethnonational rivalry and hatred, and the notorious "clash of civilizations" thesis as they apply to the region. Whereas Cigar's account of macrolevel factors is well documented and evidenced, Kaplan's journalistic impressions regarding the causes of violence and Huntington's remarks, which I briefly look at below, will exemplify in particular why top–down analyses should be corrected and complemented by views "from below."

The Grand Picture and Its Dominant Colors

Cigar (1995) traces the roots of Serbian nationalist expansionism, whose culmination was the war, to the goals explicitly voiced in a document produced in 1986 by the Serbian Academy of Arts and Sciences, the *Serbian Memorandum*. Drafted in a Westphalian spirit, this document envisaged the foundation of a pure Serbian state encompassing all Serbs regardless of which former Yugoslav republic they were living in. In Cigar's words, "Coming at a time of impending change and uncertainty, the *Memorandum* seemed to answer the need for a national strategy blueprint for Serbia" (Cigar, 1995, pp. 23–24). The implementation of the *Memorandum* could only come about by uprooting other ethnicities of the former Yugoslav republic, which is precisely what Serbian nationalism sought to do with the war, as indicated by the forced displacement of several hundred thousand Bosnians now scattered across Europe and the United States. Thus, the post-Tito Serbian nationalism found its most obvious expression in the statements of Serbia's academic elite. This was followed by the stereotypification of would-be victims, in particular Bosnian Muslims, in and through popular culture. An example discussed by Cigar (1995) is the description of Bosnian Muslims as aliens, inferiors, and cold-blooded murderers by a best-selling novelist named Vuk Draskovic, whose writings influenced no less a figure than the commander of the Serbian Guard, who admitted to having beaten Muslims (and Croatians) because of the fury ingrained in him through these writings (1995, p. 25).

Next came the work of Serbian scholars specializing in the study of Islam. This work represented Islam and its adherents as backward, hostile to European civilization, and fundamentalist masterplanners of Serbian destruction. This work further disseminated the idea, frightening to the average Serb, that there were plans to repatriate more than a million Turks to Bosnia, which clearly would contribute to the Islamization of Bosnia-Herzegovina in the post-Tito era (and would indicate a reembracing of the spirit of the Ottoman Empire, which ruled over the Balkans for more than four centuries). Serbian scholars felt that these developments should be countered by any means possible. This academic effort was then bolstered by the efforts of the Serbian Orthodox Church whose representatives evidenced their claim of Muslim primitiveness by pointing to the fact that walls were built around (Muslim) Albanian houses, which to them demonstrated that Muslims (especially Muslim women) were not liberated, and "hidden behind walls" (Cigar, 1995, pp. 27–32).

The *Memorandum*, Serbian popular literature, the denigrating work by Serbian scholars of Islam, and the Serbian Orthodox Church's efforts were thus factors in the escalation of Serbian ethnonationalist exclusivism which culminated in a four-year war between 1992 and 1995 against non-Serb ethnicities. Although the macrophenomenal reality of these factors and their influence are well illustrated in Cigar's work, a more comprehensive understanding requires ethnographic particularism to visualize the processes and mechanisms in and through which such macrophenomenal realities are effectively parochialized – or structurally *simplified*. This will help in answering the question: "How were people [of the Balkans] who had lived quietly together as neighbors for forty-five years [since the end of second World War] manipulated into killing one another and burning each other's houses down?" (Besteman & Gusterson, 2005, p. 7)

Whereas accounts of the conflict in the Balkans such as that of Cigar would get enriched and not necessarily refuted or corrected by an anthropological approach, other works on the Balkans would probably have to be rewritten in view of the insights provided by an anthropological perspective. Such two works on the two supposed causes – ancient hatreds and civilization clash – of the war are Robert Kaplan's *Balkan Ghosts* (1993) and Samuel Huntington's *The Clash of Civilizations* (1993). Following is a brief overview of the arguments of these two works, and anthropological critiques of them.

For Robert Kaplan (1993), the collective violence in the Balkans was a modern-day reincarnation of ancient ethnonational feelings of hatred that all sides partaking of the violence had been breeding against one another since time immemorial. The "Balkan syndrome," as he termed it, was something like an evil gene predisposing Balkan people toward erupting in violence. Hence, there is not much reason to be startled at the atrocities that the Balkan people meted out against one another.

In a devastating critique of Kaplan's *travelogical* assumptions (my term, by which I intend to convey a sense of the unreliability of such sweeping generalizations which *do* call for an attention to detail of the anthropological kind), anthropologist Tone Bringa (2005) sets the record straight. Building on her fieldwork in central Bosnia (which I relate in more detail below) for a total period of six years, from 1988 to 1993, Bringa notes in her critique of Kaplan's work that before the war in the ethnically mixed village (Muslim Bosnians and Catholic Croats) where she carried out her fieldwork, adherents of the two separate religious communities helped each other build the village church and the mosque, attended one another's holy days, and extended a hand to one another while building houses. These observations on the ground refute Kaplan's overgeneralized, impressionistic statements about the violent nature of the region's inhabitants. The "ancient hatreds" argument is further contradicted by the work of Lockwood, another anthropologist who, as early as the 1970s, documented in his ethnography *The European Moslems* (1975) how Serbs, Croats, and Muslims were peacefully woven into the social fabric through the integrative mechanism of the marketplace.

In a tone somewhat more sophisticated and ostensibly more scholarly than that of Kaplan, Samuel Huntington sees the violence in Bosnia as an instance of a clash of three civilizations, namely the Western, Islamic, and Eastern Orthodox ones. This was a war occurring at what Huntington (1993) named a civilizational faultline. His analysis was contradicted when the Christian United States brokered the peace agreement – thus possibly saving Bosnian Muslims from extinction on a much larger scale than had happened thus far – and also accommodated hundreds of thousands of Bosnian Muslims as refugees during and after the war.[8] As noted by anthropologist Brown (2005), Huntington's theory that countries belonging in the same "civilizational kin group" (a term invented by Huntington, who is not a kinship theorist) was discredited by on-the-ground empirical reality. Based on his fieldwork in the region, Brown exposes how the kin links that Huntington thought were so clearly identified were much more complex given the institution of *fictive kinship* in the Balkans whereby people became related to one another through *kumtsvo* (godfatherhood) ties, which crosscut so-called civilizational attachments.

I suggested at the beginning of this paper that explanations of collective violence based solely on the macro concepts of state, nation, religion, and history tend to remain rather rigid. With reference to various treatments of the Bosnian war, I emphasize that a view from below would either substantially complement such accounts (as in the case of Cigar's macrophenomenal account of the causes of Serbian atrocities) or expose the irrelevance of them to concrete situations experienced by real human beings in real locales (as in the case of Kaplan's and Huntington's accounts of the factors behind the escalation of collective violence). An anthropological approach seems better suited to help understand otherwise unexpected cases of violence: How did ethnonationalist exclusivist discourse get structurally simplified to the village level, as a result of which neighbors, covillagers, perhaps old-time friends and confidantes turned against one another?[9] The following section seeks to describe instances of structural simplification by relying on the ethnographic work of anthropologist Tone Bringa in a central Bosnian village. By *structural simplification*, I mean that process in which a larger opposition between two overarching identities gets parochialized through the identification of any such overarching identity with its local counterpart. In this process, the differences invoked at the macrolevel (discursive or otherwise) between the larger forces of opposition are simplified and selectively appropriated to forge new identities thus filling in, or overriding, a preexisting set of local relations with new and mutually oppositional content.

The following brief discussion seeks to demonstrate the dissolution and parochialization of exclusivist nationalism in the context of the relations between Catholic Croats and Muslim Bosnians. Although the foregoing discussion has focused on the development and outcomes of Serbian nationalist aggression, in this paper I am less concerned with the origins of the ethnonationalist discourse than with the actual dynamics involved in the process of structural simplification.

STRUCTURAL SIMPLIFICATION OF ETHNONATIONALIST EXCLUSIVISM: BRINGA'S CASE OF DOLINA IN CENTRAL BOSNIA

The village where Bringa conducted her fieldwork over a period of six years is a mixed (Muslim–Croat) village located in central Bosnia, and a two hour drive to the capital Sarajevo. Bringa refers to the village with the pseudonym Dolina. A simplified, parochialized version of national superiority voiced at the macrolevel by such figures as Serbian leader Milosevic (or, alternatively, in the case of Croatian nationalism, by Croat President Tudjman) in the village is seen in the remarks of the only Serbian inhabitant of Dolina vis-à-vis his Muslim covillagers. Bringa notes that this man would say that his fellow Muslim villagers had, in fact, Serbian blood in their veins (Bringa, 1996, p. 30), which seems to be a telling example of what may be termed "consanguinal expansionism."[10] This demonstrates the structural simplification of Serbian academic exclusivism (which considers Bosnian Muslims nonentities except when they are considered Serbs) to the village context.

Another instance indicative of the simplification of supralocal nationalist rhetoric becomes manifest through villagers' changing greeting practices. While in the public space of communal interaction, village inhabitants came to use ethnicity-or religion-neutral phrases of greeting when they encountered one another during various times of the day and on different occasions (on the road, while attending a feast, in neighborly visits, etc.), and they reserved exclusive greetings for intraethnic encounters (Croat versus Croat, or Muslim versus Muslim). Eventually, the escalating symbolic-discursive and physical violence found a localized manifestation: once Croat forces gained control of the municipality to which Dolina belonged, Croat-specific greetings dominated the public realm (for example, the dealings at administrative offices and in the marketplace), thus extending macrolevel ethnic exclusivism (the idealized "Greater Croatia") to the parochial level by exerting linguistic dominion over a particular portion of everyday life through the imposition of a new greeting *structure*. As Bringa notes: "Indeed, the Catholic Croats were redefining the whole area (market town and surrounding villages) as "theirs" and transforming the local Muslims into outsiders, people who did not belong, [which] was one of the many steps in a long series of more or less violent measures to squeeze the Muslims out of their villages and the municipality" (1996, pp. 57–58).

Yet another example of the simplification of high-level nationalist politics, whereby Bosnian Muslims were represented as remnants of Asiatic darkness and backwardness, relates to Dolina's Catholic (Croat) girls' changing perceptions of Muslim girls' dressing patterns. One of Bringa's Croat informants in the village notes that whereas they have left the ways of their parents' choices in clothing behind (and have thus become less and less separable from the modern urban woman), Muslim girls keep more and more to their ways. The expression seems to be a subtle practice of "othering" whereby Muslim girls are pushed into the categories of rural and traditional (Bringa, 1995, pp. 61–62). What is interesting, of course, is the emergence of an otherwise nonexistent practice. Although each group of girls' parents did not conceptualize one another in terms of their differing clothing practices, the nationalist rhetoric – disseminated through broadcast media and enforced as law in the emerging, ethnically-drafted constitutions (Hayden, 1996) – results in the creation of a simplified mirror image of differentiation and othering in the village context via changing perceptions regarding a group's dress.

With reference to Bringa's work, we have seen some examples of how macrolevel nationalist discourse manifests itself in a village in the context of consanguinal perceptions, expressions of greeting, and dressing patterns.[11] What follows is review of some key observations made by a number of political anthropologists regarding localized manifestations of macrolevel discourses which may result in changed perceptions of old friends and existing relations.

ETHNIFICATION, FOCALIZATION, AND TRANSVALUATION: RELEVANCE OF POLITICAL ANTHROPOLOGY TO ANALYSES OF THE WAR IN BOSNIA

The structural simplification process as a result of which old-time fellows, covillagers, and neighbors begin to subtly perceive one another through a reconfigured framework of relations – that is, perceive one another as belonging to different natures, historical roots, and linguistic groups – can be referred to as a case of "ethnification." Although anthropologist Friedman (1998) uses the term ethnification as part of his Marxist approach with which he seeks to explain expressions of declining hegemony, the term has descriptive utility in the context of the war in Bosnia. In particular, Friedman suggests that ethnification, the turn toward an understanding of the nation-state "...in which the nation is dominant, where the nation-state is converted from a contractual to a familistic-ascriptive model" (1998, p. 288) is an expression of the decline of a civilizational perspective based on commercial capitalism. Thus, from the Titoist social contract in which Serbs, Croats, Muslims, Slovenes, and Montenegrins were "Yugoslav" emerged exclusivist, ethnified understandings of separate families of nations (for instance, the Serb nation idealized in the *Memorandum* as the "Greater Serbia") which admitted of no aliens: hence, Balkanization ensues

(Cigar, 1995, p. 291). In other words, regional disorder was followed by huge migratory flows and demographic exchanges in the Balkans, specifically in Bosnia, as the result of a war guided by a macropolitical *ethnified* perception of state which dictated intrastate homogeneity (that is, Serbia for Serbs, Croatia for Croats). The term can have both macrolevel and microlevel application. The Serbian villager's remark that the others too are of Serbian blood may be considered an expression of homogenizing ethnification by which the "others" are precluded from having the right to their own identity. Furthermore, the increasing visibility of Croat-specific greetings in the public space could be seen as another expression of homogenizing ethnification by which the "others" are precluded from the reconstructed public space should they decline to conform to the new linguistic habits.

Two other concepts by another anthropologist Stanley Tambiah (1996) may serve as useful heuristic devices in the context of the analysis of the war in Bosnia: *focalization* and *transvaluation*. "By *focalization* [Tambiah means] the process of progressive denudation of local incidents and disputes of their particulars of context and their aggregation. *Transvaluation* refers to the parallel process of assimilating particulars to a larger, collective, more enduring, and therefore less context-bound, cause or interest" (Tambiah, 1996, p. 192). I introduce these terms not because they are used in Tambiah's (1996) work to describe processes similar to those I have called instances of structural simplification, but because they illustrate the reverse trends (in other words, they capture what Sahlins would call *structural amplification*). For example, Tambiah employs these two terms while describing "how the original issue of the death of a schoolgirl ballooned into a more general protest against the inequities of the public transport system, and that, again, into an anti-Pathan backlash" (1996, p. 191). As I noted in the beginning, I am interested in the reverse process by which general, macrolevel conflicts and exclusivist discourses are parochialized by the receivers of such discourses. Tambiah's terms may help describe the process whereby, for example, Serbian historiography strips the Battle of Kosovo in 1389 (where Serbs were defeated by the invading Ottomans) out of its context, and instrumentalizes that event by trying to assimilate the memory of it into the larger Serbian macropolitical objective vilifying the Muslims of Bosnia (who converted to Islam following the Ottoman conquest, and therefore assumed the identity of the invader, as claimed by Serbian historiography). Thus, by placing these two terms against structural simplification, I hope to have made my terminological suggestion clearer.

CONCLUDING THOUGHTS

In this chapter, I first raised the idea that blaming collective political violence on differences in civilization, competitive ideas of statehood, and normative constructions of ethnonational group identity reveals very little, if at all, about how these differences, competitions, and vying constructions manifest themselves in the everyday practices of victims as well as perpetrators of destructive political conduct. In fact, interpreting collective violence as mere consequences of top–down orchestrations is limiting *the political* to the realm of governments, political parties, nationalist leaders, etc. Without looking at how the political is embedded in everyday practices, how it manifests itself through real human beings' dealings in such real locales as the village, the street, and the marketplace, one is unable to understand in their multifaceted dimensions the complex processes as well as instruments in and through which objectives declared, legitimized, or forced by the governmental or ruling elite get accepted and/or rejected by their addressees. Thus, when critiquing political scientist David Easton's view that there existed no such thing as political anthropology because "practitioners of this nondiscipline had utterly failed to mark off the political system from other systems of society" (Lewellen, 2003, pp. x–xi), Lewellen notes that the attempt to locate politics in everyday routines is in fact political anthropology's greatest virtue. The discussion in this paper of some instances of structural simplification shows to some extent that events in former Yugoslavia at the level of what Easton would call the "clearly marked off political system" need to be complemented and/or corrected with an eye on micropolitics. Unless we conceptualize the increased use of Croat greetings in public spaces, the commentary on Muslim girls' ("backward, rural") dressing patterns, the attempt by the Serbian villager at enhancing the scope of consanguines as *truly political* phenomena in view of the then-reigning nationalist rhetoric, we are bound to fall short of understanding the 1992–1995 war in Bosnia in its complexity. The heuristic devices of structural amplification, focalization and transvaluation are useful in conceiving of the aspect pertaining to how historically specific, localized cases are ballooned or inflated for utilization as part of larger nationalistic discourses. With the idea of structural simplification, however, we can conceptualize how broader macrophenomenal realities are locally parochialized and manifested in everyday practices. My hope is that structural simplification will yield greater understanding of what happened in Bosnia as well as serve as a useful conceptual tool in future research on political conflict.

NOTES

1. Including, but not limited to, so-called ancient ethnonational hatreds, religious radicalism, and historically motivated territorial irredentism. In general, the adjectives *macropolitical, macrostructural*, and *macrophenomenal* are used in this paper to refer to those supraindividual groups, entities, or factors ("the nation," "the state," "history," "religion," etc.) otherwise claimed to have an exclusive causative impact on the emergence and sustenance of political conflict.

2. By which Sahlins (2005) means a group of Cubans escaping Castro, traveling in a boat (or some other craft), fighting sharks across the straits of Florida as well as the US Coast Guard, and, if successful, landing in Miami.

3. I recognize that the history of the 1991–1995 Balkan conflict, which resulted in the collapse of former Yugoslavia, is a contested one. But this paper should essentially be construed as a theoretical exercise, rather than as an attempt to explain why one set of contested explanations is preferable over another. My broader aim is to apply an inversion of anthropologist Marshall Sahlins' theoretical constructs with a view to developing a heuristic device to link macrolevel factors to microlevel practices. Given the limits of this paper, I cannot do justice to all accounts of the conflict that seek to explain it from various angles. Readers interested in getting a much fuller discussion of the contested accounts may consult Ramet (2005).

4. Kosovo was an autonomous region under the Serbian republic in the former federal Yugoslav state.

5. In particular, Croatia, Bosnia, and Slovenia.

6. Including Bosnians of different ethnic backgrounds, that is, Bosnian Muslims (major victims), Bosnian Croats, and even Bosnian Serbs who refused to acquiesce to the cleansing project.

7. For more detailed accounts of the war, see Cushman and Mestrovic (1996), Mestrovic (1997), Cohen (1997), and Burg and Shoup (2000).

8. I do not have the space here to extend this critique of Huntington's work. I offer a longer discussion in Keles (2007).

9. One reviewer who commented on this article suggested that "it seems to be the macro-level politics and rhetoric (the ethno-nationalist ideal of ethnically pure interaction) that is a simplification of the complex pattern of interaction on the local level," rather than local level interactions being simplified, less complex versions of macrolevel discursive battles. Ultimately, this boils down to the question of whether macrolevel factors (for instance, nationalist, political leadership) met the public already raising exclusivist sentiments, or whether the public (otherwise *relatively* peacefully interwoven through the marketplace, intermarriage, and educational institutions) subsequently grew suspicious of one another's neighbors, coworkers, etc. Following the first track runs the risk of feeding fodder to the uncritical thesis that imagines the Balkans as a land of perpetual violence, where past grievances are never settled and latent hate is the order of the day. I am more inclined to the latter track, in view of the former U.S. President Clinton's foreword to the volume by Swanee Hunt (2004), former U.S. Ambassador to Austria, where Clinton noted: "As the war raged in Bosnia, Hunt… brought to my attention news not making headlines: that the women of Bosnia had been organizing to try to prevent the war, and they were still doing what they could… to hold together their culturally diverse

communities." Consider also what one Bosnian woman, Nurdzihana, said after the war: "I've never accepted ethnic divisions. The way I was raised, we didn't say someone belongs to this or that ethnic group. The atrocities I witnessed had no ethnicity, no religion. We lived together until the day before" (Hunt, 2004, p. 95).

10. By which term I want to refer to that effort to expand one's range of blood relatives, hence including them into an imaginary "one of us" category.

11. I acknowledge that the illustrations excerpted from Bringa's work tell only part of the story in the run-up to the war. For more detailed examples of pre-war (that is, pre-1990) happenings, one can peruse Bringa's ICTY testimony available at http://www.un.org/icty/transe16/990712it.htm (I thank an anonymous reviewer for bringing the testimony to my attention). There, Bringa discusses at some length how the increasing Croat military presence in the region and the repeated, Croat-controlled media broadcasts instilled a sense of fear which reconfigured the way in which Croat inhabitants came to see their long-time covillagers as ethnic others. What seems to have emerged from complex military objectives and carefully planned broadcasts is a divisive process that produced simple, previously nonexistent, and ethnically defined "us versus them" perceptions of a hostile nature.

ACKNOWLEDGMENT

I would like to thank Prof. Michael Freedman of Syracuse University's Anthropology Department for his extensive comments and suggestive feedback on an earlier version of this article. The usual caveat applies to any remaining errors of fact or interpretation.

REFERENCES

Besteman, C., & Gusterson, H. (Eds). (2005). *Why America's top pundits are wrong. Anthropologists talk back*. Berkeley, CA: University of California Press.

Bringa, T. (1996). *Being Muslim the Bosnian way. Identity and community in a central Bosnian village*. Princeton, NJ: Princeton University Press.

Bringa, T. (2005). Haunted by the imaginations of the past. Robert Kaplan's *Balkan Ghosts*. In: C. Besteman & H. Gusterson (Eds), *Why America's top pundits are wrong. Anthropologists talk back* (pp. 60–82). Berkeley, CA: University of California Press.

Brown, K. (2005). Samuel Huntington, meet the Nuer. Kinship, local knowledge, and the clash of civilizations. In: C. Besteman & H. Gusterson (Eds), *Why America's top pundits are wrong. Anthropologists talk back* (pp. 43–59). Berkeley, CA: University of California Press.

Burg, S. L., & Shoup, P. S. (2000). *The war in Bosnia-Herzegovina: Ethnic conflict and international intervention*. Armonk, NY: M.E. Sharpe.

Cigar, N. L. (1995). *Genocide in Bosnia*. College Station, TX: A&M University Press.

Cohen, P. (1997). *Serbia's secret war: Propaganda and the deceit of history*. College Station, TX: A & M University Press.

Cushman, T., & Mestrovic, S. (Eds). (1996). *This time we knew: Western responses to genocide in Bosnia*. New York, NY: New York University Press.

Friedman, J. (1998). Transnationalization, socio-political disorder, and ethnification as expressions of declining global hegemony. *International Political Science Review*, *19*(3), 233–250.

Gledhill, J. (2000). *Power and its disguises: Anthropological perspectives on politics*. London and Boulder, Colorado: Pluto Press.

Hayden, R. (1996). Imagined communities and real victims: Self-determination and ethnic cleansing in Yugoslavia. *American Ethnologist*, *23*(4), 783–801.

Hunt, S. (2004). *This was not our war. Bosnian women reclaiming the peace*. Durham: Duke University Press.

Huntington, S. P. (1993). The clash of civilizations? *Foreign Affairs*, *72*(3), 22–49.

Kaplan, R. (1993). *Balkan ghosts: A journey through history*. New York: St. Martin's Press.

Keles, F. (2007). The antinomies of Samuel P. Huntington: Some anthropological reflections on the American pundit. *Journal of Third World Studies*, *24*(2), 131–143.

Lewellen, T. (2003). *Political anthropogology. An introduction*. Westport, CT: Praeger Publishers.

Lockwood, W. G. (1975). *European moslems: Economy and ethnicity in western Bosnia*. New York, NY: Academic Press.

Mestrovic, S. (Ed.) (1997). *The conceit of innocence: Losing the conscience of the West in the war against Bosnia*. College Station, TX: A & M University Press.

Ramet, S. (2005). *Thinking about Yugoslavia. Scholarly debates about the Yugoslav breakup and the wars in Bosnia and Kosovo*. New York, NY: Cambridge University Press.

Rubinstein, R. A. (1994). Collective violence and common security. In: T. Ingold (Ed.), *Companion encyclopedia of anthropology* (pp. 983–1009). London: Routledge.

Sahlins, M. (2005). Structural work. *Anthropological Theory*, *5*(1), 5–30.

Tambiah, S. J. (1996). *Leveling crowds: Ethno-nationalist conflicts and collective violence in South Asia*. Berkeley, CA: University of California Press.

THE DEMOCRATIZATION OF PEACEBUILDING: DEMOCRATIC EXPOSURE AND EXTERNALLY DEMOCRATIC IDEOLOGY OF PEACEBUILDING NGOS IN NORTHERN IRELAND AND BOSNIA

Bruce Hemmer

ABSTRACT

Democratization has become the prescription for peace in conflictual societies, but often stagnates in a political standoff or devolves back to war. Sustainable and effective democracy in these societies requires a citizenry which actively guides and pressures political leaders toward effective policy making for peace. But in societies with little or no democratic tradition, it takes time to develop the attitudes and organizations required. This study examines the relationship of democratic exposure to the development of the ideology of external political participation among peacebuilding NGOs. Using original field interview data, it compares the ideology of 28 peacebuilding NGOs in Northern

Pushing the Boundaries: New Frontiers in Conflict Resolution and Collaboration
Research in Social Movements, Conflicts and Change, Volume 29, 71–111
Copyright © 2008 by Emerald Group Publishing Limited
All rights of reproduction in any form reserved
ISSN: 0163-786X/doi:10.1016/S0163-786X(08)29004-X

Ireland to 37 in the less democratic context of Bosnia. The study examines the effects of exposure to democracy on "externally democratic ideology," defined as an ideology of participation in the political processes of society external to the organization. Three aspects of exposure to democracy are examined: societal democratization, internal democracy in the NGO, and mentorship by outsiders from established democracies. The findings are that internal democracy is associated with externally democratic ideology, but outsider mentorship is not, even when controlling for dominating relationships, and neither is societal democracy, except indirectly via its effect on internal democracy. Implications for theory, policy, and future research are discussed.

With the collapse of communism, democracy has become the presumptive international prescription for peace[1] in the generally intrastate, and mostly ethnic, conflicts[2] of the post Cold War world. Democratization is thus a central element of most peace agreements. Yet, while *well-established* democracies do not war with each other (Russett, 1993), and have fewer civil wars, countries in *transition* to democracy have *more* civil wars than either established democracies or autocracies (Hegre, Ellingsen, Gates, & Gleditsch, 2001). If democratization is to serve its goal of peace, then we must improve our understanding of how to democratize peacefully. One important piece of this puzzle is developing a politically engaged,[3] peace-oriented civil society to guide and pressure political leaders[4] toward more effective policy-making for peace.

Political leaders who are accustomed to autocratic rule have enough trouble adjusting to the democratic norms and procedures of compromise, open debate, questioning of authorities, and sharing and alternation of power. This is only made more difficult in a context of recent violent conflict. Some leaders may be so invested in or accustomed to the conflict that even after a peace agreement, their actions do more to maintain the conflict as a political stalemate than to take effective action to move beyond it and build a true and lasting peace. In Bosnia, for instance, the state parliament established by the peace agreement could not agree on a single law for years. Laws as basic as establishing a common currency and flag had to be imposed by the High Representative of the international community.

In developed democracies, nongovernmental organizations (NGOs)[5] and other civil society groups are important links in the democratic process, bringing issues to the attention of political leaders, suggesting solutions, pressing for action, and assisting government in implementing solutions. Ideally, in democratizing societies, civil society would be motivating and aiding political leaders in creating and implementing policies that support and build peace, rather than maintain or exacerbate conflict.

But citizens of societies with little democratic tradition are less likely to be oriented toward political participation as an appropriate, safe, or effective role (Almond & Verba, 1989/1963; Dalton, 1994; Verba, Schlozman, & Brady, 1995). Democratizing countries tend to be less developed economically, resulting in not only less human and physical capital being available to associations, but also more traditional, inflexible, and authoritarian values and practices (Inglehart, 1990, 2000). Furthermore, economic development is associated with stronger traditions of civic organization and action that is independent of established authorities[6] (Putnam, Leonardi, & Nanetti, 1993). These trends are intensified by violent ethnic conflict, which not only worsens socioeconomic conditions, but leaves ethnic groups strongly rallied around authoritarian ethnic leaders in self-defense. Citizens in these conditions are more likely to expect political leaders to be unappreciative or even repressive of civic input. Even those citizens who have decided to take matters in their own hands by becoming NGO activists are likely to view political leaders with fear or contempt, and not as partners in solving problems.

In relatively democratic societies experiencing violent conflict, when the political leaders failed to make peace or faltered in implementing peace agreements, peace-oriented elements of civil society have sought to influence them. Sometimes this involves quietly bringing them new perspectives and skills, or facilitating communication or negotiation among them. Other times it involves changing the political environment by creating democratic pressure for peace. Such political engagement by peacebuilding NGOs has been documented in Northern Ireland, South Africa, and Israel, and is given some credit for changing the political environment to make progress in the official peace process possible, especially in Northern Ireland (Bloomfield, 1997; Fearon, 2000; Fitzduff, 2002; Gidron, Katz, & Hasenfeld, 2002; Golan & Kamal, 2000; McCartney, 2000; Saunders, 1999). But such activity generally has been avoided by peacebuilding NGOs in less democratic conflict zones such as Nagorno-Karabakh, Georgia/Abkhazia, Moldova-Transdniestria, and Kosovo (Garb & Phillips, 2001). In these societies, NGOs tend to focus on interpersonal peacebuilding among ordinary citizens, such as treating war trauma, teaching conflict resolution skills, or fostering inter-communal contact and cooperation, often avoiding publicity or masking their activities as other types of humanitarian work.

How do civil society organizations in less democratic societies develop sufficiently positive attitudes toward political engagement that this vital democratic link can develop? More specifically, since not all types of civil society organizations would aid peaceful democratization,[7] how do peace-oriented civic organizations such as peacebuilding NGOs develop positive attitudes toward political engagement? Peace, after all, can be a highly charged political topic, and those daring to promote it in the political arena risk being treated as traitors, or at least naïve amateurs, by political leaders who are invested in conflict or want the credit for any peacemaking that is done.

This paper analyzes the evidence I have collected to answer this question concerning peacebuilding NGOs in Bosnia & Herzegovina (henceforth "Bosnia" or BiH) and Northern Ireland. How do they develop the ideas that peacebuilding involves interaction with political leaders and that this is a proper, safe enough, and potentially effective role for them to undertake? How much is exposure to democracy in the society a factor, and how much do other sources of democratic exposure, within the organization, and in relationships with outsiders, compensate for low societal democracy?

THEORY

Overcoming impediments to political participation in less democratic societies is an issue which most of the peacebuilding literature has ignored. Within the peacebuilding literature, the classic "track two diplomacy" literature (Montville, 1987, p. 7) briefly mentions the concept of building public pressure for peace, but then focuses on quietly facilitating transformative dialogue between leaders out of the public limelight. This is difficult to arrange without preexisting relationships with political elites, as it requires considerable trust in the facilitators. Subsequent track two diplomacy literature has sometimes described changing public opinion through similar dialogue among ordinary citizens (Saunders, 1999), but has generally ignored the issue of how these citizens could then be brought to place pressure on political leaders in autocratic or democratizing societies. Lederach (1997), the seminal theorist on "bottom-up" peacebuilding, addresses this problem mainly by pointing to the strategic importance of mid-level political, ethnic, and religious leaders as links between the grassroots and higher levels (which squares with political science literature suggesting citizens more readily engage leaders at this middle level (Almond & Verba, 1989/1963; Diamond, 1999; Inglehart, 2000; Putnam et al., 1993; Tocqueville, 1969/1850; Verba et al., 1995)). However, established mid-level leaders in newly democratizing societies may themselves be thoroughly incorporated in autocratic structures and culture which makes them hardly more receptive to grassroots input than top-level leaders.

To address these oversights, peacebuilding theory needs to incorporate some relevant ideas in political science and sociology literature. Political participation is affected by a number of factors, including political factors such as the political opportunity structure,[8] organizational factors such as resources and legitimacy, and attributes of individual citizens such as education (McAdam, 1982; McCarthy & Zald, 1997; Verba et al., 1995). A prerequisite for any of these to actually lead to political participation, however, is the democratic ideology[9] of political participation – the positive orientation toward citizens[10] attempting to influence political leaders as an appropriate and worthwhile endeavor (Almond & Verba, 1989/1963; Dalton, 1994; Verba et al., 1995). It cannot be taken for granted in democratizing societies that such an ideology is prevalent among individual citizens, the civic organizations which educate and mobilize them, or the political leaders which either ignore, repress, or respond to citizens' attempts to influence politics. Civil society activists, being optimistic innovators by nature, are likely to be the first to adopt these attitudes. In this paper, I am focusing on the development of the ideology of political participation in societal democracy by civic organizations – specifically peacebuilding NGOs – as a critical link between citizens and political leaders and a potential engine of change in attitudes toward political participation at both these other levels.

Even though civic activists tend to be innovators, it can be difficult for an organization founded in a particular sociopolitical context to adjust to the opportunities of a new, more democratic context. Once an organization is founded with a particular ideology, suited to its original context, it is often resistant to change (Dalton, 1994). But it is possible for an organization's ideology to evolve over time. Minkoff (1999) shows that organizations sometimes change core strategies, particularly between providing services or cultural activities and advocating political change, and more rarely between advocacy through conventional politics and protest. Such a change risks organizational failure, and most organizations do it rarely – usually when older, and when there is a favorable change in available resources or political opportunity structure. These are all factors which would tend to make ideological change in favor of political participation more likely as democratization proceeds, and the ideologies of older organizations become increasingly out of tune with the current context.

In addition to these factors, I theorize that the ideology of political participation is developed in large part through *exposure to democracy*, which provides opportunities for learning democratic attitudes and skills over time. This can happen indigenously in the democratizing society in two ways. One is the slow process of general democratization of the society's political institutions, social structures, and culture. Another is experiencing democracy within the NGO itself, to the degree it adopts norms and structures of democracy in running its own affairs. Exposure to *internally* democratic ideology and practice may strengthen the members' democratic attitudes, skills, confidence, and appreciation for how a democracy should work, thereby building ideological expectations of a stronger role *externally* in societal democracy (Diamond, 1999; Eckstein, 1998). The more intimate environment of an association is a less diverse and less threatening arena, often literally filled with friends, in which participants are pulled into roles that teach them, at a larger scale than their families, how to organize activities, to speak publicly, to civilly express and tolerate differences, and to find political compromises – all skills and experiences which can transfer to organized political participation in societal democracy (Lipset, Trow, & Coleman, 1962; Polletta, 2002). Kew (2002) has shown internal democracy to be associated with political engagement by NGOs in Nigeria. Note that I am distinguishing between the ideology of *internal* participation in organizational decision making that would almost necessarily accompany democratic practices *within* the NGO, and the ideology of *external* participation in the political processes of the society. It is the external sort that is of primary interest here, which I will call *externally democratic ideology*.

Internal democracy in turn is likely influenced (but not determined) by societal democratization, especially at the time the organization is founded, as organizations may model their own structures and procedures on those they know from the society around them.[11] NGOs are influenced in these decisions by whether their founders and members are culturally democratic enough to seek democratic decision making in the organization. However, civic organizations in less democratic societies likely still provide more democratic experience to their members than the surrounding society, even if they are not as democratic as organizations in established democracies. Encompassing less diversity and having less power than a state, civic organizations have less need and less ability to repress their members, and their leaders are more easily accessed and held accountable to their members (Almond & Verba, 1989/1963; Diamond, 1999; Inglehart, 2000; Putnam et al., 1993; Tocqueville, 1969/1850; Verba et al., 1995). They thus serve as islands of democratic experience for citizens of an undemocratic society. In a more democratic society, there is less opportunity for the organization to provide a notably more democratic experience than that found in the surrounding society, and the effect of internal democracy should not be as great.

Alternatively, NGO activists may be exposed to democracy through relationships with outsiders[12] from more established democracies. I theorize that outsider relationships are also particularly important at earlier stages of democratization, where there has been little opportunity for building democratic attitudes through direct experience. Relationships with outsiders are thought to be most effective when in the form of long-term mentoring which is not overbearing, but empowering (Anderson & Olson, 2003; Carothers, 1999). Such relationships sometimes develop between a parent outsider NGO and an insider offshoot, or between an established insider NGO and an outsider NGO invited to advise it. The democratic experience of the outsider mentor can aid the insider NGO in building a political orientation by developing understandings of how democracy should work, creating a "repertoire" of skills and tactics, and building confidence. This could be particularly helpful to insider NGOs serving as early "entrepreneurs" of politically engaged peacebuilding in their societies by showing the way for other insiders (Tarrow, 1998). Studies of civic education efforts show that mentoring for political participation has to involve guided real-world activity, not just abstract classroom lessons, to be effective (Carothers, 1999, pp. 231–235). This takes time, so outsider mentorship is more likely to be effective when the relationship is medium to long term. This allows the mentor to aid the insiders in evaluating early steps and making improvements to its approach, and the insiders to aid the mentor in understanding the local situation so that the advice can be tailored appropriately and integrated with local culture (Eckstein, 1992; Garb & Phillips, 2001; Lederach, 1995; McDonald, 2002).

Such mentoring could have a positive influence on externally democratic ideology, both directly and indirectly, by encouraging internal democracy. Not only may internal democracy be the cultural norm for outsider mentors, but it has become fashionable for development NGOs and agencies to promote accountability of civic organizations to their constituents or beneficiaries.

But close mentoring, especially if tied to funding, risks becoming *domination*, where outsiders have as much say, or more, in the affairs of the organization as insiders. For instance, an insider NGO that began as a project or "local partner" of an outsider NGO may be required to seek approval of its projects by the board of the outsider NGO. Or outsiders may sit on the insider NGO's board of directors. More subtly, an NGO which started out as part of an outsider effort and later became an independent insider NGO may have retained a structure designed for implementing projects from a head office rather than eliciting input and support from the grassroots. Any of these conditions would limit the control that the members or beneficiaries of the NGO have over what the NGO does, thus reducing internal democracy. Domination could also impair the development of externally democratic ideology by orienting the organization toward outsiders, rather than insider political leaders, as authorities, and by painting the organization with a foreign identity that inhibits political participation. Also, a relationship where the insider organization is dominated by outsiders is less likely to be able to successfully adapt the international influence to the local situation, impeding any positive influence of mentorship on externally democratic ideology and internal democracy (Anderson & Olson, 2003).

Summarizing the theory, I have identified two mechanisms for developing the ideology of political participation in peacebuilding NGOs in less democratic societies. First, the NGO may compensate for the lack of societal democracy by providing democratic experience in its own internal governance. Secondly, relationships with outsiders from established democracies may compensate by providing long-term mentorship in political engagement. This should be a non-dominating relationship to avoid having a countervailing negative effect on ideology and internal democracy. Finally, an NGO's internal democracy will be affected by the norms and models of decision making available in its own culture, especially at the time of its initial formation. These relationships are depicted in Fig. 1, and will be individually examined in the analysis below. The following are specific hypotheses following from this theory, which will be tested below:

1. NGOs in less democratic societies have less externally democratic ideologies.
2. NGOs with more internal democracy have more externally democratic ideologies, especially in less democratic societies.
3. NGOs with outsider mentors have more externally democratic ideologies, especially in less democratic societies.
4. NGOs with non-dominating outsider mentors have more externally democratic ideologies.
5. NGOs with dominating outsider mentors have less externally democratic ideologies.

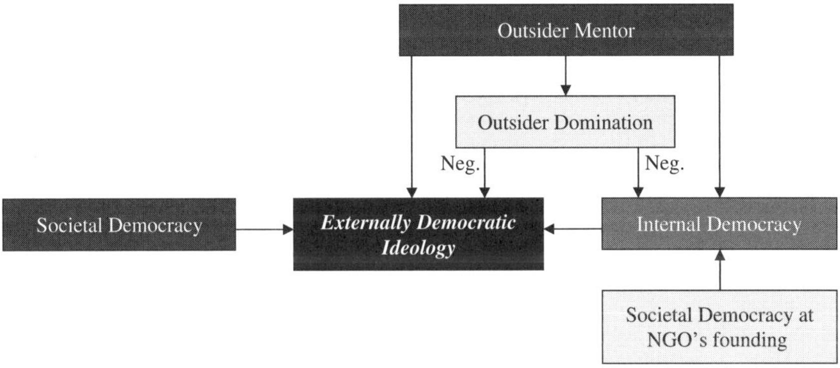

Fig. 1. A Model of Democratic Exposure Effects on Ideology.

6. NGOs with outsider mentors have more internal democracy, especially in less democratic societies.
7. NGOs with non-dominating outsider mentors have more internal democracy.
8. NGOs with dominating outsider mentors have less internal democracy.
9. NGOs founded in less democratic times have less internal democracy.

CASES AND METHOD

I have chosen to study peacebuilding NGOs in Bosnia (1991–2006) and Northern Ireland (1969–2006) because they vary in level of democracy, with Bosnia consistently trailing Northern Ireland on measures of democratic freedoms (Freedom House, 2007), as shown in Fig. 2, and democratic culture, as shown in Fig. 3 (Inglehart et al., 2005). Both have improved over time, providing variance in democracy both within and across societies. While Bosnia is also less favorable to political engagement in terms of its lower socioeconomic development and higher intensity of violence, it is common for these to covary, and democracy is the concept most immediately relevant to political engagement. Otherwise, they are similar on many points. Both are European societies which have suffered prominent violence over territorial status between religiously marked ethnic groups who had experienced ethnic violence in the past. Violence in both came to an end in the mid-1990s with international mediation and a strong influx of multilateral international aid after the peace agreement. Both also have new

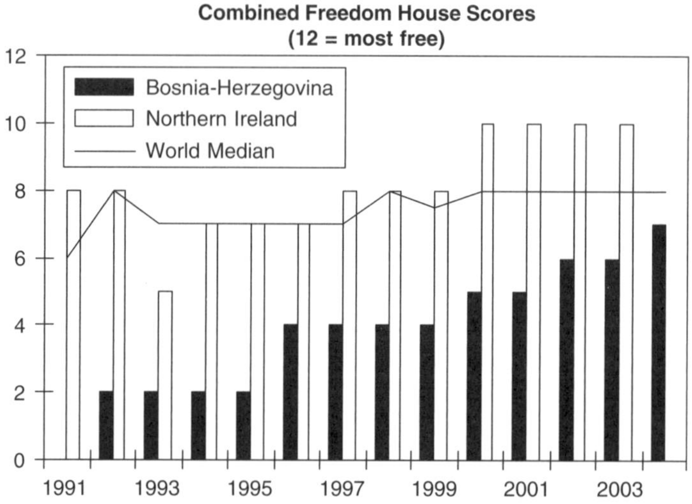

Fig. 2. Northern Ireland is Consistently Rated as More Democratic than Bosnia.

political institutions which are backed up by an outside/higher power, if they fail (the High Representative of the international community for Bosnia and the UK Parliament for Northern Ireland).

There are a number of measures of democracy available, but most focus on governmental institutions and elections, and neglect the civic aspects of democracy. The Freedom House scales focus on the ability of citizens to freely influence politics in an environment which not only holds regular free elections and permits anyone to run for office, but respects human rights such as freedoms of assembly, speech, and media, as well as the rights to fair judicial processes and freedom from abuse and terror by police or paramilitaries. Freedom House scores also happen to be available for Bosnia since 1992 and Northern Ireland for 1991–2003, while other measures are not available for substate entities such as Northern Ireland.[13] As can be seen in Fig. 2, Bosnia has consistently trailed three to six points behind Northern Ireland on the combined Freedom House scores.[14] Both are becoming more democratic, though Bosnia remains below the world median, while Northern Ireland has crossed it.

While Freedom House scores represent the rights experienced by civic groups, they do not directly measure democratic culture. Citizens can gain rights of assembly and speech without being oriented toward using them democratically to influence politics, respectfully of the rights of others. The

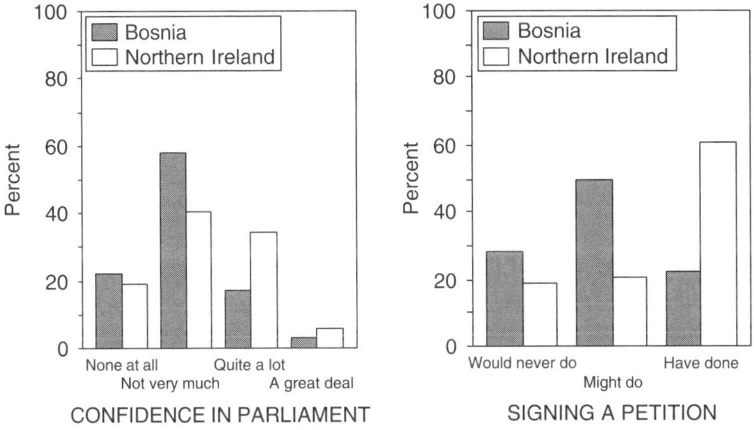

Fig. 3. Northern Ireland is More Participatory than Bosnia.

development of participatory culture and behavior in post-communist societies has lagged progress in freedoms. Post-communist societies experienced decades of repression of political expression and civic organization, except through forced participation in scripted and false ways. Post-communist societies thus suffer persisting alienation from political institutions and parties, and even from civil society organizations (Howard, 2003; Rose, Mishler, & Haerpfer, 1998, pp. 153–157). Former Yugoslavia did have somewhat more freedom to form civic associations than other communist societies, but until communism and the country began to unravel in the 1980s, such associations were either apolitical and politically monitored or effectively arms of the Communist Party. Bosnia was one of the most tightly controlled republics within Federal Yugoslavia, and the liberalization of civil society did not begin there until the last few years before war broke out and occured mostly in the capital, Sarajevo (Andjelic, 2003).

We can corroborate the indication of societal democracy given by the Freedom House scores with more direct (but less frequent) measures of democratic culture provided by the World Values Survey (Inglehart, 2005). The 2000 wave of this survey covered 68 societies, including Bosnia (2001) and Northern Ireland (1999).[15] On measures of interest in politics (not shown), the two societies are quite similar. But on measures such as confidence in political institutions or attitudes toward acts of political participation, Bosnians are less confident and less willing to participate than citizens in Northern Ireland, as shown in Fig. 3. Other World Values Survey measures not shown here show that people in Northern Ireland are more likely to participate in civil society organizations, and are also more generally trusting and tolerant.

This difference in civic and cultural democracy is consistent with the overall pattern of political engagement by peacebuilding NGOs in the two countries. In Northern Ireland, the Corrymeela Community (founded in 1965) held a major public political event involving the Northern Irish Prime Minister in 1967, just before the latest round of "troubles" began, and others in following years. They also began private political activity in this early period (McCreary, 1976). The Peace People movement formed in 1976 and began organizing massive street protests for peace which won it the Nobel Peace Prize. The Initiative '92 campaign organized public discussions throughout Northern Ireland to gather the ideas of citizens on how to move peace forward, which changed the political climate both with the resulting report and the process itself. The 1998 peace agreement referendum was supported by an active "Yes Campaign" by civic activists. Many NGOs were involved in behind-the-scenes private political activity throughout the conflict (Cox, 2003; Fitzduff, 2002, pp. 119–137; McCartney, 2000).

But in Bosnia, political engagement of peacebuilding NGOs has been much more limited. There were feeble peace protests just as the war was breaking out, but they were quickly swept away by the violence. Civil society played no role in producing ceasefires or the peace agreement, and there has been very little private political engagement. After the peace agreement, public political engagement slowly grew, so that by 2004, roughly the same proportion of peacebuilding NGOs were in some way politically engaged as in Northern Ireland, but primarily in a non-contentious and localized manner (Hemmer, 2008). There have been a few civic efforts at changing policy or laws at the highest levels of government to support peace and reintegration, and over time these have become less dependent on international actors[16] and slightly more frequent (Belloni, 2007). However, the level of ambition and impact of political engagement of peacebuilding NGOs in Bosnia still has not reached the scale found at its peak in Northern Ireland.

As part of a larger inquiry on the political engagement of peacebuilding NGOs, I have collected data on the ideology, internal democracy, and age of peacebuilding NGOs through interviews of peacebuilding NGO leaders, along with qualitative information on the causal relationships among these. I also interviewed expert observers of civil society and peacebuilding on each society (such as professors, scholar-practitioners, and officers of development aid organizations), who provide an independent source of information and a broader point of view. When available, I also collected and examined written material the NGO produced on its activities, structure, or ideology.

I had hoped to gather longitudinal data this way, but too many NGOs lacked good and accessible historical records for that to be feasible.

The difficulty of collecting this information kept the number of observations small, at around 30 NGOs per society (28 in Northern Ireland and 37 in Bosnia),[17] but this is roughly half the population of peacebuilding NGOs in each society.[18] These are NGOs for whom peacebuilding is a priority either expressed in its mission statement or clearly inherent in its choice and design of activities. They are selected to be roughly representative of the geographical spread and topical focus of the population of peacebuilding NGOs (with preference for those most strongly focused on peacebuilding).

Because the low number of observations and primarily ordinal level of measurement preclude more sophisticated multivariate analysis, the quantitative analysis of these data involves a series of bivariate or trivariate ordinal correlations, to summarize the strength and direction of relationships. An advantage of analyzing no more than three variables at once is that it is possible to use graphs to visualize the shape and strength of each relationship, which enables a richer analysis than correlation coefficients alone.

The following table provides a quick summary of the measures used, and a more detailed presentation can be found in the appendix.

Variable	High Score	Range
Externally democratic ideology	Mention of direct political engagement in mission and niche statements	0–4
Internal democracy	Frequent active mechanisms of several kinds for seeking input of beneficiaries, members, or the public on choice or design of activities	0–3
Outsider mentorship	Long-term association with an outsider organization or individual mentor from an established democracy	0–2
Outsider domination	Outsiders have at least equal say to insiders in governing the NGO	0–2 or 0–1
Societal democracy at NGO's founding	3-pt or 4-pt: Freedom House (FH) rating of "Free"	0–2 or 0–3
	2-pt: Upper half of observations on combined FH ratings	0–1

ANALYSIS

In each section of the analysis below, I will examine one part of the model shown earlier, representing at least one of the hypotheses. This begins with looking at the direct effects of each of the democratic exposure variables on democratic ideology. Then I examine the indirect effects of outsider influence and societal democracy via their effects on internal democracy.

The Effect of Societal Democracy on Externally Democratic Ideology

I will start by analyzing the bivariate relationship between societal democracy and externally democratic ideology within peacebuilding NGOs. The dataset permits doing this in two ways. Since Northern Ireland has been consistently more democratic than Bosnia, we can simply look at differences in ideology between the two societies. This version of the societal democracy variable represents difference in democratic exposure over the life spans of the NGOs, due to the consistent gap between the societies shown in Fig. 2. We can also look at the relationship between societal democracy at the NGO's founding and ideology, which focuses on a critical point in each NGO's lifespan that may have lasting effects on its ideology. Because democracy improved over time in both societies, this measure has the advantage of varying between NGOs *within* as well as across societies, helping to escape confounding effects of other societal variables. It is thus possible that younger Bosnian NGOs are founded at the same level of societal democracy as older Northern Irish ones, even though Bosnia consistently trails Northern Ireland on a year-by-year basis.[19] This will be important in the analysis below.

Often, a researcher is trying to explain why two measurements are different – but here the puzzle is why they are the same. Surprisingly, the Bosnian NGOs in the sample have ideologies that are approximately as politically participatory, on average, as their counterparts in Northern Ireland, *despite* the differences in attitudes toward political participation between the general populations of these societies, as shown above. The Bosnian NGOs appear to be ahead of their society in participatory ideology, indicating that they may be leaders of democratic cultural change, as theory predicts.

Fig. 4 helps visualize how small the difference between societies is by showing the mean level of ideology for NGOs in each society[20] (see the appendix for the distribution per society). This is not a statistically

Tau-b	Sig.	N
.049	.466	65

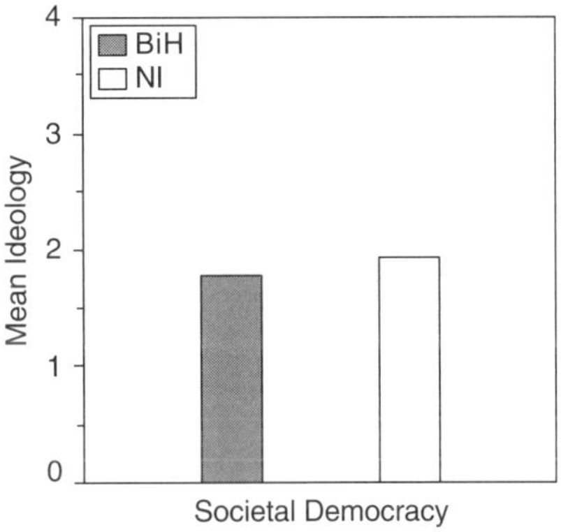

Fig. 4. Externally Democratic Ideology, *Correlated with* Societal Democracy.

significant[21] relationship according to the Tau-b correlation,[22] so I cannot say with confidence that there is a difference between the full populations of peacebuilding NGOs in these two societies. Since these societies differ in their levels of democracy, this is inconsistent with the hypothesis that societal democracy directly affects the orientation toward political participation of peacebuilding NGOs.

Looking instead at the correlation between the level of societal democracy when each NGO was founded and its current ideology also shows no significant relationship, as shown in Fig. 5. Regarding the larger (and negative) change among Northern Irish groups, although the relationship is not statistically significant, qualitative information leads me to believe there was a disengagement effect once the 1998 peace agreement was won.[23] Thus, externally democratic ideology may have been higher in Northern Ireland in the past.

It may be that ideology differed between societies earlier in democratization, but the gap closed over time, due to diminishing (or even negative) returns of societal democratization as societal democratization advanced. Unfortunately, too many NGOs lacked suitable records to establish what their ideology was at earlier time points. We shall see below that there is reason to believe that societal democratization in Bosnia caused the internal democracy and externally democratic ideology of peacebuilding NGOs to evolve, but less so in Northern Ireland. This evidence suggests there was less of an effect in Northern Ireland because peacebuilding NGOs generally began at a higher level of societal democracy and thus there was less improvement to be made.

	Tau-b	Sig.	n
Combined	.001	.697	65
Bosnia	.024	.589	37
NI	-.075	.489	28

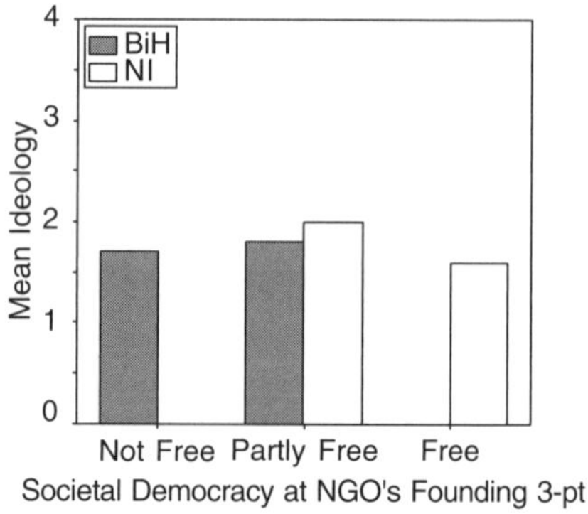

Fig. 5. Externally Democratic Ideology, *Correlated with* Societal Democracy at NGO's Founding.

	Tau-b	Sig.	n
Internal Democracy	.317	.005**	65
Outsider Mentorship	-.216	.049*	65
Outsider Domination	-.280	.017*	65
Societal Democracy at NGO's Founding, 3pt	.415	.000***	65
*p<.05, **p<.01, ***p<.001			

Fig. 6. Democratic Exposure Variables, *Correlated with* Societal Democracy.

The Effect of Societal Democracy on Democratic Exposure Variables

Before examining how the other democratic exposure variables affect externally democratic ideology, it is helpful to see how they vary with societal democracy. Unlike externally democratic ideology, the democratic exposure variables do vary significantly with the level of societal democracy, as one would expect, as shown in Fig. 6. Internal democracy is higher in the more democratic society of Northern Ireland, and outsider mentorship is higher in Bosnia, where it is theoretically needed to help compensate for lower levels of societal democracy. Outsider domination is also more likely in Bosnia, since mentorship is more likely there. Finally, the level of societal democracy at the NGO's founding is higher on average in Northern Ireland, as one would expect.

Each of these relationships is shown graphically in the appendix. There are no NGOs from Northern Ireland in the lowest category of internal democracy, or in the lowest category of societal democracy at founding, while there are no Bosnian NGOs at the highest level of societal democracy at founding. The majority of NGOs in Northern Ireland have no outsider mentor, while the majority of Bosnian NGOs do. Domination by mentors is rare, but also significantly rarer in the more democratic context of Northern Ireland. Otherwise, these variables contain substantial variation in both societies, as the graphs in the appendix show.

Now that we have verified that internal democracy and higher societal democracy at founding are more likely in Northern Ireland, and outsider mentorship and domination are more likely in Bosnia, let us turn our attention to the comparative effects of the democratic exposure variables on externally democratic ideology. Is ideology similar in the two societies because the greater presence of outsider mentorship in Bosnia makes up for less societal and internal democracy?

The Effect of Internal Democracy on Externally Democratic Ideology

Now I will test the hypothesis that internal democracy provides experience with democracy that increases ideological orientation toward engagement with political leaders external to the organization. Remember that internal democracy and external democratic ideology are different concepts, and the association is not simply what we would expect if two variables were so closely related conceptually that it would be strange if they did not correlate. Both have to do with democracy, but one is about democracy within the organization, and the other is about participation in the political process of the society. It is certainly conceivable that an internally democratic organization would not be oriented toward political participation externally, especially if the organization is focused on interpersonal issues inappropriate for government attention (some might see war trauma therapy this way, for instance). Furthermore, the former measures the actual *behavior* experienced within the organization, while the latter measures *attitudes* toward political participation externally.

The relationship across the combined sample is close to significance and mild. In Fig. 7, the relationships are graphed separately for each society, and both rise at the lower levels of internal democracy, but level off at higher levels. Looking just at Bosnian cases, the relationship is stronger than for the cases overall, but it is less significant with the lower *n*. The relationship may be weaker in Northern Ireland because observations there are concentrated at higher levels of internal democracy.

	Tau-b	Sig.	n
Combined	.181	.060	65
Bosnia	.225	.071	37
NI	.109	.380	28

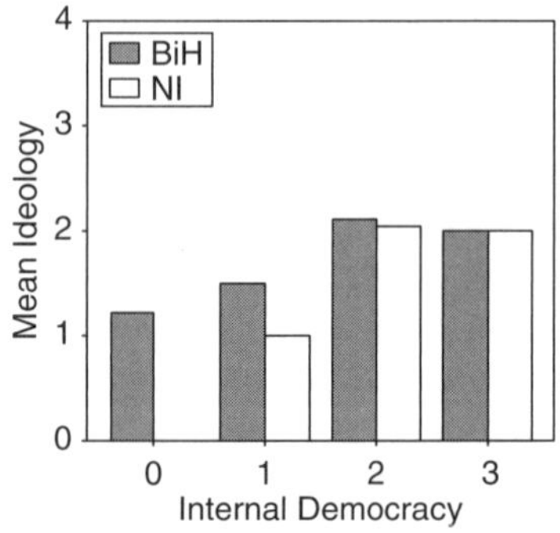

Fig. 7. Externally Democratic Ideology, *Correlated with* Internal Democracy.

	Tau-b	Sig.	n
Less Free	.310	.028*	34
More Free	.014	.813	31

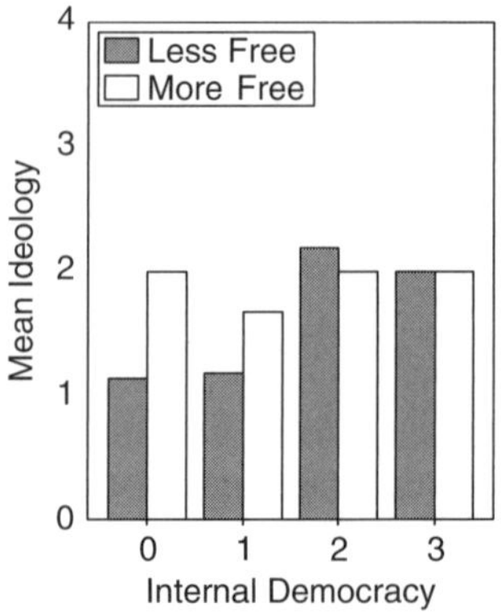

Fig. 8. Externally Democratic Ideology, *Correlated with* Internal Democracy, Controlling for Societal Democracy at the NGO's Founding.

In Fig. 8, the sample is divided roughly in half not by the society, but by the level of societal democracy at the NGO's founding (two-point scale). Three older Northern Irish groups are among the 34 NGOs in the low democracy (or "less free") group and six newer Bosnian groups are among the 31 NGOs in the high democracy (or "more free") group. Here, the relationship becomes sharper among NGOs formed at low levels of democracy, rising to .310 and significance at the .05 level. The NGOs formed at higher levels of democracy, in contrast, do not come close to a significant correlation between internal democracy and externally democratic ideology, as reflected in the flatter distribution in the graph.

The sharpening of the relationship when splitting the sample by societal democracy at NGO founding, rather than simply by society, is consistent with the idea that it is lower societal democracy that makes internal democracy an important engine of externally democratic ideology, rather than some other societal attribute (such as the more intense violence or presence of Muslims in Bosnia).

This is consistent with the theory. At higher levels of democracy, positive attitudes toward political participation are relatively easy to absorb through childhood schooling and routine examples and experiences of successful attempts by citizens to influence political leaders. Therefore, experiencing democracy within an NGO is not a new experience, and adds little to the ideology of political participation because that is already the cultural assumption. But at lower levels of societal democracy, internal democracy in an NGO is an island of democratic experience in an undemocratic sea. Members may for the first time be consulted by leaders on decisions, or find that leaders are responsive to, rather than resentful of, suggestions. They learn they cannot only question authority, but be effective in improving policy to suit their interests. Skills, experience, and ensuing confidence are built that eventually transfer into a readiness and desire to engage with political leaders in the broader society.

There is, however, an alternative explanation. NGOs which are formed with ideologies favoring external political participation could be more likely to favor internal participation in decision making, as a matter of consistency. This effect could be less pronounced in more democratic societies because the democratic model of decision making has become the cultural default mode of forming organizations, whether politically engaged or not. For example, in the United States, even garden clubs and chess clubs tend to elect their officers and have membership meetings where these officers are expected to be receptive to input.

It seems quite possible that causality actually runs in both directions in less democratic societies. Organizations formed with political engagement in mind may be philosophically inclined to be more internally democratic – but at the same time, organizations formed with internal democracy provide an arena for learning participatory attitudes that is unusual for that society. To conclusively work out this causality would require either longitudinal data on both variables or instrumental variables for a simultaneous equations model. What the present data show at this point is simply that this relationship, whatever the causality, exists only at low-to-middle levels of democracy. We shall return to this causality question at the end of the analysis.

The Effect of Outsider Relations on Externally Democratic Ideology

I will now examine whether outsider mentorship affects externally democratic ideology, especially when low societal democracy limits experience with democracy. In theory, mentorship by organizations or individuals from established democracies should increase externally democratic ideology, by nurturing the appropriate attitudes and sharing skills and experience that build confidence. We have seen above that outsider mentorship is more common in the less democratic context of Bosnia – could it explain the surprisingly similar levels of externally democratic ideology among peacebuilding NGOs across the two societies?

Fig. 9 shows there is no relationship for the combined sample, and contrary to the theory, there is no significant relationship among the Bosnian NGOs alone. Furthermore, if there is a relationship, it is in the more democratic context of Northern Ireland. This apparent Northern Irish relationship is not monotonic, but strongly hump shaped. Using Cramer's V,[24] a correlation for such non-monotonic relationships, the relationship in Northern Ireland is strong and significant, but is mild and insignificant in Bosnia. (Controlling for the level of societal democracy at the organization's founding instead of the society results in similar but weaker relationships, so this is not shown.) Middle levels of mentorship increase externally democratic ideology, but long-term mentorship appears to result in the lowest levels of externally democratic ideology. Since this Northern Ireland relationship is driven by an *n* of just two in the middle value of mentorship, it must be treated cautiously.

	Cramer's V	Sig.	n
Combined	.187	.563	65
Bosnia	.269	.484	37
NI	.517	.044*	28

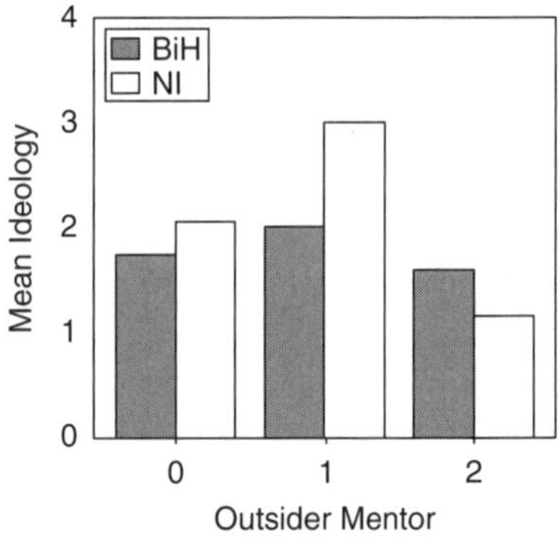

Fig. 9. Externally Democratic Ideology, *Correlated with* Outsider Mentor.

Mentorship and domination are correlated (Tau-b = .566, $p < .001^{***}$), as both require an outsider relationship, yet are theorized to work in opposite directions on externally democratic ideology. This could be confounding the above bivariate analyses, as when one variable is high, the other is likely to be also, and may be working in the opposite direction. If there is a hump-shaped relationship, it might be because mentorship helps ideology, but heavy mentorship is associated with domination, and thus a foreign orientation which inhibits orientation toward local political engagement.

In Fig. 10, the relationship is shown controlling for domination, with mixed results. Un-dominating mentorship has no effect on externally democratic ideology, as shown by the flatness of the graph. The increase at the mid-level of mentorship in Fig. 9 is oddly due to dominated cases, suggesting a positive relationship with domination. However, the drop in ideology between mid- and high-level dominating mentorship is strong and significant, suggesting a negative influence of domination. But there are only 13 cases of domination, and there are only four cases that are dominated and mid-level mentored.[25] The low *n* limits confidence in this result, but it suggests the underlying theory about domination may be partly correct, and further exploration with a larger dataset would be worthwhile. Dominating long-term outsider relationships might have a negative impact on externally democratic ideology, but less extensive mentorship that is dominating might actually improve externally democratic ideology. However, un-dominating outsider mentorship has no appreciable effect.

	Tau-b	Sig.	n
Un-dominated	-.007	.735	52
Dominated	-.533	.042*	13

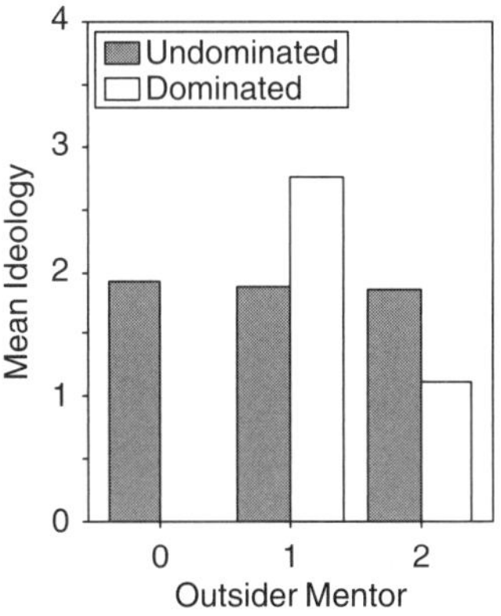

Fig. 10. Externally Democratic Ideology, *Correlated with* Outsider Mentor, Controlling for Outsider Domination.

The Effect of Outsider Relations on Internal Democracy

Now let us examine the theorized sources of internal democracy, beginning with outsider mentorship and domination. Outsider mentorship is theorized to support the development of internal democracy, especially in less democratic societies where this is not already the cultural norm. However, outsider mentorship that is dominating is theorized to have a countervailing effect on internal democracy, because outsider control interferes with the influence of members and beneficiaries over the decisions of the organization.

Fig. 11 hints at a hill-shaped relationship between outsider mentorship and internal democracy, much like that between outsider mentorship and externally democratic ideology, wherein middle levels of mentorship are slightly helpful to internal democracy. However, a Cramer's V test for this curved relationship finds only weak relationships that are not close to significance, whether for the entire sample or divided by society. Similarly to the relationship with ideology, dividing the sample by societal democracy at founding does not sharpen the relationships (not shown).

Fig. 12 shows the effect of mentorship on internal democracy, controlling for domination. For un-dominated mentorship, the relationship is now rather flat, and fails to approach significance on either the Spearman's rho or Cramer's V correlation. While dominating mentorship has a large negative correlation approaching the .1 significance level, this is driven by only four cases at the middle level of mentorship, and the nine cases at the high level of dominating mentorship have equivalent internal democracy to the non-dominating high mentorship cases. The most reasonable conclusion

	Cramer's V	Sig.	N
Combined	.200	.362	65
Bosnia	.275	.317	37
NI	.228	.421	28

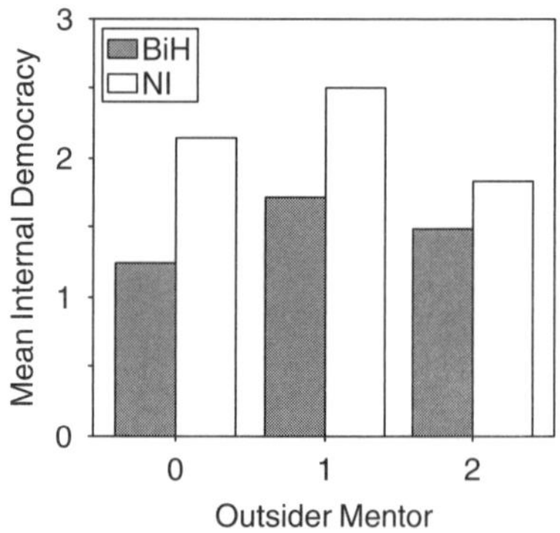

Fig. 11. Internal Democracy, *Correlated with* Outsider Mentor.

	Tau-b	Sig.	n
Un-dominated	-.060	.489	52
Dominated	-.435	.112	13

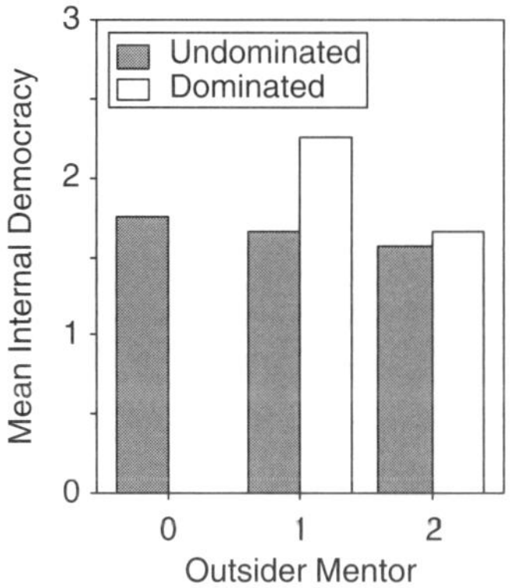

Fig. 12. Internal Democracy, *Correlated with* Outsider Mentor, Controlling for Outsider Domination.

is that mentorship does not affect internal democracy, whether dominating or not.

The Effect of Societal Democracy at the Organization's Founding on Internal Democracy

We have seen already that peacebuilding NGOs are more internally democratic in Northern Ireland than the less democratic context of Bosnia. Is this because NGOs are more likely to form themselves democratically when they observe democratic structures, procedures, and values in the society around them?

Fig. 13 shows a significant overall relationship of .280. However, this is driven by the Bosnian cases. The relationship strengthens to .333 when restricted to the Bosnian NGOs, and there is no relationship among the Northern Irish NGOs. Note that the lowest level at which an NGO was formed in Northern Ireland is the middle "partly free" level. Bosnia does have NGOs which formed at the lowest "not free" level, while lacking any at the highest "free" level. This suggests the relationship depends more on the range of democratization than the society per se. I have investigated whether this might be a spurious effect of NGO age, which is correlated with societal democracy at founding. But age is not correlated with internal democracy.

The pattern in Fig. 13 suggests that societal democracy might have more of an effect on internal democracy between low and middle levels of societal democracy. In Fig. 14, I have used a four-point version of societal

	Tau-b	Sig.	N
Combined	.280	.010*	65
Bosnia	.333	.021*	37
NI	-.102	.431	28

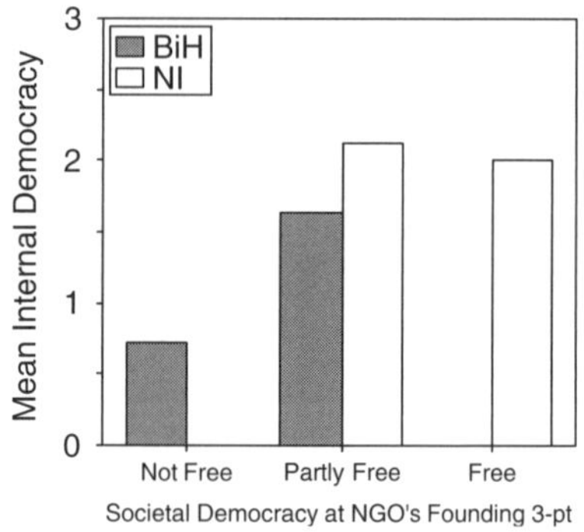

Fig. 13. Internal Democracy, *Correlated with* Societal Democracy at NGO's Founding.

democracy. This allows a more exacting examination of the relationship of societal democracy to internal democracy, separately for "less free" cases (ranging from "not free" to "quasi-free") and for "more free" cases (ranging from "mostly free" to "free"). Cases from both societies are in each of these ranges.

Though the graphs look quite similar, the correlation with internal democracy for the lower version of this scale comes out slightly stronger than for Bosnia at .353 (despite a slightly smaller *n*). This suggests it is indeed specifically moving from low to mid democracy, rather than mid to high, that produces change in internal democracy, not something else about Bosnia. Conversely, the correlation for the higher end of the scale is even less strong and less significant than for Northern Ireland, suggesting that it is Northern Ireland's higher starting point in societal democracy which results in little change in internal democracy as democratization proceeds.

The relationship at lower levels of societal democracy is consistent with the theory that the choices organizations make about how to govern their own affairs are influenced by the political culture and prevalent models of governance in the surrounding society. That this relationship disappears at higher levels of societal democracy is intriguing. It is not due to reaching some natural limit to internal democratization – some of those who formed at high levels of societal democracy do have the highest level of internal democracy, but most are middling. Perhaps NGOs formed in more democratic times feel less fervently about internal democracy, as it would no longer be novel or provide a stark contrast with the lack of democracy in the society. For NGOs in less democratic societies, internal democracy

	Tau-b	Sig.	N
Less Free	.353	.025*	34
More Free	-.057	.650	31

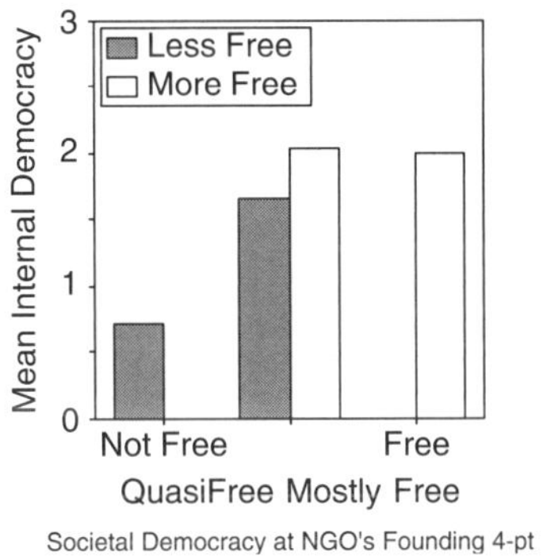

Fig. 14. Internal Democracy, *Correlated with* Societal Democracy at NGO's Founding, 4-Point Scale.

could be a subtle form of cultural resistance and a visionary statement, which becomes less important as democratization advances. It might also be due to increased professionalization (and higher salaries) of NGO staff at high levels of societal democracy, which can make internal governance more like a hierarchical for-profit firm than a volunteer or quasi-volunteer organization would be.

These results may seem contrary to the idea expressed above that NGOs serve as islands of democracy in an undemocratic society, and that they incubate which incubate externally democratic ideology. If the internal democracy of NGOs has such a strong tendency to be lower when founded in an undemocratic society, how could they be "islands of democracy?" The answer is that even if internal democracy improves along with societal democracy over time, it can still start with a large gap between internal and societal democracy, with this gap closing over time. To illustrate, I have simulated a dataset containing the same scale for internal and societal democracy, both measured at the NGO's founding, for cases in three different years. The resulting graph in Fig. 15 represents a perfect correlation between internal democracy and societal democracy at founding, while still producing an "islands of democracy" gap between societal and internal democracy at lower levels of societal democracy.

Additionally, analysis verifies that societal democracy at the NGO's founding, like general societal democracy, has no direct effect on the externally democratic ideology of peacebuilding NGOs (Tau-b = .001, $p = .697$, $n = 65$). If societal democracy affects externally democratic ideology, it is via its positive effects on internal democracy.

This supports the theorized primary causal chain of internal democracy to externally democratic ideology which is shown in Fig. 16. If the reverse were true – that internal democracy was caused by externally democratic ideology, as shown in Fig. 17, then that ideology would in turn come from either societal experience, some outside source, or independent ideological innovation. If it came from societal experience, we would expect the ideology to be associated with societal democracy at founding. But societal democracy at founding is not correlated with ideology (represented as a crossed-out arrow in Fig. 17). If alternatively the source of ideology was from outside the society, it must have been through a mechanism other than mentorship, which was ruled out above. Furthermore, if outside influence

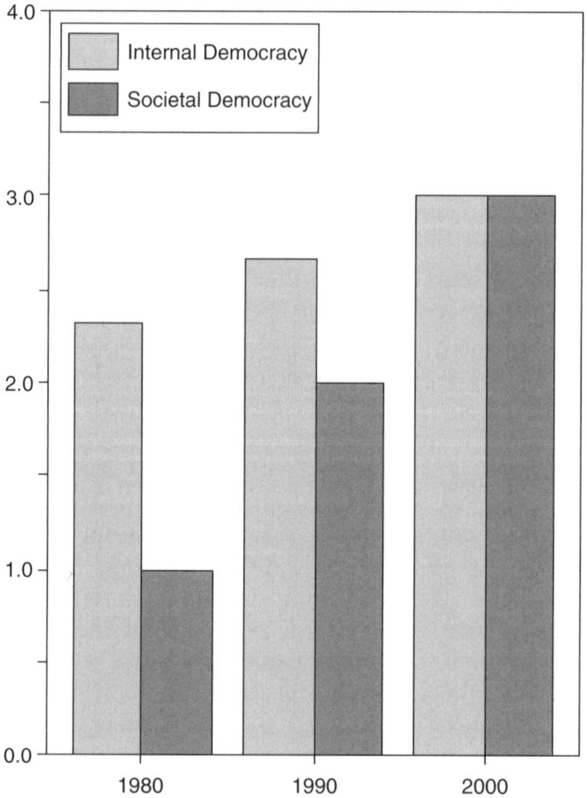

Fig. 15. Simulated Data Showing Islands of Democracy Effect When Internal Democracy and Societal Democracy at NGO's Founding are Correlated.

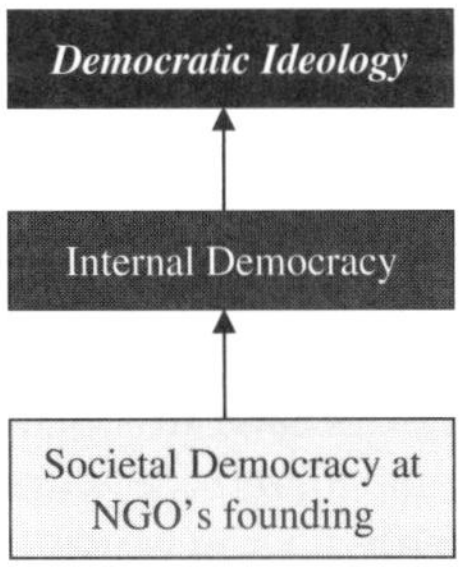

Fig. 16. Modeled Causal Relationship.

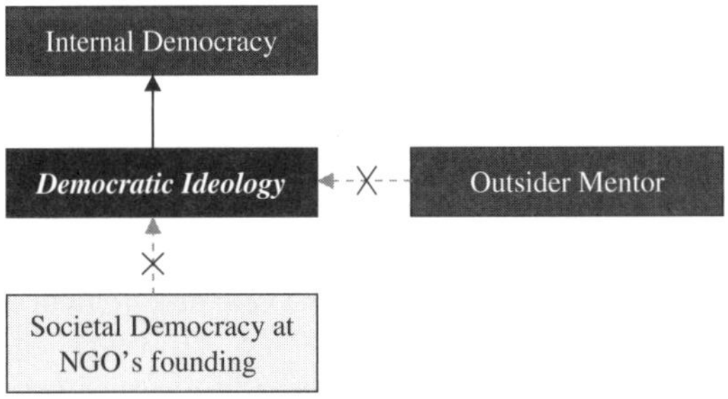

Fig. 17. Alternate Causal Relationship.

was the source of ideology, the purported result of that imported ideology (internal democracy) ought not to be associated with societal democracy at founding. Unless the NGO activists developed an externally democratic ideology independently of democratic experience through societal democracy or outsider influence, this suggests that the causality is the other way around – societal conditions influenced internal democracy which influenced externally democratic ideology over time.

CONCLUSION

The evidence presented is partly consistent with the theory that democratic experience fosters more externally democratic ideology within peacebuilding NGOs. These data (which are limited to the current time) do not support a direct link currently between societal democracy and externally democratic ideology for these two societies (contrary to Hypothesis 1). But these data are consistent with the theory that, in the early, low-to-moderate stage of societal democratization, democracy within NGOs develops as islands of democratic experience, which in turn develops externally democratic ideology (consistent with Hypothesis 2). The data also support the theory that internal democracy increases with societal democratization (consistent with Hypothesis 9), and in this way, societal democratization has an indirect, long-term effect on externally democratic ideology.

This helps explain why the Bosnian NGOs counterintuitively have similar ideology to the Northern Irish NGOs on average. Having reached mid-levels of societal democracy, Bosnian NGOs are now reaching the mid-levels of internal democracy sufficiently to have closed an ideology gap that may have previously existed between Bosnian and Northern Irish peacebuilding NGOs. This is possible despite the fact that Bosnian NGOs remain significantly less internally democratic on average, because the effects of internal democracy on externally democratic ideology occur between low and middle levels of internal democracy. Northern Irish NGOs, in contrast, were mostly formed at sufficiently high levels of societal democracy that both internal democracy and externally democratic ideology were already strong enough norms to come naturally to them.

In theory, exposure to outsiders from established democracies might also be making up the democratic experience gap. However, this dataset does not support the idea that outsider mentorship can substitute for direct insider experience. It does not show a positive effect of mentorship on either externally democratic ideology or internal democracy, even when non-dominating or in less democratic societies (contrary to Hypotheses 3, 4, 6, and 7). Furthermore, there is some reason to believe that extensive outsider mentorship of a dominating nature is harmful to externally democratic ideology (consistent with Hypothesis 5). The data do not support this conclusion regarding internal democracy, however (contrary to Hypothesis 8). It may be, however, that a more nuanced measure of outsider mentorship, including the intent of the mentor regarding political participation, would find that it can have a positive effect. Other, less directed forms of outsider influence than mentorship might also be at play, such as NGO leaders having lived or studied in democratic societies, or simply through exposure to written or recorded materials on democracy.

These findings are consistent with political culture theory that building positive orientations toward political participation requires time and is largely driven by civic associations providing forums for democratic experience in their internal governance. The finding that externally democratic ideology and internal democracy are not associated with outsider mentorship, even when non-dominating or in less democratic societies, challenges the idea that outsiders can significantly accelerate cultural democratization in such a direct manner, and further underscores the concept that cultural change takes time. These findings also provide an explanation for earlier findings that democratizing societies are most at risk for civil war. This may well be the result of a lack of political engagement of peace activists in the early period of democratization, because time is needed to develop internally democratic organizations that foster participatory attitudes. Bottom-up and middle-out peacebuilding theory should be amended to explicitly anticipate this delay in developing positive attitudes toward political engagement among civic peacebuilders in newly democratizing societies, and the importance of internal democracy in addressing it.

Future research should further examine the findings of this study with data expanded in both observations and indicators. Gathering data over time in current and future conflicts would allow more direct analysis of how externally democratic ideology evolves within NGOs, including not only which predictors are most associated with ideological change, but the time distribution of that change (neglected data of practical importance). As noted above, additional indicators of outsider mentorship which focus on the content of mentorship may produce more nuanced conclusions. The addition of other societies to the dataset would also be helpful for isolating the effects of society-level variables such as societal democracy, economic development, and violence.

Furthermore, the relationship of externally democratic ideology to actual political engagement by peacebuilding NGOs in democratizing societies should be examined, in conjunction with other factors such as organizational legitimacy and resources and political opportunity structure (see forthcoming research by this author). The relationship of internal democracy and externally democratic ideology in peacebuilding NGOs and other civil society organizations to democratic ideology among ordinary citizens should also be examined, because this affects the potential to mobilize the public for political action for peace. Finally, the link between the political engagement of peacebuilding NGOs and the peacefulness of democratizing societies in comparable danger of violent conflict should be examined.

In the meantime, this initial study sounds a policy warning that should not be ignored: a politically engaged peace movement is not likely to quickly develop in societies with little democratic experience. If outsider mentorship is ineffective, even when non-dominating, at speeding up this development, then we need to be cautious about the prospects for peaceful democratization in conflict zones with little experience with democracy. In such situations, it will take time for little islands of democracy to rise and produce the democratic experience necessary for peacebuilding NGOs to develop an ideology of political participation. Without a politically active peace movement, political leaders accustomed to and invested in violent conflict are unlikely to make new democratic institutions work well for building a new peaceful and prosperous future without, or perhaps even with, sustained strong international oversight and pressure. The continually renewed international oversight of Bosnia, now lasting 12 years with no end clearly in sight, is a case in point. The international community should anticipate a long-term commitment to peacekeeping and patiently supporting the development of internally democratic peace-oriented civil society in newly democratizing societies experiencing, recovering from, or in danger of violent conflict.

NOTES

1. For instance, UN Secretary General Boutros-Ghali's *Agenda for Peace* (1995, pp. 61–62) declares: "there is an obvious connection between democratic processes – such as rule of law and transparency in decision making – and the achievement of true peace and security in any new and stable political order."

2. Intrastate conflicts have steadily declined from a peak of 51 (34 ethnic) in 1993 to 22 (13 ethnic) in 2005, but still far outnumber interstate conflicts (Marshall, 2006). The Human Security Centre (2005, pp. 59, 148–155) attributes the decline primarily to international activism unleashed by the end of the Cold War, including by "thousands of NGOs."

3. I define "political engagement" as activity seeking to influence political leaders, expected to provoke a reaction by political leaders, or involving them in an active role, such as speaking at an event.

4. I interpret "political leaders" more broadly than simply those who hold government or political party positions, to include other authorities who are potentially targets of advocacy for policy change. This is particularly appropriate where the legitimacy of established political institutions is challenged by alternative authorities. For instance, in Northern Ireland, the Peace Train NGO pressured the IRA to cease a bombing campaign (Cochrane & Dunn, 2002, pp. 161–162).

5. NGOs are formally organized nonprofit associations, usually with professional staff, which are at least formally independent of government. They may or may not have formal members, and in either case may serve the public generally or a segment of the public (which might be larger than the membership, if any). While political parties, unions and churches, mosques, synagogues, etc., may technically satisfy this definition, they are not customarily considered NGOs, though NGOs may be associated with them (such as a religious charity). In Bosnia, a distinction is sometimes made between NGOs and "citizens' associations," a label dating back to the communist period (World Bank, 2002), but the theoretical basis of this distinction was never clear (the definition is a foggy inconsistent combination of

when they were formed, what they call themselves and where they get funding) and in practice the distinction has been deteriorating over time. Many organizations with "citizens' association" in their name also call themselves NGOs, and organizations of either label these days may get both local and international funding. Citizens' associations are considered a type of NGO for the purposes of this study.

6. The causal direction is unclear, and Putnam tentatively suggests the primary causal direction is from civil society development to economic development. But regardless of causation, we should expect less independent civic activity in less economically developed societies.

7. Berman (1997), for instance, shows that many elements of German civil society aided Hitler's rise to power, working against both democracy and peace.

8. As McAdam (1996, p. 27) defines it, the POS is more favorable when there is instability in political alignments, there are allies of the social movement among the political elite, the will and capacity for repression is limited, and political institutions are structurally open to civic input (through many points of access, for instance).

9. This concept is related to Dalton's (1994) notion of "Ideologically Structured Action" except that his study was limited to established democracies, and thus the distinction between ideologies favoring "conventional" or "unconventional" political participation, rather than whether or not to participate at all.

10. I am using this term loosely to mean "those who consider the society to be their home." Often the legal meaning of who is a citizen, and of which state, is very much contested, as in both the societies in this study.

11. Polletta (2002) discusses how founders of American social movements modeled their organizations on forms familiar to them, such as their churches. I have witnessed how communist traditions influenced the development of a youth group in postwar Bosnia (Hemmer, 1997).

12. I am using the terminology *outsider* and *insider* in place of the more common *international* and *local*, because what is international becomes confused in contested substate entities such as Northern Ireland, where one side considers the British to be foreign, and the other side sees them as domestic, and vice versa regarding the Republic of Ireland. I am using *local* exclusively in the sense of small geographic units such as cities, towns, and villages.

13. Freedom House scores are sometimes criticized as being too subjective, particularly in the 70s and 80s, but the process had been made more rigorous by the 90s, the period shown in this graph. Furthermore, Freedom House scores correlate remarkably well with other measures of democracy, even in earlier years.

14. The original Freedom House scales of Political Rights and of Civil Liberties each range from one to seven, with low scores being the most democratic. I have, as is commonly done, combined and reversed these scales by adding them together and subtracting from 14, such that the new scale ranges from zero to 12, with 12 being the most democratic score.

15. Note that these values may have improved somewhat in the six to eight years since this survey was taken. The only other WVS survey of Bosnia separately from former Yugoslavia was 1998. The four-item post-materialism score moved only from 1.71 to 1.73 (on a zero to three scale) in Bosnia in these three years, so it appears that change is slow at the societal level.

16. One of the earliest significant and clearly peace-related campaigns by Bosnian NGOs was to establish conscientious objector status, but it was occasioned by, and probably initiated by, a simultaneous push by IGOs, notably the Council of Europe. Belloni (2007) documents three cases of more truly indigenously driven peace advocacy, one beginning in 1997 and the others after 2000, all taking years of effort to have an effect.

17. In Bosnia, there have been three waves of data collection with an evolving questionnaire, April–May 2004, November 2004–July 2005, and February–October 2007. The latest wave covered 25 NGOs. However, the questions used in this paper were very similar or identical in previous waves, so the most recent data available are used, for a total of 37 NGOs. The second and third waves in Bosnia were conducted by a Bosnian research assistant, Goran Puljić. In addition, we interviewed four expert observers of Bosnian civil society/peacebuilding in August–October 2007. In Northern Ireland, I interviewed 28 organizations in November 2006–February 2007 with the current questionnaire, along with 13 expert observers. Interviews lasted one to three hours, averaging two hours.

18. A list of all peacebuilding NGOs was compiled for each society from mentions in other studies and listings in available directories. Some directories were specific to peacebuilding NGOs, and others listed all NGOs, from which peacebuilding NGOs were identified based on their mission and activities. Where possible, NGO Web sites were also consulted. Finally, the experts and NGO leaders interviewed in each society were asked to examine the list and suggest changes. This resulted in a list of 60 peacebuilding NGOs in Northern Ireland and 67 in Bosnia. NGOs were prioritized for contact based on how strongly their activities seemed related to peacebuilding. Contacts were attempted based on this prioritization in each geographical region, with attention to achieving a representative sample in terms of geographical location and topical focus of the NGOs (e.g., the proportion of NGOs focused on treating war trauma is similar in the sample and the population). It was often difficult to contact the NGOs, but repeated efforts were made with each attempted contact. Often, unresponsive NGOs turned out to be defunct, according to other NGO leaders. There were only five outright refusals, due to either time constraints (two in NI, two in Bosnia) or the NGO deeming itself to not be a peacebuilding organization (one in Bosnia). Refusals were not concentrated in particular geographical or topical areas.

19. Among the cases for which the 13-point scale is available, there is one case of a new Bosnian NGO – the Democratic Youth Movement – formed at a *higher* level of societal democracy than some old Northern Irish NGOs.

20. Since most of the variables in this study are not purely interval-level measurements, calculating a mean is, strictly speaking, inappropriate. But while I cannot say that the intervals are identical, I can say with confidence that they do not differ by a factor of ten, and probably not more than two. Thus, I present these as fuzzy means constructed from fuzzy intervals – a mean of 1.5 implies the central tendency is probably somewhere between one and two, rather than exactly halfway. Graphing the means effectively summarizes these data and corresponds well with the correlations.

21. The p values for statistical significance have been adjusted, because the sample size is large compared to the population of peacebuilding NGOs in these two countries. The formula used was: adjusted $p = p^{*}\mathrm{sqrt}((N-n)/(N-1))$.

When evaluating a relationship across both countries, $N = 127$. When evaluating a relationship for one country at a time, $N = 67$ for Bosnia and $N = 60$ for Northern Ireland.

22. In most of this analysis I use the ordinal-level Tau-b correlation, which shows a perfect relationship as ± 1 and no relationship as 0. It represents the percentage of the variance of one variable that is explained by the other.

23. Many respondents reported that after the 1998 peace agreement, which reestablished home rule with inter-communal power sharing, politicians became even more dismissive of civil society groups as competitors for power, which the politicians now wished to consolidate. The vaunted Civic Forum established by the peace agreement to advise the assembly and government was thus a flop. Many civic groups, tired from the long effort to get the politicians and paramilitaries this far, were happy enough to step back, wanting politicians to finally get things done themselves. Furthermore, the associated drop in violence and economic surge reduced the urgency for political engagement of peacebuilding NGOs. As one respondent put it, civil society's "eyes were taken off the ball" (Cochrane, 2006).

24. This chi-squared-based nominal correlation coefficient is 0 for no relationship and 1 for a perfect relationship. It represents the percentage of variance of one variable explained by the other.

25. All four of these cases are Bosnian, and have little else in common. They are a psychological care group, a youth center, a legal aid center, and an association of election officials.

ACKNOWLEDGMENTS

This research was supported by grants from the US Agency for International Development (USAID) and the following units at the University of California, Irvine: Center for the Study of Democracy, Center for Citizen Peacebuilding, Department of Political Science and School of Social Science. I appreciate the comments provided by Professors Russell Dalton, Patrick Morgan, Carole Uhlaner, John Graham, Sharon Lean, Robert Redick, and Darren Kew, as well as participants of the September 2007 conference "Cutting Edge Theories and Recent Developments in Conflict Resolution" of the Program on the Analysis and Resolution of Conflicts at Syracuse University, and three anonymous reviewers.

REFERENCES

Almond, G. A., & Verba, S. (1989/1963). *The civic culture*. Newbury Park, California: Sage Publications.

Anderson, M. B., & Olson, L. (2003). *Confronting war*. Cambridge, MA: Collaborative for Development Action.

Andjelic, N. (2003). *Bosnia-Herzegovina: The end of a legacy*. London: Frank Cass.

Belloni, R. (2007). *State building and international intervention in Bosnia*. New York: Routledge.

Berman, S. (1997). Civil society and the collapse of the Weimar Republic. *World Politics*, *49*, 410–429.

Bloomfield, D. (1997). *Peacemaking strategies in Northern Ireland: Building complementarity in conflict management theory*. New York: St. Martin's Press, Inc.

Boutros-Ghali, B. (1995). *An agenda for peace*. New York: United Nations.

Carothers, T. (1999). *Aiding democracy abroad: The learning curve*. Washington, DC: Carnegie Endowment for International Peace (Distributed by Brookings Inst. Press).

Cochrane, F. (2006). Interview by B. Hemmer. Nov. 7. Lancaster, UK.

Cochrane, F., & Dunn, S. (2002). Peace and conflict resolution organizations in Northern Ireland. In: B. Gidron, S. N. Katz & Y. Hasenfeld (Eds), *Mobilizing for peace: Conflict resolution in Northern Ireland, Israel/Palestine, and South Africa*. New York: Oxford University Press.

Cox, H. (2003). Our Friends in the North: Twenty-one years of Quaker House Belfast. http://www.quakerhousebelfast.org/page4.html

Dalton, R. J. (1994). *The Green Rainbow: Environmental groups in Western Europe*. New Haven: Yale University Press.

Diamond, L. (1999). *Developing democracy: Toward consolidation*. Baltimore: Johns Hopkins University Press.

Eckstein, H. (1992). A culturalist theory of political change. In: H. Eckstein (Ed.), *Regarding politics: Essays on political theory, stability and change* (pp. 265–285). Berkeley: University of California Press.

Eckstein, H. (1998). Congruency theory explained. In: H. Eckstein, F. J. Fleron, Jr., E. P. Hoffmann & W. M. Reisinger (Eds), *Can democracy take root in post-Soviet Russia?* (pp. 3–34). Boulder: Rowman and Littlefield.

Fearon, K. (2000). Civic society and the peace process. In: *The role of citizen peacebuilding in conflict transformation*. Irvine, California: Citizen Peacebuilding Program, University of California, Irvine.

Fitzduff, M. (2002). *Beyond violence: Conflict resolution process in Northern Ireland*. Tokyo: United Nations University Press.

Freedom House. (2007). Freedom in the world. www.freedomhouse.org

Garb, P., & Phillips, M. (2001). "Report on "The Role of Citizen Peacebuilding in Conflict Transformation," a Conference at the University of California, Irvine, June 1–4, 2000. Citizen Peacebuilding Program, University of California, Irvine, Irvine.

Gidron, B., Katz, S. N., & Hasenfeld, Y. (2002). *Mobilizing for peace: Conflict resolution in Northern Ireland, Israel/Palestine, and South Africa*. New York: Oxford University Press.

Golan, G., & Kamal, Z. (2000). Palestinian and Israeli citizen diplomacy. In: *The role of citizen peacebuilding in conflict transformation*. Irvine, California: Citizen Peacebuilding Program, University of California, Irvine.

Hegre, H., Ellingsen, T., Gates, S., & Gleditsch, N. P. (2001). Toward a democratic civil peace? Democracy, political change, and civil war, 1816–1992. *American Political Science Review*, *95*, 33–48.

Hemmer, B. (1997). Reinventing peace operations. Master's thesis, International Relations Program, Syracuse University, Syracuse, NY.

Hemmer, B. (2008). The democratization of peacebuilding: The political engagement of peacebuilding NGOs in democratizing societies. Doctoral thesis, Department of Political Science, University of California, Irvine.

Howard, M. M. (2003). *The weakness of civil society in post-communist Europe*. New York: Cambridge University Press.

Human Security Centre. (2005). *Human security report 2005: War and peace in the 21st century* (Vol. 1). Oxford: Oxford University Press.

Inglehart, R. (1990). *Culture shift in advanced industrial societies*. Princeton: Princeton University Press.

Inglehart, R. (2000). Culture and democracy. In: L. E. Harrison & S. P. Huntington (Eds), *Culture matters: How values shape human progress* (pp. 80–97). New York: Basic Books.

Inglehart, R., et al. (2005). European and world values surveys integrated data file, 1999–2002. Release I. Vol. 2005. Cologne, Germany: Zentralarchiv fur Empirische Sozialforschung (ZA)/Tilburg, Netherlands: Tilburg University/Amsterdam, Netherlands: Netherlands Institute for Scientific Information Services (NIWI)/Madrid, Spain: Analisis Sociologicos Economicos y Politicos (ASEP) and JD Systems (JDS)/Ann Arbor, MI: Inter-University Consortium for Political and Social Research, www.icpsr.umich.edu

Kew, D. (2002). Pillars of democracy? The role of civil society in Nigerian democratization and conflict resolution, 1991–1999. Dissertation thesis, Fletcher School of Law and Diplomacy, Tufts University, Medford, MA.

Lederach, J. P. (1995). *Preparing for peace: Conflict transformation across cultures*. Syracuse: Syracuse University Press.

Lederach, J. P. (1997). *Building peace: Sustainable reconciliation in divided societies*. Washington, DC: United States Institute of Peace.

Lipset, S. M., Trow, M., & Coleman, J. (1962). *Union democracy: The internal politics of the international typographical union*. Garden City, NY: Anchor Books, Doubleday.

Marshall, M. G. (2006). Major episodes of political violence 1946–2005. Vol. 2006: Center for Systemic Peace, http://members.aol.com/CSPmgm/warlist.htm

McAdam, D. (1982). *Political process and the development of black insurgency, 1930–1970*. Chicago: University of Chicago Press.

McAdam, D. (1996). Conceptual origins, current problems, future directions. In: D. McAdam, J. D. McCarthy & M. N. Zald (Eds), *Comparative perspectives on social movements* (pp. 23–40). New York: Cambridge University Press.

McCarthy, J. D., & Zald, M. N. (1997). Resource mobilization and social movements: A partial theory. *American Sociological Review*, *82*, 1212–1241.

McCartney, C. (2000). Community groups as agents of community relations and community reconciliation. In: *The role of citizen peacebuilding in conflict transformation*. Irvine, California: Citizen Peacebuilding Program, University of California, Irvine.

McCreary, A. (1976). *Corrymeela: Hill of harmony in Northern Ireland*. New York: Hawthorn Books, Inc.

McDonald, J. W., Jr. (2002). The need for multi-track diplomacy. In: J. Davies & E. Kaufman (Eds), *Second track/citizens' diplomacy* (pp. 49–60). Lanham, MD: Rowman & Littlefield Publishers, Inc.

Minkoff, D. C. (1999). Bending with the wind: Strategic change and adaptation by women's and racial minority organizations. *American Journal of Sociology*, *104*, 1666–1703.

Montville, J. V. (1987). The arrow and the olive branch: A case for track two diplomacy. In: J. W. McDonald, Jr. & D. B. Behdahmane (Eds), *Conflict resolution: Track two diplomacy* (pp. 5–20). Washington, DC: Foreign Service Institute.
Polletta, F. (2002). *Freedom is an endless meeting: Democracy in American social movements.* Chicago: University of Chicago Press.
Putnam, R. D., Leonardi, R., & Nanetti, R. Y. (1993). *Making democracy work: Civic traditions in modern Italy.* Princeton: Princeton University Press.
Rose, R., Mishler, W., & Haerpfer, C. (1998). *Democracy and its alternatives: Understanding post-communist societies.* Cambridge, UK: Polity Press.
Russett, B. (1993). *Grasping the democratic peace: Principles for a post-cold war world.* Princeton: Princeton University Press.
Saunders, H. H. (1999). *A public peace process: Sustained dialogue to transform racial and ethnic conflicts.* New York: Palgrave.
Tarrow, S. (1998). *Power in movement: Social movements and contentious politics.* Cambridge, MA: Cambridge University Press.
Tocqueville, A. (1969/1850). *Democracy in America.* New York: Perenneal.
Verba, S., Schlozman, K. L., & Brady, H. E. (1995). *Voice and equality: Civic voluntarism in American politics.* Cambridge, MA: Harvard University Press.
World Bank. (2002). *Bosnia and Herzegovina: Local level institutions and social capital study*, Vol. 1. http://go.worldbank.org/1E5B1I8NI0

APPENDIX. MEASUREMENT

Externally Democratic Ideology

This is based on analysis of answers to two questions:

1. What is the mission of your organization?
2. How do your projects fit into the overall process of building a sustainable peace in Northern Ireland? What is your organization's primary role, or contribution, in this process? What is the connection?

Each is rated 0–2 and the scores are added together.

2 = mention of actively interacting with or influencing political leaders, such as lobbying, protesting, etc.

1 = mention of supporting political participation of citizens through more indirect or diffuse means such as voter education, developing participatory attitudes and skills.

0 = none of the above (Fig. A1).

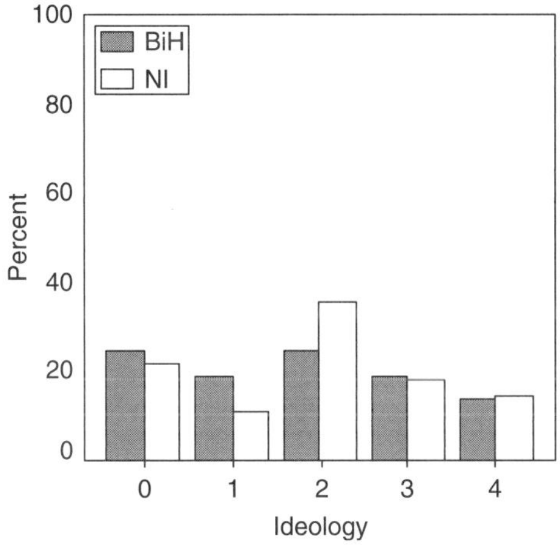

Fig. A1.

Societal Democracy

As discussed in the Cases and Method section, I feel Freedom House is the most appropriate measure of democracy for the experience of civil society. It is also available for Northern Ireland, a substate entity that is excluded from other scales. For years where scores are available, the 13-point scale was computed by adding the two 1–7 scales together and subtracting from 14 to get a 0–12 scale where most free is 12. For computing societal democracy at the NGO's founding, it was necessary to impute these scores for years other than 1991–2003 in Northern Ireland and prior to 1992 in Bosnia, based on knowledge of the history of these societies, Freedom House scores for the United Kingdom and Federal Yugoslavia in earlier years, and the Freedom House criteria as applied in Northern Ireland and Bosnia in the years where scores are provided. The three-point scale corresponds to the three-point "not free, partly free, free" scale provided by Freedom House, which splits its 13-point scale in thirds (0–3, 4–8, 9–12). This less fine scale is less sensitive to differences between my estimates and what Freedom House might have done. For the two-point scale, the sample was split in half on this variable, with three Northern Ireland cases in the low half and six Bosnia cases in the upper half. High democracy on the 2-point scale is effectively higher than 4 on the 13-point scale, or after 1976 in Northern Ireland (after the worst years of the troubles, when there is a large and sustained drop in violence following the end of large-scale internment without trial), and after 1999 in

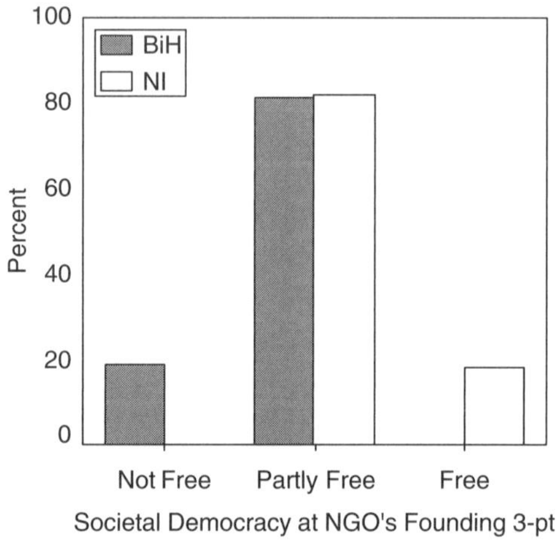

Fig. A2.

Bosnia (the 2000 elections constituted a significant alternation of power, coinciding with increased minority return). The 4-point version of the scale was created by using the 2-point version to divide the middle "partly free" category of the 3-point version (which contains over 80% of cases) in two (Fig. A2).

Internal Democracy

Do you have any structures or procedures for seeking the input of your members, beneficiaries, or the public?

If yes:

Describe them, including frequency and typical number of people participating. Do you use:

i. Surveys
ii. Meetings
iii. Request for input in newsletters
iv. Suggestion box
v. Comment form on Web site
vi. Participant evaluations
vii. Other (describe)

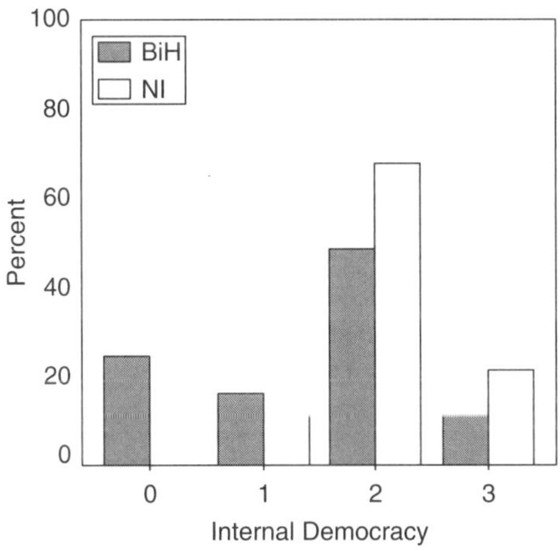

Fig. A3.

Responses are analyzed for the activeness and extent of input mechanisms and rated 0–3 as follows:

0 = none

1 = light (limited to an annual meeting, infrequent small ad-hoc mechanisms, or passive mechanisms)

2 = moderate (at least one biannual regularly occurring active method, or multiple significant ad-hoc active methods)

3 = extensive (multiple frequent, active methods, including a regularly occurring method that is at least biannual) (Fig. A3).

Outsider Relations

If you are a Northern Irish Organization, have you had a strong relationship with an organization from outside Northern Ireland, which acted as partner or mentor, either currently or in the past?

0 = no

1 = yes, in the past

2 = yes, currently

If yes (Should be yes if answer given in previous question is 2 or 3 – probe if not.)

Answer for each such organization:

a. Which organization is it?
b. What year did this relationship begin?
c. Is this relationship ongoing? (If not): What year would you say it ended?
d. During this relationship, who had the strongest role in making important decisions about your choice and design of projects, insiders to Northern Ireland, or outsiders?
   1. Outsiders played the strongest role
   2. Outsiders and insiders played equal roles
   3. Insiders played the strongest role

Mentorship is rated 0–2, where:
0 = no mentorship
1 = mentorship for up to half of the organization's lifespan
2 = mentorship for more than half of the organization's lifespan

Domination is based on part d and rated 0–2, where:
0 = no mentorship or insiders played the strongest role
1 = equal roles
2 = outsiders played larger role
(Because of low responses at the highest level, this is collapsed in most analyses to 0–1, where 1 means outsiders played at least an equal role in decisions.) (Figs. A4 and A5)

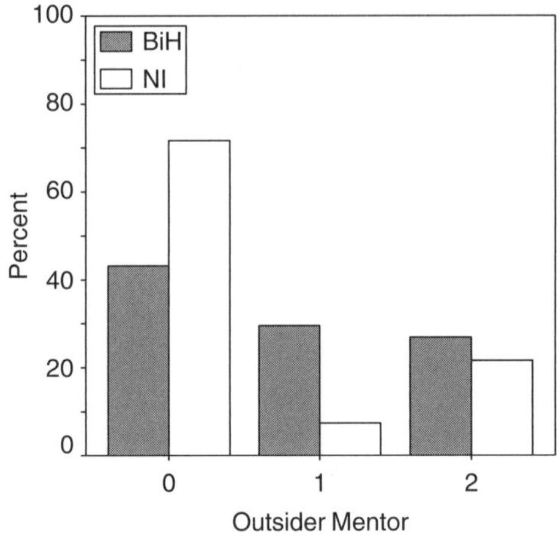

Fig. A4.

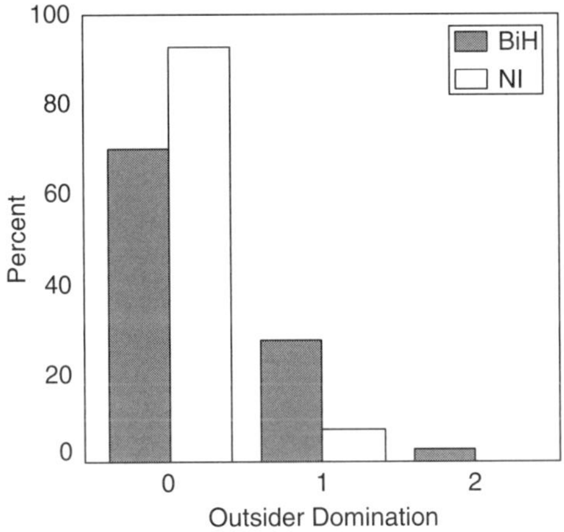

Fig. A5.

BLESSING WAR AND BLESSING PEACE: RELIGIOUS DISCOURSES IN THE US DURING MAJOR CONFLICT PERIODS, 1990–2005[☆]

Patrick G. Coy, Gregory M. Maney and Lynne M. Woehrle

ABSTRACT

Political leaders often deploy religious symbols and language to legitimate their war polices while opponents use it to forestall or control war. We examine George W. Bush's religious discourse in the post-9/11 and Iraq War era and find that it was marked by binary thinking and the demonizing of a largely religious enemy. Our analysis of the statements of 15 US peace movement organizations after 9/11 further reveals that the US peace movement had three primary responses to Bush's religiously based discourse in support of war.

First, they directly challenged his binaries and his demonizing of a broadly defined, religious enemy. Second, they harnessed the President's religious discourse to turn it against him and his policies. Third, they

[☆]The three authors contributed equally to the research and writing of this paper.

Pushing the Boundaries: New Frontiers in Conflict Resolution and Collaboration
Research in Social Movements, Conflicts and Change, Volume 29, 113–150
Copyright © 2008 by Emerald Group Publishing Limited
All rights of reproduction in any form reserved
ISSN: 0163-786X/doi:10.1016/S0163-786X(08)29005-1

constructed oppositional knowledge by providing corrective information about Islam.

By examining the movement's discourses over a 15-year period that spans five major conflict periods, our analysis also shows a close relationship between the peace movement's use of religious discourse and its identity-based talk. In addition, we found a close relationship between the movement's religious discourses and its promotion of more costly forms of politics, i.e., extrainstitutional, protest-based politics. Thus, we also argue that the US peace movement's religious discourses during major conflict periods are both strategic and driven by individual agency, are not only tactical but also expressive, and are intended to have both outward and inward effects.

> The country was up in arms, the war was on, in every breast burned the holy fire of patriotism; the drums were beating, the bands playing, the toy pistols popping ... while in the churches the pastors preached devotion to flag and country and invoked the God of Battles, beseeching His aid in our good cause in outpouring of fervid eloquence which moved every listener. (Mark Twain, The War Prayer, 1905)

Few political issues cut closer to the heart of religious sensibilities – and are, therefore, more ripe for religious discourse and activism – than a country's decision to wage war or make peace. This is not necessarily because many conflicts have religious dimensions, nor is it because some wars are waged over religious differences. Rather, it is because most religions value love, peace, charity, and justice, and most teach some version of the golden rule with its basic ethic of reciprocity (Wattles, 1996). The anthropologist Clifford Geertz (1973) developed an influential understanding of religion as a "cultural system" of symbols that provide understandings, motivations, and meanings regarding many dimensions of human experience, from the special and the peculiar to the common and everyday. This meaning-making both shapes and is shaped by social relations. "Religious symbols form a basic congruence between a particular style of life and a specific (if, most often, implicit) metaphysic, and in so doing sustain each with the borrowed authority of the other" (Geertz, 1973, p. 90). Religious people often care intensely about war and peace, and religious discourse is frequently featured in civic debates about waging wars. Religion is also important for social movements because of the legitimacy it provides through a process of ideational affiliation. That is, if believers are convinced that their gods demand certain actions, they are more likely to support policies that are in line with those demands and actions. Political leaders frequently rely on this very process to mobilize support for far-reaching and costly policies.

For example, President George W. Bush gave a speech during a religious service at the National Cathedral a few days following the 9/11 attacks. Called the "National Day of Prayer and Remembrance," the Cathedral swelled with a crowd that included his Cabinet, former presidents, large contingents from both the Senate and House, ministers, rabbis, Catholic cardinals, Muslim clerics, and many other top public and private officials. He framed his mission and that of a mourning country in what Bob Woodward called a "grand vision of God's master plan" (Woodward, 2002, pp. 66–67). The president spoke forcefully and plainly: "Just three days removed from these events, Americans do not yet have the distance of history. But our responsibility to history is already clear: to answer these attacks and rid the world of evil" (Bush, September 14, 2001). As the service ended, the entire gathering in the National Cathedral stood and sang the righteous patriotic anthem "The Battle Hymn of the Republic."

Religious discourse is a many-headed hydra. In the same way that President Bush relied on it, religion's cultural dominance means that many in the United States will be discursively attuned to and cognitively open to oppositional messages that reference common religious beliefs. Thus, religious discourse provides opportunities for movements trying to fashion oppositional cultures of counter-hegemonic resistance (Billings, 1990). Moreover, religion provides a host of other assets for social movements, many of which are rich with meaning and resonance. These assets include divine legitimation for protest activities as well as moral imperatives associated with justice, peace, charity, and equality. Religion also provides sacred rituals that uphold political engagement, and values that foster self-sacrifice and sustained activism on behalf of others. As a social institution, religion offers to movements experienced and respected leadership, financial and material resources, familiar and authoritative discourses, and even safe political or civic spaces. Last but certainly not the least, religion provides movements with preexisting solidarity networks, communication systems, and those cross-cutting collective identities that are so important to mobilization (Smith, 1996, pp. 9–22). Some of these religious riches have been hard-won in the US tradition of ideological struggle, while others have gradually and almost imperceptibly accumulated over time given the prominent place religion holds in the country's history.

OVERVIEW

We begin with an explanation of the theoretical framework. We follow that with a historically informed discussion of the influential role civil religion has played in the United States and the concomitant influence that history imparts to religious discourses. Although religion has played a prominent role throughout his campaigns and presidency, we focus the bulk of this paper on two conflict periods associated with President George W. Bush: the period immediately following 9/11 and the first two years of the Iraq War. We provide a brief overview of Bush's religiosity, followed by a detailed analysis of his religious discourse. Here we show that George W. Bush's religious discourse was marked by extensive use of binary thinking and the repeated construction and demonizing of a largely religious enemy. Having set the table in this way, we then turn to our analysis of the religious discourses of the US peace movement during the two conflict periods. Our qualitative analysis reveals that the US peace movement had three primary responses to Bush's religiously-based discourse. First, they directly challenged his reliance on binaries and his demonizing of a broadly defined enemy. Second, they harnessed the President's overt religiosity and his religious discourse and turned the power of these symbols against him and his policies. Third, many of the peace movement organizations (PMOs) constructed oppositional knowledge by focusing their statements on providing remedial education about Islam. Our quantitative analysis of peace movement discourses across five conflict periods further reveals a close relationship between the peace movement's use of religious discourse and its identity-based talk. In addition, we find a close relationship between the movement's religious discourse and its advocacy for extrainstitutional, protest-based politics.

We now turn to explaining our theoretical framework and then to setting the longer historical context for understanding religious discourse in the United States during major conflict periods.

THEORETICAL FRAMEWORK: RESPONDING TO HEGEMONY

Hegemony refers to cultural processes that aid in the reproduction of existing power relations (Gramsci, 1971; Williams, 1982; Carroll & Ratner, 1994).[1] Specifically, hegemony involves elites drawing upon a reservoir of cultural materials to frame issues (Snow & Benford, 1988). Social theorists note that enduring beliefs, images, narratives, and collective identities are circulating among the public that, because of their frequent reference by powerholders, carry uncommon authority (Steinberg, 1999; Ku, 2001; Ferree, 2003). These are the "social myths, language, and symbols" that inform how people both understand the issues they care about and their opportunities for addressing them (Gaventa, 1980, pp. 15–16). Williams (2002) refers to these familiar and authoritative materials collectively as a symbolic repertoire; we use the term "dominant symbolic repertoire" to denote both its primacy and the fact that it is available for appropriation. The resonant quality of these materials stems from their being part of taken-for-granted ways of thinking, writing, talking, and acting.

In the United States, religious symbols, beliefs, and language are deeply embedded in the dominant symbolic repertoire. Through repeated use of these materials to frame their claims, political elites link their policies with the culture's cherished symbols. As a facet of hegemony, therefore, religious discourses provide political elites with an advantage over social movements in mobilizing public support for their claims.

Yet as Michel Foucault's studies of power reveals, there is another side to the discursive coin. "We must make allowance for the complex and unstable process whereby discourse can be both an instrument and an effect of power, but also a hindrance, a stumbling-block, a point of resistance and a starting point for an opposing strategy" (Foucault, 1980, p. 101). When discursively engaging hegemony, movement groups have three options: challenging hegemony, harnessing hegemony, or some combination of the two.

When oppositional movements exploit the cultural traction that the concepts in the dominant symbolic repertoire have in order to legitimate opposition to *status quo* arrangements, we call this harnessing hegemony. With regard to peace and war, PMOs harness hegemony by positively referencing nationalist identity and cultural values (such as religious beliefs), and then appropriating them into a discourse that promotes peace and opposes war. For example, a religious peace movement organization might say that "as a 'Christian country' the United States is morally bound to cut the military budget and to fund development projects at home and abroad." We argue that by intentionally employing taken-for-granted terminology and familiar expressions of identity used by elites (i.e., "as a Christian country"), challengers tap into a deep well of discursive power that they can harness to promote alternative viewpoints.

Nonetheless, harnessing hegemony is also dangerous. Over time it may disillusion core supporters whose identities and discourses are rooted in more directly oppositional stances. Thus, PMOs may also engage in a more confrontational approach; one that rejects dominant understandings as mistaken or plainly wrong. We term this response challenging hegemony. For example, a peace group might claim that the all-volunteer armed forces relies disproportionately on recruits with lower social economic status, terming it a "poverty draft" and critiquing it as morally wrong.

Direct challenges to hegemony are not painless. They are rarely popular since they are – by definition – contrary to prevailing perceptions. When challenges to hegemony occur beyond the confines of movement adherents, common reactions range from incomprehension and disbelief to ridicule and anger. Challenging hegemony is like swimming upstream against a strong current. Consequently, we expect peace groups will often take hybridized approaches that contain elements of harnessing and elements of challenging hegemony. Moreover, we expect them to switch back and forth between the approaches, depending on the circumstances and audiences. As we analyze the religious discourses of the peace movement, we will regularly employ this interpretive schema. Before doing so, however, we first set the longer historical context for understanding religious discourses in the United States.

US CIVIL RELIGION

The Puritans believed that God had assigned a uniquely divine mission to the nation they were creating. Massachusetts Governor John Winthrop confidently proclaimed as early as 1630 that "The God of Israel is among us… We shall be as a city upon a hill" (Ahlstrom, 1975, p. 464). Notwithstanding this early ardor for joining God and state in the American experiment, the separation of church and state through the disestablishment clause of the Constitution is commonly hailed as the central and greatest political innovation of the United States (Fowler, Hertzke, & Olson, 1999, p. 11). Somewhat paradoxically, when combined with the constitutional guarantees of free speech and assembly, this separation has made religion an influential force in US history, profoundly shaping the national experience (Wills, 1990, p. 380; Heyer, 2003, p. 150). Religion has played two powerful roles: one largely a supportive, maintaining role for a government that grants it free exercise, and the other a visionary corrective to a state whose policies violate peace, justice, and equality. While religion has helped to maintain and serve the *status quo* throughout US history, it has also often been a prickly thorn in the side of a sleeping public conscience through moral judgments, protests, and political mobilizations of the faithful. These dual roles are often conceived of as competing – or complimentary – manifestations of the country's "civil religion," defined below. In the analysis that follows of White House and peace movement discourses, both of these traditions will be amply represented.

Nearly 40 years ago, sociologist Robert Bellah argued that the United States is marked by a civil religion, "a collection of beliefs, symbols, and rituals with respect to sacred things and institutionalized in a collectivity" (2005, p. 46). While many of these beliefs and symbols are culturally associated with the Jewish and Christian tradition in particular and a transcendent dimension more generally, others are also intimately connected to the country's political history and the values of freedom, liberty, and democracy associated therein. Many scholars have used Max Weber's basic distinctions between the priestly and prophetic leadership types played by religion to identify not a single unified American civil religion, but two primary strains (Williams & Alexander, 1994; Fairbanks, 1981). The first is state-centered and priestly with its focus on the United States as a chosen nation with exceptional responsibilities to do God's will on earth; this is often associated with the doctrine of the United States' "manifest destiny." This doctrine has fueled US neoimperial interventions from Mexico to the Philippines to Chile and, arguably, to Iraq. The second includes a prophetic vision that not only cares about justice at home but also turns outward to globally promote cooperation, disarmament, internationalism, and equality (Wuthnow, 1988, pp. 244–257; Billings & Scott, 1994; Kent & Spickard, 1994).

Civil religion in the United States is remarkably strong, especially from a comparative perspective. Following his tour of the young United States in 1831, Alexis de Tocqueville reported that "There is no country in the world where the Christian religion retains a greater influence over the souls of men than in America" (Lipset, 1996, p. 62). It is well known that the United States is predominantly a Protestant country. What is less often realized is that national opinion polls by Gallup and others indicate that Americans are not only the most churchgoing in Protestantism but the most fundamentalist in all of Christiandom (Lipset, 1996, p. 61). Meanwhile, according to the most recent World Values Survey (2005), 81% of the US citizens surveyed report that they describe themselves as religious persons – independently of whether or not they go to church. In comparison, for selected European countries (Austria, East Germany, West Germany, France, Italy, Netherlands), the number was on average significantly lower (55%).[2]

THE RICHES OF RELIGIOUS DISCOURSES

Given the strengths of the religious tradition in the United States, religious discourse itself may be the most valuable aspect of what religion offers to social movements (Billings, 1990, p. 4). This is because it is widely available and easily understood across the US population, including as a framework for thinking about the moral dimensions of public life (Williams, 2004). How else can one make sense of the contradictory public policies that Reverend Pat Robertson and Reverend Jesse Jackson manage to advocate while relying upon strikingly similar religious symbols and language? Civil religion is, at base, a public religious discourse; it is a complex of cultural practices and religiously infused traditions available to various groups to deploy on behalf of their own interests and agendas (Williams & Demerath, 1991). We think it best to conceive of this US civil religious discourse as the distinctly religious dimension of the dominant symbolic repertoire – the vast stock of durable images, ideas, and beliefs whose frequent use by authority figures (both secular and religious) over time infuses it with more resonant and more potent meanings (Coy et al., 2003; Maney et al., 2005, 2008; Coy et al., 2008a; Woehrle et al., forthcoming). Consequently, it is not just presidents or pastors who can make use of the images associated with civil religion, as demonstrated by this quotation from Pax Christi from the first weeks following 9/11:

> We need to honor those impulses as a nation and in our faith. Our call to be the peace of Christ will take the same courage and creativity, strength and honesty to live out the best of US traditions – those which reflect Christ's discipline of love: affirming the human dignity in ourselves, our neighbor (especially the vulnerable), and our enemy alike. These "better angels of our nature," as Abraham Lincoln called them, are embodied in a vision that presents an alternative to war – neither excusing nor fueling acts of terror. (Pax Christi, September 25, 2001)

Here the peace group extolled the moral teachings not only of Jesus Christ but also of Abraham Lincoln, a venerable US figure, and fused their teachings tightly to a national identity that is said to eschew war.

When religious discourse is further wrapped in a package of nationalist symbols and myths of origin, not only is it widely available for appropriation, but also its resonance and its potency is multiplied. Just as the Battle Hymn of the Republic song in the National Cathedral gave President Bush religious legitimacy for war abroad and repression at home, oppositional groups may achieve similar effects from their use of other nationalist hymns. In the example below from a public letter to President Bush during the run-up to the Iraq War, the American Friends Service Committee (AFSC) harnessed elements from the dominant symbolic repertoire in the form of a beloved and often-sung national hymn. A plea to President Bush was wrapped in the deeply religious lyrics of a national song in order to cajole the President to enact policies that live up to the hymn's lofty promises and national symbols. What it means for a country to be a "great power" was redefined as the peace group created what we call "oppositional knowledge" (Coy & Woehrle, 1996; Coy et al., 2008b; Woehrle et al., forthcoming) around this issue:

> Each stanza of our great national hymn, "America the Beautiful," turns from celebration of the bounty and strength which God has granted us to a prayer of thanksgiving and petition. In that hymn we pray: "America, America, God mend thy every flaw, confirm thy soul in self-control, thy liberty in law." That prayer is the burden of this letter.
>
> The mark of a truly great power is that it exhausts every opportunity of negotiation and diplomacy, bears even the most excessive frustrations and challenges, rather than resort to its military might. For the great power, war is the very last resort, not the exercise of a preemptive option. We urge you, Mr. President, to show us the self-control, patience and long-suffering appropriate to a great power. Use the good instruments of international law, international institutions such as the United Nations, World Court and International Court of Justice to resolve our conflict with Iraq. (American Friends Service Committee, September 20, 2002)

METHODS

The data for this paper consists of press and media releases, printed statements, editorials, and public calls to action from 15 US PMOs, issued in the name of the organization as a whole (usually by the national office).[3] Information on the 15 groups is included in the appendix. We intentionally included some of the oldest, largest, and most well-known peace movement groups as well as some newer groups. We also included a range of religious groups and secular groups, including a Muslim group, pacifist and policy groups, women's groups, labor groups, African-American groups, and online groups. We aimed for a sample that was broadly representative of the larger movement.

The data collected stretches from August 1990 to March 2005 and includes 510 documents issued during five conflict periods. These statements were typically released to the mainstream media and/or posted to the organization's Web site. They not only represent the public face and voice of the organization, but they are arguably the best record of an organization's evolving official positions. Such statements provide a tangible representation of the organization's framing work and as such can be effectively used in data analysis. They also create a historical record of an organization's words and actions, demonstrating how these groups contribute to the discursive processes that create social knowledge and shape public policy. Just as important, the statements are not subject to the vagaries of an individual's memory, or of the face-saving and after-the-fact reconstructions that often accompany later interviewing (Polletta & Amenta, 2001).

Fifteen organizations and five conflict periods support comparative analysis and interpretations that reveal the dynamic nature of peace movement discursive practices (Table 1). The data stretches across three presidential administrations encompassing both Republican and Democratic leadership. The conflict periods differed in terms of available political opportunity and national emotional climate, offering rich comparative opportunities. The diversity and breadth of organizations represented, combined with the longitudinal nature of the data set, makes it an important contribution to the study of social movements, particularly during conflict periods. The size of the data set provides a unique collection of documents on the US peace movement, and allows for greater generalizability of the findings.

We suggest that social movement strategists, i.e., those who monitor and respond discursively in resonant ways to structural and cultural changes, are something like farmers. All successful farmers know they not only have to monitor the weather but that they must also regularly test their soils. As both the weather and the soil changes, so too must their tilling, planting,

Table 1. Data Profile.

Conflict Period	No. of Peace Movement Organizations	No. of Peace Movement Documents	No. of Presidential Documents
Gulf War	5	94	
Iraq Bombing 1998	7	20	
Kosovo/a 1999	6	22	
9/11 and Afghanistan War	9	58	95
Iraq War (first 2 years)	15 (Data for 5 orgs. across all conflict periods)	316	
Total		510	

and fertilizing or they risk poor or unsustainable harvests. Similar principles also apply to social movement activists as they track cultural trends and monitor shifting structural conditions. One of the reasons why this dynamic relationship between structure, culture, and agency has been too seldom demonstrated empirically is because of the difficulty of collecting longitudinal data on the same social movement actors over many years and across multiple periods of contention. Our data set on the statements from five PMOs (American Friends Service Committee [AFSC], Fellowship of Reconciliation [FOR], Peace Action, Pax Christi, and Women's International League for Peace and Freedom [WILPF]) across five different conflict periods (Gulf War, Iraq 98, Kosovo/a, 9/11, Iraq War) over 15 years (1990–2005) overcomes this historic difficulty. Whenever we present longitudinal analysis (across multiple time periods), we base those findings only on the data drawn from the five organizations for which we have statements for all five conflict periods.

In our data analysis, we weave deductive and inductive thinking together and combined quantitative and qualitative methodologies. Computer-assisted analysis eased the challenge of accurately analyzing large amounts of textual data. We used the data-mining and analytical modeling program N-Vivo to inductively code the documents for ideas. Files from N-Vivo can be exported to SPSS (directly) and to Stata (via Excel). These statistical packages were used to analyze data weighted to control for variations in the amount of text produced by different organizations as well as across conflict periods.

The coding process involved a series of developmental analytical stages. Codes emerged inductively from the data and others were added from existing ideas in the literature. All three researchers participated in the coding process. To develop our initial coding strategy and to ensure shared understandings and uniformity, randomly chosen documents were coded by all three researchers and compared. Based on the refined coding strategy, the data set was then split into three parts, and each document was coded by a primary coder who then sent it to be coded by a secondary coder. The secondary coder suggested revisions. The resulting dialogue between the researchers established the final coding.

In order to analyze the dialogical dimensions of peace movement discourses, we also collected and coded all statements from President Bush in the immediate post 9/11 period (September 11 through December 31, 2001) available from the online White House archives (www.whitehouse.gov/), excluding joint press conferences with other world leaders. We gathered and used 75 presidential statements in this analysis. This data included formal speeches to Congress and other groups and institutions, press conferences, and radio addresses. The coding strategy we employed for this data was similar to the one we used for the 15 PMOs. The code lists were somewhat different than that used for the peace movement statements since the coding categories for each set of data were developed inductively.[4]

We turn next to a profile of Bush's religiosity and his discourse, focusing on his constructions of a religious enemy, followed by analysis of the peace movement's religious statements in response.

BUSH'S RELIGIOSITY

When Texas Governor George W. Bush began his presidential push, he called influential religious leaders from the region to the governor's mansion. They performed a ritualized "laying on of hands" on the soon-to-be candidate that served to religiously validate for evangelical Christians his "calling" to the presidency. Not long after, in December 1999, Republican candidates in a presidential primary debate were asked which political philosopher had the most impact on their political beliefs. Bush stunned many by promptly and boldly replying, "Christ, because he changed my heart." The candidate's spiritual autobiography, *A Charge to Keep*, which also appeared in 1999, recounts a series of conversion experiences and religious "testimonies" cast in traditional terms and apparently meant to define and promote his born-again religiosity. Bush constructs a narrative in which he has other figures suggesting to him that he is called to be today's Moses, chosen by God to courageously lead the United States in its presumed mission to spread freedom, democracy, and moral values (Bush, 1999, pp. 8–13, 136–139). Bush's national prominence increased significantly as he highlighted his conversion experiences and increased his devotion to the evangelical Christian agenda (Gurtov, 2006, p. 36).

Some have claimed that no modern White House occupant has ever cast his presidency in such deeply spiritual terms as George W. Bush (Urban, 2006). Empirical evidence supports this, with the possible exception of Ronald Reagan. Analysis of State of the Union addresses from Franklin Roosevelt in 1933 to George W. Bush in 2005 shows that Bush engaged in more "God talk" than any other president, with Reagan running a close second. Significantly, Reagan and Bush were also much more likely to posture as prophets. That is, they linked their discourses about God and freedom and liberty with suggestions that they had personal knowledge of God's desires or intentions in these matters (Coe & Domke, 2006, pp. 309–330), as in the example below, which we've taken from a Bob Woodward interview with Bush:

> I say that freedom is not America's gift to the world. Freedom is God's gift to everybody in the world. I believe that. As a matter of fact, I was the person that wrote that line, or said it … And it became part of the jargon. And I believe that. And I believe we have a duty to free people. I would hope we wouldn't have to do it militarily, but we have a duty. (Woodward, 2004, pp. 88–89)

This sort of discourse from the president of a military superpower is rather sobering. When the commander-in-chief of the US military conflates his mind with the mind of God, debate is stifled, alternatives go unexamined, and missions considered to be God's may become one with the national mission, all as defined by the president himself.

Even more challenging for oppositional social movements, however, may be that for many US Christians, so little of this was problematic. Reverend Pat Robertson resigned as president of the Christian Coalition in December, 2001 after Bush ramped up his religious rhetoric in response to 9/11. As influential Christian conservative Gary Bauer put it, "I think Robertson stepped down because the position has already been filled. There was already a great deal of identification with the president before 9–11 in the world of the Christian right, and the nature of this war is such that it has heightened the sense that a man of God is in the White House (Milbank, 2001, p. 2)." A former Christian Coalition head, Ralph Reed, commented on the new role of the evangelical movement in national politics by saying that it had succeeded in electing Bush. "You're no longer throwing rocks at the building; you're in the building (Milbank, 2001, p. 2)." Actually, they have come a long way from throwing rocks at the White House, or even just getting in the door. The fusing of Christian fundamentalism with White House policies under George W. Bush was coupled with the centralizing of authority and increased levels of secrecy within the Executive Branch of government. The constriction of policy-making dialogues that resulted created grave dangers for the future of democracy in the United States (Hedges, 2006, p. 254).

BUSH'S BINARIES

In keeping with some traditions of religious fundamentalism, George W. Bush's presidency was marked by an absence of doubt, an unwavering certitude even with regard to complex and complicated foreign policy issues (Woodward, 2004, pp. 139–140). Bush consistently employed a dichotomy between the forces of good (the United States) and the forces of evil (terrorists, Islamic fundamentalists, and all those who "hate America"). One of the more famous examples of this dichotomous thinking infused with religious power occurred during his address to a joint session of Congress on September 20, 2001:

> Every nation, in every region, now has a decision to make. Either you are with us, or you are with the terrorists (Applause) … . Freedom and fear, justice and cruelty, have always been at war, and we know that God is not neutral between them (Applause). Fellow citizens, we'll meet violence with patient justice – assured of the rightness of our cause, and confident of the victories to come. In all that lies before us, may God grant us wisdom, and may He watch over the United States of America. (Bush, September 20, 2001)

David Domke's (2004) comparative analysis of Bush's discourse both before and after 9/11 revealed that the President's usage of the good/evil binary nearly tripled in the period immediately following the attacks and up to his "mission accomplished" speech when he prematurely claimed from an aircraft carrier that major combat operations in Iraq were over. In our own research, we analyzed 75 statements from President Bush in the immediate post 9/11 period (September 11 through December 31, 2001). Forty-six (61.3%) of those presidential statements included binary thinking of the "good versus evil" variety. Clearly, this rhetorical device (and way of interpreting the world) was repeated frequently by the President of the United States in many different ways and in scores of different contexts.

Within discursive politics, binaries advance the agendas of powerholders in three ways. First, they discount certain ways of thinking and being. In so doing, they create a powerful interpretive hierarchy where one way of viewing the world soundly trumps the other one. Second, insofar as they are often rooted in fundamentalism, they carry a moral and even religious power that can influence popular opinion. For example, empirical research shows that during the run-up to the Iraq War, the potential influence of presidential moralizing was magnified, thanks to a subservient mainstream print media whose editorial pages largely excluded criticisms of the invasion on moral grounds (Nikolaev & Porpora, 2007).[5] Third, binaries are easily understood, all the more so if they have a religious hue. They take little ink and, therefore, promptly become a favored device in both the mass media and in the popular mind. For example, David Domke also compared the presence of the good–evil binary in newspaper editorials in 20 major newspapers published in the two days following each presidential address. They increased by nearly sixfold relative to newspaper editorials appearing in the two days following each presidential address in the pre-9/11 period

(Domke, 2004, pp. 33–42). This substantial "echo effect" granted to moralizing presidential discourses by the mainstream media contributes to political closures and shapes political discourse.

FROM BINARIES TO ENEMIES

Our analysis found that one of the binary-based discursive approaches taken by President Bush was to construct enemies within the context of his religious discourse. Constructing a loathsome enemy who represents the worst of humanity is a common accompaniment to armed hostilities (Keen, 1985). The us versus them thinking inherent in enemy images produces a kind of group think that focuses public attention and constricts other formulations (Merskin, 2004). As a hegemonic device, well-defined enemy images divert awareness from potentially problematic domestic policies (such as civil liberties repression) outwards toward a shared enemy instead – all the more so if the enemy constructions can be given a religious or, at least, a moralized overlay. Of the 60 paragraphs we coded for religion in statements by President Bush during the 9/11 period, nearly a quarter of them (23%) are focused on the President's constructions of a religious enemy. Collectively, he paints a stark and forbidding portrait of terrorists, the Taliban, Al Qaeda, Osama bin Laden, and generic Islamic extremists. The Bush quotes below are a partial listing of the enemy images he constructed within the context of his religious discourse in the post-9/11 period.

According to the President, the "Islamic extremists" who he defines as the country's enemy:

- have tried to hijack a great religion,
- hate Christians and Jews,
- love only one thing – they love power,
- celebrate death,
- despise creative societies and individual choice,
- have no home in any faith,
- have a special hatred for America,
- are heirs to fascism,
- want to force every life into grim and joyless conformity,
- encourage murder and suicide,
- are isolated by their own hatred and extremism,
- destroy religious symbols of other religions,
- are drug dealers,

- are murderers,
- are barbaric in their meting out of justice,
- dare to ask God's blessings as they set out to kill innocents,
- have no place in any culture,
- resent and resist freedom,
- are the likes of which we have never seen before,
- are incredibly ruthless,
- gloat over killing fellow Muslims,
- can't stand what America stands for,
- hate women,
- disrupt humanitarian supplies,
- have no conscience,
- don't educate children,
- forbid children to fly kites, or sing songs, or build snowmen,
- imprison women in their homes,
- dictate how to think and how to worship,
- deny women basic healthcare and education,
- steal food from starving people,
- beat girls for wearing white shoes,
- are evil and determined,
- commit mass murder against innocents,
- destroy great monuments of human culture.

And finally, the President claims they

- are so evil that those of us in America can't possibly comprehend why they do what they do.

President Bush clearly evinced a propensity to address important and complex policy choices through the extensive use of simple binaries that are embedded within religious discourse. When this is combined with his repetitive and stark constructions of a religious enemy, we would expect the US peace movement to respond in its own discourses. We turn to our analysis of those responses below.

THE PEACE MOVEMENT'S RELIGIOUS DISCOURSES

The peace movement's religious discourses, have at least two origins. First, for at least some of the organizations, it emanates from deeply held values associated with religious identities. That is why the AFSC would often preface their statements with the phrase "as Quakers," while the FOR would say "as faith-based pacifists," while Pax Christi would say "as Catholics" or "as followers of the nonviolent Jesus." Peace groups publicly construct their identities like this not only to introduce and explain their more radical policy positions but to "credential" and legitimate them (Coy & Woehrle, 1996). Second, PMOs are strategic as they talk back to powerholders in a dialogical fashion (Steinberg, 1999). Here they appropriate and attempt to undermine the religious dimensions of the dominant discourse that legitimates power and lends religious credibility to Presidential policies. Both of these approaches are well represented across our data set.

As our longitudinal analysis across the five conflict periods shows (see Fig. 1), the peace movement responded to the religious discourse of George W. Bush with their own extensive religious rhetoric. Our "identity politics-religion code" is defined as "spiritual beliefs and/or religion as a means of organizing people to resist, including appeals to a person's

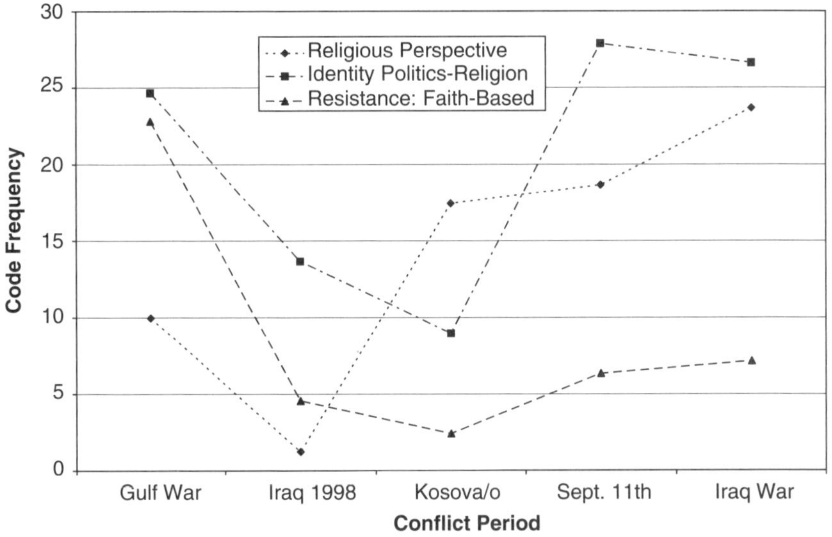

Fig. 1. Code Frequencies in PMO Statements by Conflict Period. *Notes:* Analysis based on weighted data controlling for differences in the volume of text between organizations as well as across conflict periods. Only data from the five PMOs issuing statements in all five conflict periods included (American Friends Service Committee, Fellowship of Reconciliation, Pax Christi, Peace Action, Women's International League for Peace and Freedom).

religious identity." The movement's use of religious discourses based on identity-politics was highest during the two periods associated with George W. Bush's presidency (9/11 and the Iraq War), and was rivaled only by his father's presidency (Gulf War). In addition, our "religious perspectives" code is defined as "articulation of a religious tradition and/or what its teachings say." As Fig. 1 also shows, the movement's use of a more generalized religious perspective discourse was highest during the Iraq War period, and comparatively high during the 9/11 period as well.

There were three primary ways in which the peace movement responded to Bush's religious discourse and his enemy constructions during 9/11 and the Iraq War: (1) by challenging what was seen as divisive demonizing; (2) by harnessing the President's self-presentation as a man of faith; and lastly, (3) by doing remedial education on Islam. We will treat these three approaches in turn.

DEBUNKING THE DEMONIZING

A few days after the beginning of the Iraq War, Mary Ellen McNish, the general secretary of the AFSC critiqued an invasion that it opposed on religious grounds. She put the Iraq War in the context of contemporary US political history by noting that the primary proponents of the war within the George W. Bush administration were hardline neoconservatives who had been deeply disappointed by the first Bush administration's failure to depose Saddam Hussein during the earlier Gulf War.[6] Their subsequent blueprint for US global military dominance, dubbed "The Project for a New American Century," favored unilateralism over cooperation and partly tied the United States' greatness to the degree to which others held it in awe and fear.[7] These neoconservatives and President Bush utilized the moral shock of the 9/11 attacks to justify a newly aggressive, preemptive set of foreign policies in Afghanistan, Iraq, and elsewhere. The president's much used terminology of an "axis of evil" is discursively emblematic of these developments.[8] The AFSC chief harnessed the axis of evil discourse by dipping into the historic well of Quaker humanitarian service to redefine the nature of evil and the country's true enemies. Here poverty, militarism, and environmental decay are labeled the true axis of evil about which all good-thinking Americans ought to be concerned.

> When Americans cried 'Why?' in the face of 3,000 dead at the World Trade Center, they were offered a list of scapegoats, an Axis of Evil. They [the Bush administration

> neo-conservatives] offered America their vision of what true safety required. They knew what they believed, and they spoke with great confidence. In opposition to this vision, Quakers and the other peace churches had another vision to offer. We saw the same facts, but the eyes of our historic witness made us see those facts very differently. Our experience tells us, and you may have heard me say this before, that the true axis of evil is pandemic poverty, environmental degradation, and a world awash in weapons. (American Friends Service Committee, March 27, 2003)

Shortly after 9/11, when President Bush's rhetoric was most intense, some groups named and then directly challenged the President's lack of distinctions and his ready reliance on binaries, as Pax Christi does here.

> Right now across the Islamic world, innocent people are living in terror, wondering what President Bush may do to them. The President says, "We shall make no distinctions between the terrorist and countries that harbor them." Shall a whole country be condemned for the actions of its leaders? (Pax Christi, September 26, 2001)

During the Iraq War, the FOR also took a challenging approach to the demonizing issue. In a statement titled "Torture in Iraq: No Monopoly on Capacity for Evil," the interfaith group addressed the root causes of the abuse of Iraqi prisoners by US troops at Abu Ghraib. The FOR laid responsibility for the abuse at the feet of the President due to what the organization called his "cavalier" attitude and because of his "ongoing demonization of the Arab and Muslim world." The FOR used the abuse to argue that facile distinctions between the enemy and US citizenry are fundamentally false and morally bankrupt.

> The violence of the last few weeks [at Abu Ghraib by the US and in Fallujah by insurgents] throws light on an essential truth: The "enemy" holds no monopoly on evil and "our side" no monopoly on good. All humankind has the capacity to perpetrate evil and violence upon its fellows. All violence, whether depicted graphically in photographs and videos, or taking place anonymously, out of the camera's range, is an affront to the God-given humanity of all. Americans now face the humbling task of asking themselves and their government how it could possibly have been in any nation's interests to provoke such violence by invading and occupying a nation that never attacked us. (Fellowship of Reconciliation, May 14, 2004)

The US peace movement engaged the President's demonizing language by challenging it directly from a variety of approaches. The Islamic group, Council on American-Islamic Relations (CAIR), took their challenge into the Washington, DC marketplace by hosting an interfaith memorial at the Capitol Reflecting Pool to mark the second anniversary of the 9/11 attacks. They framed this action as a direct "challenge [to] those who seek to divide America along religious or ethnic lines" (Council on American-Islamic Relations, August 28, 2003). In the passage below, the Black Radical

Congress (BRC) rejects the president's divisive approach not only on religious grounds, but also quite overtly on racial identity grounds. Note, too, how religious faiths of all persuasions are presumed to lead each believer to oppose the Iraq War.

> The Black Radical Congress opposes the war against the Iraqi people and call on all black, brown, red, yellow, and white people (in short, the majority of the peoples of the world) to oppose this war. The attempts to use religion to divide the non Islamic peoples of the USA from the peoples of the Islamic faith must be opposed. Peoples of all religious faith and all spiritual orientation must call on their innermost powers to oppose the war. (Black Radical Congress, March 20, 2003)

HARNESSING A RELIGIOUS PRESIDENT'S DISCOURSE

When powerholders utilize elements of the dominant symbolic repertoire, including religious language and images, they open themselves to counter-challenges that harness the same language and images. In the example below, the FOR accused the President not only of exploiting religion, but also of engaging in an "extremist rhetoric" that was akin to none other than Osama bin Laden's. Here the peace group turns the rhetorical tables on the President by labeling him with the same language and enemy images that he painstakingly constructed in his own religious discourse.

> The religious language used by the President (evil, God, US as the agent of God to give freedom to the world, and faith-based initiatives) attempts to claim righteousness for policies that disregard the public opinion of the world and the substantial moral objections of many Americans. This obvious manipulation of religion for political ends comes at a time when the overwhelming majority of US religious leaders have spoken out against the Administration's war in Iraq and have questioned the morality of such an aggressive policy. It is a direct parallel of the extremist rhetoric of Osama bin Laden, and is leading us in a very similar direction. (Fellowship of Reconciliation, January 30, 2003)

There is no question that George W. Bush's courting of the evangelical Christian vote through his overt expressions of religiosity – first on the campaign trail and later during his first term in the White House – reaped significant electoral dividends. What is too often overlooked, however, is the other half of this equation. As the president used religious discourse to his advantage and to promote his policy agendas, it made him and his policies vulnerable precisely on those same religious grounds. As the AFSC put it at the beginning of the Iraq War, "It is surprising that a man who says he is guided by faith has ignored the council [sic] of major religious leaders in this country and internationally, who condemn this action as an unjust war" (American Friends Service Committee, March 21, 2003).

About two weeks following the invasion of Iraq, a coalition of religious groups including Pax Christi and the FOR organized a demonstration at the White House that featured the arrest of 68 prominent religious leaders. Pax Christi's press release on the arrests is rich with examples of the "harnessing hegemony" dynamic as the religious PMOs turned the moral demands of Christianity squarely back on the Bush administration. For example, although President Bush had frequently emphasized the "born-again" nature of his Christianity, he is actually a member of the United Methodist Church. Thus, Pax Christi strategically highlighted the words of United Methodist Bishop C. Joseph Sprague at a press conference just prior to the action, where the Bishop explained why he felt compelled to commit nonviolent civil disobedience at the White House. Pax Christi's statement also included Catholic Bishop Thomas Gumbleton's moral condemnation of Bush's war policies in explaining why he too was arrested, along with a group of Nobel Peace Prize Laureates.

> "The United Methodist bishops have sent four letters to the president and vice president, whom many of you know are both Methodists, seeking a meeting to discuss this war," stated Sprague. He went on to say that that they only received "'one terse reply" from the Bush administration and no meeting .... [Catholic] Bishop Gumbleton of Detroit, who traveled to Iraq in January, was among those arrested in Wednesday's action. "As people of faith and conscience, we proclaim that it is a grave sin to support this war," said Gumbleton. "We cannot stand silent while the Bush administration murders innocent men, women and children." (Pax Christi, March 27, 2003)

When President Bush scheduled an audience with Pope John Paul II during his 2004 reelection campaign, Pax Christi took him to task for ignoring the counsel about the war even while the President exploited his connections to those same religious leaders. Pax Christi released a statement in advance of Bush's Vatican visit highlighting the ways that Catholic religious figures worldwide were using the President's appearance with the Pope to ramp up their moral critiques of Bush's war. Pax Christi quoted far-flung Bishops and Cardinals who were each criticizing the invasion and occupation of Iraq from a religious perspective. They also called the President out for his selective use of religious teaching to further his own electoral needs.

> President Bush should have used today's meeting [with the Pope] to offer explanations why the opinions of the world's religious leaders are ignored by himself and others in his administration ... Instead, what we see is blatant political opportunism, orchestrated to confuse US Catholics into thinking that President Bush is in tune with the principles of their faith. (Pax Christi, June 4, 2004)

Religious discourse is so deeply a part of the US culture that it is democratically available (Williams, 2002, p. 251), at least in the sense that one need not be a believer to use religious discourse and its powerful symbols. While we think there are credibility concerns – in that some are more able to use religious discourse more effectively than others – the point still holds generally true, as it also does when quoting historic religious figures. In fact, we found that secular groups also used religious discourse, especially by quoting historic leaders like Reverend Martin Luther King, Jr. When PMOs challenge the state as it goes to war, the political deck is heavily stacked against them, thanks to the legitimated political closure that follows the decision to wage war. Rallying around the flag in the moment trumps attempts to discuss the long-range consequences of war. In such a game, activists find they are dealt a rather hapless hand, with few cards to play of consequence. But religious discourse – and the moral authority and the political legitimation that accompanies it – can help to level the playing table. And when the discourse is harnessed to especially hallowed and resonant figures like Reverend King, even quite radical critiques can be proffered.

For example, in a statement focused on the domestic needs going unmet due to the costs of the Gulf War, the secular group Peace Action used King's words to raise the issue of the spiritual health of the national soul: "A nation that continues year after year to spend more money on military defense than on programs of social uplift is approaching spiritual death" (Peace Action, 1991). When President Bush laid a wreath at King's tomb on the national holiday devoted to him, the FOR called it a "cynical gesture" since his preemptive war to bring "liberation" to Iraq is contrary to what Rev. King taught. The FOR quoted King to the effect that history was cluttered with the wreckage of those who came killing in the name of liberation and peace. This is a clear example of our argument that when powerholders use elements of the dominant symbolic repertoire, it provides opportunities for challenging groups to hold powerholders accountable to the same standards that they used in their own discourses.

Similarly, in the passage below, the secular War Resister's League (WRL) reports on the arrest of 46 of its members at the US mission to the UN during the Afghanistan war, following a four-day series of presentations and training reflecting on the life of the religious leader:

> Dr. King's dream of a just society has yet to be realized. As King said, "The greatest purveyor of violence is my own country" .... This is still true, and our collective conscience calls us to confront not only the violence committed on behalf of Americans, but also the institutions committing those acts. (War Resisters League, January 22, 2002)

Most Americans are resistant to the notion that the United States is the greatest purveyor of violence; it doesn't square with prevailing versions of national identity. Thus, this is never an easy argument to make. Making this point only four months after 9/11, the WRL risked easy rejection and self-righteous ridicule. Yet by standing behind the frock of the widely respected Reverend King, the WRL presumably prevented reflexive rejection of their argument.

REMEDIAL EDUCATION ON ISLAM

The third primary way that PMOs responded to the administration's rhetoric and to events in Iraq and the United States was to create what we refer to as "oppositional knowledge" (Coy & Woehrle, 1996; Woehrle et al., forthcoming). They did this by disseminating alternative information about religion in general and about Islam in particular. In addition, many groups emphasized constructive commonalities between religions, as CAIR did below:

> Over the last few weeks, Americans of all faiths have been horrified by images of violence in the Middle East. The Iraqi prisoner abuse scandal does not represent America or Christianity. The Israeli missile that killed innocent Palestinian children in Gaza does not represent Judaism. And the beheading of an innocent American man, Nicholas Berg, does not represent Islam. Islam, Christianity and Judaism share the basic values necessary to create a world in which tolerance and peace prevail. We have an opportunity to build bridges between our faiths and to challenge those who attempt to divide humanity along religious and ethnic lines. (Council on American-Islamic Relations, May 26, 2004)

Already faced with the scapegoating of American Muslims five days after 9/11, CAIR offered the country oppositional knowledge by reminding the country of the significant contributions made by Muslims to the United States.

> It was a Muslim who was the architect for the Sears Tower. Islam is the fastest growing religion in America and in the world. We are doctors, lawyers, engineers, mechanics, teachers, and store owners. We are your neighbors. (Council on American-Islamic Relations, September 16, 2001)

It was not just the Islamic group in our study that attempted to stem the tide of religious intolerance that intensified after 9/11 by creating oppositional knowledge about Islam. The AFSC, BRC, New York Labor Against the War (NYCLAW), FOR, and Pax Christi also offered the country many lessons about Islam, as demonstrated by the example below from the FOR:

> The religion of Islam, which claims more than one billion global adherents including eight to nine million within the USA alone, cannot be characterized as being "extreme" or "violent". Individuals who engage in acts of war against civilians violate the most sacred tenets of Islam. Muslims of all nationalities who reside in the United States vigorously condemned the events of September 11 and are actively involved in all aspects of humanitarian relief and recovery following this tragedy. (Fellowship of Reconciliation, September 19, 2001)

The taking of civilian hostages became widespread in Iraq in the summer of 2004, including some high-profile US hostages. In this shifting political context, the CAIR used its standing in the religious community to organize US Imams to issue a declaration – released at a Capitol Hill press conference – which condemned hostage-taking as a violation of Islamic beliefs and called for the release of all hostages in Iraq, no matter their faith or nationality. CAIR also launched an online petition drive called "Not in the Name of Islam" that was designed to disassociate Islam from the violent acts of some Muslims. CAIR hoped that Muslims would sign the ad and work to correct misperceptions of Islam and the Islamic stance on religiously motivated terror. Over 50,000 Muslims signed the petition within the first two weeks. As this excerpt shows, the strongly worded petition is a splendid example of a PMO creating oppositional knowledge, in this case about the nature of the Islamic faith.

> We, the undersigned Muslims, wish to state clearly that those who commit acts of terror, murder and cruelty in the name of Islam are not only destroying innocent lives, but are also betraying the values of the faith they claim to represent. No injustice done to Muslims can ever justify the massacre of innocent people, and no act of terror will ever serve the cause of Islam. We repudiate and dissociate ourselves from any Muslim group or individual who commits such brutal and un-Islamic acts. We refuse to allow our faith to be held hostage by the criminal actions of a tiny minority acting outside the teachings of both the Quran and the Prophet Muhammad, peace be upon him. (Council on American-Islamic Relations, August 31, 2004)

The final way that the PMOs built bridges across faith traditions, provided remedial education on Islam, and challenged the President's dichotomous discourse was by organizing solidarity actions with the Islamic community. The religious groups in particular (AFSC, FOR, Pax Christi) made extensive use of this approach, urging people to study Islam, to visit Mosques, and to reach out in many different ways to American Arabs and to Muslims. We present only one example below – Pax Christi's call for acts of spiritual solidarity during the month of Ramadan. Note the subtle ways that the PMO tries to lead its readers into creating oppositional knowledge by advising them on how to dive deeply into the spiritual riches of Islam. Here is a view of Islam that is radically different from the dominant one in the United States.

> During the upcoming season of Ramadan, we want to show a gesture of respect and appreciation for Muslim brothers and sisters and to learn from them. We welcome an opportunity to be in solidarity with Muslims who rely on the month of Ramadan to help inculcate values of simplicity, service, sharing, compassion and mercy. We recognize the need for these virtues in our own lives. We invite you to join us in this effort of solidarity with our Muslim brothers and sisters, as a shared prayer and action for peace that depends on conversion from ways of injustice and reliance on war … . The intent of this call is to urge people to grow closer to our Muslim brothers and sisters through whatever gesture of solidarity they can make beginning October 26 and continuing through the following four weeks. (Pax Christi, October 11, 2003)

Offering a corrective to dominant understandings of Islam was only one way that some movement organizations developed their religiously infused oppositional politics in response to the religiously infused hegemonic discourse. Since war and peace concerns are oftentimes paramount for religious believers, we also wanted to understand the relationships between the religious discourses of the US peace movement during wartime and the construction of organizational identities. In addition, we investigated associations between religious discourse and the political tactics the peace movement promoted. We turn to this quantitative analysis in what follows.

RELIGIOUS IDENTITIES AND TACTICAL REPERTOIRES

McVeigh and Smith's (1999) US-focused survey research found that compared to the nonreligious, Christians were at least two times more likely to have engaged in institutional politics like lobbying rather than taking no political action. In addition, frequent church attendance was found to significantly increase the likelihood that individuals would engage in protest compared to institutional forms of politics. More specifically with regard to social movement organizations, some studies have found empirical evidence that religious and faith-based PMOs tend to support and engage in "unruly," noninstitutional forms of political engagement – including nonviolent forms of protest and civil disobedience (Epstein, 1990; Pagnucco, 1996; Nepstad, 2004). Finally, religion is frequently a highly salient factor in the development and refinement of a peace movement organization's identity (Coy & Woehrle, 1996; Smith, 1996, p. 380). Our analysis of the discourses of the US peace movement from 1990 to 2005 supports these findings.

Table 2 shows those codes that most frequently appeared within the same passage, i.e., paragraph, with our two primary religion-related codes: "religious perspectives," and "identity politics-religion." As explained earlier, religious perspectives are defined as "articulation of a religious tradition and/or what its teachings say." The identity politics-religion code is defined as "spiritual beliefs and/or religion as a means of organizing people to resist, including appeals to a person's religious identity." The first finding to take note of is the high concurrence of the "organizational identity" code with these two religion codes. This suggests that religious discourse is critical to organizational identity construction.

The code most associated with our "identity politics-religion" code across the five conflict periods (i.e., the code that most often appears in the paragraphs coded as identity politics-religion) was the "faith-based

Table 2. Frequency of Code Concurrence in Same Passage.

Coupling Codes	No. of Base-Code Passages	% of Base-Code Passages	No. of Base-Code Documents	% of Base-Code Documents
Base code – Religious perspectives				
Identity politics-religion	30	16.7	18	17.8
Organizational identity	22	12.2	20	19.8
Violence condemned: costs	17	9.4	15	14.9
Nonviolence supported	16	8.9	15	14.9
Civil liberties	16	8.9	11	10.9
Resistance: faith-based	11	6.1	8	7.9
Base code – Identity politics-religion				
Resistance: faith-based	65	26.1	38	32.5
Nonviolence supported	48	19.3	36	30.8
Organizational identity	37	14.9	33	28.2
Religious perspectives	30	12.0	18	15.4

Notes: Base codes are religious perspectives and identity politics-religion. For each of the base codes, 83 code couplings were examined. Results presented in the table are limited to code couplings whose number of passages or number of documents is two standard deviations above the mean for all code couplings examined. It includes documents from all five conflict periods. Only the five PMOs for which there is data for all five conflict periods are included (American Friends Service Committee, Fellowship of Reconciliation, Pax Christi, Peace Action, Women's International League for Peace and Freedom).

resistance" code. The latter code has to do with PMO calls for resistance to war activities, specifically resistance work that includes a religious faith component. The concurrence within the same paragraph between these codes was quite substantial, over 26%. The code that appears second most often with identity politics-religion across the five conflict periods is "nonviolence supported," which is defined as explicitly advocating for nonviolent action and conscientious objection. The concurrence within the same paragraph here was also substantial (over 19%). Equally important, if we look at concurrence within the same document, it is over 30% in both cases. The "nonviolence supported" code is also closely associated (from a comparative perspective relative to possible code-couplings) with the more generalized "religious perspective" code across the five conflict periods. The "faith-based resistance" and the "nonviolence supported" codes each relate to mobilization, more particularly with encouraging engagement in potentially costly, extrainstitutional politics to challenge hegemony, such as the civil disobedience at the White House profiled earlier in the paper. Consequently, these findings suggest an important role for religiously-based identity politics in mobilization efforts by the US peace movement.

The PMOs' general discourse (religious and secular) around nonviolent action and costly forms of resistance was wide-ranging. Across the conflict periods, the tactical repertoire promoted by the peace movement to directly challenge hegemony included: calls for and reports on demonstrations, pickets, pray-ins, various kinds of civil disobedience, breaking the embargo on Iraq by shipping humanitarian and medical supplies there, engaging in citizen diplomacy by traveling to Iraq, fasting and donating money saved to humanitarian needs, disruptions of events where high-level Bush administration figures would be appearing, boycotts, work stoppages, labor union refusals to transport war-related materials, women shaving off their hair in front of the Liberty Bell, vigils, war-tax resistance, conscientious objection, providing sanctuary for objectors and military resisters, die-ins, burning of tax forms, sit-ins and obstructions at military recruitment centers and congressional offices, delivering the names of those killed in war to the White House and to Dover Air Force Base, holding nonviolent action trainings, and more.

As the above list implies, engaging in nonviolent action may entail high risks for the affective, political, social, and financial dimensions of an activist's life. For example, social stigmatization and political ridicule can combine with lost wages for practitioners of nonviolent civil disobedience in ways that seriously dampen mobilization efforts. Identity construction, validation, and appeals to a sense of belonging can help overcome these obstacles to mobilization. Strategically highlighting religious commitments and moral values to boost positive identification with being a nonviolent resister to the hegemony of violence was a common tactic for the faith-based groups, and was even used by some secular groups.

The religious PMOs for whom we have data for all five conflict periods (i.e., AFSC, FOR, Pax Christi)[9] often tied their nonviolent action mobilization efforts directly to their religious identities, to those of their members, and even to the wider US public. In other words, they appealed to religious identities and sensibilities while trying to mobilize extrainstitutional forms of resistance to war and militarism. Pax Christi did this more often than any other group, and frequently fashioned its identity appeals to match the target audience and forms of contention requested. They were strategic about when they would use sectarian appeals, sometimes highlighting themselves as "Catholics," as "Catholic Christians," or as "followers of the nonviolent Jesus." However, when appealing to a larger audience, they often described themselves as "people of faith," or even more generically simply as "citizens," or as "people of good will."

Finally, it is useful to note that violence is tied to the hegemonic dimensions of US society. Violence is featured, if not lionized, in a majority of media formats from children's cartoons to video games to Hollywood movies to nightly TV news programs. With regard to international affairs in particular, it is commonly presumed that the United States has a wide-ranging right to use its violent might. When presidents wrap in religious garments their calls for war, a militarized economy, and civil liberties repression at home, the hegemony of violence is strengthened. In short, violence is culturally routinized and normalized and, therefore, difficult to directly challenge effectively. Equally important is the fact that violence is also normalized through its coupling with religious discourses that legitimate it. In the context of what is generally presumed to be a "Christian country," where Christian broadcasting on television and radio is ubiquitous and where the foreign policy utterances by Christian leaders like Reverend Pat Robertson and others are commonplace, it may become even more important for oppositional voices to respond to these religiously-based calls to arms. Peace activists must contest and redefine the meaning of religious identities much in the same way they contest nationalist identities (Coy & Woehrle, 1996). Those who want to mobilize others must utilize cultural materials, themes, and collective identities – including religious identities – that have enough potency and resonance to stand against the powerful position of violence in the US culture. In this regard, and as our final example, below Pax Christi attempted to harness none other than the symbol of Jesus Christ on the first day following September 11:

> As people of faith and disciples of the nonviolent Jesus, we must be willing, even now in this darkest moment, to commit ourselves and urge our sisters and brothers, to resist the impulse to vengeance. We must resist the urge to demonize and dehumanize any ethnic group as "enemy." We must find the courage to break the spiral of violence that so many in our nation, we fear, will be quick to embrace.
>
> We therefore call for restraint on the part of our nation's civilian and military leaders. The appropriate response to this despicable act is not a despicable act of violence in kind. Vengeance is not justice. The only kind of justice that will honor the memory of all those who lost their lives is a justice based on international law, not reckless retribution.
>
> To follow the nonviolent Jesus in the midst of unimaginable violence is the call and the challenge to which we remain committed. (Pax Christi, September 12, 2001)

CONCLUSION

Religious discourse is a site of contentious politics. As the passage from Mark Twain's "War Prayer" that opens this paper suggests, and as our analysis of the Bush statements further demonstrates, religion is often put to work on behalf of the nation and of the state's war policies. Too rarely have scholars demonstrated the obstacles that religion in the service of hegemony presents for social movement mobilization. The political closure always associated with decisions to go to war makes added demands on PMOs. During war, it is difficult for oppositional groups to get a hearing, much less to have their alternative perspectives taken seriously and given credence.

Our findings clearly demonstrate that peace movement groups both harnessed and challenged hegemony through their own discourses, religious and otherwise. Our analysis of Bush's presidency showed his overt religiosity, his reliance on binary thinking, and his propensity to demonize a religious enemy. This research also demonstrates that when powerholders utilize elements of the dominant symbolic repertoire – including religious language and images – they open themselves to counter-challenges that harness the same language and images. The importance of this finding to theory-building in social movements scholarship is increased by its companion dimension, i.e., we show that even secular PMOs harnessed religious elements from the dominant symbolic repertoire. Harnessing the dominant religious discourse casts a strong moral spotlight upon power-holders. By exposing gaps between religious rhetoric and the actual policies of powerholders, cracks in their wall of legitimacy are created and widened. The rich and malleable qualities of religious discourse were strategically used to confront the hegemony of violence in US foreign policy, to appeal to members and bystanders, and to provide a sense of meaning, purpose, and legitimacy marked by transcendent dimensions. In this way, our research demonstrates not only the strategic but also the expressive dimensions in social movement organizing.

PMOs also directly challenged Bush's reliance on binaries and the demonizing of a broadly defined enemy. Challenging binaries and creating shades of gray through education are major counter-hegemonic projects. This is particularly significant insofar as the moral certainty and religiously informed devotion to his and to the country's "calling" that so marked President Bush was a potentially perilous combination for the country, and even the world. Such a combination residing in the hands of the leader of the world's sole "superpower" may easily change an already problematic US exceptionalism into an even more problematic US adventurism in foreign affairs (Gurtov, 2006, p. 36.). We have also shown that PMOs harnessed the President's overt religiosity and his religious discourse and tried to turn the power of these symbols against the President and his policies.

In addition, we found that many of the PMOs constructed oppositional knowledge by focusing their statements on providing remedial education about Islam. For some groups, like the FOR, this was a dominant dimension of their statements following 9/11 and into the Iraq War period. We show that creating and disseminating oppositional knowledge is a vital aspect of the peace movement's counter-hegemonic project. This was done as a bulwark against both the real and the potential scapegoating of Muslims in the United States and elsewhere. We have identified and analyzed four forms of oppositional knowledge created by the US peace movement in work related to that presented here (Coy et al., 2008; Woehrle et al., forthcoming). The findings here suggest that more research should be done on why, when, and how different social movements create various forms of oppositional knowledge focused around religion. Equally important are our findings that US peace movement groups quoted familiar and authoritative religious leaders like the Rev. Martin Luther King, Jr., and spotlighted the civil disobedience of Methodist and Catholic Bishops and Nobel Peace Prize winners to bolster movement positions and to increase the likelihood that the more radical of their critiques might enjoy some resonance among the general public.

We must also remember, however, that while even secular groups deployed religious discourses strategically, for the faith-based groups it was often rooted in deeply held beliefs and principles that defined some of the organizations and their members. Our findings of the association of identity talk with religious discourses in the peace movement statements support this interpretation. Moreover, religious values and discourse were associated with support for engaging in extrainstitutional politics like nonviolent action, offering not only inspiration and motivation but also the potential of individually validated rationales. In other words, effective mobilization often entails linking identity to action, as in, "to be an authentic Christian during war, one must take risks while acting for peace." These findings suggest that religion may nurture sustained, disruptive challenges to dominant discourses. Religious PMOs appeared to put the agency of the individual activist in the political foreground, fostering an activism that might be uncommonly genuine and authentic in its meaning-making, and therefore have longer staying power as a challenge to hegemony than purely secular appeals to action.

Finally, we believe our research further suggests that peace movement discourse may, over time, influence civil religion itself. This influence will likely take the shape of transforming civil religion in ways that constrain powerholders rather than facilitating their agendas. In this way, the dominant priestly strain of US civil religion may be undermined while its dissenting prophetic strain would be strengthened.

NOTES

1. In the explanation of our theoretical framework that follows, we rely upon and draw directly from some of our other publications (including Coy, Maney, & Woehrle, 2003; Coy, Woehrle, & Maney, 2008a, 2008b; Maney, Woehrle, & Coy, 2005, 2008; Woehrle, Coy, & Maney, 2009).

2. Ronald Inglehart's World Values Survey data is available online at: www.worldvaluessurvey.org/

3. We have collected a large set of data. Although we utilize specific parts of that data set in different research articles, overall the data was collected, coded, and analyzed in highly similar ways for our various research papers and for our book. It therefore seems reasonable to write the methods sections of our different papers in similar ways. Consequently, some of the language in this methods section has also appeared in the methods section of our other publications that are based on parts of the same larger data set (Coy et al., 2003, 2008a, 2008b; Maney et al., 2005, 2008; Woehrle et al., 2009).

4. A listing of the codes used for the PMO documents and for the Bush documents, with definitions, is available from the authors upon request.

5. Nikolaev and Porpora (2007) examined 292 editorials and op-eds published during the two months preceding the Congressional authorization vote to use force

against Iraq in four leading mainstream newspapers (*New York Times*, *Washington Post*, *Christian Science Monitor*, *Wall Street Journal*) and two leading news magazines (*Newsweek* and *Time*).

6. For an insider's view of the significant influence of the neoconservatives on G. W. Bush's policies, see former Treasury Secretary Paul O'Neill's account of Bush's candidacy and the early years of his presidency (Suskind, 2004, pp. 80–82).

7. This helps explain why the invasion of Iraq was dubbed by these same neoconservatives with the widely publicized code name, "Shock and Awe."

8. One revealing account of how the "axis of evil" terminology emerged within the Bush White House in the post 9/11 period attributes it to Michael Gerson, the Bush speechwriter primarily responsible for the President's State of the Union address four months after the attacks. Gerson, a theology graduate from religiously conservative Wheaton College, was a self-described evangelical Christian whom Bob Woodward reports found a way to fuse "biblical high-mindedness and the folksy" in many speeches he drafted for Bush throughout the months following the attacks (Woodward, 2004, pp. 86–87).

9. The Muslim group, Council on American-Islamic Relations (CAIR), was added to our data for the last two conflict periods: 9/11 and the Afghanistan War; and the Iraq War. Interestingly, CAIR made no mention of nonviolence whatsoever during either of the two periods, and there was only one instance of "resistance-costly" in both periods combined. This is likely due to two factors. First, among all the organizations in our data set, CAIR is the least oriented toward "peace" as a descriptor of its fundamental organizational identity, being somewhat more of a civil-rights-oriented organization. Second, CAIR's use of religious discourse was overwhelmingly (10 of the 12 passages in six documents) associated with teaching the media and public about Islam generally, and protecting Islam by correcting misperceptions about it more specifically (e.g., seven of the ten religious discourse-related passages had to do with disassociating Islam from terrorism). Since Islam is not part of the dominant symbolic repertoire and is widely disparaged by power-holders, CAIR had to be on the discursive defensive rather than the discursive offensive like Christian groups. Their statements are an instance of articulated assimilation, highlighting the facets of Islam compatible with religious elements of power-holder discourse.

ACKNOWLEDGMENTS

This research was partly funded by a grant from the National Science Foundation (SES 043289) and from the American Sociological Association's Fund for the Advancement of the Discipline. We are grateful to Christopher Bellas, David Castillo, Denise Dollar, Michelle Prescott, Musa Tuzuner, and Douglas McKinzie for their research assistance. We also thank Jeffrey Anderson, Rachel Fleishman, and three anonymous reviewers for their helpful comments. Much of this article appears as chapter 6 in Lynne M. Woehrle, Patrick G. Coy and Gregory M. Maney, *Contesting*

Patriotism: Culture, Power and Strategy in the Peace Movement, forthcoming late in 2008. It is included here with the kind permission of Rowman and Littlefield Publishers.

REFERENCES

Ahlstrom, S. (1975). *A religious history of the American people* (Vol. 1). Garden City, NY: Image Books.

Billings, D. B. (1990). Religion as opposition: A Gramscian analysis. *American Journal of Sociology*, *96*(1), 1–31.

Billings, D. B., & Scott, S. L. (1994). Religion and political legitimation. *Annual Review of Sociology*, *20*(August), 173–201.

Bush, G. H. W. (2001, September 20). *Address to a Joint Session of Congress and the American People*. Whitehouse, Washington, DC, Retrieved July 12, 2003 (http://www.whitehouse.gov/news/releases/2001/09/print/20010920-8.html).

Bush, G. W. (1999). *A charge to keep*. New York, NY: Morrow.

Carroll, W. K., & Ratner, R. S. (1994). Between Leninism and radical pluralism: Gramscian reflections on counter-hegemony and the new social movements. *Critical Sociology*, *20*(2), 3–26.

Coe, K., & Domke, D. (2006). Petitioners or prophets? Presidential discourse, God, and the ascendancy of religious conservatives. *Journal of Communication*, *56*(2), 309–330.

Coy, P. G., Maney, G. M., & Woehrle, L. M. (2003). Contesting patriotism by the post 9/11 peace movement in the United States. *Peace Review: A Transnational Quarterly*, *15*(4), 463–471.

Coy, P. G., & Woehrle, L. M. (1996). Constructing identity and oppositional knowledge: The framing practices of peace movement organizations during the Gulf War. *Sociological Spectrum*, *16*(3), 287–327.

Coy, P. G., Woehrle, L. M., & Maney, G. M. (2008a). Discursive legacies: The US peace movement and 'Support the Troops'. *Social Problems*, *55*(2), 161–189.

Coy, P. G., Woehrle, L. M., & Maney, G. M. (2008b). Reclaiming democracy: Oppositional knowledge and the US peace movement. *Sociological Research Online*, *13*(4), http://www.socresonline.org.uk/13/4/3.html

Domke, D. S. (2004). *God willing?: Political fundamentalism in the White House, The "war on terror", and the echoing press*. London: Pluto Press.

Epstein, B. (1990). The politics of moral witness: Religion and nonviolent direct action. In: S. Marullo & J. Lofland (Eds), *Peace action in the eighties: Social science perspective* (pp. 106–124). New Brunswick, NJ: Rutgers University Press.

Fairbanks, J. D. (1981). The priestly functions of the presidency: A discussion of the literature on civil religion and its implications for the study of presidential leadership. *Presidential Studies Quarterly*, *11*(2), 214–232.

Ferree, M. M. (2003). Resonance and radicalism: Feminist framing in the abortion debates of the United States and Germany. *American Journal of Sociology*, *109*(2), 304–344.

Foucault, M. (1980). *Power/knowledge: Selected interviews and other writings, 1972–1977*. New York, NY: Pantheon Books.

Fowler, R. B., Hertzke, A. D., & Olson, L. R. (1999). *Religion and politics in America: Faith, culture, and strategic choices* (2nd ed.). Boulder, CO: Westview Press.

Gaventa, J. (1980). *Power and powerlessness: Quiescence and rebellion in an Appalachian valley*. Urbana, IL: Universtiy of Illinois Press.
Geertz, C. (1973). *The interpretation of cultures: Selected essays*. New York, NY: Basic.
Gramsci, A. (1971). *Selections from prison notebooks*. London: New Left Books.
Gurtov, M. (2006). *Superpower on crusade: The Bush doctrine in US foreign policy*. Boulder, CO: Lynne Rienner Publishers.
Hedges, C. (2006). *American fascists: The Christian right and the war on America*. New York, NY: Free Press.
Heyer, K. (2003). US Catholic discipleship and citizenship: Patriotism or dissent? *Political Theology*, *4*(2), 149–174.
Keen, S. (1985). *Faces of the enemy: Reflections of the hostile imagination*. San Francisco, CA: Harper and Row.
Kent, S. A., & Spickard, J. V. (1994). The 'Other' civil religion and the tradition of radical Quaker politics. *Journal of Church and State*, *36*(2), 373–388.
Ku, A. S. (2001). Hegemonic construction, negotiation and displacement: The struggle over right of abode in Hong Kong. *International Journal of Cultural Studies*, *4*(3), 259–278.
Lipset, S. M. (1996). *American exceptionalism: A double-edged sword* (1st ed.). New York, NY: W.W. Norton.
Maney, G. M., Woehrle, L. M., & Coy, P. G. (2005). Harnessing and challenging hegemony: The US peace movement after 9/11. *Sociological Perspectives*, *38*(3), 357–381.
Maney, G. M., Woehrle, L. M., & Coy, P. G. (2008). Ideological consistency and contextual adaptation: US peace movement emotional work before and after 9/11. *American Behavioral Scientist*, *52*(4).
McVeigh, R., & Smith, C. (1999). Who protests in America: An analysis of three political alternatives: Inaction, institutionalized politics, or protest. *Sociological Forum*, *14*(4), 685–702.
Merskin, D. (2004). The construction of Arabs as enemies: Post-September 11 discourse of George W. Bush. *Mass Communication and Society*, *7*(2), 157–175.
Milbank, D. (2001, December 21). Religious right finds its center in the oval office. *Washington Post*.
Nepstad, S. E. (2004). Disciples and dissenters: Tactical choice and consequences in the plowshares movement. In: D. J. Myers & D. M. Cress (Eds), *Research in social movements, conflicts and change* (Vol. 25, pp. 130–159). Oxford, UK: Elsevier Science.
Nikolaev, A. G., & Porpora, D. V. (Eds). (2007). Talking war: How elite US newspaper editorials and opinion pieces debated the attack on Iraq. *Sociological Focus*, *40*(1), 6–25.
Pagnucco, R. (1996). A comparison of the political behavior of faith-based and secular peace groups. In: C. Smith (Ed.), *Disruptive religion: The force of faith in social movement activism* (pp. 205–222). New York, NY: Routledge.
Polletta, F., & Amenta, E. (2001). Conclusion: Second that emotion? Lessons from once novel concepts in social movement research. In: J. Goodwin, J. M. Jasper & F. Polletta (Eds), *Passionate politics: Emotions and social movements* (pp. 303–316). Chicago, IL: University of Chicago Press.
Smith, C. (1996). Correcting a curious neglect, or bringing religion back in. In: C. Smith (Ed.), *Disruptive religion: The force of faith in social movement activism* (pp. 1–25). New York: Routledge.
Snow, D. A., & Benford, R. D. (1988). Ideology, frame resonance and participant mobilization. In: B. Klandermans, H. Kriesi & S. Tarrow (Eds), *International Social Movement Research* (Vol. 1, pp. 197–217). Greenwich, CT: JAI.

Steinberg, M. W. (1999). The talk and back talk of collective action: A dialogic analysis of repertoires of discourse in nineteenth-century English cotton spinners. *American Journal of Sociology*, *105*(3), 736–780.
Suskind, R. (2004). *The price of loyalty: George W. Bush, the White House, and the education of Paul O'Neill*. New York: Simon & Schuster.
Urban, H. B. (2006). The secrets of the kingdom: Spiritual discourse and material interests in the Bush administration. *Discourse*, *27*(1), 141–165.
Wattles, J. (1996). *The golden rule*. New York, NY: Oxford University Press.
Williams, R. (1982). *The sociology of culture*. New York, NY: Schocken Books.
Williams, R. H. (2002). From the 'beloved community' to 'family values': Religious language, symbolic repertories, and democratic culture. In: N. Whittier, D. S. Meyer & B. Robnett (Eds), *Social movements: Identity, culture, and the state* (pp. 247–265). New York, NY: Oxford University Press.
Williams, R. H. (2004). The cultural contexts of collective action: Constraints, opportunities, and the symbolic life of social movements. In: D. A. Snow, S. A. Soule & H. Kriesi (Eds), *The Blackwell companion to social movements* (pp. 91–115). Malden, MA: Blackwell Publishing.
Williams, R. H., & Alexander, S. M. (1994). Religious rhetoric in American populism: Civil religion as movement ideology. *Journal for the Scientific Study of Religion*, *33*(1), 1–15.
Williams, R. H., & Demerath, N. J., III. (1991). Religion and political process in an American city. *American Sociological Review*, *56*(4), 417–431.
Wills, G. (1990). *Under God: Religion and American politics*. New York, NY: Simon and Schuster.
Woehrle, L. M., Coy, P. G., & Maney, G. M. (forthcoming). *Contesting patriotism: Culture, power and strategy in the peace movement*. Lanham, MD: Rowman and Littlefied.
Woodward, B. (2002). *Bush at war*. New York, NY: Simon and Schuster.
Woodward, B. (2004). *Plan of attack*. New York, NY: Simon and Schuster.
Wuthnow, R. (1988). *The restructuring of American religion: Society and faith since World War II*. Princeton, NJ: Princeton University Press.

APPENDIX. ORGANIZATIONAL PROFILES

Note: Parts of these descriptions are taken directly from the organizations' self-descriptions on their respective Web sites.

American Friends Service Committee (AFSC) – Religious. Established in 1917 to address humanitarian concerns worldwide and to promote actions on peace and war. Affiliated with the Religious Society of Friends (Quakers). Data included for all periods.

Black Radical Congess (BRC) – Secular. Founded in Chicago in June 1998 with the objective of bringing together varied sections of the Black radical tradition to work for peace and justice. Data included for 9/11 and Iraq War periods.

Black Voices for Peace (BVFP) – Secular. Founded in 2001 as a national network of people of African heritage and others working for peace with justice at home and abroad. Data included for Iraq War period.

CODEPINK – Secular. Founded in 2002 as a women-initiated grassroots peace and social justice movement working to end the war in Iraq, stop new wars, and redirect resources into healthcare, education, and other life-affirming activities. Data included for Iraq War period.

Council on American-Islamic Relations (CAIR) – Religious. Founded in 1994, it is now the mission of the largest Islamic civil liberties group in the United States, CAIR, to enhance the understanding of Islam, encourage dialogue, protect civil liberties, empower American Muslims, and build coalitions that promote justice and mutual understanding. Data included for Iraq Bombing 1998, 9/11, and Iraq War periods.

Fellowship of Reconciliation (FOR) – Religious. FOR-USA was founded in 1915 by religious pacifists in response to the outbreak of World War I. FOR is the largest and oldest interfaith peace and justice organization in the United States and is committed to exploring the power of love, truth, and nonviolent action for resolving human conflict. Data included for all periods.

MoveOn.org (Moveon) – Secular. Founded in 1998, MoveOn.org has two functional arms. One focuses on education and advocacy while the other mobilizes people online to fight important battles in Congress and help elect candidates who reflect progressive values. Data included for Iraq War period.

New York Labor Against the War (NYCLAW) – Secular. Founded at "Ground Zero" as the first antiwar labor body established in the United States after 9/11. NYCLAW is committed to opposing war, multiracial leadership, broad alliances, and democratic processes. Data included for 9/11 and Iraq War periods.

Pax Christi – Religious. Pax Chritis USA was founded in 1972 to create a world that reflects the Peace of Christ by witnessing to the call of Christian nonviolence. It has four primary foci: primacy of conscience, economic and social justice, and respect for creation. Data included for all periods.

Peace Action – Secular. Originating in peace organizations founded during the Cold War (including SANE in the 1950s and the FREEZE campaign in the 1980s), the organization that would be Peace Action was formed in 1987, and then renamed again in 1993. Campaigns to end the nuclear threat, create a more peaceful economy, and apply nonviolent resolutions to international conflicts. Data included for all periods.

TrueMajority – Secular. Founded by Ben Cohen, cofounder of Ben and Jerry's Ice Cream. True Majority was started to compound the power of all those who believe in social justice, giving children a decent start in life, protecting the environment, and having the United States work in cooperation with the world community. TrueMajority monitors politics in Washington and sends mobilization alerts through email networks. Data included for Iraq War period.

United States Labor Against the War (USLAW) – Secular. Founded in 2003 as a national network of 69 unions and other labor organizations opposed to the Iraq War, USLAW wants a just foreign policy for working people, an end to US imperialism, and the redirecting of resources from the military to human needs. Data included for Iraq War period.

Women's Action for New Directions (WAND) – Secular. Founded in 1982 as Women's Action for Nuclear Disarmament, the group was renamed Women's Action for New Directions after the Cold War ended. It advocates for alternatives to violence and for shifting to a civilian-based economy that will meet human, economic, and environmental needs. The group also promotes the prevention of violence against women as well as increases in women's political leadership. Data included for 9/11 and Iraq War periods.

War Resister's League (WRL) – Secular. Founded in 1923 by secular pacifists who opposed WWI. Believing that war is a crime against humanity, the League works for a society that is democratic and free of economic, racial, and sexual oppression. The methods WRL uses range from education to demonstrations to lobbying to nonviolent direct action. Data included for Iraq Bombings 1998, Kosovo/a 1999, 9/11, and Iraq War periods.

Women's International League for Peace and Freedom (WILPF) – Secular. Founded in 1915 by women from warring countries to address the root causes of World War I and to redefine the notion of security. The group rejects war-making and military domination as the path to security and advocates the equality of all people in a world free of sexism, racism, classism, and homophobia, as well as the guarantee of fundamental human rights including the right to sustainable development. Data included for all periods.

Statements by Peace Movement Organizations Quoted in the Text

American Friends Service Committee, 2002, September 20. "Letter to George Bush."

American Friends Service Committee, 2003, March 21. "AFSC Sees Hope in International Peace Movement Revitalized by Iraq War."

American Friends Service Committee, 2003, March 27. "No One Is Our Enemy."
Black Radical Congress, 2003, March 20. "BRC Calls for Total Opposition to the War and for Renewed Resistance."
Council on American-Islamic Relations, 2001, September 16. "Muslim Condemnations of the September 11 Attacks."
Council on American-Islamic Relations, 2003, August 28. "Muslims to Hold 9/11 Vigil at US Capitol."
Council on American-Islamic Relations, 2004, May 26. "US Muslims Publish Ad Denouncing Terror, Bigotry: Effort part of CAIR 'Not in the Name of Islam' Campaign."
Council on American-Islamic Relations, 2004, August 31. "CAIR's 'Not in the Name of Islam' Petition."
Fellowship of Reconciliation, 2001, September 19. "Talking Points: September 11, 2001 Terror Attacks."
Fellowship of Reconciliation, 2003, January 30. "Talking Points: The State of the Union Address."
Fellowship of Reconciliation, 2004, May 14. "Torture in Iraq: No Monopoly on Capacity for Evil."
Pax Christi, 2001, September 12. "Pax Christi USA Statement on the Devastation of September 11th."
Pax Christi, 2001, September 25. "Dialogue Starters: 'Talking Points' Toward an Alternative Vision as We Respond to Acts of Terror."
Pax Christi, 2001, September 26. "Darkness Cannot Drive Out Darkness: A Pax Christi USA Call to Break the Cycle of Violence."
Pax Christi, 2003, March 27. "Nobel Peace Prize Laureates, Religious Leaders Arrested in D.C. Action: Nonviolent Civil Disobedience Aimed at Stopping the War in Iraq."
Pax Christi, 2003, October 11. "Ramadan 2003 Statement."
Pax Christi, 2004, June 4. "Pope's Criticism of President Bush Should Not be Obscured by Medal Photo-Op."
Peace Action, 1991, nd. "The Cost of the Persian Gulf War: Unmet Needs At Home."
War Resisters League, 2002, January 22. "46 Arrested at US Mission to the U.N. Urging Changes in US Foreign Policy."

RECONSIDERING LEADERSHIP THEORY AND PRACTICE FOR COLLABORATIVE GOVERNANCE: EXAMINING THE U.S. COAST GUARD

Heather Getha-Taylor

ABSTRACT

Traditional leadership theory and practice in the public sector has focused on leading within bounded hierarchies. However, the demand for collaborative governance requires new approaches to leadership. The question for scholars is: what is collaborative leadership and how does it compare to traditional leadership thought? *To investigate this question, personal interviews were conducted with experienced collaborators in the federal government, with special emphasis on executives in the Department of Homeland Security (DHS). Interview data were analyzed alongside three public leadership models. Analysis revealed that four strengths are fundamental to collaborative leadership: (1)* oral communication, *(2)* external awareness, *(3)* continual learning, *and (4)* interpersonal skills. *In the context of collaboration, leadership contrasts significantly from traditional public sector leadership models, which emphasize directive action rather than supporting, or human relations–focused action. While*

Pushing the Boundaries: New Frontiers in Conflict Resolution and Collaboration
Research in Social Movements, Conflicts and Change, Volume 29, 151–173
Copyright © 2008 by Emerald Group Publishing Limited
All rights of reproduction in any form reserved
ISSN: 0163-786X/doi:10.1016/S0163-786X(08)29006-3

there was considerable congruence among interviewees with regard to the core skills necessary for collaborative leadership, U.S. Coast Guard (USCG) respondents value creativity/innovation as a collaborative leadership attribute, which seems to be in contrast with the organization's formal command-and-control structure.

According to the 2007 National Leadership Index, 77% of Americans agree that our nation is in the midst of a leadership crisis (National Leadership Index, 2007). A full 79% of respondents believe that "unless the country's leaders improve, the United States will decline as a nation." Further, the 2005 version of this study found that Americans have little confidence in the ability of state and local leaders to work collaboratively with federal officials in the event of a disaster. On a scale of one to four, where one is not confident at all and four is very confident, the mean score was 2.65, indicating a serious lack of confidence in the ability of our nation's leaders to work collaboratively, or across organizational boundaries, to solve shared problems (2005, p. 12).

The reliance on collaboration as a means to solve society's most complex problems requires a fresh look at leadership theory and practice. According to Bardach (1998, 2001) the lack of competent leadership is one of the key threats to effective collaboration. However, our traditional approaches to understanding leadership have focused on understanding the ways in which individuals motivate others within bounded, hierarchical organizations. Collaboration, or achieving results through a network of partners, represents a shift in traditional leadership thought. According to Seiling (1999), the contemporary emphasis on collaboration places new demands on leaders. "Leaders serve as moral models by actively creating partnerships across blurred lines" (p. 19). A 2001 report by the Office of Personnel Management affirmed Seiling's point by stating that it is the responsibility of organizational leaders to model collaborative behavior, and thus, "institutionalize new ideas and practices" (p. 9).

How to best model and institutionalize collaborative leadership values and behavior is the foundation of this chapter. First, this chapter investigates the question, *what makes collaborative leaders so successful in working across boundaries?* And closely following, *what lessons can be applied to guide future theory and practice?* Examining this concept in the context of homeland security, where collaboration is critical for performance, can provide important lessons for practitioners and scholars alike.

By investigating collaborative leadership practices, we can better understand the ways in which existing leadership theory can adapt to accurately represent the demands of collaborative governance in the public sector.

REVISITING TRADITIONAL LEADERSHIP THOUGHT

Excellence in public service, says Huddleston (1999), requires excellent public leaders. This connection between executive leadership and public sector performance is a long-standing component of the public management research agenda. For example, Riccucci's (1995) work illustrated the importance of executive leadership in the federal government. "The American people often overlook the fact that it is not just the people we elect to government office who make social and political decisions about how this country is run. There is also a layer of high-level civil servants in the federal bureaucracy who are responsible for decisions and policies that affect our lives in vital ways..." (p. 2). This research continues in Riccucci's tradition by examining executive leaders (rather than political appointees) in the context of collaboration. According to Lawler (1992, 1996), changing organizational forms that move beyond hierarchy require new sets of leadership skills at all levels of an organization.

Traditionally, scholars have studied leadership in one of three ways: (1) studying characteristics of the leader such as traits, skills, or tactics, (2) studying characteristics of the followers to understand trust, task commitment, or satisfaction, and (3) studying characteristics of the situation to connect the task with the organizational and environmental complexities. Yukl (2002) explains that the trait approach to leadership study focused on task-oriented, relations-oriented, and change-oriented behaviors. A comprehensive review of leadership trait studies dating from 1948 to 1999 revealed that while providing a number of lists of leadership traits, there was very little overlap in terms of findings. Among the findings, only self-confidence was linked to leadership in a majority of the studies (Judge, Ilies, Bono, & Gerhardt, 2002). The lack of consistency in trait studies led to new approaches, which emphasized the characteristics of the followers or of the situation.

This new approach highlighted the belief that much of leadership is contextual (Doig & Hargrove, 1990). The leader who is successful in one situation may fail in another, due to changing organizational and policy contexts. In the context of collaborative governance, the question becomes, *which leadership behaviors are most effective?* Given that collaboration, or working across boundaries to achieve shared goals, necessarily involves an ability to motivate others to adopt a vision that transcends narrow interests, the work on transactional and transformational leadership is relevant. Burns (1978) first differentiated transactional leadership from transformational leadership. While transactional leaders motivate followers by recognizing their needs and providing rewards to fulfill those needs in exchange for performance, transformational leadership takes an altogether different approach. Transformational leaders motivate others to transcend narrow self-interests in pursuit of goals that benefit a larger group. Bass' (1985, 1998) work further illustrates the difference in these approaches. Bass indicated that while transactional leaders rely on rewards and punishments to ensure compliance, transformational leaders use visioning, encouragement, and leading by example to motivate others.

While informative, both the transformational and transactional leadership models focused on leading within bounded, hierarchical organizations. According to Alexander and Wilson (1997), the need for boundary-spanning leadership is now apparent. The authors examine boundary spanning in the context of globalization, stating "exercising leadership in this demanding environment calls for new capacities in many leaders and new thinking about their organizations." According to the authors, boundary-spanning leaders share five key attributes: heightened self-awareness, the habit of inviting feedback, a thirst for learning, work–life integration, and respect for differences in others. While meant to capture the attributes of global leaders, the authors believe it is appropriate to say these traits are necessary in all future leaders. "Even if the leader does not operate directly in an international setting, she or he must be able to reconcile differences and assume a global perspective that transcends parochial boundaries. If the workplace of the future is certain to have one characteristic, in addition to constant change, it is its widely divergent points of view" (p. 294).

Van Slyke and Alexander (2006) noted that in the context of public management, boundary-spanning leadership represents a "significant departure from leading large, centralized, hierarchically arranged institutions" (p. 364). The authors go on to say that "understanding the interactions between the micro-level attributes of the individual leader (trait, characteristics, and competencies) and the macro-level attributes of the organization (structure, culture, environment, products, people, and partnerships) is critical for discovering and developing appropriate models of public sector leadership" (p. 366). In the case of leading via networks, such a dramatic new paradigm is needed to begin to analyze leadership. Huxham and Vangen (2000) comment on the changing nature of leadership in the context of collaborative initiatives.

> The implication that there is a formally acknowledged leader with managerial responsibility and a hierarchical relationship with followers does not apply in collaborations because the individuals involved come from different organizations or groups. The leadership challenge, in any case, is concerned with influencing or transforming individuals only (or at least largely) to the extent that such transformation may, in turn, affect the behavior of organizations. (p. 1159)

Chrislip and Larson (1994) note that collaborative leaders differ from leaders in hierarchies in some important ways: "... Leaders are those who articulate a vision, inspire people to act, and focus on concrete problems and results ... collaboration needs a different kind of leadership; it needs leaders who can safeguard the process, facilitate interaction, and patiently deal with high levels of frustration" (p. 42).

Bardach (2001) illustrates the centrality of leadership to interorganizational collaborative capacity. Leadership, says Bardach, helps define mission and goals, diagnose areas for improvement, and nurture an environment of trust (p. 157). Not only does leadership help enhance collaborative capacity, but the absence of capable and competent leadership, says Bardach, may serve as the death knell for collaborative efforts (p. 308). Leadership in an interorganizational collaboration, says Bardach (1998), "is a difficult and sometimes dangerous job, often without adequate compensation and unsupported by staff or other resources" (p. 33).

Bardach indicates that collaborative leadership requires a radically new approach. According to the author, traditional "heroic" or "top-down" leadership styles are suspect in collaboration. Instead, members of a collaborative effort prefer leaders who engage in "servant" or "facilitative" leadership as conceptualized by Svara (1994). Among the many characteristics that Bardach attributes to such leaders a number are worth mentioning, including "appropriate self awareness," "a natural gift for diplomacy," "cross-disciplinary training and experience," "a relatively positive personality," and "a personality that welcomes risk-taking and desires achievement" (p. 226). While Bardach is clear about the importance of leadership in collaboration, he does not attempt to study leadership behaviors in the context of interagency collaboration. This is an important gap that this research serves to fill.

CUTTING-EDGE THEORY: COLLABORATIVE LEADERSHIP

Understanding why some leaders and organizations collaborate more successfully than others is an important research task that has only just begun. Both theory and practice must now acknowledge the demands for collaborative governance, or the need to work across organizational boundaries to achieve results. Traditionally, leadership theory has focused on how leaders influence followers in Weberian-style bureaucracies. Even network theory, which Rainey (2003) lauds as a "very interesting and original" approach to analyzing public leadership, assumes some degree of hierarchy. Yet, as clearly illustrated in the response to such "wicked problems" as Hurricane Katrina, public sector problems extend beyond traditional organizational boundaries and thus challenge public leaders to lead beyond boundaries as well.

A report by Agranoff (2003) notes that "most public executives today have been trained to deliver results via the traditional hierarchy. And they got to where they are by performing well within their own organizations. But to be successful tomorrow, government executives must increasingly be able to deliver through networks, partnerships, and the use of collaboration" (p. 5). Agranoff stresses the importance of creating coalitions, especially by Senior Executive Service (SES) members, who are expected to demonstrate proficiency in this area. The U.S. Office of Personnel Management has identified three associated skills that are included as subcomponents of "Building Coalitions." These three skills – partnering, influencing, and political savvy – are widely acknowledged to be analogous to collaborative leadership skills. This chapter examines that contention.

In his pioneering work on the theoretical construct of collaborative capacity, Bardach (2001) identified leadership as a foundational component in the ability of organizations to work successfully across boundaries. However, Bardach's work leaves much to be desired in terms of understanding exactly how leadership is conceptualized and exercised in such collaborative situations. Examining exemplary and average collaborative leaders, this chapter focuses specifically on collaborative leadership in the U.S. Coast Guard (USCG) to illustrate the contrast between traditional leadership theory, which emphasizes leading through hierarchy and authority, and contemporary collaborative leadership challenges.

The rationale for focusing on the U.S. Department of Homeland Security broadly – and the USCG, specifically – is multifaceted. First, the Partnership for Public Service (2006) found that there are significant discrepancies between the USCG and other DHS organizations on leadership indicators. The Partnership made special note of the differences between the USCG and the Federal Emergency Management Agency (FEMA): "FEMA's largest problem is their employees' lack of confidence in the leadership ... FEMA falls below the government average for their confidence in both immediate supervisors and senior leaders." However, the Partnership found that "Coast Guard is well above the government average for every question within the leadership category. Their employees feel well informed, empowered, and have a great deal of respect for their organization's leaders." Further, the Government Accountability Office (GAO) found that the USCG utilizes "new and expanded partnerships inside and outside the federal government" to "improve operational effectiveness and efficiency" (GAO, 2006). To examine collaborative leadership in the context of homeland security, the USCG offers a fitting organization for study.

A 2005 working paper from Harvard University's Center for Public Leadership asked the following: "if leadership, as traditionally understood, is working to build the capacity within organizations, then what different brand of leadership is necessary to get beyond that silo thinking to achieve the cross-agency coordination of effort...?" Drawing on personal interviews with senior executives, this chapter seeks to answer questions related to those posed by this 2005 report. First, *what makes collaborative leaders so successful in working across boundaries?* And closely following, *what lessons can be applied to guide future theory and practice?*

DATA AND METHODS

To answer these questions, this chapter examines personal interview data alongside three models of leadership in the context of collaborative governance. According to Lawler (2003), organizations can build leadership capability by "identifying a group of 'high-potential' executives who exhibit the skills and competencies that senior executives need" (p. 211). For the purposes of this research, two such leaders were identified: Admiral James Loy and Admiral Thad Allen. Both Loy and Allen served as leaders of the USCG but were also asked to take on other significant leadership roles in DHS, where collaboration was linked to meeting organizational goals.

To examine the questions of interest, Admirals Loy and Allen were interviewed to elicit their personal leadership styles. The Loy and Allen models of leadership are compared, along with the U.S. Office of Personnel Management's Executive Core Qualification (ECQ) model, against interview data to understand how these three public leadership models are supported by evidence from exemplary ($n = 22$) and average ($n = 23$) collaborators. Interview data were coded using an axial process, using the three leadership models as guides (Strauss & Corbin, 1990). In each model, the component strengths are defined (see, for example, Tables 2 and 3), providing the necessary "axes" for data coding.

To differentiate and compare responses from average and superior collaborators, a proxy for collaborative ability was identified. As there currently exists no government-wide award for collaborative success, the Presidential Rank Award represents the next best metric. This federal award recognizes the top one percent of career senior executives "who have demonstrated exceptional performance over an extended period of time" (U.S. OPM, 2007). The ability to work across boundaries to achieve results (referred to as *building coalitions*) is an important component of the selection criteria.

Of the interviews used in this research, 12 (26%) represent executives from the USCG and are examined separately. Data from interviews with 13 federal personnel managers are also included to examine the congruence between the strengths that excellent collaborators view as essential to collaborative leadership versus the strengths that human resource managers view as such.

COLLABORATIVE LEADERSHIP EXAMPLE

Admiral Thad Allen and Hurricane Katrina

One of the most notable examples of collaborative leadership failure and then redemption was the federal response to Hurricane Katrina, which as DHS Secretary Michael Chertoff said, "will go down as the largest natural disaster in [U.S.] history" (CNN, 2005). The federal response was blasted not only by the media, state and local officials in the Gulf Coast, and Congress, it was also criticized by the very citizens that the government worked to serve. This criticism was widespread: a September 2005 poll by CBS News showed that 77% of Americans did not think the federal government's response to Katrina was adequate. Much of the criticism focused on failures of leadership, particularly in the FEMA. This failure was most clearly articulated by the House committee that investigated the response to Katrina. The committee deemed that FEMA Director Michael Brown was "clueless" (CNN, 2006). Following Brown's poor performance, then Vice-Admiral Thad Allen of the USCG was called in "to bail him out" (Washington Post, 2005).

Allen, in contrast to Brown, was praised as "experienced," "unflappable," and "intensely organized" (*ibid.*). Allen successfully directed the collaborative efforts of public, private, and nonprofit organizations, as well as faith-based groups and citizen volunteers who together responded to the disaster. The Partnership for Public Service commended both the Coast Guard and leaders such as Allen for illustrating the importance of effective training and field-level decision making. In a 2006 report, the Partnership recommended that other organizations follow the Coast Guard example by "creating a top-notch federal workforce that is able and empowered to innovate during crises." The White House's (2006) report on lessons learned from the Hurricane Katrina response echoed the Partnership's recommendation and called for building a corps of federal leaders "who are prepared to exhibit innovation and take initiative during extremely trying circumstances." Most importantly, the White House report identified *leadership* as the key element in building the critical *collaborative relationships* that facilitate federal performance.

COLLABORATIVE LEADERSHIP EXAMPLE

Admiral James Loy and the Establishment of TSA

The Transportation Security Administration (TSA) was established immediately in the wake of the September 11 terrorist acts as a result of the Aviation and Transportation Security Act. TSA met some seemingly impossible goals in its early days. The organization was tasked with recruiting, assessing, hiring, training, and deploying security officers for 450 commercial airports from Guam to Alaska in 12 months and providing 100% screening of all checked luggage for explosives within 13 months of being established. The organization's success in meeting these goals was attributed in large part to the leadership of TSA's first director, Admiral James Loy, formerly of the USCG.

Collaboration, said Loy, was a necessary tool for accomplishing his goals, but one that simply made sense, particularly as it relates to leadership. According to Loy, "at the end of the day people that come to the table will not be protecting turf and all of those kind of things at the expense of what they can collectively know to be the greater performance indicators for the organization as a whole. That is what leadership is all about. The ability to inspire those kind of relationships within the organization to persuade as necessary, inspire as necessary, direct as necessary. And then forge, as a result, the relationships, alliances, the kinds of things that really make a difference in breeding collaborative capacity" (Interview, September 6, 2006).

COLLABORATIVE LEADERSHIP MODELS

Executive Core Qualifications

To identify indicators of collaborative leadership, it is important to first examine existing models of leadership that are intended to capture such skills. The first place to start is the Executive Core Qualifications (ECQs), as described by the U.S. Office of Personnel Management. The ECQs contain a section for "Building Coalitions/Communication" that hypothetically includes collaborative leadership skills, including partnering, political savvy, and influencing/negotiating. Table 1 presents the entire ECQ leadership model as drafted by the U.S. Office of Personnel Management. The competencies of interest are separated and described in Table 2.

During the interviews conducted for this research, both Admirals Loy and Allen were asked to indicate the skills that are necessary for effective

Table 1. Executive Core Qualifications: Overview.

Leading Change	Leading People	Results Driven	Business Acumen	Building Coalitions/ Communications	Fundamental Competencies
Creativity/ innovation	Conflict management	Accountability	Financial management	Partnering	Interpersonal skills
External awareness	Leveraging diversity	Customer service	Human capital management	Political savvy	Oral communication
Flexibility	Developing others	Decisiveness	Technology management	Influencing/ negotiating	Continual learning
Resilience	Team building	Entrepreneu- rship			Written communication
Strategic thinking		Problem solving			Integrity/honesty
Vision		Technical credibility			Public service motivation

Source: U.S. Office of Personnel Management (2001).

Table 2. Building Coalitions.

Subcomponents	Definition
Partnering	Develops networks and builds alliances; collaborates across boundaries to build strategic relationships and achieve common goals.
Political savvy	Identifies the internal and external politics that impact the work of the organization. Perceives organizational and political reality and acts accordingly.
Influencing/ negotiating	Persuades others; builds consensus through give-and-take; gains cooperation from others to obtain information and accomplish goal

Source: U.S. Office of Personnel Management (2001).
Note: This core qualification involves the ability to build coalitions internally and with other Federal agencies, State and local governments, nonprofit and private sector organizations, foreign governments, or international organizations to achieve common goals.

collaborative leadership. Both Admirals provided their own leadership models, which they indicated accurately represent their philosophies on leadership with regard to working collaboratively.

COLLABORATIVE LEADERSHIP MODELS

Loy Model of Leadership

Admiral Loy has coauthored with Donald Phillips his own personal leadership model, which is named the "Architecture of Leadership" (Phillips & Loy, 2008). In this model, a set of character traits and values (including honesty, courage, integrity, respect, commitment, ethics, trust, and hard work) serve as the foundation for all leadership behavior. The drive to achieve and the capacity to care serve as the two additional foundational elements. From that base, a series of eight innate traits and 14 acquired skills are hypothesized to be key to effective leadership performance. With these traits and skills, the effective leader can perform when given the opportunity.

According to Loy and Phillips, "the Coast Guard gets the job done by empowering its people with solid leadership fundamentals." The authors attribute the organization's successful response to such disasters as Hurricane Katrina to the shared organizational commitment to leadership development: "the Coast Guard has proven that the optimal way to imbue leadership throughout an organization is for the senior executives to

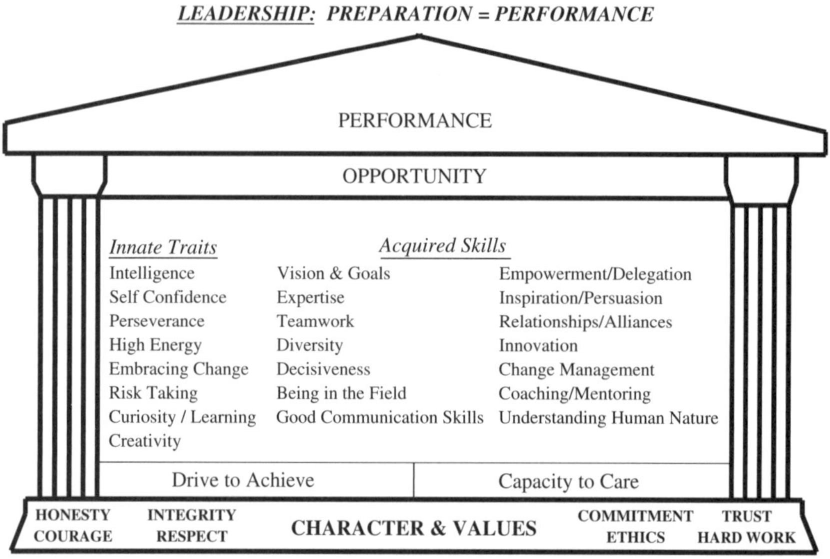

Fig. 1. Architecture of Leadership (Loy Model). Adapted from Phillips & Loy (2008).

design their leadership continuum *through* their own people – and then live it on a day-to-day basis." The Loy model of leadership is presented in Fig. 1.

COLLABORATIVE LEADERSHIP MODELS

Allen Model of Leadership

Like Admiral Loy, Admiral Allen indicated that he has a leadership philosophy to which he subscribes. This model, conceptualized in a 2005 Center for Public Leadership Working Paper is entitled "Meta-Leadership." This approach captures ten fundamental strengths that are necessary to connect "the purposes and the work of different organizations or organizational units" (p. 44). The paper indicates that "meta-leaders" are those individuals who are able to "influence and accomplish such collaboration of effort across organizations" (p. 44). The ten key principles of meta-leadership are detailed in Table 3.

Table 3. Meta-Leadership (Allen Model).

Courage	Requires the judgment to accurately calculate risk, take risks as appropriate, and face consequences; overcomes resistance and personal attacks to focus on mission at hand.
Curiosity	Willing to venture into substantive matters of policy where proficiency and comfort are lacking; includes communication skills such as listening and thoughtful questioning.
Imagination	Ability to envision what cannot be seen using imagination paired with strategic planning; requires fresh insights into problems.
Organizational sensibilities	Ability to link organizational systems and envision ways to build capacity; requires new methods and models of action.
Persuasion	Creating and communicating plans, which speak to the needs of diverse audiences.
Conflict management	Ability to resolve differences and maintain mission focus; requires consensus-building skills and the ability to use authority when necessary to resolve disputes that threaten effectiveness.
Crisis management	Ability to reshape plans as necessary to meet changing circumstances; quick thinking and improvization are valued.
Emotional intelligence	Emotional intelligence indicates an ability to draw steadiness, security, and support from within; includes self-awareness, self-regulation, motivation, empathy, and social skills.
Persistence	Commitment of time and effort outside of one's job description; willingness to engage in efforts not tied to promotion.
Values meta-leadership	Recognizes the importance of working with others to solve shared problems; invests in relationship building.

Source: Adapted from Center for Public Leadership (2005).

TESTING THE MODELS

There is significant overlap among the ECQ leadership model, the Loy model of leadership, and the Allen model of leadership. The commonalities among the three models include the following nine concepts: (1) persuasiveness, (2) interpersonal skills, (3) external awareness, (4) creativity, (5) integrity, (6) learning, (7) communication skills, (8) resilience, and (9) partnering. Of these nine shared leadership attributes, analysis of personal interview data reveals that four of these are identified as collaborative leadership strengths not only by both superior and average collaborators, but also by human resource management experts (see Tables 4–6). The four strengths are *oral communication*, *external awareness*, *interpersonal skills*, and *continual learning*.

When evidence from the criterion (superior collaborators), comparison (average collaborators), and expert (federal personnel managers) samples

Table 4. Collaborative Leadership Indicators: Overall.

Rank	Collaborative Leadership Indicators	Supported by Interview Data ($n = 58$) (%)
1	Oral communication	93
2	Continual learning	70
	Interpersonal skills	70
	Partnering/alliances	70
5	Developing others/empowerment	68
6	External awareness	67
7	Empathy/capacity to care	65
8	Political savvy	60
	Leveraging diversity	60
10	Strategic thinking	51
	Public service motivation	51

Table 5. Collaborative Leadership Indicators: Expert Panel.

Rank	Collaborative Leadership Indicators	Supported by Interview Data ($n = 13$) (%)
1	Oral communication	69
2	Technical credibility	61
	Integrity/honesty	61
4	External awareness	53
	Flexibility	53
	Interpersonal skills	53
	Continual learning	53
8	Conflict management	46
	Developing others	46
	Influencing/negotiating	46
	Public service motivation	46

is integrated, oral communication is mentioned significantly more often (in 93% of interviews) than all other skills as critical to collaborative leadership. Following oral communication are a commitment to learning, interpersonal skills, and partnering/alliances (all of which were mentioned in 70% of interviews). These findings reflect little congruence with the three subcomponents of the "building coalitions" portion of the Executive Core Qualifications model. Of the top ten leadership strengths revealed via interview analysis, only partnering and political savvy ranked. Influencing/negotiating, also believed to be critical to "building coalitions," did not receive sufficient support to be listed within the top ten collaborative leadership strengths overall.

Table 6. Collaborative Leadership Indicators: Superior and Average Collaborators.

Rank	Collaborative Leadership Indicators: Superior Collaborators	Supported by Interview Data ($n = 22$) (%)	Rank	Collaborative Leadership Indicators: Average Collaborators	Supported by Interview Data ($n = 23$) (%)
1	Oral communication	100	1	Oral communication	100
	Developing others/empowerment	100	2	Empathy/capacity to care	86
3	Leveraging diversity	90	3	Partnering/alliances	78
4	Technical credibility	86	4	External awareness	69
5	Continual learning	85		Strategic thinking	69
6	Interpersonal skills	81		Political savvy	69
7	Partnering/alliances	77		Interpersonal skills	69
8	External awareness	72	8	Continual learning	65
10	Political savvy	68	9	Leveraging diversity	56
	Empathy/capacity to care	68		Field experience	56

It is important to note that there exists significant divergence between the strengths that excellent collaborators attribute to collaborative leaders and those that human resource managers attribute to effective collaborative leaders. Interview analysis finds agreement on six items: the four core collaborative leadership strengths (oral communication, external awareness, interpersonal skills, and continual learning) as well as technical credibility and empowerment. However, superior collaborators believe that leveraging diversity, empathy, partnering, and political savvy are key to collaborative leadership, while human resource managers believe that integrity, flexibility, conflict management, influencing, and public service motivation are important to collaborative leadership.

The agreement on six key concepts is promising and suggests that when incorporated into evaluation systems, these six items will likely be favored by both human resource managers and skilled collaborators as valid measures of collaborative leadership. However, the divergence suggests that human resource managers risk measuring and rewarding those activities that may not be as important to collaborative leadership. As a result, public organizations may not be developing collaborative leaders as effectively as possible.

Further, this divergence is interesting in that in interviews, skilled collaborators support two of the three "building coalitions" strengths (partnering and political savvy), while interviews with human resource managers support only one of the three "building coalition" components (influencing/negotiating). While human resource managers were quick to equate the "building coalitions" ECQs as "collaborative skills," when asked to describe excellent collaborators, their descriptions did not fit the ECQ definitions provided by the U.S. Office of Personnel Management. This finding suggests that either human resource management experts espouse different definitions than those offered by OPM, or that their espoused "theories of action" do not match with "theories in use" (Argyris & Schon, 1974). Comparisons of the two groups as described above are presented in Tables 5 and 6.

CORE COLLABORATIVE LEADERSHIP STRENGTHS

The following section integrates scholarly literature and interview transcripts to describe the four primary collaborative leadership strengths identified via interview analysis: *continual learning, external awareness, oral communication*, and *interpersonal skills*.

Continual Learning

The finding that continual learning is a valued collaborative leadership strength supports Bardach's model of collaborative capacity mentioned previously. This finding suggests that collaborative leaders support learning in collaborative efforts via their own example. While Bardach contends that learning is the pinnacle of collaborative capacity, he is careful to note that learning must have a purpose. In public sector collaboration, that purpose typically centers on creating public value. As Bardach (1998) says, the possibility of creating new value "must be attractive enough to spark at least some collective hopefulness and enthusiasm" (p. 7). Collaborative leaders spark that hopefulness and enthusiasm by their own desire to learn and improve. As one interviewee pointed out, what may be viewed as collaborative failure, where a key goal was not achieved, may not be a real failure if learning took place. This interviewee said that it is important to remember that "you have still accomplished something" by creating relationships and learning new lessons. "Take those lessons and apply them to your organization ... and remember them for next time."

External Awareness

According to Gray (2000), collaboration presents leadership challenges since "stakeholders with an interest in the problem domain can no longer take unilateral action to control the direction of the domain toward their own desired ends" (p. 243). As a result, collaborative leaders must be aware of the needs of their collaborative partners and must balance these with uniquely public sector concerns: political accountability and responsiveness. Van Slyke and Alexander (2006) note that "challenges in coordination, information exchange, and the degree to which government leaders have to collaborate with an extensive network of intergovernmental and private and nonprofit organizations presents leadership opportunities and potential barriers that may well be different than in other sectors" (p. 368). External awareness, a core collaborative leadership trait, fits that description. Admiral Allen's commitment to external awareness was made evident in interviews for this research. As one USCG employee said, "he truly presses us toward collaboration. I've heard him say that [he] believes that leadership in the Coast Guard means to understand and advocate for things beyond just the Coast Guard, but things that are for the department or for the nation."

Interpersonal Skills

According to Gormley (2002), one of the antecedents of interorganizational cooperation is the creation of a culture based on trust. According to Keast, Mandell, Brown, and Woolcock (2004), trust is formed by relationship building. This research supports these claims by noting the centrality of interpersonal skills in effectively leading collaborative efforts. These findings indicate that collaborative leaders must be attuned to the needs and motivations of others in order to lead collaborative efforts. This finding also supports Bardach's (1998) contention that members of a collaborative effort prefer leaders who engage in "servant" or "facilitative" leadership. The importance of interpersonal skills was reflected in interviews with USCG members, including one who highlighted the positive example of Admiral James Loy, whose behavior under fire was inspirational. "Loy was phenomenal in Congress. One second he is getting the crap beat out of him in testimony, the next second he is shaking hands with that same guy. You know, business is business, but I still want to have a relationship with you. That pays off in the long term. They got what they needed, and they are willing to work with you. You see that and you go: if he can do it, I have to be able to do it."

Oral Communication

It is worth noting that the single most important collaborative leadership strength, as identified by this study, is oral communication. This finding supports Agranoff's (2003) work, which said that collaborative networks are promoted and sustained by ongoing communication, especially face-to-face communication. This finding also supports Bardach's (1998) work, which indicates that communication is necessary to solve conflicts within collaborative efforts. Interviews for this research also reinforce the importance of communication by organizational leaders. As one USCG employee said, Admiral Allen's communication style is engaging and personal: "He remembers names, he remembers facts, he does not use cue cards." In addition, this employee added that after giving a major speech, Admiral Allen met with audience members to listen to their questions. He never said, "I'll have my staff look into this. He gave his heart to heart answer." That honest and open communication, said this employee, made him want to join Allen's organization: "Wow, sign me up ... I'm there with you." This ability to communicate effectively, said the interviewee, is a key component in Allen's collaborative success.

COLLABORATIVE LEADERSHIP AND THE U.S. COAST GUARD

When separated by organization, USCG responses nearly mirror the responses of their counterparts in other organizations. Further, their preferences support two of the three Executive Core Qualifications "building coalitions" skills – partnering and political savvy. While USCG interviews generally overlap on most dimensions, one stands out as unique: *creativity/innovation*. This dimension does not rank in any of the other analyses, except among USCG respondents (see Table 7). It should be noted that both the Allen and Loy models of leadership emphasize creativity and innovation as well. Given the small sample size for this finding, it would be necessary to investigate further to understand the role of creativity/innovation in the USCG.

This finding is interesting in that the USCG is a hybrid organization, consisting of both military and civilian components. As such, it maintains a hierarchical command-and-control structure. This finding suggests that while the formal organizational structure favors command-and-control

Table 7. Collaborative Leadership Indicators: USCG Sample.

Rank	Collaborative Leadership Indicators	Supported by Interview Data ($n = 12$) (%)
1	Oral communication	100
2	Partnering/alliances	83
	Continual learning	83
3	External awareness	75
4	Interpersonal skills	66
	Political savvy	66
6	Creativity/innovation	58
	Leveraging diversity	58
	Strategic thinking	58
	Empathy/capacity to care	58

processes, the informal culture (i.e., leadership, training) promotes creativity and innovation throughout the organization. This commitment is reflected in the USCG Core Values, which were drafted by Admiral Loy. In addition to *Honor* and *Devotion to Duty*, all USCG members embrace the value of *Respect,* which includes: "We encourage individual opportunity and growth. We encourage *creativity* through empowerment. We work as a team" (USCG, 2008, emphasis added).

Admiral Loy's coauthored "Architecture of Leadership" (2008) explains this commitment further: "all Coast Guard personnel from the youngest recruit to the senior-most admiral are immersed in the culture of leadership, taught leadership skills, and expected to practice it on a daily basis." This commitment to creativity and working outside of the traditional hierarchy was reflected in a 2006 personal interview with Admiral Allen who said that innovation was necessary in the response to Hurricane Katrina because "there was no command-and-control infrastructure in New Orleans."

RECONSIDERING LEADERSHIP THEORY AND PRACTICE

Traditional models of public sector leadership assume some level of authority to direct work within hierarchical organizational structures. This approach is contrasted by such authors as Page (2003), Kanter (1989), and Chrislip and Larson (1994), who contend that leading across boundaries requires new approaches to leadership than those typically employed to lead within hierarchies. In a classic study of organizational leadership, Reddin

Table 8. Collaborative Leadership Style.

Concern for People	Concern for Task	
	Low	High
High	*Collaborative leadership* Supporting, or human relations style Concerned with developing relationships	Coaching, or participative style Concerned with setting standards for others
Low	Delegating, or laissez-faire style Concerned with rules and procedures	*Traditional leadership* Directive, or autocratic, style Concerned with directing others

Source: Adapted from Reddin (1987).

(1987) identified four basic leadership styles that reflect a leader's concern for task and people: (1) supporting, or human relations style, (2) coaching, or participative style, (3) delegating, or hands-off style, and (4) directing or autocratic style (Table 8). The best style to employ depends on the situation.

In the context of collaboration, the core leadership strengths identified in this research (oral communication, continual learning, external awareness, and interpersonal skills) best fit the supporting, or human relations, style of management. In this style, leaders illustrate an above-average concern for people and relationship building. This style contrasts with the typical bureaucratic style of leadership, which centers on task-oriented behaviors stemming from the directing or autocratic style as conceptualized by Reddin. These findings support the assertion that leadership practice is changing and that leadership theories should adapt as well to maintain their relevance.

CONCLUSION

According to Trinka (2003), "most great leaders are not superheroes, in that they normally only possess a few profound strengths that they leverage to achieve outstanding results. Knowing this, we might ask which core areas should we ask our managers to concentrate on and what characteristics or competencies differentiate great leaders from good ones. After all, good does not equal great, and all organizations need more great leaders." This research addresses this challenge by identifying the collaborative leadership strengths that superior and average collaborators, as well as human resource management experts, identify as significant. This study revealed that among these strengths, four are essential: interpersonal skills, oral communication, external awareness, and continual learning.

The agreement on these four strengths presents an opportunity to examine leadership theory and development. To ensure that collaborative leadership skills are being developed in the public sector, it is important that human resource management tools, including assessments and rewards, reflect measures for these aptitudes. Further, it is up to leaders to institutionalize these strengths in organizational cultures by leading by example (i.e., modeling collaborative behaviors) and ensuring that these behaviors are properly valued and recognized. Finally, leadership theory should continue to develop to reflect these changing priorities. While Reddin's model of leadership styles captures collaborative strengths, it is far from a perfect fit. Additional work must be done to explain the necessary behaviors for effective collaborative leadership.

An August 2006 report described DHS's ongoing leadership vacuum, characterized by dramatic losses of key personnel and an inability to fill leadership positions. According to former inspector general Clark Kent Ervin, this is a serious concern because "it only hampers the effectiveness of a department everyone agrees is ineffective" (Federal Times, 2006). This report further illustrates the importance of leadership, particularly in an organization where the critical mission requires leaders who are committed and able to meet goals collaboratively with a variety of public, private, and nonprofit homeland security partners.

ACKNOWLEDGMENT

This research was supported in part by the Volcker Junior Scholar Research Grant.

REFERENCES

Agranoff, R. (2003). *Leveraging networks: A guide for public managers working across organizations*. Arlington, VA: IBM Endowment for the Business of Government.

Alexander, J., & Wilson, M. S. (1997). Leading across cultures: Five vital capabilities. In: F. Heselbein, M. Goldsmith & R. Beckhard (Eds), *The organization of the future*. San Francisco: Jossey-Bass.

Argyris, C., & Schon, D. A. (1974). *Theory in practice: Increasing professional effectiveness*. San Francisco: Jossey-Bass.

Bardach, E. (1998). *Getting agencies to work together: The practice and theory of managerial craftsmanship*. Washington, DC: Brookings Institution Press.

Bardach, E. (2001). Developmental dynamics: Interagency collaboration as an emergent phenomenon. *Journal of Public Administration Research and Theory*, *11*(2), 149–164.

Bass, B. M. (1985). *Leadership and performance beyond expectations*. New York: Free Press.

Bass, B. M. (1998). *Transformational leadership: Industrial, military, and educational impact*. Mahwah: Erlbaum.

Burns, J. M. (1978). *Leadership*. New York: Harper & Row.

Chrislip, D. D., & Larson, C. E. (1994). *Collaborative leadership: How citizens and civic leaders can make a difference*. San Francisco: Jossey-Bass.

CNN News. (2005). The aftermath of Katrina. September 3.

CNN News. (2006). Report: Katrina response a "failure of leadership." February 14.

Doig, J. W., & Hargrove, E. C. (1990). *Leadership and innovation: Entrepreneurs in government*. Baltimore: Johns Hopkins.

Federal Times. (2006). Leadership vacuum hobbles DHS. August 7.

Gormley Jr., W. T. (2002). Reflections on terrorism and public management. In: *Governance and public security*. PricewaterhouseCoopers Endowment for the Business of Government. Syracuse, NY: Campbell Public Affairs Institute, Syracuse University.

Gray, B. (2000). Assessing inter-organizational collaboration. In: D. O. Faulkner & M. DeRond (Eds), *Cooperative strategy: Economic, business, and organizational issues*. Oxford: Oxford University Press.

Huddleston, M. W. (1999). *Profiles in excellence: Conversations with the best of America's career executive service*. Arlington, VA: The PricewaterhouseCoopers Endowment for the Business of Government.

Huxham, C., & Vangen, S. (2000). Leadership in the shaping and implementation of collaboration agendas: How things happen in a (not quite) joined-up world. *Academy of Management Journal*, *43*(6), 1159–1166.

Judge, T. A., Ilies, R., Bono, J. E., & Gerhardt, M. W. (2002). Personality and leadership: A qualitative and quantitative review. *Journal of Applied Psychology*, *87*(4), 765–780.

Kanter, R. M. (1989). *When giants learn to dance: Mastering the challenge of strategies, management and careers in the 1990s*. New York: Simon and Schuster.

Keast, R., Mandell, M. P., Brown, K., & Woolcock, G. (2004). Network structures: Working differently and changing expectations. *Public Administration Review*, *64*(3), 363–371.

Lawler, E. E., II. (1992). *The ultimate advantage: Creating the high-involvement organization*. San Francisco: Jossey-Bass.

Lawler, E. E., II. (1996). *From the ground up: Six principles for building the new logic corporation*. San Francisco: Jossey-Bass.

Lawler, E. E., II. (2003). *Treat people right! How organizations and individuals can propel each other into a virtuous spiral of success*. San Francisco: Jossey-Bass.

National Leadership Index. (2007). *National leadership index 2005: A national study of confidence in leadership*. Cambridge, MA: John F. Kennedy School of Government, Harvard University.

Page, S. (2003). Entrepreneurial strategies for managing interagency collaboration. *Journal of Public Administration Research and Theory*, *13*(3), 311–340.

Partnership for Public Service. (2006). *Best places to work*. Washington, DC: Partnership for Public Service.

Phillips, D. T., & Loy, J. M. (2008). *Architecture of leadership*. Annapolis, MD: Naval Institute Press.

Rainey, H. G. (2003). *Understanding and managing public organizations* (3rd ed.). San Francisco, CA: Jossey-Bass.

Reddin, W. J. (1987). *How to make management style more effective*. Maidenhead: McGraw Hill.

Riccucci, N. M. (1995). *Unsung heroes: Federal execucrats making a difference*. Washington, DC: Georgetown University Press.

Seiling, J. G. (1999). Reaping the rewards of rewarding work. *The Journal for Quality and Participation, 22*(2), 16–20.

Strauss, A., & Corbin, J. (1990). *Basics of qualitative research: Grounded theory procedures and techniques*. Newbury Park, CA: Sage.

Svara, J. H. (1994). *Facilitative leadership in local government: Lessons from successful mayors and chairpersons*. San Francisco: Jossey-Bass.

The White House. (2006). *The federal response to Hurricane Katrina: Lessons learned*. Washington, DC: The White House.

Trinka, J. (2003). Developing "great" leaders. Unpublished monograph.

U.S. Coast Academy (2008). Core Values of the Service. August. Accessed at: http://www.uscga.edu/display.aspx?id=339

United States Government Accountability Office. (2006). Hurricanes Katrina and Rita: Coordination between FEMA and the Red Cross should be improved for the 2006 hurricane season. 06-712. Author.

United States Office of Personnel Management. (2001). *Guide to the senior executive service*. Washington, DC: United States Office of Personnel Management.

United States Office of Personnel Management. (2007). Senior Executive Service Recruitment and Selection: Executive Core Qualifications. May. Accessed at: http://www.opm.gov/ses/recruitment/overall_ecq.asp

Van Slyke, D., & Alexander, R. (2006). Public service leadership: Opportunities for clarity and coherence. *American Review of Public Administration, 36*, 362–374.

Washington Post. (2005). Coast Guard's Chief of Staff to Assist FEMA Head Brown. September 7. Accessed at: http://www.washingtonpost.com/wp-dyn/content/article/2005/09/06/AR2005090601677.html

Yukl, G. (2002). *Leadership in organizations* (5th ed.). Upper Saddle River: Prentice-Hall.

REVERSING THE DESTRUCTIVE DISCOURSES OF DEHUMANIZATION: A MODEL FOR REFRAMING NARRATIVES IN PROTRACTED SOCIAL CONFLICT THROUGH IDENTITY AFFIRMATION

Thomas E. Boudreau and Brian D. Polkinghorn

ABSTRACT

Groups often perpetuate conflict by developing and enforcing hostile, dehumanized, and objectified images of the "other" with whom they intentionally engage in conflict. The thesis of this article is that if the double hermeneutics of identity "framing processes" (Lewicki, Gray, & Elliot, 2003) drive the dehumanization of the excluded or enemy other, then these same processes can be a factor in the social reconstruction of another's humanity. Specifically, a model of identity affirmation is posited that can ideally challenge and change the dominant discourses and narratives that go into the in-group's social construction of a dehumanized out-group. As such, the process of identity affirmation is designed to be

Pushing the Boundaries: New Frontiers in Conflict Resolution and Collaboration
Research in Social Movements, Conflicts and Change, Volume 29, 175–205
Copyright © 2008 by Emerald Group Publishing Limited
All rights of reproduction in any form reserved
ISSN: 0163-786X/doi:10.1016/S0163-786X(08)29007-5

used to rehumanize a once ethnic, excluded, or even enemy "other." This model was inspired by, and is applied to, a brief case study outlined in the essay involving the Onondaga Sheriff's Department headquartered in Syracuse, New York, and the Onondaga Indians who are part of the Iroquois Confederacy.

INTRODUCTION: THE DYNAMICS OF DEHUMANIZATION

The social construction of a dehumanized enemy other is a prevalent practice in intense protracted social conflicts (Azar, 1990; White, 1968). Yet, there is no word in the English language to "rehumanize" an individual or group that has been profoundly dehumanized. In an attempt to address and amend this, this essay will present a model of identity affirmation (Boudreau, 2003; Polkinghorn & Boudreau, 2007) that entails a process of the social reconstruction of one's humanity that has been progressively degraded or deconstructed in prolonged social conflict. This model was inspired by an actual case study involving the Iroquois Indians and the sheriff of Onondaga County in upstate New York in 1983. In examining this case study, the authors postulate that the same "framing processes" (Lewicki, Gray, & Elliott, 2003) involved in the social deconstruction of a person's or group's humanity could be used in reverse in order to rehumanize the excluded or enemy other.

Dehumanization depends on dueling social constructions that emphasize that the "other" is morally culpable of great crimes, thus less than human and deserving of punishment. If "dehumanizing" processes are to be reversed, the current dominant discourse concerning how each group simultaneously frames itself and the other must be continually challenged, changed, and reconstructed through the actual deeds, including symbolic ones (Schirch, 2005), by the current "in-group." This is obviously very difficult, though not impossible, to do. In particular, this article argues that a conflict between groups can be lessened by the explicit affirmation by one group of the other group's identity, including recognition of its past pain, defeats, and collective losses, when appropriate. In fact, the following case study actually *inspired* the sustained reflection and inquiry concerning the meaning and necessary stages of rehumanization that eventually resulted in the model of identity affirmation contained in the final part of this chapter.

THE BEGINNINGS: THE BONES OF CONTENTION

We start this essay by including a short news story on the repatriation of Native American Indian bones as reported by Brenda Cawthon in the Syracuse *Post Standard* on June 30, 1983. The meeting took place just outside the Onondaga Nation Territory about five miles south of Syracuse, New York:

> Old Bones Given to Onondaga Indians
>
> A small group of newsmen gathered in the parking lot of a Nedrow café to witness the end of a recent debate over the centuries-old remains of an unknown Indian woman.
>
> The bones that caused all the furor were packed in a plain cardboard box resting on the back seat of Onondaga County Sheriff John Dillon's car.
>
> Lee Lyons, brother of Onondaga Indian Chief Oren Lyons, drove into the lot, shook hands with the sheriff and received the bones. It took about two minutes to settle the latest quarrel in a longstanding feud between Indians and archaeologists over the treatment of Native American burial grounds.
>
> "We see this as being a very important move," Lyons said. "We've been working to establish a rapport with archaeologists across the state .... We certainly would not go down and dig up your cemeteries."
>
> "The skeleton will be reburied in a private ceremony on the Onondaga Reservation," Lyons said.
>
> The bones were discovered on June 11 by two children playing in an Ellisburg sandpit. State police unearthed the remains and turned them over to Syracuse University anthropologist Mark Fleischman.
>
> It was Fleischman who determined the bones were those of an Indian woman who probably lived in the 17th century or earlier. Although the skeleton is similar to many others found in New York State, he said, the dimensions of the skull and other features provided clues to its origins.
>
> Many Native Americans perceived disruption of the burial site as another violation of their heritage by white society.
>
> "Archaeologists are always saying 'we're doing this for you,'" Lyons said. "We have yet to have an archaeologist come to the Longhouse and say, "This is what we learned."

The Onondagas, part of the Iroquois Confederacy, were particularly upset that the New York State Police turned the bones over to the Anthropology Department at Syracuse University. In the past, many archeology or anthropology departments and museums saw such human remains as simply "scientific" evidence or data (Bray, 2001). However, to many American Indian nations, this was an affront to their humanity and a dishonor to their dead (Echohawk & Echohawk, 1996). The Onondagas thought that the bones should be turned over to them directly or at least to the county's medical examiner's office, where human remains are normally taken. Once the remains were identified as most likely Indian and those of a female, the matter became more contentious as the Onondagas are a matriarchal society whereby much of the social structure revolves around clan mothers.

The Sheriff's Department of Onondaga County is traditionally the "point agency" for federal, state, and local law enforcement agencies concerning any legal or criminal matters or other issues dealing with the Onondagas. This tradition sometimes breaks down as state police enter the territory in reputed "hot pursuit" or in search of a fugitive. Federal law enforcement agencies have also tried to pursue or investigate individuals on the nation. So the Sheriff's Department seems to be the precarious point agency in this shaky law enforcement alliance that reaches back to the federal government in Washington, DC. As a result, the Onondagas are usually very wary of any police activity on or near their territory.

Even so, from a legal or administrative standpoint, the Onondaga County Sheriff's Department did not have to get involved in the issue of the contentious bones at the time. This episode of the exchange of the bones between the Onondaga Nation and Sheriff Dillon is notable because it occurred well before the current Native American Graves Protection and Repatriation Act was passed by the US Congress in 1990 (Trope & Echo Hawk, 2001). The return of ancestral remains to Native American communities was by no means assured in the early 1980s when Sheriff Dillon decided to act; in fact, the reverse was often the case (Trope & Echo Hawk, 2001). In view of this, during the 1970s and 1980s, the issue of the protection and repatriation of American Indian remains was a growing concern to native peoples in the United States and Canada (Bray & Killion, 1994). Native Americans were also increasingly concerned about other issues like tribal identity, the protection of known burial sites, and return of sacred artifacts (Cornell, 1988). Their growing concern over these issues was part of a resurgence of interest, especially among younger Native Americans, in the unique identity and ancient traditions of their peoples (Nagel, 1997). Under these circumstances, the improper handling of Indian remains became a "flash point" in an already strained relationship.

Hence, Sheriff Dillon's act of returning the bones, observed from a distance by one of the authors of this article, represented a singular yet significant shift in police policies in upstate New York towards Native

Americans. To understand this seemingly simple act, we need to probe deeper into the social and conceptual structures and resulting narratives of human conflict in general, and specifically into the possibilities for conflict transformation through identity affirmation and the subsequent social reconstruction of the dehumanized "other" into a rehumanized group or individual, which is what Sheriff Dillon, wittingly or unwittingly, initiated on that June day south of Syracuse.

Specifically, the sheriff's seemingly simple act of transferring the bones to the Iroquois actually represents the complex transformation of a once dehumanized people into a recognized and affirmed group rightly recognized as fellow human beings. The dynamics of such rehumanization and conflict transformation begins with the *epistemic encounter or engagement* between groups or individuals representative of their respective groups involved in a social conflict. As we shall see, the key to conflict transformation in such an epistemic encounter is for one group to move from a "will to power" over the other group to a "will to empower" shared by both groups simultaneously (Boudreau, 2008). This can be done only by changing both the internal definition and dominant dialogues and narratives among the in-group, its "identity frame," as well as changing the "characterization frame" concerning how the parties perceive each other (Lewicki et al., 2003). These processes of identity and characterization framing are both a function of a dynamic double hermeneutics (Gadamer, 1960; Giddens, 1984; Ricour, 1986; Jackson, 2006) resulting from the epistemic encounter.

For rehumanization to occur, both of these images or acts of framing processes must often be challenged or changed. Once this is done, the rehumanization of the once excluded or enemy "other" becomes a distinct possibility in theory, though it is often very difficult to do so in practice. We will argue below that this is what the sheriff did through the process of identity affirmation. Yet, before doing so, we must establish the basic building blocks concerning the social construction and reconstruction of one's humanity. Such an analysis begins with the epistemic encounter.

THE DYNAMICS OF REHUMANIZATION: THE EPISTEMIC ENCOUNTER

The epistemic encounter is the basic social encounter or engagement between two or more human beings who are simultaneously active hermeneutical agents that are continually interpreting or reinterpreting, not only their surrounding social context, but also each other, in a constant process of social construction, cooperation, competition, and conflict (Boudreau, 2008). Lewicki et al. (2003) best capture this simultaneous hermeneutical phenomenon in their concept of framing dynamics in which participants in a conflict create multiple frames of reference and narratives at the same time concerning their own self image and identity, as well as the characterization of the other groups or individuals.

From a social constructionist perspective, such an encounter is fundamentally epistemic in that each participant, as an active hermeneutical agent, is capable of creating, interpreting, building, refining, and testing his or her knowledge claims concerning ensuing social realities resulting from an episodic or ongoing engagement with the other or others. In this way, the epistemic encounter between two knowing and interpretive beings or groups distinguishes the ensuing construction of social reality from the basic "empirical encounter" between a "subject" and "object" posited in the natural sciences or the realists' correspondence theory of knowledge (Goldman, 1986).

There are three key characteristics of the epistemic encounter. First, the epistemic encounter assumes that each subject in the exchange is an active agent of interpretation, who initially plays a *unique* role of interpreting, constructing, and participating in the world that he or she purports to describe. This is especially true, as we shall see, when the subjects encountering each other come from completely different cultural backgrounds, such as Sheriff Dillon and the Iroquois clan mothers and chiefs. Thus, the epistemic encounter or engagement of reciprocally knowing and interpreting subjects in a specific time and place defies the positivist idea in the sciences or social sciences of the isomorphic, and hence interchangeable, knower of an "objective reality."

Hence, the epistemic encounter is qualitatively different than an encounter between a "subject" and an "object." According to the realist school of correspondence theory, an initial encounter occurs between "a sensate being and the facticity of the world" (Goldman, 1986). Realists of this persuasion believe "the world is prestructured into truth-like entities (facts), and that truth consists in language or thought mirroring a precategorized world" (Goldman, 1986). The role of the subject as sensate being is simply to record the cumulative encounters with this precategorized "objective" reality.

In contrast, the epistemic encounter in social conflicts results in ongoing social constructions that are rarely, if ever, isomorphic as *each representative* of their relevant epistemic community will initially interpret his or her contextual situations in a partial, perspectival (Nietzsche, 1974; Merleau-Ponty, 1963), and "prejudiced" (Palmer, 1969; Gadamer, 1960) manner; in other words, each participant in an epistemic encounter will interpret his or her life world (Habermas, 1987) and, in particular, encounters with others according to antecedent and ongoing cultural, normative (Kratochwil, 1989), and self-defining (Kelman, 1997a, 1997b) processes of social construction (Pouliot, 2007). As a result, each subject or party in an encounter, especially in a prolonged or violent social conflict, will struggle to define and defend its own self-image and interpretation of events, not simply as a knowledge claim, but as "The Truth." This results in simultaneous dual (or multiple) interpretations, a *double hermeneutic* (as defined here), concerning the origins, nature, objectives, or limits of the ensuing contested knowledge claims that supposedly "objectively" define and describe social construction of a "lethal contest" (Tilly, 2003).

Hence, the double hermeneutic is a second characteristic of the epistemic encounter. In the current context, the double hermeneutic can be defined as the *simultaneous acts of interpretation* and self-definition by each agent in an epistemic encounter concerning his or her own self-image and identity, which is inevitably related to his or her primary group allegiances. This is a close, though not an isomorphic, definition of the double hermeneutic developed by Anthony Giddens (1987). For Giddens, sociological knowledge can be interactive in a way that scientific knowledge can't be in that it influences how people act, thereby creating new interpretations. The phenomenon of the double hermeneutic and its dynamics has also been explored and defined in various and somewhat different ways by Gadamer's "the fusion of horizons," Ricour's "objectification of meanings," as well as Giddens' interactive element in interpretation, similar to Immanuel Kant, between the "knower and the known" (Gadamer, 2004[1960]; Ricour, 1986; Giddens, 1987). Within the social sciences, Vincent Pouliot seems to define the double hermeneutic in the following way: "Interpretation means not only drawing inferences from data, as even diehard positivists do, but also recognizing (and taking advantage of) the fact that 'an important part of the subject matter of social science is itself an interpretation – the self interpretation of the human beings under study' (Neufeld, 1993). A constructivists social science develops meanings about meanings" (Pouliot, 2007). Or, as Patrick T. Jackson concisely states, the double hermeneutic involves the dual interpretive processes of "making sense of making sense" (Jackson, 2006).

In an intensely contested epistemic encounter, the double hermeneutic that usually ensues is closer to Giddens' original definition which involves a twofold *interpretive and interactive process*. Specifically, a double hermeneutic initially develops as both or all groups involved in a conflict *simultaneously* interpret the same events from their own point of view, which is usually intensely partisan. This framing process of the conflict first occurs *within each contesting group* as elites vie with each other for the privilege of articulating the dominant discourse for, and identity of, the group as a whole. While a dominant discourse and identity is established within a contesting group, this same process of hermeneutical struggle is simultaneously occurring within the other group or all groups involved in a prolonged violent conflict. This is a variety of the process of "identity framing" posited by Lewicki et al. (2003).

Unfortunately, the epistemic encounter becomes more complex when involving a prolonged (long standing) social conflict (Azar, 1990). This is because one's own group identity can become intensely intertwined in this ongoing hermeneutical process of interpreting a prolonged social conflict with the "other." In such a situation, a *dueling* double hermeneutic develops and evolves between the rival groups, each struggling to assert the dominant discourse and definitive narrative that will provide, so they hope, the most convincing and accepted characterization of the origins and nature of the contest, and consequent blame for the ensuing strife and even violence. Ethnocentric in-group images (Levine and Campbell, 1972) and stereotypical thinking (White, 1968) often results as the in-group inevitably sees itself as "superior," "virtuous," and "peaceful," and the out-group is consequently "inferior," "immoral," and violent" (Sumner, 1906, 1927). As a result, almost inevitably, the other group is deemed less than human by the in-group and subsequently dehumanized for its alleged approval of and actual involvement in attacks against civilians, destruction of homes, murder, assassinations, or other atrocities. A *double hermeneutic of dehumanization* occurs when both or all sides do this simultaneously in a prolonged social conflict. This process of how parties to a conflict define each other is described by Lewicki et al. (2003) as "characterization framing."

This framing process of the out-group presents significant challenges to peacemaking since extremists from a group involved in a lethal contest often *define themselves* in terms of a demonized and dehumanized enemy "other." The accumulation of such socially constructed extremists' self-images often creates an accompanying group-think (Janis, 1982) as well as self-replicating economies of scale that financially and emotionally benefit the extremist communities. Such communities can present a significant challenge to peaceful change since they have a vested interest in an insecure and sometimes violent *status quo*. We will come back to that problem when we address the processes of reframing dynamics in the following section on identity affirmation.

Second, the dueling double hermeneutic is a function of *epistemic pluralism,* which can be defined as the presence of competing knowledge claims made by competent subjects concerning the same apparent factual situation. In the context of our current discussion, this can be more precisely defined as the presence of intense *competition* between the different knowledge claims being espoused by different groups in prolonged social conflict. There can be a wide variety of such claims and counterclaims, especially in lethal contests in which each side is intent on destroying the rival claimants to the supposed "truth" of violent human conflict. The presence of epistemic pluralism concerning the seemingly same objective and "factual" situation on the ground challenges a key assumption of scientific modernity that the same or similar subjects, with the same or similar education, will see the objective "facts" in the same way (Gaukroger, 2007). In violent social conflict, because of the presence of a dueling double hermeneutic between subjects, this is patently not the case.

All too often, scholars or academics may be tempted to attribute the competition of truths to a "lack of objectivity," a lack of reasonableness, or simply a distortion of the data (Goldstein & Pevehouse, 2007). Such criticisms assume a common rational or positivistic framework for evaluating a phenomenon. However, the issue and the key prize in an intensely conflicted situation is often *precisely* the intensely waged overt or latent struggle over *which* epistemic framework should be privileged and used to interpret subsequent events.

So, if we are to successfully reverse the dynamics concerning the dueling hermeneutics of dehumanization, then the reality of profound epistemic pluralism in prolonged social conflicts (Azar, 1990) or lethal contests (Tilly, 2003) must be recognized and addressed. We will come back to this point when we discuss the model of identity affirmation later in this paper.

Third, the dueling hermeneutics is often a result of the *differing epistemic communities* to which the contesting participants belong. The participants' willingness to cooperate, compete, or conflict with another group or individual in an epistemic encounter depends, in significant ways, upon the perceptions and resulting interpretations or identity "images" that each brings to and takes away from a meeting with the "other" (Stein, 2001; Eldridge, 1979).These interpretations are, in turn, reflective of the perceived power balances and imbalances and resultant levels of perceived friendliness or threat that each might have of the other. Often, the perceived power relationship between individuals in such an epistemic encounter is socially defined by existing patriarchal, racial, religious, or other ethnic structures. These structures, in turn, reflect the larger epistemic and social communities in which individuals reside and refer to as their dominant identity group or groups.

Thus, the epistemic encounter can best be understood as an inevitable extension and constituent activity of epistemic communities (Adler & Haas, 1992), whether such communities be collegial, competitive, or intensely conflicted. The concept of epistemic communities as "networks of knowledge-based experts" (Haas, 1992) is broadened within the current context to include competitive, incompatible, or contested *beliefs within* and *between* each group involved in prolonged policy or social conflict (Mitchell, Herron, Jenkins-Smith, & Whitten, 2007). Each subject of an epistemic encounter presumably comes from a larger ethnic, indigenous, religious, or national group and identity. Thus, the group or nation as a whole is construed here as the epistemic community.

In this context, the idea of "networks of knowledge-based experts" (Haas, 1992) is construed more narrowly as an *epistemic elite*, or elites. Group identities themselves are in the process of constantly being redefined, contested, and developed or deconstructed as internal and external epistemic elites compete to articulate the dominant discourse of a group during the course of a prolonged social conflict. In short, such epistemic elites vie with each other in a prolonged social conflict to provide the dominant discourse and selective narratives of groups as a whole, including their own as well as the ethnic, excluded, or enemy "others."

Understanding the dynamics of dueling double hermeneutics between epistemic elites and communities opens up possibilities for challenging or changing, however incrementally, the dominant discourses and interpretations of each group locked in a prolonged social conflict with another. These discourses are multiple, interactive, and layered both within and between the competing groups (Ford, 2007). For instance, both Sheriff Dillon and the Iroquois were undoubtedly involved in these dual framing dynamics in their encounter with each other. They each had to overcome negative images of the other, especially back in their respective groups, simply in order to meet. For the sheriff, it was the law enforcement community, especially within the New York State Police, and for the Onondagas it was the Six Nations of the Iroquois. They also shifted from a singular "will to power" characteristic of intense zero sum conflicts and redefined themselves in terms of a "will to empower" each other (Boudreau, 2008). In doing so, they revealed some of the key framing dynamics for ending the cycles of dehumanization and "mirror imaging" (White, 1968) of each other that had occurred in previous years. We will explore these framing dynamics further when we develop the model for identity affirmation of the excluded or enemy "other."

DUELING SOCIAL CONSTRUCTIONS AND IDENTITY AFFIRMATION

From the perspective of realistic group conflict theory, groups compete with each other for land, scarce resources, and relative, if not absolute, security. Influenced by Simmel and Coser, Levine and Campbell (1972) state that, from the perspective of this theory, the presence of a perceived threat from the outside consolidates the group's boundaries, solidifies group membership, and heightens the costs of a member's defection (Coser, 1956; Simmel, 1964). They point out that groups under threat or with a besieged mentality often develop a hardened self-image, or so it seems to outside observers. The resulting image of the group under threat is often one of rigid, almost fossilized formation with little or no diversity of discourses and competing narratives among elites or the membership at large, nor any variation in the perception of "threat" from a hostile or "enemy" other.

Yet, such a static conception of group identity, as presented in realistic group conflict theory, overlooks the dynamics and competitive processes of negotiating identities that can potentially operate within and between groups (Kelman, 1997a, 1997b). In short, it overlooks the *dueling double hermeneutics* at work in almost every lethal contest. Expanding upon this idea, we focus first on the selective definition of a group's identity with an emphasis on its framing processes of dynamic self-definition. In doing so, we assume an alternative view concerning the social construction of group identity, even under a perceived threat, which is much more dynamic and more complex than realistic group conflict theory presents concerning the competition within and between groups over the dominant discourses and characterization of a prolonged social conflict. Such an alternative view of social construction allows for the selective redefinition of a group through identity affirmation by an out-group.

The main premise of identity affirmation is that the tensions and mistrust associated with past conflict between groups, or even between nation-states, can be lessened, and perhaps even healed, by the explicit affirmation of another group's identity, and especially the deliberative acknowledgment of each group's past pain, struggles, and losses, which Vamik Volkan (1998) defines as its "collective loss." This premise is, in turn, based upon two implicit and interrelated axioms, namely that: (1) group identify is largely a social construction that involves a dynamic process of selective self-definition and (2) the selective self-definition of the group's histories and psycho-cultural boundaries includes its history of traumatic experiences or, more precisely, the traumatized self-representation" (Volkan, 1998) of the group. It is within this process of group self-definition that one can fully understand and appreciate Volkan's problematic terms: "chosen traumas" and "chosen glories."

These deposited traumatized self-representations of the group can be addressed and, over time, partially healed by an explicit affirmation of the in-group's identities, including its selective self-definition of the group's triumphs and tragedies. The key is to view the act of identity affirmation as an attempt to influence *a group's own interior set of selective and privileged discourses* among its elites and members concerning its view of itself as well as out-groups that are potentially or actually a threatening enemy other. These selective sets of interior interpretations, dialogues, and privileged discourses are occurring *simultaneously* in each conflicting group – hence the double hermeneutic. The goal of identity affirmation, at the very least, is to try to transform the potential or actual conflict by addressing over time each of these simultaneous, interior discourses (Boudreau, 2003). In the language of Lewicki et al. (2003), the first goal of identity affirmation is to attempt to transform the identity-framing processes *within each group* involved in a conflict.

At the same time, the process of identify affirmation seeks to transform how each group selectively defines, deconstructs, and dehumanizes the excluded or enemy "other" involved in a prolonged social conflict. How each group selectively interprets, stereotypes, and demonizes other groups in a lethal contest creates a *dueling* double hermeneutic that constitutes, in essence, a profound struggle over the characterization framing of a conflict (Lewicki et al., 2003). As we shall see, the most dangerous moment for a political leader is when he or she simultaneously tries to transform the interior identity framing of his or her own group *as well as* the characterization framing of another group. This is especially true since the image of the "other" as being less than human or dehumanized often becomes part of *one's own self or group image* and is, thus, very difficult to change or transform. This leads us to the problem of conflict transformation.

CONFLICT TRANSFORMATION

The concept of identity affirmation grows directly out of the ongoing research on conflict transformation. For instance, Raimo Vayrynen (1991) identifies several ways in which conflict transformation takes place. His ideas complement those of Galtung (1984), who emphasizes the analysis of interparty and intraparty conflicts in their structural, cultural, and behavioral contexts. According to Miall, Ramsbotham, and Woodhouse (1995), one of the key ways of reducing conflict is through personal and group transformation. Citing Galtung (1984, 1996) and Vayrynen (1991), they point out that "conflict transformation requires real change in parties' interests, goals or *self-definition* (Emphasis Added). These may be forced or encouraged by the conflict itself, or may come about because of intra-party changes, shifts in the constituencies of the parties or changes in the context in which the conflict is situated" (Miall et al., 1995, p. 158). In conflict reduction through identity affirmation, the purpose is transformation of the group's interior processes of selective self-definition that can, in turn, open up new possibilities for intergroup peace.

In her article, "Image, Identity and The Resolution of Violent Conflict," Janice Gross Stein proposes a process very similar to identity affirmation. She states that in "both enduring interstate rivalries and bitter ethnic conflict, interests are shaped by images that in turn are partially shaped by identity" (Stein, 2001, p. 189). Like Kelman, she states, "The identities that shape images are not given but are socially reconstructed as interactions develop and contexts evolve over the trajectory of a conflict" (Stein, 2001, p. 189). She especially emphasizes the importance of leadership in initiating a series of challenges and changes to the group's self-image, and its image of the other group.

Furthermore, Stein points out that once "leaders or groups begin to change their image of their adversary and are interested in attempting to resolve their conflict, they must also change the image their adversary has of them if conflict reduction is to make any progress" (Stein, 2001, p. 201). This psychologically makes sense as people have a tendency to see cognitive consistency in making sense of the world. Following and developing Stein's argument, we refine the role of leadership in the process of identity affirmation by specifying the critical *and most dangerous moments* for leaders when trying to change the in-group's perception of the out-group. As we shall see, leaders often try to first change the "image their adversary has of them" *without first successfully transforming their own group's image of their adversary*. The failure of transforming one's own group perception of the other can be catastrophic. Timing or "ripeness" in starting such "turning point" processes is critical and even the best of intentions can lead to disaster, as is evidenced with such individuals as Gandhi, Sadat, and Rabin (Boudreau, 2003). All three were assassinated by a member of their own primary identity group as they were engaged in a prolonged peace process in which they were trying simultaneously to challenge their own group's selective definitions of itself, as well as their own group's characterization of the other. These tragic examples vividly illustrate the need to understand the dynamics of peacemaking and identify affirmation more carefully; otherwise, the assassin's wish to demonize and dehumanize the "other" may well succeed.

CONFLICT REDUCTION THROUGH IDENTITY AFFIRMATION: THE DYNAMICS OF SELF-DEFINITION

A dynamic understanding of a group's selective self-definition provides for the distinct possibility of intergroup conflict reduction through identity affirmation that results in the incremental, or even dramatic, changes in the in-group's internal discourses and perceptions of an out-group. In effect, one group is trying to negotiate or renegotiate its identity *first within itself* and, secondly, with another group. Kelman points out concerning this secondary process that "how a group defines itself has significant consequences for others… its chosen identity has an impact on the interests, rights, and identity of other groups. Such groups do, therefore, have a legitimate concern about and a stake in the way in which a given group defines itself. For this reason, national identity, even though it is a psychological fact created by the way a group chooses to define itself, is a legitimate subject for negotiation with other groups … that are affected by this self-definition" (Kelman, 1997b, p. 337).

Identity affirmation works best when it manages to *dislodge or displace* simultaneously: (a) the internal discourses and narratives concerning *one own's self-identity* defined in terms of defiance or disregard, i.e., "benign neglect" of the enemy other; (b) how one's in-group primary discourses and narratives negatively characterize the out-group. This can be done only by changing both the internal definition and dominant dialogues and narratives among the in-group, its "identity frame," as well as simultaneously changing the "characterization frame" concerning how the parties perceive each other (Lewicki et al., 2003). Both these processes of identity and characterization framing are a function of the double hermeneutics resulting from the epistemic encounter. In essence, one is trying to displace or transform the dueling double hermeneutics of dehumanization through identity affirmation.

In conflict reduction through identity affirmation, one group is trying to undertake one or all of the following four changes or transformations:

(1) change or, in Kelman's words, "negotiate" the in-group's identity among its own elites and members; (2) challenge and attempt to negotiate the perception of the out-group concerning its own collective identity and ethos; (3) challenge and attempt to negotiate the out-group's perception of one's own group; and (4) change or negotiate simultaneously new narratives and discourses within *one's own group* concerning its collective mythos and selective self-definition, which includes simultaneously undertaking an affirmative action to transform the group's own *enemy image* or characterization of another group (Boudreau, 2003). This is, in effect, trying to engage and partially heal one's own group's innermost hurts, fears, and traumas, and by doing so change its image of the out-group. All of these steps presuppose that a group's identity is socially constructed and subject to competing or alternative internal discourses concerning its collective mythos and selective self-definition.

In other words, using the language of Lewicki et al. (2003), the first two changes identified above are "identity framing," while the last two are examples of "characterization framing." As we have seen, a leader's most dangerous moment may well be step 4 when he or she attempts to transform *simultaneously* a group's interior processes of identity and characterization framing of the "other." In doing so, such a leader gets *caught in the crossfire of a dueling double hermeneutic*. A leader in this situation is first trying to transform how his or her own group defines itself in terms of an identity presumably *heavily invested in its "heroic" and "righteous" defense against the enemy other*. Simultaneously, he or she is trying to change how the parties define each other, and it's very difficult to convince people that a former or current enemy who has killed large numbers of one's group members can now be trusted not to do so. Hence, more modest steps might first be recommended. Using the process of identity affirmation, each type of change could be specifically selected by an in-group in an attempt to transform prevailing stereotypes and dehumanized images held by a group.

So the question presents itself: *How* should such affirmations be carried out and completed? Obviously, there is no factual formula that can be universally applied to each and all situations, especially where intergroup conflicts are persistent and severe. In short, no set formula is exclusive – each unique situation calls for an identity affirmation process that is tailored to local and historical circumstances. It may not work in some situations at all. Given these limitations, it may be useful nevertheless to outline a tentative model for conflict reduction through identity affirmation, to be tried and tested in actual and ongoing disputes.

THE ELEMENTS OF IDENTITY AFFIRMATION: A MODEL

As Edward Azar (1990) states, prolonged social conflicts possess identity elements in terms of actual or perceived violation by one party of another. This is where claims or warrants by one against the other originate. However, if the arguments are framed in norms violations or legal breeches, the identity element might not manifest itself unless, of course, the violation occurred precisely because of who the alleged victims are. The violation must, therefore, be internalized. Even so, a violation that touches on the emotional or psychological harm inflicted by one group on another could arguably fit into the identity-based category.

Now, to reverse the thought process, it goes to reason that if certain identity affirmation elements are present in the conduct of the parties, then the collective emotional and psychological part of the conflict may be addressed. One example is a case in which two police officers in South Africa brutally beat a young man to death. They later sought amnesty, confessed in public to what they had done, and went one step further to ask for forgiveness from the young man's mother. The mother granted it, based not on the fact that the truth was told, but because the men who murdered her son spoke of him in a humane way. The same form of de-escalation can be seen when someone delivers a sincere apology. This example illustrates the importance of humanizing even a murdered victim as part of conflict reduction or resolution.

The potential limitations of identity affirmation include the obvious caveat that the process probably can't work while direct physical violence and assaults against human beings are occurring or escalating; in all likelihood, its success depends on the *absence* of continued violence and attacks, or a prolonged stalemate on the ground. Furthermore, it might not work very well when and if used by the group or government perceived to be "weaker" in a conflict, since the mere attempt may be interpreted as a sign of further weakness by the stronger party. Yet, weakness and strength are relative terms, especially in a violent conflict. The Iroquois still tell of the time when the French to the north, in what is today Canada, mistook the Iroquois peace emissaries as a sign of weakness and initiated further hostilities. The French lost all of their Indian allies and perhaps even Canada to the British as a result (Wallace, 1980). So much depends on the context and the relevant parties' perceptions concerning the appropriate timing and potential effectiveness of identity affirmation.

In essence, identity affirmation attempts to do *on a group or international level* what Martin Buber (1970) describes as an essential, if not the essential, transformation of relationships on the individual level – changing an "I-it" relationship into an "I-thou" relationship. This requires challenging the in-group history of hostility towards an out-group through its own processes of selective self-definition and social construction. This is admittedly a daunting task even in the best of times, but as we shall see, there are historical examples in which people have reached out over the great divide of intergroup conflict and sought conflict reduction, even resolution, through identity affirmation.

The basic argument is that certain elements should be present in a conflict for the model to be effective. More specifically, there are four elements in the proposed model of conflict reduction through identity affirmation: leadership, recognition, validation, and the transparency of future time. We believe that each of these elements can help in rehumanizing the once excluded or enemy "other." They do so by trying to influence a group's dominant interior discourses of self-definition and the negative framing processes of the other group. We will examine how this is done in the following four sections.

Initiatives: Reaching Out to Others: Track I Diplomacy

The first element of identity affirmation is initiatives, or leadership. As Janice Gross Stein (2001) notes, dynamic leadership is required to initiate the process of conflict reduction with an out-group. When we think of public leadership, we often think of our political leaders and diplomats, but they are not the only ones who could undertake such an initiative. Public leaders in their official capacity are obviously prime candidates for initiating the process of conflict reduction through identity affirmation. This is often referred to as Track I diplomacy, which usually consists of official diplomacy by governmental officials. President Anwar Sadat's unilateral initiative in the fall of 1977, which led to his trip to Jerusalem and contributed, eventually, to the Camp David Accords, is an example of this type of Track I diplomacy. In essence, a well-timed, sincere, and meaningful act on the part of an adversary can have immense emotional and psychological impacts on the out-group.

In our case study, both the Onondaga County sheriff and the Onondagas exercised their political power in order to initiate the ensuing encounter and exchange. The sheriff discovered that he had legal jurisdiction over all human remains found in Onondaga County and, upon this basis, negotiated the return of the contentious bones from Syracuse University. He then took the initiative to set up the meeting with the Onondagas on the border of their land to return the remains. In turn, the traditional chiefs and clan mothers are governed by the Iroquois' famous *Great Law of Peace* that encourages them to take the initiative in establishing the "right relationship" with their neighbors and even with their enemies (Wallace, 1980). The Great Law also recognizes the leadership roles of the clan mothers and of the chiefs. Hence, their delegate's meeting with the sheriff was in full accordance with their own law and traditional power as leaders of their peoples. In fact, if the meeting for some reason failed to result in a successful outcome, the Onondagas were required by the Great Law to make at least two more initiatives or attempts at a resolution before deciding that the intentions of the other party are hostile (Wallace, 1980). In short, the clan mothers and chiefs were ready to make further initiatives and overtures to local law enforcement in order to secure the return of the bones.

But sometimes the political leadership of a group or groups in conflict can't or are not ready to act. In such cases, track II diplomacy may be useful in helping to restore the humanity of the other.

Track II or Multitrack Leadership: Nonofficial Initiatives

Because the risks to leaders who seek to challenge the collective mythos of their own group are often great, the initiative to affirm the identity of an out-group can fall on leaders and participants of nonpolitical organizations. Ambassador John McDonald, Harold Saunders, Joseph Montville, and others have defined and developed the concept of Track II or citizen diplomacy (Saunders, 2005; Diamond & McDonald, 1996; Volkan, Julius, & Montville, 1991).

Track II diplomacy consists of local, religious, economic, or other nonpolitical leaders or simply private citizens who engage in citizen diplomacy and constructive engagements with citizens of the out-group or even with the "enemy." For instance, citizen initiatives were helpful during the end of the Cold War in transforming the dynamics of dehumanization of the Russian people by challenging the prevalent dialogues, images, and narratives of the demonized Soviet "other" in the West (Ross, 2003). By doing so, such citizen diplomats take the initiative to implicitly or explicitly affirm the identity of the excluded group while simultaneously beginning the long process of transforming the image of the "other" within the in-group. This may make it safer for political leaders to take such initiatives in the future.

The ideal outcome is that the initiative of the leader to affirm the "other" will be accepted by his or her society as a whole, and may be eventually embedded in the very social fabric of the in-group. We will come back to this problem – that of embedding a new relationship between groups, creating in essence a new collective mythos or at least transforming critical parts of the old one – in the forthcoming discussion on "the transparency of future time."

Recognition: The Basic Building Block

In normal times, recognizing the other as a human being entitled to certain basic rights is a quintessential condition of the epistemic encounter; it is the often assumed and implicit basis for most cooperative contact and communication between interpretive subjects, especially those who share a similar familial, communal, or cultural background. Yet in a prolonged or violent conflict, the basic act of recognition becomes extremely problematic if not sometimes impossible. It is also difficult when two or more groups share a common history of deep mistrust, conflict, or violence, such as in our original case study where New York State and local law enforcement agencies had an extremely problematic relationship with the Iroquois in the past. So let's first look at what recognition means within the context of the social construction of a protracted social conflict, and then we will try to apply these precepts to the case study between the sheriff and the Onondaga Nation.

First, recognition of the "other" in its most basic form affirms the inherent right of the other to exist as part of the human family. As such, it is the basic foundation to identity affirmation. Cast in basic terms, recognition fundamentally means that the "we-group" no longer seeks to destroy or annihilate the "out-group." In less extreme circumstances, it means the in-group will not seek to humiliate or denigrate the customs, religions, and culture of the out-group. In the case study, Sheriff Dillon expressly recognized the laws, customs, and traditions of the Onondaga people. Recognition also implies and requires acceptance of the moral obligation by the in-group that *reciprocity* and not repression will govern the relationship between the groups in the future.

Reciprocity, in turn, means that the in-group will demand no rights for itself that it denies to the out-group. Finally, it requires that the in-group will make no demands upon the out-group that it refuses to accept for itself. In essence, reciprocity affirms that the in-group recognizes its moral and legal obligations to treat the out-group as equals. Recognition also includes an appreciation of the other in regard to their inherent worth as individuals and as a group. In effect, *recognition acknowledges each other as equals*, at least in the sense that the individuals or groups involved in an epistemic encounter are equally recognized as human beings. In doing so, recognition widens the borders of the in-group's moral community to include the out-group. Let it be clear that this is a moral transformation and not a superficial form of assimilation. Both individuals and groups are recognizing each other as equally human, or in Martin Buber's terms as an "I-Thou," not as an "I- it" (Buber, 1970). This is the first key step in a model of identity affirmation.

In our case study, a remarkable example of *mutual* recognition is implicit in the encounter. Several factors, unmentioned in the newspaper accounts of the exchange at the time, reveal the sheriff's sensitivity to the Onondagas and their concerns in this exchange of the contentious bones.

First and foremost, the Nedrow café mentioned in the article sits on the border of the Onondaga Nation Territory. By meeting right on the border, Sheriff Dillon was *explicitly recognizing* the Onondagas as coequals; specifically, he was recognizing the limits to his own jurisdiction as well as the sovereignty of the Onondagas over their own lands. By doing so, he was recognizing the coequal jurisdictions of the Sheriff's Department and of the traditional chiefs and clan mothers. This was in sharp contrast at the time to the New York State Police, who practiced a policy of "hot pursuit" deep into the Onondaga Nation Territory. One such incident contributed to the death by heart attack of one of the Onondaga chiefs who tried to intervene. In contrast, it was Sheriff Dillon who first contacted the traditional chiefs of the Onondaga Nation, the legal government of the Onondagas, and made arrangements to turn the bones over at the border of the Onondaga territory; he and his deputies had no intention, he told the chiefs, of coming onto their land.

The chiefs and clan mothers were deeply impressed by the sheriff's willingness to recognize the borders of their sovereign nation. They were more used to the threats of local, state, and even federal law enforcement officers to come upon the nation's territory to seize a suspect or enforce legislation. Despite the past relationships between law officials and the chiefs, Sheriff Dillon was, in effect, announcing his acceptance of the traditional chiefs as governmental and jurisdictional equals. This approach forged a stronger relationship between local law enforcement and the Onondaga Nation. In short, the sheriff was saying in *deeds, not merely words*, that he would respect their sovereignty and traditions as coequal to his own.

Such an overt act of explicit recognition helps to dislodge the dominant negative images that one side may have of the other. It adds an element of "cognitive dissonance" (Festinger, 1957) that disrupts the established narratives, discourses, and resulting hostile images of the in-group concerning the once or ongoing demonizing of the other group. Specifically, an act of unilateral or mutual recognition can help *dislodge* the framing processes that contribute to the double hermeneutic of dehumanization. This can occur when clear evidence in deeds matches the accompanying discourse that challenges not only the hostile image of the out-group, but also challenges the internal narratives concerning the out-group's supposedly "true nature" as less than human. Such an abrupt disruption of once dominant and negative framing processes is what the sheriff and chiefs seem to accomplish together. By agreeing to meet, and recognizing each as equals, they also prevented or interrupted the negative framing of each other that could contribute to the perpetuation of a dueling hermeneutic in the future.

In this way, Sheriff Dillon and the chiefs and clan mothers of the Onondagas were able to overcome any lingering suspicions and meet each other as equals. This is the second necessary – but not sufficient step – in identity affirmation. Much more is usually needed to overcome hostile and negative stereotypes of the other.

Validation by Word and Deed: The Foundation Stone of Identity Affirmation

Validation is the emotional core of identity affirmation. This is because a critical aspect of identity affirmation is recognition *and* validation of the out-group's past experiences of traumas, pain, and defeats, especially if inflicted by the in-group that now seeks to affirm its former opponents. The validation of pain means the in-group takes responsibility, when appropriate, for the trauma and suffering it has caused the out-group in the past. Or validation may simply mean to acknowledge the past pain of an out-group or enemy, even when the in-group is not responsible. This is what President Kennedy did in his famous Commencement Address at American University in June 1963. In contrast to his predecessors during the Cold War, he openly and publicly acknowledged the suffering and losses of the Soviet peoples in his speech by stating: "And no nation in the history of battle ever suffered more than the Soviet Union suffered in the course of the Second World War. At least twenty million lost their lives. Countless millions of homes and farms were burned or sacked. A third of the nation's territory, including two-thirds of its industrial base, was turned into a wasteland – a loss equivalent to the devastation of this country east of Chicago" (Kennedy, 1963). He also announced an immediate suspension of above ground nuclear testing by the United States and invited Soviet reciprocation. The speech led directly to the opening of talks to complete the partial Test Ban Treaty and to the beginning of détente.

The political, not to mention the emotional, impact of Kennedy's speech in recognizing and validating the still fresh wounds of the Soviet people were apparently great. President Kennedy's science advisor, Jerome Wisner, stated that intelligence reports indicated the speech was published in all of the Soviet major newspapers and that Chairman Khrushchev said it was the best speech ever made by an American President (Etzioni, 1970). Unfortunately, the "peace process" that President Kennedy initiated at American University seemed to die with his assassination five months later and the subsequent US escalation of the Vietnam War.

Validation, if done with integrity and credibility, appeals directly to the emotional core of the out-group. Sometimes, simple statements and deeds can thaw the hostility simply because of the sincere validation of the other. In the case of returning the bones, the validation came from Sheriff Dillon's prompt action in arranging for and actually returning the bones on the border of the Onondaga Nation Territory; his actions allowed for the reburial of the bones on the ancestral lands of the Iroquois. These actions validated the Onondagas' belief that the *remains of their ancestors are sacred*, and *should be regarded as such*, and that they deserve a proper reburial (with traditional rites) if discovered. This deeply held belief, shared universally by other Indian nations and tribes, was a large factor in the popular pressure that encouraged and supported Congressional passage of the Native American Graves Protection and Repatriation Act of 1990.

Most importantly, Sheriff Dillon was implicitly (or explicitly, depending on his motivation) recognizing that the chiefs, clan mothers, and Onondaga people had been wronged and emotionally pained by the state's treatment of these remains as simply a subject of academic or anthropological curiosity. His quick and decisive actions seemed intended to minimize or even reverse this perceived injury. By returning them at the edge of the nation's territory, he was paying respect to their past pain, in part by assuring them through his act that *no new pain* would be inflicted or endured over the fate of these silent, solemn bones. Forgiveness begins with a word or *act* of apology.

In doing so, Sheriff Dillon was explicitly contradicting any negative image or narrative that the Onondagas and the Sheriff's Department may have had concerning each other in the past. In effect, he was vigorously challenging through an actual deed the *negative characterization framing process* of the Onondaga Nation's members who might be understandably tempted to characterize the "white man's attitude" toward native peoples' own dead as universal, extremely hostile, and thus "less than human." By returning the remains, Sheriff Dillon was probably able, at least initially, to *dislodge or displace* the Onondagas' previous primary discourses and narratives that could justly and negatively characterize the European out-group as enemies. In essence, he was able to displace the dueling hermeneutics of dehumanization through validation of their past and present pain caused by the State Police's perceived cavalier treatment of the sacred remains. In doing so, he decisively broke with past or enduring practices of the "white man" and validated the Native Americans' emotional pleas that the bones should be returned and buried in their ancestral homeland.

At the same time, Sheriff Dillon was undoubtedly sending a message back to his own and other law enforcement agencies. (In this regard, it is important to note that Sheriff Dillon showed up at the meeting unarmed and dressed in no uniform; he was accompanied by two uniformed and armed deputies, one of whom was a member of the Iroquois Confederacy.) He was demonstrating through a seemingly simple deed that mutual respect and not recrimination did and would govern his department's relationship with the Onondagas. The symbolism was not missed.

As Chief Oren Lyons later stated, "[It] begins with the word 'respect.'... Respect begets respect, and that begets peace" (Cousineau, 2006). For Oren Lyons, his brother Lee (who was present for the Onondagas when the bones were exchanged) and the rest of the nation, returning the bones was proof of the "respect" the sheriff and his department had towards them. In doing so, it helped to destroy both group narratives, especially those held by extremists leading to mutual dehumanization. Specifically, the dueling double hermeneutics of dehumanization were being replaced, at least initially, by a new story or narrative that both groups could now share and tell from a positive point of view.

Transparency of Future Time: Transforming the Framing Dynamics of Self-Identity

The last element in the identity affirmation model is creating a relationship between the two groups characterized by the "transparency of future time."

This means that the in-group will attempt to build a new and nonthreatening relationship with the hitherto excluded group by taking concrete steps and immediate behavioral actions – as distinct from mere verbal promises – to make their future relationship as predictable, certain, transparent, and hence peaceful as possible. In his book, *Evolution of Cooperation*, Robert Axelrod (1984) discusses extending the "shadow of the future" over current interpersonal interactions as one way to insure continuous cooperation. The idea is that the prospect and promise of having a continuous and mutually beneficial relationship in the future is one way to engender or enhance cooperation in the present. Basically, the in-group is demonstrating by current and concrete actions that it is no longer a threat to the out-group in the future.

Extending the shadow of the future is a powerful way to communicate with a once excluded enemy other that the in-group no longer seeks a contested relationship based upon a sheer "will to power"; instead it conveys the new reality that the once hostile in-group has a new "will to empower" each other, and thus jointly prosper. The United States seemed to successfully do this after World War II by inviting both the Japanese and Germans to become dominant trading partners instead of military rivals with the United States. Through the Marshall Plan and other initiatives the United States, in an explicit decision and subsequent policy of sharing its power, convinced their once implacable enemies that joint prosperity was preferable to continued hostility (Ikenberry, 2000). In essence, in the interest of insuring their own peace and prosperity, the United States postwar policy was one of a joint "will to empower" by make trading partners of Germany and Japan, rather than render the vanquished enemy other as impoverished, vassal states.

More importantly, the prospect and promise of a new and cooperative relationship in the future between two hitherto hostile groups *forces a reconsideration of each group's self-image* as one defined in terms of defiance or hostility toward the once dehumanized other. It introduces new and positive discourses in the social construction of a self-image. Specifically, extending the shadow of the future over recently hostile groups holds out promise that the competing groups will now be governed by, and internally described as, a new relationship of mutual respect and tolerance in the future. By doing so, the reframing process of self-identity becomes possible as old dominant discourses or negative narratives become dislodged and displaced by the *clear evidence* of a new relationship. In other words, holding out the prospect of a new cooperative, prosperous, and mutually supportive relationship between all groups involved in the future is a powerful way to dislodge the extremists in both or all groups, and gradually displace an *internal self-image* held by each group that is based upon hostility and dehumanization of the once excluded ethnic or enemy other.

Both the Onondagas and the sheriff made it quite apparent to each other in this case, and in many other subsequent interactions, that they wanted and treasured a positive relationship with each other; most importantly, they made it clear to each other that they *wanted to continue this cooperative and positive relationship in the future, and they did.* The ensuing years tested this cooperative relationship. For instance, there was the highly publicized and contentious Dennis Banks affair. (Dennis Banks, one of the cofounders of the American Indian Movement (AIM) sought sanctuary for more than a year with the Iroquois from federal and state law enforcement agencies.) Another acrimonious internal dispute within the Onondaga Nation involved the Sheriff's Department for months and concerned the sale of tax-free cigarettes. This resulted in arson on the Onondaga Nation Territory and ongoing disruption of traffic to and from the "tax-free" stores. (The Sheriff's Department had to police the on and off ramps of local highways, as well as separate the protestors for or against the families selling the cigarettes.) So their future relationship after the brief exchange involving the "bones of contention" was by no means uneventful. Yet, both sides persevered in the goodwill, mutual respect, and identity affirmation of each other that was evident in June 1983. Because of this, in part, they were able to work together to negotiate successful outcomes to subsequent problems. To this day, the Onondaga Sheriff's Department prides itself on its legacy of good relations with the Onondagas.

This mutual process of identity affirmation is not necessarily a new idea. Gandhi said he never really had an enemy and thus he treated others with such respect that his British opposition, especially those in the Labour Party, had a hard time disliking him. One particular practice of Gandhi's was to announce to the other side what he planned to do well in advance down to the exact action, the specific time, and specific place so that the other side would not be surprised or humiliated. This was extending the shadow of the future even in the midst of a serious nonviolent campaign that pitted enormous social and economic forces against each other. As a result, some of his biggest support came from the British themselves, as his personal visits to the working class districts around and outside of London attested. This complete transparency of the self and of the intended actions performed by Gandhi and his followers was an extension of humility, respect, and, most of all, trust. Gandhi always emphasized that there should be no place for hatred in the self-image of the newly empowered Indian people.

A related concept, developed by Osgood (1962), is GRIT or the gradual reduction in tension. This, too, is a means of reducing conflict by announcing, often in a unilateral manner, a specific action that is designed to de-escalate the rhetoric and action of the contending parties by undertaking an activity that sends a signal to the other groups that they wish to improve the dynamics, change the course of action between the groups, and to otherwise provide some reason to begin to trust the group undertaking GRIT.

Transparency of future time, as is seen in the deliberate actions of Gandhi or through the idea of GRIT, works to reestablish some sense of trust. Deutsch and Coleman (2000) speak of two types of trust: identity-based trust (IBT) and calculus-based trust (CBT). IBT is the kind you experience in close relationships where the other and you have a great deal of personal characteristics in common. It can be based on family, clan, and tribe, or perhaps other larger group characteristics, such as gender, race, or ethnicity. IBT allows individuals to undertake activities with others that may be considered risky if done with a stranger. On the other hand, CBT is often seen in conflict settings and where relationships are strained. CBT operates on individuals or groups doing stated activities that the other can check off as they are completed. If a spouse cheats on his or her companion, the relationship is strained or broken. In the case of strained relationships, there may be some opportunity to repair it, and this is where individuals and groups may see successful results using GRIT. Misperceptions, misattribution, misjudgment, and misunderstanding can be addressed and the process of repairing and reframing the relationship can begin.

In some cases, problem-solving workshops by Kelman and Burton (1984), or Fisher (1997) have been used to bring conflicting parties together to reduce the objectification of each other and to work on each group's understanding of their future. John Cleese of Monty Python fame talks about a "time-space oasis" where groups can remove themselves from the context and experience the company of the other group while working out how the future will unfold. In this way, the dueling double hermeneutics of dehumanization can be gradually replaced, or even suddenly transformed, into a mutually empowering rehumanization of each other. The practical application of this element of the model is difficult, but is built upon the success of recognition, initiatives, acceptance, and validation. In the "transparency of future time," the parties are encouraged to define new dominant discourses and narratives of themselves and of other groups, based upon the new evidence of cooperation and trust by the once dehumanized and demonized other.

CONCLUSION

The process of rehumanizing the excluded or enemy other through identity affirmation assumes that three basic dynamics are at work in most prolonged social conflict settings. First, such dueling social constructions fundamentally involve an "epistemic encounter" or engagement (Boudreau, 2008) between two or more groups and representative individuals. In turn, the epistemic encounter does not presuppose nor require the interchangeable or *isomorphic knower* predicated in positivism or in the predictive sciences. In contrast, most individuals or groups involved in a major conflict interprets the excluded or enemy other in unique ways, at least initially.

Second, this epistemic encounter or engagement produces a "double hermeneutic" operating within *and* between both or all sides of the conflict. In a violent social conflict, the dynamics of the double hermeneutic resulting from this encounter can become particularly deadly since both or all sides are often engaged in a prolonged deconstructive process of dehumanizing the other group. Through the pernicious process of dehumanization, the most extreme narrative or internal discourse deconstructs the identity of an excluded or enemy other to such an extent that members of the excluded or "out-groups" (Sumner, 1906, 1927) are viewed as less than human and thus deserving of punishment (White, 1968) and even individual or group destruction.

Third, this process often takes place within a larger group or nation in which epistemic communities vie with each other to provide the dominant discourse and selective narratives of the conflict with another group. Because of this, the social construction of a conflict can be a very contentious framing process within each group as epistemic elites within each community vie for power and dominance via a process of selective definition of one's own identity. As a result, the extremists in each group may have an initial advantage, especially in an escalating conflict, since they often provide the most demonized and dehumanized version of the other that facilitates and legitimates the ensuing violence.

Identity affirmation probably can't work while violence against each other rages. In fact, identity affirmation may require a prolonged stalemate on the ground, or a period of uneasy peace after prolonged hostilities before it can possibly work. Much depends on the unique historical circumstances and timing involved in each case. Yet, the potential for reframing the conflict by attempting to change the dominant discourses and framing processes among the participants should not be overlooked by members of each group as well as interested third parties.

The key to identity affirmation is to reverse these same framing processes of dehumanization by trying to influence *a group's own interior set of selective and privileged discourses* among its elites and members concerning its socially constructed identity. These selective sets of interior interpretations, dialogues, and privileged discourses are occurring *simultaneously* in each conflicting group – hence the double hermeneutic. The goal of identity affirmation, at the very least, is to try to transform the potential or actual conflict by addressing over time each of these simultaneous, interior discourses (Boudreau, 2003). In the language of Lewicki et al. (2003), the first goal of identity affirmation is to attempt to transform the identity framing processes *within each group* involved in a conflict.

At the same time, the process of identify affirmation seeks to transform how each group selectively defines, deconstructs, and dehumanizes the excluded or enemy other involved in a prolonged social conflict. How each group selectively interprets, stereotypes, and demonizes other groups in a lethal contest creates a *dueling* double hermeneutic that constitutes, in essence, a profound struggle in the characterization framing of a conflict (Lewicki et al., 2003). As we have seen in our case study, the leaders of two intensely suspicious groups – law enforcement and the Native Americans – were able to change their interior narratives, meet together, and exchange a set of bones that had been at the center of a controversy threatening to drive their respective communities apart. In short, they affirmed the identity of each other by simultaneously changing their "framing processes" of themselves and of the once excluded or enemy other group. In this way, they provided an inspiring example of identity affirmation that challenges other groups or nations to attempt and emulate.

REFERENCES

Adler, E., & Haas, P. M. (1992). Conclusion: Epistemic communities, world order, and the creation of a reflective research program. *International Organization*, *46*, 390–397.

Axelrod, R. (1984). *The evolution of cooperation*. New York, NY: Basic Books.

Azar, E. (1990). *The management of protracted social conflict: Theory and cases*. Aldershot: Dartmouth.

Boudreau, T. (2003). Intergroup conflict reduction through identity affirmation: Overcoming the image of the ethnic or enemy 'other'. *Peace and Conflict Studies*, *10*(1), 87–107.

Boudreau, T. (2008). Human agonistes: Interdisciplinary inquiry into ontological agency and human conflict. In: D. Sandole & S. Byrnes (Eds), *Handbook on conflict resolution*. London: Routledge.

Bray, T. L. (Ed.). (2001). *The future of the past*. New York, NY: Garland Publishing Inc.

Bray, T. L., & Killion, T. W. (1994). *Reckoning with the dead: The Larsen Bay repatriation and the Smithsonian institute.* Washington, DC: Smithsonian Publishing.
Buber, M. (1970). *I and thou.* New York, NY: Charles Scribner & Sons.
Burton, J. W. (1984). *Global conflict: The domestic sources of international crisis.* Sussex, Great Britain: Wheatshef.
Cornell, S. (1988). *Return of the native: American Indian political resurgence.* Oxford: Oxford University Press.
Coser, L. A. (1956). *Functions of social conflict.* New York, NY: Free Press.
Cousineau, P. (2006). *Huston Smith in conversation with native Americans on religious freedom.* Berkeley, CA: University of California Press.
Deutsch, M., & Coleman, P. T. (Eds). (2000). *The handbook of conflict resolution: Theory and practice.* San Francisco, CA: Jossey-Bass.
Diamond, L., & McDonald, A. J. (1996). *Multi track diplomacy: A systems approach to peace.* Bloomfield, CT: Kumarian Press.
Echohawk, R. C., & Echohawk, W. R. (1996). *Battlefields and burial grounds: The Indian struggle to protect ancestral graves in the U.S.* Minneapolis, MN: Lerner Publishing Group.
Eldridge, A. F. (1979). *Images of conflict.* New York, NY: St. Martins Press.
Etzioni, A. (1970). The Kennedy experiment. In: A. Etzioni & M. Wenglinsky (Eds), *War and its prevention.* New York, NY: Harper and Row.
Festinger, L. (1957). *A theory of cognitive dissonance.* Stanford, CA: Stanford University Press.
Fisher, R. (1997). *Interactive conflict resolution: Pioneers, potential and prospects.* Syracuse, NY: Syracuse University Press.
Ford, M. (2007). Situating knowledges as coalition work. *Educational Theory, 57*(3), 307–324.
Gadamer, H.-G. (2004[1960]). *Truth and Method.* New York: Continuum.
Galtung, J. (1984). *There are alternatives! Four roads to peace and security.* Nottingham: Spokesman.
Galtung, J. (1996). *Peace By peaceful means: Peace and conflict development and civilization.* London: Sage.
Gaukroger, S. (2007). *The emergence of a scientific culture and the shaping of modernity 1210–1685.* Oxford: Oxford University Press.
Giddens, A. (1984). *The constitution of society: Outline of the theory of structuration.* Berkley, CA: University of California Press.
Giddens, A. (1987). *Social theory and modern sociology.* Cambridge: Polity Press.
Goldman, A. I. (1986). *Epistemology and cognition.* Cambridge: Harvard University Press.
Goldstein, J., & Pevehouse, J. C. (2007). *International relations* (8th ed.). New York, NY: Pearson Longman.
Haas, P. (1992). Introduction: Epistemic communities and international policy coordination. *International Organization, 46*, 1–35.
Habermas, J. (1987). In: T. McCarthy (Trans.), *The theory of communicative action. Vol. 2. Lifeworld and system: A critique of functionalist reason.* Boston: Beacon Press (first German edition published in 1981).
Ikenberry, G. J. (2000). *After victory: Institutions, strategic restraint and the rebuilding of order after major wars.* Princeton, NJ: Princeton University Press.
Jackson, P. T. (2006). Making sense of making sense: Configurational analysis and the double hermeneutic. In: Y. Dvora & S.-S. Peregrine (Eds), *Interpretation and method: Empirical research method and the interpretive turn.* Armonk, NY: M.E. Sharpe.

Janis, I. (1982). *Groupthink: Psychological studies of policy decisions and fiascos* (2nd ed.). Boston, MA: Houghton Mifflin.

Kelman, H. (1997a). Group processes in the resolution of international conflicts: Experiences from the Israeli-Palestinian case. *The American Psychologist*, *52*(3), 212–220.

Kelman, H. (1997b). Negotiating national identity and self-determination in ethnic conflict: The choice between pluralism and ethnic cleansing. *Negotiation Journal*, *13*(4), 327–340.

Kennedy, J. F. (1963). *Commencement address at American University*, Washington, DC, www.cs.umb.edu/jfklibrary/j061063.htm

Kratochwil, F. (1989). *Norms, rules, decisions*. Cambridge: Cambridge University Press.

LeVine, R. A., & Campbell, D. T. (1972). *Ethnocentrism: Theories of conflict, ethnic attitudes and group behavior*. New York, NY: Wiley.

Lewicki, R. J., Gray, B., & Elliott, M. (Eds). (2003). *Making sense of intractable environmental conflicts: Concepts and cases*. Washington, DC: Island Press.

Merleau-Ponty, M. (1963). In: Alden Fisher (Trans.), *The structure of behavior*. Boston, MA: Beacon Press.

Miall, H., Ramsbotham, O., & Woodhouse, T. (1995). *Contemporary conflict resolution*. Malden, MA: Blackwell Publishing.

Mitchell, N. J., Herron, K. G., Jenkins-Smith, H. C., & Whitten, G. D. (2007). Elite beliefs, epistemic communities and the Atlantic divide: Scientists' nuclear policy preferences in the United States and European Union. *British Journal of Political Science*, *37*, 753–764.

Nagel, J. (1997). *American Indian ethnic renewal: Red power and the resurgence of identity and culture*. Oxford: Oxford University Press.

Neufeld, M. (1993). Interpretation and the "Science" of international relations. *Review of International Studies*, *19*(1), 39–61.

Nietzsche, F. (1974). In: W. Kaufman (Trans.), *The gay science*. New York, NY: Random House.

Osgood, C. E. (1962). *An alternative to war or surrender*. Urbana, IL: University of Illinois Press.

Palmer, R. (1969). *Hermeneutics*. Chicago, IL: Northwestern University Press.

Polkinghorn, B. D., & Boudreau, T. (2007). Bones of contention: Applying an identity affirmation conflict reduction model to a case study of repatriating of ancestral remains. *Race, Gender and Society*, *13*(3–4), 143–161.

Pouliot, V. (2007). "Sobjectivism": Toward a constructionist methodology. *International Studies Quarterly*, *51*(2), 359–384.

Ricour, P. (1986). *Du texte a l action. Essais d hermeneutque [From text to action: Essays in hermeneutics, 2]*. Paris: Seuil.

Ross, F. (2003). Call to action to elders: The need to highlight their abilities, wisdom and compassion as citizen diplomats. *Peace and Conflict Studies*, *10*(1), 116–123.

Saunders, H. (2005). *Politics is about relationship: A blueprint for a citizens' century*. New York, NY: Palgrave Macmillian.

Schirch, L. (2005). *Ritual and symbol in peacebuilding*. West Hartford, CT: Kumarian Press.

Simmel, G. (1964). *Conflict and the web of group affiliations*. New York, NY: Free Press.

Stein, J. G. (2001). Image, identity and the resolution of violent conflict. In: C. Crocker, et al. (Eds), *Turbulent peace*. Washington, DC: US Institute of Peace.

Sumner, W. G. (1906). *Folkways: A study of the sociological importance of usages, manners, customs, mores and morals*. New York, NY: Dover Publishers.

Sumner, W. G. (1927). *The science of society*. Yale, CT: Yale University Press.

Tilly, C. (2003). *The politics of collective violence*. Cambridge: University of Cambridge Press.
Trope, J. F., & Echo Hawk, W. R. (2001). The Native American Graves Protection and Repatriation Act: Background and legislative history. In: T. L. Bray (Ed.), *The Future of the Past*. New York, NY: Garland Press.
Vayrynen, R. (Ed.) (1991). *New directions in conflict theory: Conflict resolution and conflict transformation*. London: Sage.
Volkan, V. (1998). *Blood lines: From ethnic pride to ethnic terrorism*. Boulder, CO: Westview.
Volkan, V., Julius, D., & Montville, J. (1991). *The psychodynamics of international relations: Unofficial diplomacy at work*. Latham, MD: Lexington Books.
Wallace, P. (1980). *White roots of peace*. Philadelphia, PA: University of Pennsylvania Press.
White, R. K. (1968). *Nobody wanted war: Misperception in Vietnam and other wars*. Garden City, NY: Doubleday.

CATALYSTS OF CHANGE: APPLYING NEW FORMS OF PRACTICE TO THE CONTEXT OF NIGERIA'S DEMOCRATIC DEVELOPMENT

Marie Pace and Darren Kew

ABSTRACT

Conflict resolution efforts have larger implications for democratic development: they provide a valuable discursive space *where social change can be collectively conceptualized and negotiated to the benefit of democratic development, and where participants gain* democratic experience, *providing a constructive catalyst in the ongoing social transformation of values, norms, and political cultures. Through a fusion of discourse-based and democratic culture analysis of the Nigerian case, we explore how conflict resolution practices may better engage and catalyze public discourses that promote processes of constructive social change, and how conflict resolution practices can help to build democracy and good governance. We use the example of Nigerian discourses on democratic governance to investigate the broader importance of recognizing and engaging discursive realities. Secondly, we explore how transformative conflict resolution methods, such as workshop models,*

Pushing the Boundaries: New Frontiers in Conflict Resolution and Collaboration
Research in Social Movements, Conflicts and Change, Volume 29, 207–231
Copyright © 2008 by Emerald Group Publishing Limited
All rights of reproduction in any form reserved
ISSN: 0163-786X/doi:10.1016/S0163-786X(08)29008-7

promote democratic values at the same time that they provide a valuable democratic experience.

Conflict resolution efforts have larger implications for democratic development. Conflict resolution workshops and programs provide a valuable *discursive space* where social change can be collectively conceptualized and negotiated to the benefit of democratic development, and where participants gain *democratic experience*, providing a constructive catalyst in the ongoing social transformation of values, norms, and political cultures. In addition to the good news for democracy, this impact may also have noteworthy implications for conflict resolution and peacebuilding practices themselves. Based on separate and joint research efforts we have conducted in Nigeria, our goal is to provoke reflection and provide insights about how conflict resolution practices may better engage and catalyze public discourses that promote processes of constructive social change, and how conflict resolution practices can help to build democracy and good governance. We do not seek to introduce new empirical research; rather, we draw on our separate works in order to raise new theoretical possibilities by a fusion of discourse-based and democratic culture analysis. In addition, we outline and suggest new avenues for possible research.

As a country prone to violent conflict, Nigeria has become host to an increasing number of conflict resolution/peacebuilding programs and projects since it began its latest endeavor to build democratic rule in 1999. These efforts aim to address the growing violence in the Niger Delta, ethno-religious violence in the centrally located states of the Middle Belt, and episodic outbreaks of clashes across the country, including those linked with elections and the struggle for political advantage. While the characteristics of these three arenas of conflict – the Niger Delta, ethno-religious conflict, and politically motivated violence/conflict – each have distinct features and are generally addressed as such, they are significantly linked through the common context of Nigeria's governance crisis and ongoing struggle toward democratic consolidation.

During the past two years, while participating in and observing a number of these workshops, we noted participants readily linking issues of peace with issues of good governance, regardless of the specific topic. In the Niger Delta, participants readily point to the failures of local governance structures to generate public benefits (such as jobs, education, and infrastructure) from oil dividends as they demand renewed moral fortitude among officials to resist corruption. A common theme in the Middle Belt region is the partiality among government officials when it comes to addressing ethnic and religious conflicts. In these and other examples, the cry for accountable government authorities committed to public welfare, and the rule of law is directly linked to conflict resolution strategies. Nigeria's 2007 general election in particular provokes reflection about promising discursive and experiential trends that can be linked to conflict resolution efforts.

In approaching this question of how conflict resolution efforts may provide a constructive catalyst in Nigeria's struggle toward democratic consolidation, we turn to two emerging lines of thought within the field. First, we use the example of Nigerian discourses on democratic governance to investigate the broader importance of recognizing and engaging discursive realities. Second, we explore how transformative conflict resolution methods, such as workshop models, promote democratic values at the same time that they provide a valuable democratic experience. Many theorists in the conflict resolution literature have called upon practitioners to better engage the socially constructed and value-laden realms of worldviews and discourse. Through the Nigerian context, we explore the possibilities and limitations for practitioners interested in applying these new models of practice both in Nigeria and elsewhere. While exploring these two interrelated themes of discourses and democratic experience, we look at the importance of specificity, and how, as practitioners, we might better learn to engage and respond to the particular contexts in which we work. In particular, we examine the overarching theme of democratic governance and its relationship to what we do as conflict transformation practitioners.

THE ROOTS OF CONFLICT IN NIGERIA

Much of the source of Nigeria's social conflicts – and its struggles for democratic consolidation – is rooted in resistance to the authoritarian political cultures that remain prevalent across much of Africa. These cultures reflect an authoritarian pattern that is typically called neopatrimonialism, what Nigerians call "godfatherism" or the "Big Man" problem. Typically, authoritarian rule in Africa in the 1970s and 1980s centralized both political power and economic industry in the hands of government, such that the few individuals who controlled the government became fabulously rich and influential. These "Big Men" utilized their wealth and power to build networks of clients, sometimes even across ethnic lines, in a pyramid fashion. In return for these material rewards and access to the largesse of the state, "clients mobilize political support and refer all decisions upward as a mark of deference to patrons" (Bratton & Van de Walle, 1994, p. 458). Consequently, the early stages of democratization tend to resemble competitive oligarchy, during which the Big Men and their client pyramids struggle for control of state power and its resources, and loyalty to the Man at the center often trumps the rule of law in determining political behaviors.

Nigeria exemplifies this pattern. As a result of over 20 years of military rule, political and economic power became consolidated at the federal level, a circumstance that was further institutionalized in the 1999 constitution. By the time of the most recent transition to a civilian government in 1999, Nigeria's neopatrimonial system of elitist politics had become characterized by vast patronage networks of elites – Nigeria's Big Men – arranged in a pyramid fashion, with the occupant of the Presidency and its control of massive oil resources typically situated to be the most influential of these mandarins. This system of elitist politics encourages self-serving perspectives among power seekers, while the interests of the Nigerian people remain largely ignored. In many parts of the country, for instance, basic public infrastructure such as electricity, roads, and health care remain as dilapidated as they were under military rule. Even though annual oil revenues accrue in the billions of dollars, 92% of the population continues to live on less than 2 dollars per day (see, http://devdata.worldbank.org). Within this overarching context of patrimonial politics and socioeconomic disparities, Nigeria faces significant challenges in the form of violent internal conflicts.

In Nigeria's oil-producing Niger Delta region, uneven distribution of oil revenues and environmental degradation have been the sources of mounting tensions between local communities, the government, and oil companies. This conflict has escalated since the late 1990s as youth gangs and militia groups have been acquiring and stockpiling alarming numbers of weapons. Through the acquisition of arms, youth groups have arguably managed to leverage greater political relevancy for themselves, albeit, as of yet, with few constructive outcomes to show for it. With this development comes the growing concern that militias are beginning to reason that they will yield political gains from being drawn into political squabbles. Given Nigeria's elitist, Big Man political culture – where the unwritten conventions of power and the high oil stakes often combine to generate unscrupulous behaviors – the situation is fraught with the dangers of escalation. Already many of the political mandarins have built alliances with these militias and are engaging them in their political and financial disputes.

Since the return of democracy to Nigeria in 1999, Nigeria has also experienced a series of communal and ethno-religious violent crises. The worst affected areas have been in the Middle Belt region, also known as the North-Central and much of the Northeast zones, where violent episodes have resulted in widespread death, destruction, and displacement since 1999. In Plateau State, for instance, it is estimated that over 50,000 people have died from conflicts since September 2001, a third of these children, with a further 300,000 persons who have been displaced (Agence France-Presse, 2004). Within the context of ethno-religious conflict in Nigeria, the interplay between local and elitist dynamics is particularly significant. On the level of elite politics – which can itself be divided between national, state, and local elites – there is a continual jostling for position that plays out. Among the elites at each of these levels – some are in government, and some are on the outside, like the godfathers – a range of realpolitik strategies are consistently in play. On the level where the majority of the population carries on with their lives, it is the larger trends of ethnicity, religion, and poverty that tend to dominate. While the elites, aided by the media, can divisively or inadvertently engage these larger themes, they cannot fully dictate how events will unfold. Things can and do get out of control at times and, to echo the title of Chinua Achebe's famous novel, can even "fall apart." Local skirmishes involving individuals from different ethnic groups have on numerous occasions led to riots and counter riots against immigrants of one group living in the core territories of the other.

SIGNPOSTS OF CHANGE

Within this overarching context of disparities and Big Man politics, there are notable signs of some democratic consolidation on the one hand, and an increased capacity on the part of civil society and other stakeholders to constructively address inter-communal conflict and political grievances on the other. These trends manifest in distinct ways. On the one hand are signposts of institutional and structural changes, on the other hand is evidence of a deeper, more diffuse and intangible shift in values. In the course of highlighting these trends and how they manifest themselves, what is revealed is a tension in the core fabric of Nigerian society, suggesting a struggle over identity and meaning that is bound in competing visions for Nigeria's social and political future.

A milestone in Nigeria's progress toward democratic consolidation was reached in May 2006, when the National Assembly, bowing to tremendous public pressure, rejected President Obasanjo's gambit for a third term in office through an amendment to the constitution. This action showed that Nigerian democracy has made great strides toward building some check on the overwhelming powers of the presidency, and more importantly, that the public, media, and civil society are increasingly willing and capable of mobilizing to defend democracy and the public interest. This event suggests a strengthened and emboldened democratic system on the one hand and growing civic demands for responsive, effective, and transparent leadership on the other. The vehicle for this civic demand has been a growing democratic discourse calling for, among other things, popular choice of rulers and government accountability.

With most African countries at some stage in transition to democracy, executives retain predominant power in ways that reflect neopatrimonial political cultural patterns of behavior developed during authoritarian times. Constitutions may say that legislatures hold formal fiscal responsibilities and judicial decisions must be obeyed, but in practice, executives often wield far more power or control than democratic checks and balances would demand. This is not because legislators or judges have not read the constitution, but because neopatrimonial patterns of authoritarian governance remain firmly ingrained. Since Nigeria's transition to democratic rule in 1999, a struggle between formal and informal patterns of political behavior have dominated the political discourse, as expressed by the media, civil society, and increasingly, politicians themselves. At the heart of this tension are efforts to reject the corrupt status quo and to consolidate the values, norms, and institutions that will better ensure accountability and representation.

Relevant to these developments is a litany of disappointments Nigerians have suffered from their fledgling democracy. President Olusegun Obasanjo began his first term in office with bold promises about how he would clean up corruption and improve the country's failing electricity supply and other basic services. The first four years of his presidency were marked by a list of initiatives that promised much, but in the end delivered little that was perceptible to the nation's mostly poor masses. Many believe that public expectations for what the civilians could deliver during the first four years were unrealistically high (Smith, 2007, p. 115). Nonetheless, the failures of the civilian administration to deliver the expected dividends of democracy, compounded by deeply flawed elections in 2003, contributed to the widespread perception that corruption in the new civilian government was just as bad, if not worse, than under the military (Smith, 2007, p. 115). In response, frustration and disappointment have become a powerful narrative of complaint. Anthropologist Dan Smith provides a vivid portrait of Nigerian corruption and its discontents. What he demonstrates is how both corruption and the discourses of complaint it generates are at the core of contemporary events, shaping collective imagination and driving social action (Smith, 2007, p. 8).

In an important sense, the increasing Nigerian demand for more accountable and responsible leadership – the call for good governance – emerges from narratives of popular discontent, and in many respects these have become two sides of the same coin. While on one side of the coin are expressions of a deep-rooted cynicism about their own society, on the flip side are expressions of an optimism and expectation that the country can and should be doing better. Inherent in these discursive realities, therefore, is an emerging collective vision for how Nigeria can overcome some of its most intractable problems. Through these discursive narratives, Nigerians are imagining and recreating the relationship between state and society. And in so doing, they may be forging the means for constructively engaging and transforming Nigeria's three core, inter-related arenas of conflict.

THE PEACE AND GOOD GOVERNANCE LINK

Nigeria provides an important context for examining the linkage between conflict resolution practices and democratic governance. Overall, the resources committed to conflict resolution, prevention, and management in conflict-prone regions of the developing world have expanded substantially since the end of the Cold War. Nigeria exemplifies this trend. Within the context of Nigeria and elsewhere, training in conflict resolution and management has become a mainstream feature of development assistance programs. "Bilateral agencies such as the US Agency for International Development (USAID), the Canadian International Development Agency (CIDA), and the UK Department for International Development (DFID), as well as several UN agencies, all support capacity-building initiatives in peacebuilding, conflict management, and conflict prevention throughout the developing world". In Nigeria alone, countless conflict resolution, conflict prevention, and conflict management trainings have been carried out since 1999. Key actors from other sectors have also brought significant resources to bear on addressing violent internal conflict. The Nigerian government, under the presidency, supports the Institute for Peace and Conflict Resolution (IPCR). Although primarily devoted to research, IPCR regularly partners with UN and bilateral agencies to host conflict-related training and workshops. This extends to the private sector as well; in 2006 alone, over 500 staff working for Shell Corporation in Nigeria received training on both human rights and conflict resolution awareness (Shell Global.com).

Importantly, the linkages between peace and good governance have been embraced by the larger world of policy makers and international development agencies alike. In Africa in particular, the role of good governance – generally defined as democratic governance – is thought to be essential to transforming the decades of conflict that have plagued post-colonial state building. As a result of these assumptions, multilateral and bilateral agencies have poured millions of dollars into increasing the democratic governance capacities of African states to deliver stable peace and security for the continent (USAID.gov).

DISCURSIVE WINDS OF CHANGE

The notion of discourse provides a particularly important analytical tool in the African context, where informal patterns of political behavior are often stronger than the formal patterns demanded by political institutions. Nigerian discourses on matters of peace and governance are central to the theme of this paper. Discourse refers to the vocabulary, expressions, and perhaps also the style commonly used to communicate on a specific topic. It assumes that shared ways of thinking and talking are contextual, representing the boundaries of communication – the style, vocabulary, and expression – relative to geographical, social, and historical locations. As such, a discourse signifies the collective expression – albeit not a monolithic one – of values and norms generating shared meanings, or a shared sense of reality, that can be linked to patterns of behavior. Thus, discourses can be treated as social sites where shared notions of what is true and real are continually contested and negotiated – for instance, what constitutes appropriate expressions of democratic leadership (Foucault, 1970). Because such discursive contexts are not fixed or stable realities, they are fertile arenas where social change is collectively imagined and negotiated, as established power structures are challenged and resisted through everyday speech and action. As such, discursive contexts are sites of reciprocal interaction among various groups, where meaning is continually contested, negotiated, and renegotiated.

Recent contributions from the social sciences to the conflict resolution field point to the importance of discursive realities to the analysis, resolution, and transformation of conflicts. Helpful to an understanding of this development is a look at current forms of practice and their theoretical underpinnings, which have informed work being carried out by agencies, donors and other key actors in conflict-prone regions of the developing world. It further provides relevant context for emerging conversations in the field, which point to discourse as the latest frontier of engagement.

The 1990s saw the emergence of new approaches to transforming intractable conflict situations in response to prevalent changes in the nature of social conflict. These approaches call for integrated, comprehensive methods of conflict resolution and peacebuilding that reach beyond state institutions and state actors. It has now come to be generally accepted that inter-communal, or social, conflicts have roots that reach deep into the fabric of the society. But these assumptions arose with a shift in thinking that occurred at the end of the Cold War with the breakdown of the bipolar system, followed by persistent conflicts such as in the Middle East, the Balkans, and Rwanda. The sources of these conflicts are embodied in the institutions, policies, and practices of governance, but they are further understood to be embodied in the human core of the culture, values, needs, and experiences of parties in conflict, as expressed from within the various interwoven stratum and sectors of the society. Thus the multileveled or multichanneled approach to conflict transformation that emerged prioritizes both state and non-state actors, and calls on leadership from top to middle to grassroots levels of society to contribute to the goal of peacemaking (Lederach, 1997; Saunders, 1999; Diamond & McDonald, 1996).

These approaches focus on strengthening national, state, and local governance capacities in conflict management and prevention, and on strengthening and empowering community and civil society actors and leaders to play their part in addressing conflict in constructive ways. The prevalence of trainings in Nigeria and elsewhere in the developing world that aim to build capacities in conflict-related skills is a direct response to this thinking. The multichanneled nature of this approach is in contrast to the top-down thinking of the Cold War era that focused predominately on state-level actors. The movement of thinking – from top-down to multichanneled approaches to conflict – can be characterized by its increased inclusiveness (more social actors), its increased holism (more dimensions of society), and its concern with culture, values, and needs as experienced from multiple locations within society. Pushing the direction of this thinking even further are research and theories that call for the further inclusion of discursive realms of values, perceptions, and norms.

Researchers and practitioners are beginning to explore the relationship of perceptions or worldviews to conflict and conflict resolution practices.

As an example, Jane Docherty studied the clash of worldviews between the Branch Dividians and the FBI in Waco, Texas (Docherty, 2001). Her work highlights the tragic confrontation between the Branch Dividians and the FBI. She poignantly demonstrates the centrality of socially constructed, discursive realities to the business of conflict resolution. Her work points to the need for studies that deepen our understanding of the dynamic and specific nature of these socially constructed worlds. Also responding to the intangible dimension of worldview, LeBaron (2002) applies a similar line of thinking to the world of practice. Her claim is that it is in this intangible realm of worldviews that the cutting edge – *third wave practices*, as she calls them – of the conflict resolution field can be found. Third wave practices highlight evolving perceptions and understandings about personal and social transformation, particularly as they relate to conflict resolution processes. Focused on *worldviews*, third wave practices are concerned with the symbols, perceptions, identities, and meanings that give rise to conflict and their transformation (LeBaron, 2002, p. 7). As she explains, the impetus for this emerging new wave of practices are as follows:

> [Conflicts] are bound up with stories we tell, the ways we order and structure our thoughts and our feelings, and the cultural messages that shape our perceptions... If we want to bridge differences durably and respectfully, we cannot use a strategy centered in problem solving or in improving communication alone. We have to begin by acknowledging that our logic and common sense about how to communicate arise from our own ways of knowing – the ways we make meaning of our lives. These ways are influenced by culture, personality, context, and a whole system of knowing called our worldview (LeBaron, 2002, p. 8).

LeBaron (2002) is advocating for sensibilities and processes that extend beyond established territory. Primary to this aim are critical, self-reflective capacities that can identify and locate the socially constructed features of any relational context. It further suggests that the power of our practices, like the power of direct nonviolent action, is located in part in the immaterial, symbolic terrain of discourse, and in the collective imagination.

Affirming the importance of collective imagination, John Paul Lederach articulates further the focus of these third wave sensibilities: To engage evolving perceptions and understandings about personal and social transformation is the essence of peacebuilding. According to Lederach, the essence of peacebuilding is deeply grounded in the realities and circumstances giving rise to conflict, but – and this is crucial – it is not limited by them. Present, therefore, is the capacity to "[give] birth to that which does not yet exist." Rooted yet not bound, the collective or *moral* imagination contains the power to create new possibilities that are relevant to existing realities and challenges (Lederach, 2004). Within the Nigerian context, what is of interest is how Nigeria's moral imagination may be contained within democratic discourses that express both complaint and expectation. It may be through these discursive narratives that Nigerians are imagining and recreating the relationship between state and society. And in so doing, they may be forging the means for constructively engaging and transforming Nigeria's three core, inter-related arenas of conflict.

Suggesting that Nigeria's moral imagination is at work through discourses on democratic consolidation has implications for practitioners in several respects. First, when it comes to capacity building trainings in conflict-related skills, it suggests that greater relevancy and effectiveness can be achieved by those with *third wave* sensibilities that can attune to the significance of discursive themes. Underscoring the importance of *knowing thy context*, attunement to constructive and creative discourses requires a specificity of knowledge about that particular context. Yet, it further suggests that in-depth knowledge alone will not guarantee a capacity to hear, and thus respond to, transformative discourses. Thus, a specificity of knowledge works hand in hand with third wave sensibilities. Nonetheless, to suggest that practitioners are strengthened through a capacity to attune to creative or moral discourse that is informed by an in-depth understanding of a particular context, does not necessarily tell us what to do next. In other words, how to catalyze and engage creative discourse, particularly in the workshop or seminar setting, is an additional matter for inquiry and speculation.

Within the Nigerian context, being alert to the underlying importance of discussions that vacillate from peacebuilding to governance strategies is an important first step for the third wave practitioner. When discussions about how to create meaningful employment for youth in the Niger Delta are melded with outcries for electoral reform, for instance, we are well served to hear the moral logic at play. Corrupt politicians who hire armed youth to hijack elections provide an example of the kind of dynamics that regularly undermine social and economic renewal projects and programs. Contained in that linkage is, thus, a popular understanding of one of the root causes of the conflict. Also contained in that linkage is a critique of this status quo and an assertion of public values and norms that challenge and reinvent it. Once practitioners have achieved the capacity to *hear* moral discourse at work, we then have the possibility to reflect purposefully on what we hear so that, as with the case of Nigerians, they have the possibility to better hear themselves and one another.

Arguably in every society, moral imaginations are wrestling to create solutions to the most vexing social problems. Yet the self-reflective capacity to capture collective solutions and inspire action is critical, and often lacking. To this effect, workshops and seminars offer an important environment. Given its structure and purpose, the workshop setting provides a valuable context to reflect and inform the constructive and creative solutions that are being generated through popular discourse. While the content of conflict-related capacity-building workshops and programs convey valuable analytical tools and problem-solving skills, the emphasis here is on the process of delivery and engagement. Regardless of the curriculum content, practitioners apply third wave sensibilities through their capacity to listen reflectively, to apply positive inquiry, and to reframe messages. Through skillful reflection, practitioners can capture the diffuse power of discursive themes, distilling and amplifying key messages. Through careful inquiry and reflection, for instance, practitioners may probe Nigerian complaints about corruption, insightfully reframing them to reveal the positive values being expressed and collectively affirmed. In so doing, practitioners are well positioned to catalyze social processes that envision constructive responses to conflict-generating social issues.

CONFLICT RESOLUTION AND DEMOCRATIC EXPERIENCE

While the starting place for this paper is an observation specific to Nigeria – about how peace and governance is linked through popular discourses – this linkage may apply elsewhere as well. Conflict resolution methodologies may in fact support democratic development, such that conflict resolution scholars and democracy theorists are "relatives from the same village," working toward a host of common, mutually reinforcing goals. Noting that the fundamental values that underpin transformative conflict resolution methods, such as problem-solving workshops, are identical to those of democratic political culture, we trace the impacts of these methods on democratic processes.

Democratic forms of governance are commonly assumed to provide a better guarantee that sources of conflict will be addressed given the emphasis on responsive and accountable leadership. Democracy is believed to facilitate constructive means for addressing social conflicts in two overarching ways. First and most commonly, democracy is presumed to provide structures and institutions through which conflicts can be channeled and, ultimately, rationally negotiated in a peaceful manner. Second, democracy inculcates a *culture* of negotiation over time that allows society to resolve conflicts outside formal political processes. Democratic culture furthermore brings extra social weight that ensures formal democratic processes are followed and eventually consolidated.

Organizers and facilitators of conflict resolution workshops may never mention the word democracy explicitly during the process, and may, in fact, never be conscious of any democratic impacts their efforts may have. Nonetheless, most workshop models are structured in a fashion that is based on democratic values, such as respect for opposing points of view, principled compromise, freedom of speech, and accountability (see appendix). Consequently, when participants take part in transformative conflict resolution processes like workshops, they walk away with a *democratic experience*. This experience can help to inculcate and reinforce democratic values (Kew, forthcoming). In Nigeria, this experience can inculcate and reinforce democratic values that further challenge the authoritarian norms embodied in neopatrimonial systems of governance.

The analytical concepts of discourse and political culture both explain the persistence of neopatrimonialism in Nigeria and provide a vehicle for understanding how processes of ongoing democratic consolidation may be linked to conflict resolution practices. Political culture reflects "people's predominant beliefs, attitudes, values, ideals, sentiments, and evaluations about the political system of their country, and the role of the self in that system" (Diamond, 1994, p. 7). Political culture, like culture itself, is the collected, common experiences of a group of people over time, disseminated to differing degrees in each member of the group, but on the aggregate reflecting what a group has learned from its experiences (Avruch, 1998, pp. 17–18). Consequently, political culture reflects a profile of key norms, values, and judgments that members of a group share together on average in a discernable pattern that is generally different from members of other groups (although groups may, of course, hold similar values).

Importantly, however, no individual belongs to a single group – be it ethnic, religious, organizational, professional, or social. All individuals, therefore, carry multiple layers of culture within themselves that reflect the many groups to which they belong (Avruch, 1998, pp. 17–18, *see also* Tajfel & Turner, 1986). Values and ideas learned or experienced within one group to which an individual belongs may be carried into the context of another group to which she or he is a member. A trade unionist, for instance, who learns to respect opposing points of view during an election for his union officers, may take that value into his church group, where he then is more open to opposing perspectives. Values learned at the micro-level within small groups can also impact the values of the largest groups to which individuals belong, including the state. Just as experience within a neopatrimonial pyramid can shape norms of clientelism and corruption, group experiences within democratically structured organizations inculcate and reinforce democratic values for members of the group and have a strong impact on democracy-promoting behavior (Kew, forthcoming).

Since culture is a derivative of group experience, it follows reasonably that conflict resolution processes can promote democratic political culture. Thus, individual-level democratic experiences in conflict resolution processes can serve to inform democratic discourses and political norms. Discourses informed and shaped within the context of groups or social environments can contribute to shifts in the larger patterns of values, norms, and behaviors that constitute political cultures within a polity. Kew (forthcoming) finds, in fact, that civil society organizations are strongly inclined to promote democracy vigorously at the national level *if* they resolve their internal conflicts in a fashion that is essentially the same as the approach in workshop models. Rather than simply being an outgrowth of democratic structures, however, democratic political culture can be a catalyst for democratizing authoritarian political structures and promoting the peaceful resolution of conflicts. If the political values of the public change to favor democracy for a sustained period of time, an authoritarian system may be forced to adjust (Huntington, 1991). The recent declaration of assets by the newly inaugurated President Yar'Adua, against the advice of his counsel, is an example of how this can work. That values of transparency are beginning to permeate the level of national politics is a direct result of NGO advocacy.

Consequently, the impact of conflict resolution efforts on national political cultures through the direct inculcation of democratic values within the context of these efforts is of tremendous importance. For instance, as Nigerian civil society organizations with their diverse mandates interact with like-minded regional and international organizations, a process of exchange occurs serving to inform and reshape dimensions of a discursive topic – say, human rights. As the discourse on human rights strengthens in coherency and finds increased outlets for public articulation, it can engage and challenge the dominant national political discourse on the rights of individuals, negotiating for new values, norms, meanings, and behaviors. In this manner, various threads of discourse – such as those on human rights, democratic governance, environmental sustainability, coexistence, and conflict resolution – are arguably moving African polities away from neopatrimonialism and toward democratic political culture.

NIGERIA'S MORAL IMAGINATION

The 2007 Nigerian general elections arguably illustrate Nigeria's moral imagination at work. They demonstrate how third wave sensibilities that are attuned to creative discourse can be of value to analysts and practitioners alike. In order for our practices to invoke and sustain innovative collective responses to the roots of conflict, we must recognize such sensibilities when visible through a constructive read of evidence and the historical context from which these events emerge. Importantly, Nigeria further demonstrates how the ripples of conflict-related training programs are visibly entangled within democratic political culture and events. In this way we suggest how conflict resolution tools and capacities have become a part of Nigeria's democratic arsenal in its popular struggle toward democratic consolidation.

The elections were a greatly anticipated event as the first civilian handover of power between one democratically elected president to another. In the run-up, popular enthusiasm for the upcoming elections was widely expressed. Also, preparations included generous amounts of attention and support from the international community. Despite this popular enthusiasm and anticipation, clues that suggested underhanded motives began to appear. Nigeria's then-President Obasanjo had appointed a chairman of the election commission who was the target of much criticism by the media and other observers for "calculated incompetence" that persistently threatened to upset the scheduled election calendar. In spite of a number of logistical obstacles, a lack of materials, and a questionable voter's registrar, elections did take place as scheduled. They occurred despite a backdrop of skepticism and doubt on the part of a wide spectrum of observers. From ordinary voters to international observers, this skepticism endured through the lead-up and into the final Election Day. While elections did indeed take place, most election observers concluded it was a "fraudulent election," marked in most parts of the country by massive rigging, voter intimidation, and outright fabrication of many of the election results (Observer Reports of the European Union, National Democratic Institute (NDI), International Republican Institute (IRI), and Transition Monitoring Group (TMG)). In line with earlier suspicions, many also believe that President Obasanjo – having been thwarted from his third term ambitions in 2006 – planned on creating an election crisis in order to provide himself an excuse for annulling elections, declaring a state of emergency, and extending his stay in office past the constitutionally mandated end of his term in May 2007 (Pace, Personal Communication, 2007a; Senior Nigerian Political Leader, August

2007). From this view, the poor election preparations were part of a package of provocations aimed to set off a volatile public.

Other strange events, increasingly assumed to be staged, fuel these suspicions. In the volatile northern city of Kano, tensions rose when a prominent sheik was killed in a mosque while leading his congregation in prayers just days before the presidential election. In the midst of this tense moment, with religious leaders working hard to diffuse the threat of violent outbursts among their populations, a group of over 200 fighters, which the media claimed were "Nigerian Al Qaeda" suddenly appeared and attacked the outskirts of a northern city. Government troops returned fire, pursued the departing attackers, and claimed to have routed them, and yet not a single dead body of "Al Qaeda" has ever been produced, nor has a single member been captured. Meanwhile in the nation's capital of Abuja on the eve of the presidential elections, police "uncovered" an unmanned fuel tanker at the top of a hill overlooking the electoral commission's national office, with a rock on its gas pedal. This potential bomb, apparently aimed to blow up the electoral commission headquarters, instead swerved and hit a tree. Photos of this near-catastrophe were front-page news in all the major newspapers. How a vehicle as obtrusive as a fuel tanker managed to sneak past the manned security gates that stood before the top of this sloped driveway was a widely articulated question, revealing a popular skepticism about the truth of this story.

At the same time that there was much targeted public speculation and criticism about the motives and tactics of President Obasanjo, the behavior of the political class was also widely called into question. According to the ruling party and the national electoral commission, it was "those enemies of democracy" who were inhibiting their good intentions when it came to elections. Opposition cried foul to these claims. At the same time, scattered reports of election-related incidents of violence fueled *more* speculation that the opposition was aiming to derail the election process. In either scenario, Nigeria's elites, espousing the norms of neopatrimonial culture, were steering to control the outcome of events at the expense of democratic processes and an expectant public.

Yet, while Nigeria's neopatrimonial, Big Man culture was the underpinning of events that led to a fiasco election process and other conflict-provoking events, Nigerians remained calm. This was in spite of many predictions of an explosive response on the part of the Nigerian public. For civil society leaders, international election experts, and observers, Nigerians' seeming docility became a perplexing focus of frustration and disappointment and the subject of much speculation. At the same time, when many feared widespread protest would result in violence, others were hopeful that Nigerian civil society had reached a level of sophistication where this would not happen. Some held the hope that Africa's velvet revolution would begin here, as small pockets of Nigerians across the nation came out in nonviolent protest of their stolen mandate and the grossly flawed election process. As a result, development professionals and political officials speculated quietly among themselves about whether they may have overestimated the sophistication of Nigerian civil society and the degree to which democracy has taken root in the hearts and minds of most Nigerians.

A counterview holds that democratic values and aspirations were indeed alive and well during Nigeria's election events. This view highlights Nigerians' active refusal to be manipulated into violence and their rejection of the authoritarian, neopatrimonial inclinations of many Nigerian politicians and collaborators. This was accomplished primarily through a strong public conviction that elections, along with a democratic handover of power to a new administration, must take place. This view was strongly articulated by civil society activists and ordinary voters alike. During actual elections, although voter turnout was low to moderate, observers throughout the country reported lines of patient but insistent voters, many of whom waited hours in grueling heat for polls to open and to vote. While frustrations did result in outbreaks of violent protest, and some nonviolent protest also occurred, Nigeria did *not* see the anticipated velvet revolution or the explosion of riots and other forms of violent protest. While the 2007 general elections were grossly flawed, many Nigerians expressed their preference for a peaceful handover of power from one civilian president to another and underscored their support for the democratic process. This is a significant democratic milestone for Nigeria, despite how elections transpired and the fallout of issues that Nigeria must still grapple with as a result. Crucial to the achievement of this milestone was the Nigerian public. Far from apathetic, as many outside commentators concluded, a creative, constructive, collective logic was arguably in motion, refusing the bait of an irresponsible elite that sought to provoke them to violence for its own ends.

One particular event demonstrates the power and logic of Nigerian democratic discourse to inspire active resistance to events perceived to threaten democratic stability. It furthermore reveals the influence of conflict resolution efforts in shaping this active resistance. One day before the April 2007 governorship elections, a popular Islamic scholar, Sheikh Jaffar Adam, and two of his assistants were murdered by gunmen during morning prayers in a mosque in Kano state. The killing was widely believed to be politically motivated, stirring up religious turmoil in an effort to disrupt the next day's elections. Kano's history of religious-based violence prompted fears that this event would trigger riots, but this did not happen.

Conflict resolution responses to prior violent episodes in the region may have contributed to the overall calm public response to these provocations. In February of 2000, over 2,000 residents of Kaduna died in Muslim-Christian violence, after the Muslim governor implemented a version of the Shari'a criminal code in his state. Nigeria is evenly divided between Muslims and Christians, and the fault line runs right through the middle of Kaduna state. In the wake of this tragedy, conflict resolution activists moved to reconcile the two communities. An interfaith NGO led by a Muslim imam and a Christian pastor – Muhammad Ashafa and Pastor James Wuye – held a series of workshops with local faith leaders, politicians, and community associations. Their efforts produced several compromises among religious leaders that provided the framework used by the governor and the state legislature to pass the "Kaduna Compromise," in which only partial elements of the Shari'a code were implemented and additional protections for Christians were introduced.

Like the Kaduna Compromise they helped to broker, Imam Ashafa and Pastor Wuye themselves are "products" of earlier conflict resolution efforts in Kaduna. When talking about their transformative journey, they make distinct reference to conflict resolution workshops funded by both USAID and the US Institute of Peace (Pace, Personal Communication, April 2007b). Both men were leaders of militant groups involved in conflict between Muslims and Christians in Kaduna. Both suffered deep personal loss from violence and both are today at the forefront of initiatives to promote interfaith coexistence (see www.fltfilms.org.uk/imam.html). They continue to apply their conflict resolution training as they work to cultivate inter- and intra-faith networks throughout Nigeria's Muslim-Christian fault lines.

During a visit to Kano and Kaduna the week that the sheik was killed, Pace interviewed Imam Ashafa and Pastor Wuye, along with other leaders of the religious community. These leaders all emphasized the role of these religious networks in putting out messages of nonviolence for the coming election, and in response to the killing of the sheik. In an effort to avert violence, these leaders were actively "working their phones" to be in touch with their constituencies and other religious leaders. In the end, there were no violent outbreaks in Kano and Kaduna during the election period. As with most other parts of the country, these states remained relatively calm. It appears that religious leaders played an important role in inspiring this "mature" public behavior, as one religious leader labeled it. These same religious leaders have been informed, influenced, and inspired by conflict resolution training and workshops. At the same time that they worked to avert violence, they worked to protect democratic processes. These events are suggestive of how conflict-related training programs and the tools and capacities they impart may have become mainstreamed into the struggle for coexistence between Nigeria's Muslim and Christian populations, and how this struggle – together with these tools and capacities – may be entwined with the struggle toward democratic consolidation through democratic discourse and political culture.

CONCLUSION

Nigeria's recent general election was site to a monumental battle between neopatrimonial and democratic forces. Arguably, this battle took place most poignantly on the discursive plane, where societies struggle to define who they are. Social discourses are powerful because of their capacity to shape and reshape a sense of what is real and true. In the course of doing so, discursive realities provide the foundation of a society's ethical and moral logic about good and bad, right and wrong, and they form the everyday logic through which actions are taken. Without the discursive logic of voter's rights and accountable, legitimate leadership, Nigerians would have seen no point to standing in line for hours in the hot sun to vote, especially given a clear uncertainty about whether or not the polls would even open.

The millions of Nigerians who came out to vote waged a powerful challenge to the discursive logic of neopatrimonialism. Their actions were consistent with a multichannel understanding of how the sources of conflict permeate the fabric of a society. To challenge neopatrimonialism discursively – rather than targeting elite actors and institutions per se – is to challenge the internalized neopatrimonial values and norms of behavior that have seeped through every layer of Nigerian society. In the buildup and during elections, citizens who chose not to participate could be heard expressing a sense of futility about the election process, believing that Nigeria's Big Men keep a tight stranglehold on Nigerian political processes. Struggles between those cynical and hopeful about Nigerian democracy are evident from the level of the household all the way to the Presidential Villa, as Nigerians wrestle within themselves over the implications of these competing worldviews. One commentator made sense of this by saying: "There is a war going on right now over the soul of Nigeria" (Pace, Personal

Communication, Nigerian high official, 2007c). This discursive war is good news for democrats and conflict resolvers alike.

One of the important promises of democracy is that it increases a society's capacity to deal with conflict in constructive ways. It follows that through imagining and recreating the relationship between state and society, Nigerians are developing the means to transform their conflicts. These linkages have implications for practitioners and for our field. On the one hand, we examine calls to develop discursive sensibilities and to integrate these into our practices and, on the other hand, we examine more broadly the linkages between conflict resolution and the needs and demands for good governance. These two directions reveal two cutting edges of our field's development. On one hand is the call for third wave sensibilities and practices that can hear and engage creative, moral discourse, as well as a call for greater depth to our practice. To reach into the realm of discourse is to reach deep into processes of social transformation and peacebuilding, where Lederach tells us that the moral imagination resides. On the other hand, through developing stronger linkages between conflict resolution and governance, the span of our field is stretched. Through extending the theoretical and practical reach of our field to governance capacities, we scale up the scope of our potential and targeted impacts. As the case of Nigeria demonstrates, through increasing both the depth and the span of our work, we increase our potential for both effectiveness and relevance.

To suggest that democracy is strengthened as a result of transformative conflict resolution work raises important issues and questions for our field. Most obviously, it suggests the need for conflict resolution practitioners to think more deeply about the democratic impacts of their efforts. To more explicitly identify democratic and political development as an objective and outcome could appeal to donors with a duel interest in addressing conflict and building democracy. Further, these linkages offer an analytical approach to gauge the longer term impacts of conflict resolution efforts, so as to counteract growing donor frustrations with the seemingly undetectable evidence of success from such interventions. Evidence of increased peace in a nation as a result of workshops and other efforts has been difficult to prove in many cases, but growing democratic discourses and subsequent democracy-promoting behaviors among workshop participants can be verified more readily. The relationship between these variables is not, of course, incontestable, but the political and institutional impacts of conflict resolution on democracy building offer a rich array of data and subjects through which to trace this relationship. These unintended outcomes also indicate that conflict resolution efforts could perhaps have an even greater democratic impact if their connections to political cultural development are considered in a more strategic fashion. How can we plan our workshops and other interventions with an eye toward even greater democratic impacts *without* undermining or neglecting our priority goals of resolving the conflicts in question? Can we consciously introduce more complicated elements targeting democratic discourse into our workshops – perhaps even consciously encouraging participants to think discursively – without introducing a host of additional governance issues that will dilute the discussion and divert participants from the goals of peacemaking? Lastly, these findings raise a host of rich but thorny questions for theory building in conflict resolution. First and foremost, transformative models are a diverse bunch. Do some transformative models build democracy better than others? What is the best approach for testing them? And what about settlement-oriented approaches – approaches that seek an immediate deal as opposed to addressing the roots of the conflict? Do they also contribute to democratic discourse and inculcate democratic culture? If so, this would imply that every participant in a mediation, including the likes of Slobodan Milosevic and Franjo Tujman in Richard Holbrooke's 1995 Dayton effort, comes out more of a democrat. Although the evidence suggests he did not, we can say that gauging such impacts from settlement-oriented mediations are likely to be more difficult to measure than transformative ones, given the overall shorter timeframes and the lower priority that deeper psychosocial concerns are typically given in such interventions. The list of overlapping values between democratic political culture and conflict resolution workshops, found in the appendix, does not indicate which of these values is more important, if any. For instance, is respect for opposing views more important than principled compromise for democratic discourses and inculcating democratic culture? If there is such a hierarchy of impacts among these values, then we should give such elements greater priority in our workshop planning if we intend to promote democracy through our efforts.

Nigeria provides a provocative case study of these two cutting edges of our field because of the apparent convergence between creative discourses and democratic consolidation. To assume that this convergence has application elsewhere is to potentially over-privilege the promise that democratic processes hold for resolving social conflicts. While it is arguably true that democratic practices do provide the means for constructively dealing with conflicts, the whole point of third wave practices is to set aside ready-made answers and imported frameworks of analysis and to listen and respond to struggles over how meaning is being made within a particular context. By their very nature, third wave practices and discursive analysis are leery of overarching theories about what conflict transformation processes should look like. Rather, they aim to be grounded practices that emerge in response to local specificities. A rigorous discursive analysis of Nigerian political discourses would reveal a lot about Nigeria's competing worldviews not captured through the initial observations contained in this paper. Jane Docherty's study of the Branch Dividians and the FBI provides a useful model for such an analysis and demonstrates the value of what can be revealed through such a study. Rather than importing set goals, third wave sensibilities can serve to inform and shape conflict resolution outcomes and goals in response to a given context. Despite these important reservations, it can also be argued that third wave sensibilities enable the capacity to hear and respond to values that address the structural roots of conflict that are not being expressed through western frameworks of understanding. These include values that support justice systems or the fair distribution of resources. In other words, discursive sensibilities can correct the tendency to reduce democratic values to the western (typically free-market) expression of these values.

Overall, third wave sensibilities and democratic theories can both make important contributions to our practices. In particular, democratic theory may have impacts beyond just the immediate goals of the transformative processes utilized. Democratic development can benefit from our peace-building work, undermining neopatrimonialism, as it contributes to a more peaceful society. In the case of Nigeria, these goals can be enhanced through the engagement of discourses that seek to move the country in the direction of democracy. Elsewhere, discursive sensibilities can allow us to identify and more effectively engage a society's moral imagination as it seeks to creatively transform conflict situations. Conflict and democratic theory have much to learn from each other, which in turn can have important implications for policy and practice in both fields. Third wave practices as well have important implications for both how we do our work, and, when it comes to democracy, how we frame and pursue this as a goal. In both cases, the parameters of the field are being stretched into new and potentially promising directions.

REFERENCES

Agence France-Presse. (2004, 7 October). More than 53,000 Nigerians killed in three years of ethnic strife.

Avruch, K. (1998). *Culture and conflict resolution.* Washington, DC: USIP Press.

Bratton, M., & Van de Walle, N. (1994). Neopatrimonial regimes and political transitions in Africa. *World Politics*, *46*(4), 458.

Diamond, L. (1988). *Class, ethnicity, and democracy in Nigeria: The failure of the first republic.* Syracuse, NY: Syracuse University Press.

Diamond, L. (Ed.). (1994). *Political culture and democracy in developing countries.* Boulder, CO: Lynne Rienner Publishers.

Diamond, L., & McDonald, J. (1996). *Multi-track diplomacy: A systems approach to peace.* West Hartford, Conn.: Kumarian Press.

Docherty, S. J. (2001). *Learning the lessons from Waco: When the parties bring their gods to the negotiation table.* Syracuse, NY: Syracuse University Press.

FLT Film, London. A recent documentary film highlighting their journey from perpetrators of violence to instigators of peace is currently being screened within interfaith and coexistence circles throughout the world. www.fltfilms.org.uk/imam.html

Foucault, M. (1970). *The order of things.* New York, NY: Vintage Books.

Global Shell. http://www.shell.com/home/content/envirosoc-en/case_studies/shell_in_society/soc_nigeria_0504.html

Hill, B. J. (1982). An analysis of conflict resolution techniques: From problem-solving workshops to theory. *Journal of Conflict Resolution, 26*(1), 113–114.

Huntington, S. (1991). *The third wave: Democratization in the late twentieth century.* Norman, OK: Oklahoma UP.

Kew, D. (Forthcoming). Classrooms of democracy? Civil society, conflict resolution, and building democracy in Nigeria. Manuscript under contract with Syracuse University Press, subject to external review.

LeBaron, M. (2002). *Bridging troubled waters: Conflict resolution from the heart.* San Francisco, CA: Jossey-Bass.

Lederach, J. P. (2004). Keynote presentation delivered to the Association of Conflict Resolution 2004 Annual Conference.

Lederach, J. P. (1997). *Building peace: Sustainable reconciliation in divided societies.* Washington, DC: United States Institute of Peace Press.

Obasanjo, O., & Mabogunje, A. (Eds). (1992). *Elements of democracy.* Abeokuta: ALF Publications.

Observer reports of the European Union, NDI, IRI, and TMG.

Pace, M. (2007a). Personal Communication, interview with a senior Nigerian political leader, August 9, 2007; interview with the head of a leading election monitoring NGO, August 7, 2007. These comments echoed similar conclusions made about Obasanjo's intentions in the media and among politicians in ruling and opposition parties.

Pace, M. (2007b). From conversations with Pace, April 12, 2007 and repeated at a public address given for the event of a birthday celebration for Judy Asuni.

Pace, M. (2007c). Interview with Nigerian government high official describing the internal resistance to Yar'Adua's recent move to declare his assets.

Saunders, H. (1999). *A public peace process: Sustained dialogue to transform ethnic conflicts.* New York: St. Martin's Press.

Sklar, R. L. (1996). Toward a theory of developmental democracy. In: A. Leftwich (Ed.), *Democracy and development: Theory and practice.* Cambridge, MA: Polity Press.

Smith, D. J. (2007). *A culture of corruption: Everyday deception and popular discontent in Nigeria.* Princeton, NJ: Princeton University Press.

Tajfel, H., & Turner, J. C. (1986). The social identity theory of inter-group behavior. In: S. Worchel & L. W. Austin (Eds), *Psychology of intergroup relations*. Chicago, IL: Nelson-Hall.
USAID. USAID's democracy and governance budget and approach: http://www.usaid.gov/our_work/democracy_and_governance/
World Bank, see http://devdata.worldbank.org

APPENDIX. COMMON VALUES OF CONFLICT RESOLUTION METHODS AND DEMOCRATIC POLITICAL CULTURE

Conflict Transformation Value (Hill, 1982, pp. 113–114)	Associated Democratic Political Cultural Value (Diamond, 1988; Sklar, 1996; Obasanjo & Mabogunje, 1992)
Equality within the context of the negotiation	Equality before the law
Right of participants to discuss or not discuss issues as they see fit	Freedom of speech
Right of participants to participate, and to control the pace and direction of the discussion	Participation, self-determination
Notion that participants are representative of key interests and/or points of view within their communities, although they may or may not be formally elected or selected representatives	Representation
Parties will return to their communities after the workshop with whatever new perspectives were forged	Accountability, legitimacy
Responsive third-party assistance and oversight	Responsive governance and judicial recourse
Integrity and security of participants within the workshop and after they return to their respective communities	Freedom of person/right to life
Interest-based (basic human needs) negotiation, under the belief that individuals are the key unit of politics, and that they are rational (pursue their own self-interests)	Principled compromise, citizenship, and rationality

APPENDIX. (*Continued*).

Conflict Transformation Value (Hill, 1982, pp. 113–114)	Associated Democratic Political Cultural Value (Diamond, 1988; Sklar, 1996; Obasanjo & Mabogunje, 1992)
Respect for opposing points of view when expressed in a generally respectful manner; tolerance	Respect for "loyal opposition" parties, groups, and opinions; tolerance
Political conflict is inevitable, but violent, unjust outcomes are not; individuals are adaptable and capable of learning and/or modifying their behaviors	Nonviolent political competition; individuals are adaptable and capable of learning and/or modifying their behaviors

CONSTRUCTING A BASELINE UNDERSTANDING OF DEVELOPMENTAL TRENDS IN GRADUATE CONFLICT RESOLUTION PROGRAMS IN THE UNITED STATES

Brian D. Polkinghorn, Haleigh La Chance and Robert La Chance

ABSTRACT

The graduate field of conflict resolution is composed of an eclectic mix of programs, departments, centers, institutes, and think tanks which conduct a wide range of theory development, basic and applied research, service and teaching functions. Prior research on the graduate field has been limited mainly to either direct comparisons between a few graduate programs or summaries of progress made by program clusters, with the largest being a study of 18 programs. The composition and activities of the graduate field as a whole are not well understood, yet are hotly debated. This research attempts to fill part of this knowledge gap by specifically examining all known graduate programs in Peace Studies

Pushing the Boundaries: New Frontiers in Conflict Resolution and Collaboration
Research in Social Movements, Conflicts and Change, Volume 29, 233–265
Copyright © 2008 by Emerald Group Publishing Limited
All rights of reproduction in any form reserved
ISSN: 0163-786X/doi:10.1016/S0163-786X(08)29009-9

(PS), Alternative Dispute Resolution (ADR) and Conflict Resolution (CR) in the United States that award verifiable graduate credentials (i.e., certificates, masters, or doctoral degrees) in PS, ADR, or CR. *The participants in this study therefore constitute the entire known population (*N = *94) of graduate credential granting programs in the United States that collectively award roughly 164 certificate and/or degree options. The results of this study constitute a baseline from which to specifically examine and compare program factors including: program location, size, student composition, faculty credentials and areas of expertise. This study also examines program content, including curriculum content, design, and delivery, areas of training specialization; and those elements that participants report make their programs unique. These and other results provide a means of comparing program types and individual program innovations in regard to curriculum, service, research agendas, and areas of practice. The study concludes with participants' ideas on what program development trends we can expect to see in the coming years as well as where the academy is or is not meeting social needs.*

This chapter presents findings from a multiyear survey research study on the graduate field of "conflict resolution" in the United States. For the purposes of this article, "conflict resolution" describes a broad category of degree-granting graduate programs that focus a major portion of their mission and vision on conflict analysis, dispute resolution, and/or peace-building. More importantly, it refers to programs that have established their curriculum, theory development, research agendas, and, if present, faculty and student practice on dispute/conflict analysis, prevention, management, and/or transformation.

In addition, due to historical developments, we have divided the field into three interrelated groups of programs. The first and oldest group is composed of degree-granting Peace Studies (PS) programs, as well as some certificate programs in labor relations. The second group is a conglomerate of Conflict Resolution (CR) programs that generally cling together based on their common curricular foci and overall program mission. Some of these programs are direct evolutionary offshoots of PS programs, while others have deliberately distinguished themselves from PS programs. The third group is Alternative Dispute Resolution (ADR) programs. ADR is a general reference to decision-making or settlement options other than those used by courts (e.g., adjudication, litigation, and other forms of prosecution), such as negotiation and mediation. Not surprisingly, these programs are largely found in law schools. These three categories are not mutually exclusive, as quite a few CR programs consider themselves to be closely aligned to PS programs, while quite a few ADR programs are remarkably similar to CR programs. This "bleeding over" creates unique programs that borrow from many academic paradigms and traditions, which reinforces the flexible and evolutionary nature of the field. Common roots, similarities, and differences between PS, CR, and ADR programs will be discussed in the "History of the Field" and "The Present State of Wave Four" sections.

RATIONALE FOR THE STUDY

Over the years, a variety of studies have been done on developments within specific parts of the field. The literature is rich and encompasses many interrelated topics. Indeed, taken as a whole, it presents an interesting visual mosaic of the field. Specific research will be discussed in depth in the literature review.

What is lacking is a broad, empirical accounting of what constitutes the field in terms of its composition, size, breadth, or depth; locations within the academy; areas of specialization; or emerging areas of program development. In fact, some of the research forays into these topics are, by many authors' own accounts, based largely on good faith, educated guesswork, and are focused on a specific area within the field. A few scholars, such as Ron Fisher in an unpublished report, conducted detailed comparative analysis of three different types of graduate programs. William Warters' (1999) Delphi study of Hewlett-funded programs provides an excellent examination of survey results from 22 colleagues in graduate programs, while Timothy Hedeen and Pat Coy (1996) conducted a study of undergraduate CR programs. In addition, several directories list many types of programs at the undergraduate and graduate level, including those that teach courses but do not offer academic credentials. These include the Consortium on Peace Research, Education, and Development (COPRED) directory, the Peace and Justice Studies Association (PJSA) directory, and the listing available on www.CRinfo.org.

In short, there has been no research study whose end result attempts to present a panoramic view of the entire graduate field, or that provides a means of accounting that allows researchers to conduct across-the-board comparisons between programs. The current study provides a starting point from which to begin the long-term process of framing many of the great advances that have and will take place within our field. It also provides a starting point for other cross-comparison work on the rich and eclectic range of programs that constitute the field, both current programs and those being developed. Finally, it provides a greater understanding of the core elements that bind programs together into one field of study.

HISTORY OF THE FIELD

A review of literature on the history of the field's development and curriculum changes is necessary in order to properly ground the results of the research on current trends in graduate education and the future projections. CR, PS, and ADR graduate programs have an intriguing and interconnected history. Ironically, this history has become the focus of quite a few heated debates in recent years, as some individuals and programs jockey for the "pioneer" status position. Others debate where the field began, under what conditions it evolved, and which group or individual gets credit for discovering or leading this academic enterprise. This study indicates that there is enough good work and recognition to go around.

Some see PS, CR, and ADR as having completely distinct origins that have only recently merged, like streams into one river. However, that analogy works only if one fails to see the overlap between the three areas of the field. For this reason, we are adopting Carolyn Stephenson's wave development analogy to discuss the history of the field.[1]

Like waves reaching a beach, it is sometimes difficult to draw a clear line between one wave cresting and another one receding. Some of the developments in various parts of the field have occurred at the same time, and some have occurred in isolation. In other words, the wave analogy depicts motion that is impacted by past and current forces – a reality of the field. This "wave" history of the field also provides a context within which to place the current research, and from which to launch into a discussion on the future trends – both internal and external to the academy – that will shape the field in the coming years.

Historically, the three areas of the field (CR, PS, and ADR) have gone through several overlapping and intertwined, yet distinct, phases or waves of development. To some degree, each wave has been propelled by a combination of major social forces, including labor unrest, war, legal reform, religious teaching on day-to-day social responsibility and social justice, consumer demand, and changes within the academy itself. Some members of the field see these changes within a social movement framework, while others see them as a response to job market forces. Still others describe these changes as the melding of established disciplines that are making unique contributions to this multidisciplinary field of practice. Whatever the thinking behind how individuals frame the field, it is clear that these social dynamics form part of the root system that supports the present base. And, over time, numerous evolutionary branches have jutted off in new and unforeseen directions, giving way to unique specialized areas of theoretical development, new areas of basic and applied process research, and specialized forms of practice. Current graduate programs, whether knowingly or not, have been strongly influenced by these past social forces.

Wave One

The first wave of graduate education began soon after World War II, in the early 1950s, with the advent of PS as a discipline.[2] While it is difficult to pinpoint an exact beginning for any field, most scholars would agree that PS began during this first wave, as early as 1948, with the program at Manchester College (Dugan, 1989; Lopez, 1989; Stephenson, 1999). Dugan and Carey (1996) observe three developments to signify the "birth" of an academic discipline: the development of published journals, professional associations, and academic programs in colleges and universities (p. 85). The first journal specific to PS was the *Bulletin of Research Exchange on the Causes of War*, published in 1952 (Stephenson, 1999), followed by many other journals throughout the 1960s. Professional associations also began to develop at that time; the first PS conferences were held in the United States, Sweden, and the Netherlands (Stephenson, 1999).

These early programs were primarily research-oriented. In fact, many early researchers were mathematicians and quite a few of the doctoral degrees were in mathematics with an emphasis in peace research (Dugan, 1989). While such origins produced excellent theoretical foundations and empirical results, it offered little in the way of practical application to resolving current day-to-day conflicts. In a related vein, Princeton and Harvard University mathematicians, economists, and physicists began experimenting with game theory and rational choice models of decision-making, ranging from interpersonal cooperative-competition (e.g., the Nash equilibrium) to large-scale nuclear war simulations.

The after effects of World War II and the beginning of nuclear proliferation strongly impacted the theories taught and the research conducted during this time. Research was based on the beginning assumption that conflict, especially war, was negative (Poundstone, 1992). The primary focus was on the quick cessation of physical violence (or "negative peace," as it was later dubbed) and other means of de-escalation that led to détente, rather than the resolution of deep-rooted social problems. A decided split was developing at this early stage during the Cold War, which would begin to separate the field by research agenda, activism, and politics.

Throughout the 1960s, as this first wave of PS was drawing to a close, these assumptions about conflict began to change, especially as Galtung's (1969) theories of positive peace and structural violence gained momentum. The advent of the modern PS movement began as researchers came to embrace ideas such as the positive potential of conflict and Coser's (1964) functions of social conflict, and began studying the presence or absence of structural violence rather than more strictly defined armed conflicts (Wehr & Washburn, 1976).

While scholars in PS did make significant headway in developing the beginnings of a discipline, the field was still very broad and usually interdisciplinary (Lopez, 1989; Scott, 1984). Many universities, rather than starting an entirely new program, would draw courses and faculty from other departments, further straining already limited resources (Rank, 1989).

During this first wave, when PS dominated the academic scene, there were some early, limited forays into CR (Kriesberg, 2005). The University of Michigan started the Center for Research on Conflict Resolution in 1959. Though it was in operation for only 12 years, the Center and staff made significant headway in developing CR as a separate discipline from PS. While the goals of the Center were fairly conventional, its scope and ambition was broad, distinguishing it from other PS centers being developed in this same time period, such as those at Stanford and Northwestern.

Many of the problems plaguing the early CR "movement" in the academy in the late 1960s, and leading to the Center's closure in 1971, were the same problems that PS faced in the early 1990s. Harty and Modell (1991) theorize that "perhaps because the movement had emerged as a joint project of a large group of scholars from a variety of disciplines, and because it was always plagued with obstacles in the recruitment of the new young scholars, no single theoretical framework, set of variables, or terminology had gathered enough proponents to become the interdisciplinary theory of conflict resolution" (p. 735). Indeed, the lack of a canon or a coherent connection between theory development, research agendas, and their combined impact on practice is an ongoing challenge for the field.

Also during this first wave, law schools created a parallel track in making significant curriculum reform toward a focus on trial and appellate procedure. While ADR was not introduced at this time, the reform would set the groundwork for ADR to take root in legal education in the 1970s.

Wave Two

The second wave began in the early 1970s, following the height of the civil rights movement and the end of the Vietnam War, and continued through the mid-1980s. During this wave, the number of graduate programs in PS grew quickly, and there was also significant growth at the undergraduate level (Stephenson, 1989; Dugan & Carey, 1996). While scholars were unsure if the first wave of PS could truly justify its position as an independent academic discipline, by this second wave of development PS was most certainly an academic field (Lopez, 1985; Carey, 1980). Though many programs still lacked resources and institutional support, the rise of journals, professional organizations, and conferences offered a new legitimacy to the field.

During this wave, both curriculum and research shifted dramatically in response to significant cultural and societal changes. Though the nation was still embroiled in the Cold War, with the Vietnam War drawing to a close, curricula began focusing less on individual choices for peace and more on the practical application of peace research at the personal, group, national, and international levels.

The focus of research shifted, becoming more action-oriented or activist in nature rather than strictly empirical. Research and teaching began to focus more on current political conflicts, particularly nuclear disarmament, and processes of resolving conflict. Debate arose as to the role of peace research in a time of peace activism. Some scholars argued that research should be empirical and neutral; others argued that research should have an overt goal of ending violence. The balance between activism and neutrality is an issue still faced by academics and practitioners today.

Though the early efforts in CR, such as those at the University of Michigan described above, tapered off or ended in the late 1960s, some level of development did continue between that time and the late 1980s when CR really began to flourish as its own field. A growing number of universities began offering isolated courses in mediation and negotiation skills, teaching students to put those skills to use in resolving disputes in their own daily lives (Kriesberg, 2005).

Also during the second wave, in the 1970s and 1980s, ADR courses began appearing in law school curricula. Some of this rise can be attributed to a growing social awareness of nonviolence and the growing legitimacy of PS in liberal arts education. Sacks (1984) argues that this dual development (both social and academic) created not only the demand for ADR courses, but also the pedagogical basis for its continued growth. Another contributing factor was the introduction of moot courts, trial skills, and theories from other disciplines into law school curricula. In 1981, the University of Massachusetts Amherst opened the Mediation Project, which allowed law students to practice ADR techniques and by the mid-1980s, several law programs had an ADR focus in their curricula or research.

Wave Three

The third wave of PS began as a massive expansion in the mid-1980s. In fact, "the campuses that did not offer at least some type of peace studies courses were few and far between" (Lopez, 1989, pp. 67). That expansion quickly gave way to the development of CR graduate programs as an independent academic field, with significant changes in curricula, philosophy, and pedagogy, with the first program at George Mason University in 1983 (the Institute for Conflict Analysis and Resolution, or ICAR) in 1983. As CR programs continued to expand through the late 1980s and early 1990s, the growth of PS programs slowed. The shift to CR was so drastic that some scholars no longer considered PS a field on its own but rather a subset of CR (Rank, 1989; Katz, 1989), though many would still argue that PS stands alone.

Literature on PS throughout the late 1970s to the mid-1980s expressed concern over perceived vulnerabilities in the field. Several areas were noted in which programs must evolve to keep up with changing political and academic trends, in order to stay relevant as a field throughout the 1990s. The primary concern seemed to be a lack of structure, both at the University level (Wehr & Washburn, 1976) and in the field as a whole (Lopez, 1985). At the University level, programs were often interdisciplinary, lacking any real framework in terms of learning goals, curriculum, and courses: "Too often, PS programs are mere amalgams of existing courses with a new title affixed" (Wehr & Washburn, 1976, p. 48). At a broader level, there was again very little framework delineating the boundaries or goals of the field or the curriculum. Leaders in the field, when writing about goals, were split between educating students about causes and consequences of conflict and actively training students to be advocates for peace, similar to the research split described above.

CR programs grew rapidly beginning in the mid-1980s.[3] In Paul Wehr's survey of 500 programs, he found that 294 offered at least one course in CR (Warters, 1999).[4] Within another ten years, those course offerings had rapidly evolved into undergraduate and graduate programs (Warters, 1999). Much of the quick development was a result of a growing social movement in nonviolence and political changes toward the end of the Cold War (Kriesberg, 2005). During the 1980s, the Hewlett Foundation began to directly support CR programs, especially in the area of theory development. Support of "Hewlett Programs," as they came to be known, lasted until the early 2000s.

CR programs differ significantly from the earlier PS programs. Generally speaking, the primary difference is CR's mix of practical experience, skill-building and theory, as compared to PS' almost exclusive focus on theory and research. At least in part, the academic shift from PS to CR can be ascribed to the differences between PS' primarily theory-based curriculum and the experiential learning component present in most CR programs. For instance, in 1987, Dr. James Laue and the Conflict Clinic, Inc. joined George Mason University's ICAR program and, with some student involvement, provided mediation services to the community, a practical concept that has been duplicated across the country. This difference is crucial, since "few colleges or universities have successfully incorporated an experiential component into their [Peace Studies] academic programs" (Bing, 1989, p. 48).

A second difference between the two subfields can be seen in the research each produces. While PS was originally quantitative in nature and provided statistics on the effects of and reasons for war, CR research typically focuses on specific, isolated conflicts and offers practical solutions for resolution.

As CR courses and programs were gaining momentum, the curriculum typically focused on domestic conflicts and the dispute resolution skills necessary to effectively intervene. While some theory and research was taught in most programs, this usually took second place to skills training in mediation, arbitration, and negotiation. Even though labor relations programs had been in existence for many decades, it now became one of the primary areas in which students began putting these practices to use. Indeed, many of the CR organizations today evolved directly out of labor relations departments' attempts to professionalize their own field. It wasn't until CR scholars began taking those theories and skills that were working so well in labor relations and applying them to international crises, a concept which PS was only approaching in a theoretical manner, did CR really take off.

Also during wave three, the ADR movement in law schools grew rapidly. In 1986, 43 law schools reportedly offered ADR courses, representing almost a quarter of law schools at the time. Just three years later, 550 ADR courses were being offered in 174 law schools. By 1997, that number had jumped to 714 courses in approximately 177 law schools, representing most US law schools at that time (Moberly, 1998).

The emergence of ADR courses, clinics, and degree-granting programs in law schools came not only from increasing social and academic interest in ADR as described above, but also from the growing use of it in the civil legal system. Many states encourage or require some form of ADR for civil cases, especially in family courts. Another factor is the general public's ongoing dissatisfaction with the administration of justice and the American Bar Association's willingness to make adjustments. As negotiation and mediation became common means of dispute resolution in the justice system, and as lawyers began using these skills in their daily practice, the number of ADR courses offered in law schools increased.

This growth was also facilitated by a small group of pioneering law faculty who wanted to reinforce a holistic approach to client needs. They reinvigorated the curriculum, all the way down to first-year doctrinal courses, by focusing on the breadth of needs-based services that the traditional, adversarial approach to legal education had largely ignored.

During this wave, there was some debate as to how ADR should be incorporated into law school curricula. The Missouri Plan, articulated by Leonard Riskin in 1984, attempted to challenge the adversarial bias of the standard curriculum by incorporating the skills, theories, and practices of ADR into each of the first-year courses. While students did learn the processes of mediation, arbitration, and negotiation, the plan was not as successful as hoped when it came to shifting the focus of students from adversarial trial law to a more needs-based approach (Pipkin, 1998). Other attempts to introduce ADR into the curriculum include adding basic theories to specific first-year courses (i.e., civil procedure and basic legal skills) (O'Neill, 1998; Vaughn, 1998) or dedicating third-year courses to skills training in ADR processes (Moberly, 1984).

WAVE FOUR: RESEARCH ON THE CURRENT STATE OF THE FIELD

The field has again undergone significant changes in curriculum, focus, and mission due to social forces, planting us firmly within a fourth wave of development. The results of this study present a clear understanding of this current state of the field. Before going directly to the results, a brief discussion on the background and research methods used in the study is in order. For those wishing to skip this section and go directly to the results, please see "The Present State of Wave Four" section below.

This study began in 1995 when the Department of Conflict Analysis and Resolution (DCAR) at Nova Southeastern University was taking part in the University's reaccreditation process. An external reviewer asked the department how it compared to similar programs in terms of curricular and programmatic specialization, faculty competencies and qualifications, postgraduate student job placement, and a variety of other key program indicators. A review of the literature revealed no studies that addressed these questions. We therefore undertook a series of studies, one internal and the other an external study that canvassed the field, to meet the reviewer's request for information (Polkinghorn, 1998; Polkinghorn & Chenail, 2000). Our departmental colleague, William Warters, conducted his 1999 Delphi study on Hewlett Programs during this time period. These studies provided us with evidence that the field was in the midst of rapid change in curriculum, program focus, and program location throughout a wide range of schools and colleges. In 2001, the project took on added significance when a request was made to begin preliminary work on a master's program, this time at Salisbury University. A more complex research tool and protocol was developed and administered to all graduate programs in the United States.

RESEARCH TOOLS, PROTOCOL, AND SUBJECTS

The current study builds on these previous inquiries. More than ten years in the making, this research has continuously tracked the development of the field that now constitutes 94 US-based graduate CR programs. Members of the research team have been able to personally visit most of the programs. From our survey research, semistructured interviews and analysis of written documents, Web pages, and literature reviews, the following profile is made possible.

The primary research instrument is an extensive survey, completed over the phone or in person with program directors or key faculty members, usually requiring at least an hour.[5] Questions fell into six areas of inquiry: history of the program, location within the University or College structure, demographics on the students and faculty, curriculum delivery, content and areas of specialization, and the uniqueness of each program.

These extensive surveys completed with each program comprise the primary research data.[6] In addition, a separate survey was developed and administered to students in four graduate programs as supplemental information. Two programs completed it online and two chose to administer it face to face. We chose the programs for student interviews based on four criteria: (1) if the program director was amenable to it, (2) how long the program had been in operation, (3) geographical location, and (4) the area or field in which the program is located (i.e., law, international, domestic/social, or PS). Finally, after the data had been collected on 94 programs and a preliminary analysis of the data had been conducted, the last step was to interview the second group of nearly 30 senior academics.[7] Most of these individuals have had a major impact on the field and provided a wide range of thoughts. Their perspective on the history of the field, in relation to the findings from the study, has provided critical insight into the identification of long-term trends. Their participation has also helped make sense of some of the history behind a few of the data trends. For that we are grateful.

PROGRAM SELECTION

The threshold criteria for a program to be included in the study are straightforward. The "entity" (i.e., school, department, institute, center) housing the program must have the authority to award academic credentials (certificates or degrees), which must appear and be verified on a student's official university or college transcript. This means that the institution where the program is located has granted the program permission to confer graduate certificates or degrees, including Master of Arts, Master of Science, Master of Divinity, Juris Doctorate, Master of Law, MBA, or Doctorate.

In order for the program to be included in this study, the degree must be directly in CR (recall this can be labeled conflict management, conflict transformation, PS, peace and justice, ADR or a host of other related names) or the degree must have a verifiable designation, concentration or track in CR. So, for instance, a doctoral program in Sociology or International Relations with a concentration in CR would be included.

The certificate awarded by programs must be in an area of CR, PS, or ADR, and/or specialized areas such as environmental, international, or cross-cultural CR. If the program does not offer a degree option, the certificate must appear on student transcripts.

account for this decline. Survey participants were asked two important questions: What forces helped shape the field? Where do you want to see your program evolve? Three answers were the most common. First, the program simply morphed from PS to CR, although some ADR directors disagree. Second, the politicization of "peace" has forced a shift in program focus and goals. Third, the market for skilled practitioners and researchers in both the public and private sector led to a surge of CR programs.

The next generation of programs in CR, found more often in traditional liberal arts departments and university public outreach programs, has come to comprise more than half of the graduate programs in the field (58%). This is followed by the relative latecomer – ADR law school programs (24%), and finally PS programs (14%).

Likewise, the sudden shift from PS programs being alone in the field to a surge in the development of CR and ADR programs produced a configuration of clusters. Taking a closer look at the CR and ADR clusters, a detectable, but more gradual, corresponding shift in the types of institutions that house these programs is evident. They moved from being overwhelmingly private to an increasingly more in public institutions. However, about two-thirds of programs, roughly 62%, are still found in private universities, with another 37% found in public universities and one percent in a public/private university.[9]

Recall that Fig. 1 shows a high concentration of programs (about 34%) in the northeast, stretching through the Ohio Valley. These programs are primarily housed in private institutions that typically have some affiliation to a religious organization. They are also older and more firmly established.

Taking this as a starting point, it is interesting to note the relationship between the specific type of program (PS, CR, and ADR) and the type of institution housing it. From interviews with participants, we hypothesized that both PS and CR programs would be more likely to be found in private institutions, but for different reasons. It is reasonable to think that PS programs are more likely to be found in institutions with affiliations to religious organizations that are without exception private. On the other hand, we think CR programs are often found in private institutions, since private institutions have the ability to quickly respond to emerging areas of research and practice, as well as changes in the job market, by moving into new areas of study. It is also worth noting that, overall, 80% of the schools and colleges that house CR programs are in both research and teaching institutions with student populations of less than 17,500. Because ADR programs are largely in law schools, and therefore subject to American Bar Association rules and consistent market trends, we did not think there

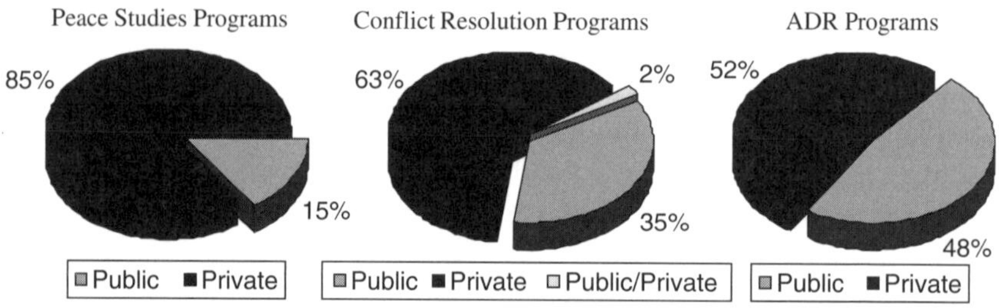

Fig. 4. Breakdown of Programs by Private or Public Institution.

would be much difference in degree-granting program locations. However, we hypothesized that certificate programs, which are less subject to outside requirements, would more likely be found in private law schools. Indeed, certificates are found in nine private and six public institutions. All three suppositions were correct. Not surprisingly, Fig. 4 indicates that a majority of PS programs are found in private institutions (85%), as are CR programs (63%), while not surprisingly, ADR programs are fairly well distributed between private (52%) and public (48%) institutions.

Program Evolution

Because of its eclectic composition, as well as the various developmental paths many programs have taken, the story of the evolution of field is complex. It certainly isn't as clear as the development of fields like psychology or sociology. The evolution of individual programs is similarly complex. For instance, most of the master's programs in the field have evolved from one of the following sources: individual classes or a concentration in CR (36%); a graduate certificate program (18%); a PS undergraduate program, although not necessarily a degree-granting program (9%); an undergraduate program other than PS such as criminology or sociology (13%); or a university outreach or service center (9%). A majority of master's programs that evolved from certificate programs have kept their certificate programs running. In fact, it is rare for a program to begin by offering a master's degree and later add a certificate option. When this does happen, these certificates are for areas of specialization (e.g., environmental, cross-cultural, international, or peace education). Of the master's degrees offered throughout the field, most are Master of Arts, followed by Master of Science, Master of Law or Master of Divinity degrees. The remaining master's programs (e.g., MBA) offer various concentrations and minor options.

The doctoral programs within the field have evolved in a much more predictable and structured manner. Only two programs in the United States offer a doctorate directly in the field. The oldest is the doctoral program in Conflict Analysis and Resolution at George Mason University. The other is the doctoral program in Conflict Analysis and Dispute Resolution at Nova Southeastern University. Two master's programs in the southeast United States plan to launch doctoral programs in CR over the next two years. (Worldwide, there are 14 programs that offer a doctorate directly in the field.) Of the 11 remaining doctoral programs found in the United States, eight are degrees in a variety of disciplines with a concentration in CR and one with a concentration in PS. The remaining two offer minors in the field (one CR and one PS).

For the most part, the development of CR graduate programs appears to be largely an internal graduate school evolutionary phenomenon. There seems to be less impact from external sources such as undergraduate programs, certificate programs, or the morphing of centers or institutes into degree-granting programs. Overall, the field is dominated by master's programs; this is highly predictable and expected. A master's degree acts as the first level of entrée into most fields of practice, while doctoral programs are reserved for specialized work, usually of a research nature. This heavy weight toward master's programs in the field mimics the structure of most social science and humanities disciplines across the nation. The wide range of offerings and requirements for certificate programs is too lengthy to describe in detail here.

Program Curriculum Content

From the previous studies, we found that for the purposes of data analysis, it made sense to divide the curriculum into five tracks: practice, theory, process, research, and substantive areas of specialization. Using the five tracks, an across-the-board examination shows which courses are taught and which are required. This provides the first real opportunity to examine which areas students are being trained.

Two-thirds of the programs (66%) offer field practice or supervised practicum course work, while two-fifths of the programs (39%) require a practicum. A total of 73 programs (78%) offer theory courses, and of those, 68% indicate that these are specific to their program. Sixty percent of programs indicate that theory courses are required. This means that roughly three-fifths of the programs have theory and practice built into their curriculum.

Eighty-five percent of programs offer processes courses (i.e., mediation, negotiation, arbitration, facilitation) and 70% require them. Half of the programs offer at least one research methods course. However, of those, (using cross tabulation) we note that 23% offer research courses taught by a different department that may not be specifically geared to the program and 56% of programs do not require research courses at all. See Table 2 for more details.

Specialization Courses

Specialization courses are offered in most programs (81%). Often there is a direct correlation between the program size (number of faculty and students) and age of the program to the number of specialized courses offered. About one quarter (24%) of the programs offer both required and elective specialized courses. Offering a variety of specialized courses is an indicator of multiple credentialing options. Indeed, one program in the Western United States offers multiple degrees and numerous areas of certification, and delivers more than a dozen specialized courses. Another program, this time on the East coast, offers a master's degree and more than 40 specialized one-credit skills courses annually. There are roughly six programs that have a large full-time and part-time faculty who offer between 30 and 52 distinct courses in CR annually. These programs do not represent the average faculty size or curriculum profile.

Participants' listing of specialized area courses offers an insight into the many areas of theory, research, and practice that are currently being taught within their program. When asked to list specialized courses, participants easily provide 365 responses that constitute 54 distinct areas of curricular specialization. Table 3 provides more detail.

In order to understand the vastness of the curriculum across the field, a quick examination of these specialization areas is necessary. The above topics can be broken down into three broad categories: practice and process areas of specialization, substance areas of specialization, and specialized areas of study.

The practice and process area of specialization is fairly straightforward. These courses primarily focus on training in various traditional and hybrid conflict intervention processes. Some programs teach strictly third-party process and human factor skills, making use of various training models and role-plays, while others blend theory and research to analyze processes, such as organizational conflict or dispute system design.

Table 2. Program Content.

Course Types	Offered		Program Specific[a]		Required		Electives	
	Yes (*n*, %)	No (*n*, %)	Yes (*n*, %)	No (*n*, %)	Yes (*n*, %)	No (*n*, %)	Yes (*n*, %)	No (*n*, %)
Field practice/practicum	62, 66.0	25, 26.6	50, 53.2	37 39.4	37, 39.4	50, 53.2	28, 29.8	59, 62.8
Internship	45, 47.9	41, 43.6	36, 38.3	51, 54.3	22, 23.4	65, 69.1	23, 24.5	64, 68.1
Theories	73, 77.7	13, 13.8	64, 68.1	22, 23.4	56, 59.6	30, 31.9	25, 26.6	61, 64.9
CR/ADR processes	80, 85.1	5, 5.3	70, 74.5	15, 16.0	66, 70.2	19, 20.2	29, 30.9	56, 59.6
Specialized content areas	76, 80.9	10, 10.6	65, 69.1	21, 22.3	36, 38.3	50, 53.2	57, 60.6	29, 30.9
Research methods	47, 50.0	39, 41.5	36, 38.3	50, 53.2	33, 35.1	53, 56.4	17, 18.1	69, 73.4

Note: There is overlap between courses that are offered as an elective or as a required course. This is due to the particular program offering multiple courses within that particular category (in the case of internships or practicum, the program in question allows students to receive additional credits as an elective after required course work is completed).

[a]By program specific, we are referring to those courses taught directly in the program. A research methods course, for example, that is offered to all humanities students would not be considered program specific, while a research methods course directly in PS or CR would.

Table 3. Areas of Curricular Specialization.

Responses	Frequencies	Percentage
Negotiations (including collective bargaining)	20	5.5
International conflict	19	5.2
Cross/multicultural conflict issues	19	5.2
Environmental issues and conflict resolution (including ecology and sustainable development)	17	4.7
Mediation	16	4.4
Organizational conflict analysis and dispute systems design	15	4.1
Religion and conflict dynamics	15	4.1
Law and applications of conflict resolution	14	3.8
Workplace and/or organizational conflict dynamics	13	3.6
Peace Studies (including peace-building and nonviolence)	12	3.3
Restorative justice and/or trauma reconciliation	11	3.0
Family conflicts (including domestic violence)	10	2.7
War & conflict (including mass violence & genocide)	10	2.7
Gender and conflict studies	9	2.5
Ethnicity and conflict studies	8	2.2
Justice studies	8	2.2
Human rights and civil rights	8	2.2
Conflict analysis and intervention (including processes)	8	2.2
Communication and conflict theory	7	1.9
Arbitration	7	1.9
Conflict management	7	1.9
Business applications of conflict resolution	6	1.6
Race and conflict studies	6	1.6
Conflict Resolution processes in schools (peer mediation)	6	1.6
Facilitation	6	1.6
Public policy and administration (including urban planning)	6	1.6
Ethics (legal, business, religious)	6	1.6
Large-group conflict resolution theories & processes (including group dynamics)	6	1.6
Identity-based conflict	5	1.4
Trial advocacy (including appellate advocacy)	5	1.4
Violence & nonviolence studies (including social movements)	5	1.4
Decision-making and leadership	5	1.4
Conflict transformation	4	1.1
Economics	4	1.1
Education and conflict resolution	4	1.1
Social work and human services	4	1.1
Violence prevention	3	0.8
Counseling	3	0.8
Psychology	3	0.8
Interpersonal relations and conflict resolution	3	0.8
Political science and political conflict studies	3	0.8
Critical thinking	2	0.5
Community conflict	2	0.5
Middle-east conflict studies	2	0.5

Table 3. *(Continued)*

Responses	Frequencies	Percentage
Theories of conflict resolution	2	0.5
Class-based conflict studies (rank and privilege)	2	0.5
Parish leadership and youth ministry	2	0.5
Behavior science (including behavior modification)	2	0.5
Criminology	1	0.3
Human resources systems	1	0.3
Healthcare	1	0.3
Faith -based conflict resolution education	1	0.3
Western cosmology	1	0.3
Skills training	1	0.3
Total	365	100.0

Substance areas of specialization refer to specific social, political, legal, or other topics of inquiry. This category includes such topics as social movements, peace and justice, philosophy, international conflict, peace education, legal, violence and violence prevention, service provision, and religion and spirituality. In terms of curriculum development trends, it is highly likely that this category will show the most growth in the years to come as faculty and students explore more areas of specialized theory development and practical applications.

The final category mentioned is specialized areas of study, specifically those curricular areas that programs report as being directly tied to their specializations. In many cases, these courses are the primary self-reported source of what makes the programs unique within the field and correspond to faculty expertise and research. Such areas include gender, ethnicity, class or racial conflict studies, theory development, or conflict in specific regions, such as the Middle East.

Fieldwide Comparison of Credit Requirements

Certificates

Many certificate programs are attached to either a master's or a law degree program. Therefore, some of the required courses in these programs can count toward both the certificate and degree completion. Overall, there is a wide variation in credit requirements for these certificate programs. Most require between 9 and 15 semester hour credits. A completely different strategy for programs is to offer a variety of stand-alone certificate programs without offering a degree option. These programs tend to require between 15 and 21 semester credits and may, for example, require students take a prescribed number of courses from an approved list. Courses range from general conflict courses to areas of substantive specialization within the degree program such as international, cross-cultural, PS, environmental, social movements or education.

Master's Degrees

There is a huge range of credit requirements across master's degree programs. On the lower end of the scale, master's programs with "minors" or concentrations in the field require require between 9 and 18 semester credits. semester credits. Note that this is for the minor or concentration, not the overall degree. On the other end of the spectrum are divinity and seminary programs that traditionally require up to 63 semester credit hours.

If all programs are weighted evenly on a semester credit system (rather than quarter or trimester credits), the average program requires 36 credits. The range of credits is 9 to 63 semester credit hours, with the outliers mentioned above.

Doctorates

Credit requirements for four of the 13 doctoral programs are unavailable.[10] The two doctoral programs in directly CR require 57 and 82 credits. The program with the fewer credit requirements also, remarkably, provides the most curricular flexibility, allowing students to take courses in a variety of departments. The other program is more structured and allows far fewer opportunities to take courses in other departments or schools. One of the doctoral programs that offers a minor requires 15 semester credits. The remaining doctoral programs are those with a concentration in CR, and these have a wide variation in credit requirements. Some of the concentrations require a substantial percentage of the coursework in CR, and it is a highly emphasized part of the program.

Examining credit requirements is one means of making direct comparison between programs. It provides some sense of the number of courses (though not content) necessary for each program. With some programs requiring only a few core courses and others more than 20, it is reasonable to think there might be differences in regard to expertise and preparedness in graduates.

Fieldwide Comparison of Program Faculty

The strength of a program is related to the quality of and, to a lesser degree, the number of faculty. Inquiries were made about the number of full-time, part-time, and adjunct faculty[11] and how many faculty members possess terminal degrees. This measures one aspect of program strength, and the level of commitment by the host institution and/or student demand.

The number of program faculty is often a function of program growth and corresponding institutional support. However, some programs are heavily reliant on part-time faculty, who are either borrowed from other programs or are hired adjuncts. Few programs have more than ten full-time faculty. In fact, 90% of the programs have nine or fewer full-time faculty and 80% of programs have nine or fewer part-time faculty members. Excluding those programs not reporting on faculty numbers ($n = 14$), programs have a mean of just over four full-time faculty members and close to five part-time faculty members. Sixty-nine percent of the programs operate between a range of one and ten total faculty members. Any programs that have ten or more full-time faculty members are considered outliers. In order to better understand the relationship between full-time and part-time faculty member composition, each "dot" in Fig. 5 represents the count of part-time and full-time faculty for each program reporting. Note,

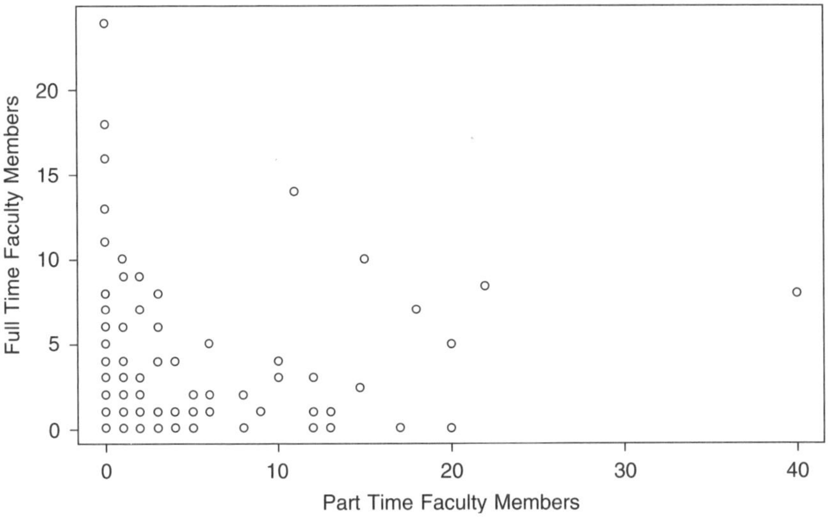

Fig. 5. Scatter Plot of Part-Time to Full-Time Program Faculty.

however, that some programs have the same configuration of faculty (e.g., three part-time and two full-time faculty members), so each dot may represent more than one program.

Fig. 5 shows the results of a comparison between full-time (vertical) to part-time (horizontal) faculty for each program.[12] Recall that 14 did not report on their faculty composition; additionally, at least 14 programs have no part-time faculty and at least 11 programs have no full-time faculty. Most programs cluster within the bottom-left portion of the chart, with fewer than 20 faculty members (ten part-time and ten full-time faculty members). A few programs are worth pointing out. On the far left side of the chart, notice that five "elite" programs have no part-time faculty (zero on the horizontal axis), but anywhere from 13 to 24 full-time faculty. These are typically law school programs or long-established master's or doctoral programs. Likewise, in the middle of the chart and to the far right of the chart, there are programs that have anywhere from 5 to 15 full-time faculty, along with 13 to 40 part-time faculty. Upon further investigation of programs with a large part-time faculty, it appears that they usually operate summer institutes, winter terms, and weekend courses (in an "institute" format) that are largely taught by part-time and/or adjunct or visiting faculty. This means that student demand and delivery method impact the size of the faculty.

The study also examines the credentials of the faculty, as that too is a measure of program strength. Not shown here is the breakdown between program types and terminal degrees. PS programs have the smallest number of faculty and ADR programs have the largest number. Likewise, nearly 100% of ADR programs report that their faculty possess a terminal degree (JD or higher), while in CR and PS programs, the range varies widely from 0% to 100% of faculty possessing terminal degrees. Across the board, 82% of programs report that all of their full-time faculty members possess terminal degrees, while 58% of programs report that all their part-time faculty members possess terminal degrees.

Program Resources

Another area of inquiry relating to program development and growth examines resource allocation and external funding. Programs reported on their use of grants for research, service provision, or other projects. They also reported on whether or not they are seeking long-term endowments, since some programs exist solely on those funds; in fact, three programs

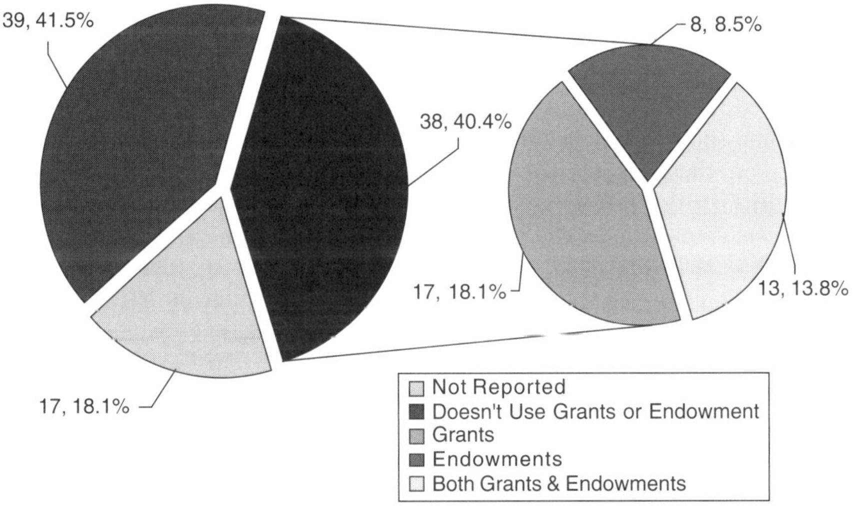

Fig. 6. Programs Reporting Grants and Endowments Activity.

have endowments of more than $50 million. Examining a program's grant activity is not only an indication of research and scholarship activity, but is also a sign of the addition of value to the program. It also is an indirect indicator of increased resources. Likewise, evidence of endowment activity is one indication of program stability, at least in economic terms. Programs that seek grants and endowments may be more strategically situated to weather major shifts in the field. Yet, Fig. 6 indicates that more than two-fifths of the programs undertake none of these activities. Eighteen percent of programs seek grant activities while 14% have or are working on an endowment campaign. The remaining 9% seek both grant and endowment opportunities. Not shown in Fig. 6 is the difference between programs in public versus private institutions that seek either grants or endowments. Programs in private colleges or universities are more likely to seek grants and endowments than those in public institutions.

WHAT DOES THE FUTURE HOLD?

The following discussion comes from a variety of sources. First, participants – mostly programs' directors or key faculty members – were asked: "In an ideal scenario, where you have unlimited resources to work with, what would you do to build the ideal graduate program?" Second, students were asked: "What do you seek in a CR graduate program?" And third, additional information was obtained from the senior leaders of the field, who were interviewed after the first analytical run of the data.

Faculty members indicate that in order for a program to thrive it needs increased scholarships and resources for students (10%), more faculty dedicated to the direct support of the program (9%), funding for more hands-on experiences (7%), and more specialized courses or tracks (5%). They also express a desire for visiting faculty, endowed chairs to bring in notable professors to help anchor their programs, a lecture series to draw public attention and more professional development opportunities for faculty and students.

For the most part, students want superior faculty, in particular those with firm credentials directly in the field rather than those migrating from other disciplines. They also want faculty who actually practice conflict intervention, or that train or otherwise engage in activities that are taught in the courses. To a lesser extent, but still prominent on the list, are faculty who generate new knowledge, whether in the form of new practice or process innovations, theoretical development, or basic and applied research endeavors. In other words, students are demanding competent teachers who practice and produce scholarship to be their mentors and guides.

The senior faculty, quite a few of whom have been professional leaders in the field for more than 50 years, uniformly look at the big picture in terms of how to connect all the various current trends into a coherent whole.

PROJECTING INTO THE FUTURE

The above analysis covers only a few notable highlights of the data collected. The future trends for the field, outlined below, are based on the analysis of all the empirical data gathered, taken together with information from the three groups mentioned above and within the context of the field's historical development.

From that, we can project some trends that will impact the direction of our current wave four of the field. These partially include:

1. There will be more meshing of specific professional occupations (i.e., law, business, counseling, and even accounting) and public administration with CR/ADR to produce greater specialization expertise. Expect to see more dual-degree programs.

2. Programs will begin to adjust their development plans, in part, based on employer and social demands. Currently, this is not happening fast enough.
3. The 94 programs in this study are spread out in more than 20 different departments and schools. (Note: Some clusters of CR programs are found more frequently in Sociology and Social Psychology than in, for example, History departments.) This wide-ranging growth will continue, but may eventually be impacted in terms of where growth will occur by the influence of megaprograms, i.e., heavily endowed programs with large faculties that draw students from around the world or have broad curricular offerings.
4. In order to meet student demand and employer needs, expect more programs to form consortiums to offer extracurricular opportunities for such things as specialized field work, practice courses, training programs (certificate sharing), and overseas experiences that increase student marketability.
5. Following national trends, expect to see more programs offering a variety of flexible curriculum delivery formats. (The current breakdown includes 18.9% online courses, 24.2% distance learning, and 35.8% weekend formats.) While there is ongoing debate about online instruction in a practice-oriented field, some programs will not have the resources to resist and will even make this a hallmark of their program. Programs with more resources will be in a position to either resist or adapt to some parts of this trend.
6. We can learn from past mistakes. There are three common reasons why programs fail. First, curriculum planning is based on what the faculty want or can teach, rather than students' desire or what various sectors of the job market demand. Second, too narrow a specialization may create students who are experts in one aspect of the field, but are otherwise unmarketable. And third, there is lack of institutional commitment, competent faculty, or internal program leadership. Also, universities should avoid the temptation to build a program around one faculty member. Programs that strike a balance in program focus, perhaps theory to practice, and that build institutional support will do well.
7. Expect process-heavy programs to emphasize courses that focus on marketable skills including training, workshop development, and other consultative skills.
8. Rather than "reinventing the wheel," programs are beginning to adopt courses from other established programs and modifying them to meet

their own program focus. This is indicative of an emerging core curricular canon across the field.

9. There will be more growth in specialization certificates as a value-added component to existing degree programs.
10. In the law school arena, we can expect to see more growth in certificate programs but less in degree-granting programs.
11. More graduate programs will continue the trend of beginning to branch into undergraduate instruction by offering certificate programs or minors; however, fewer will develop undergraduate majors.

CONCLUSION

This article shows some of the many across-the-field comparisons that can be made between the 94 programs that constitute our field. This study is the first to thoroughly account for the composition of the field in these areas, and provides both a grounding and the means to further track the evolution of the field. The study describes a field in the process of formation with few across-the-board stated guidelines on such things as curriculum content and focus, practice competencies, an established canon or coherent framework for theory development, or overarching research agendas. The study also indicates that there are clustered sets of standard requirements for faculty credentials (especially in law and doctoral programs) but, in other parts, the standards are not based on any particular set criteria other than that of the host institution.

Additionally, it shows that the field is growing in a flexible manner, which strengthens the scope and utility of the field from theoretical, research, and especially practical ends. The findings also indicate that the field is composed of programs that provide an exceptionally rich variation in course content, program specializations, areas of practice, and, to lesser extent, variation in degree requirements. As the field continues to develop, we will experience further growing pains (tension) between old and new programs as developments in theory, practice, and new orientations challenge older, established program agendas. This can be based to some degree on generational differences, ideological shifts, political preferences, and substantive similarities creating new "forces" within the field, along with a sense of growing urgency to try and establish some sense of common goals. This should be the basis of the fifth wave. In other words, we are exactly where we should be.

NOTES

1. Stephenson's wave analogy was developed and published in 1989 as a basis to examine the development of PS programs, and is broken up into distinct waves based on identifiable social influences. CR and ADR programs, though coming to the group much later than PS, were impacted by the same social forces and can fit within Stephenson's wave analogy. Additionally, these waves correspond to Lopez's (1989) eras of development.

2. PS was obviously researched and practiced prior to the 1950s, most notably by Wright and Richardson. This date refers to the advent of PS as a recognized field of study within higher education.

3. Although the field has certainly grown, based on prior research there seems to be little verifiable agreement on exactly what parts have grown and by how much. Many reports mention a rough number of programs that exist (anywhere between 50 and 500) without providing either a research protocol or other direct evidence to back up the assertion. Some rely on the opinion of experts in the field, while others rely on preexisting program lists such as COPRED. Many articles that touch on this subject also fail to mention the exact parameters used to decide which programs are included in the program count. Is it the number of colleges or universities that periodically teach a course or two in peace and conflict? Is it an actual program on the campus regardless of whether or not it teaches any courses at all? Does the program provide a minor, a major, or graduate credentials in PS? Without answers to these questions, we can't begin to examine the inner workings of individual programs, much less be able much less be able to make across-the-board comparisons.

4. This study predominantly focuses on undergraduate programs.

5. In many instances, it was left to a staff member to assist us by gathering more detailed data. Because of this, we were able to collect more data from some programs such as annual reports; curriculum projects; lists of key course materials including books, course exercises, and syllabi; brochures and other promotional materials; and, remarkably, four book manuscripts (all of which have been published).

6. Only highlighted results will be presented in this article. The full data analysis is too detailed to be included here but will be available in a forthcoming book.

7. This group is composed of senior program directors and leading theoreticians, researchers, and practitioners in PS, CR, and ADR programs.

8. Table 1 provides the self-reported answers to the question: "Where is your program housed?" Many smaller universities clump all graduate programs into a "Graduate School" rather than having separate schools or colleges for each discipline. Almost a quarter of the programs reside in the "School of Arts and Humanities," as expected, but programs are also housed in other locations such as the "School of Management" or the "Public Resources Department," a growing and interesting trend.

9. Statistics indicate that there are more private universities than public in the United States.

10. These four doctoral programs have no set credit requirements for entering students. Instead, a personal program is built with faculty advisors and/or the

dissertation committee. Therefore, a comparison of their requirements to those programs with set requirements is inapplicable.

11. Part-time faculty members are those who teach more than one course and/or have additional responsibilities in the program, including faculty from other departments; adjunct faculty typically teach one course and have no extra responsibilities in the program.

12. As noted, a few programs reported no full-time or part-time faculty. Each course was taught by faculty members who work full time in another department.

REFERENCES

Bing, A. I. (1989). Peace studies as experiential learning. *The Annals of the American Academy of Political and Social Science*, *504*, 48–60.

Carey, D. (1980). A discipline development model for peace studies. *Peace And Change: A Journal of Peace Research*, *6*, 90–98.

Coser, L. (1964). *The functions of social conflict*. New York, NY: Free Press.

Dugan, M. A. (1989). Peace studies at the graduate level. *The Annals of the American Academy of Political and Social Science*, *504*, 72–79.

Dugan, M. A., & Carey, D. (1996). Toward a definition of peace studies. In: R. J. Burns & R. Aspeslagh (Eds), *Three decades of peace education around the world: an anthology*. New York, NY: Garland Publishing.

Galtung, J. (1969). Violence, peace, and peace research. *Journal of Peace Research*, *6*, 167–191.

Harty, M., & Modell, J. (1991). The first conflict resolution movement, 1956–1971: An attempt to institutionalize applied interdisciplinary social science. *The Journal of Conflict Resolution*, *35*, 720–758.

Hedeen, T., & Coy, P. G. (1996). Please don't tell me you teach that book: Charting the state of peace and conflict studies undergraduate degree programs in the US and Canada. Paper presented at the annual meeting of the International Peace Research Association, Brisbane, Australia, 8–12 July.

Katz, N. H. (1989). Conflict resolution and peace studies. *The Annals of the American Academy of Political and Social Science*, *504*, 14–21.

Kriesberg, L. (2005). Contemporary conflict resolution applications.. In: C. A. Croker, F. O. Hampson & P. R. Aall (Eds), *Turbulent peace*. Washington, DC: United States Institute for Peace Press.

Lopez, G. A. (1985). A university peace studies curriculum for the 1990s. *Journal of Peace Research*, *22*, 117–128.

Lopez, G. A. (1989). Trends in college curricula and programs. *The Annals of the American Academy of Political and Social Science*, *504*, 61–71.

Moberly, R. B. (1984). A pedagogy for negotiation. *Journal of Legal Education*, *34*, 315–325.

Moberly, R. B. (1998). Introduction: Dispute resolution in the law school curriculum: Opportunities and challenges. *Florida Law Review*, *50*, 583–588.

O'Neill, K. (1998). Adding an alternative dispute resolution (ADR) perspective to a traditional legal writing course. *Florida Law Review*, *50*, 709–718.

Pipkin, R. M. (1998). Teaching dispute resolution in the first year of law school: An evaluation of the program at the University of Missouri-Columbia. *Florida Law Review*, *50*, 609–666.

Polkinghorn, B. D. (1998). An examination of current trends in graduate alternative dispute resolution programs. *Alternative*, *16*(8), 115–121.

Polkinghorn, B. D., & Chenail, R. (2000). *Current trends in graduate ADR programs: Preliminary findings*. Conflict Management in Higher Education Report, Vol. 1, No. 2.

Poundstone, W. (1992). *Prisoner's dilemma*. New York, NY: Anchor Books.

Rank, C. (1989). The interdisciplinary challenge of peace studies. In: D. C. Thomas & M. T. Klare (Eds), *Peace and world order studies: A curriculum guide* (5th ed.). Boulder, CO: Westview Press.

Sacks, A. M. (1984). Legal education and the changing role of lawyers in dispute resolution. *Journal of Legal Education*, *34*, 237–244.

Scott, P. D. (1984). Introductory essay. In: B. J. Wein (Ed.), *Peace and world order studies: A curriculum guide* (4th ed.). New York, NY: World Policy Institute.

Stephenson, C. M. (1989). The evolution of peace studies. In: D. C. Thomas & M. T. Klare (Eds), *Peace and world order studies: A curriculum guide* (5th ed.). Boulder, CO: Westview Press.

Stephenson, C. M. (1999). Peace studies, overview. In: L. Kurtz (Ed.), *Encyclopedia of violence, peace and conflict* (vol. 2). San Diego, CA: Academic Press.

Vaughn, L. B. (1998). Integrating alternative dispute resolution (ADR) into the curriculum at the University of Washington School of Law: A report and reflections. *Florida Law Review*, *50*, 679–707.

Warters, W. C. (1999). Graduate studies in dispute resolution: A Delphi study of the field's present and future. *Online Journal of Peace and Conflict Resolution*, *2*, 1–14.

Wehr, P. E., & Washburn, M. A. (1976). *Peace and world order systems: Teaching and research*. Beverly Hills, CA: Sage.

REFLECTION AND COMMENTARY: CONFLICT RESOLUTION CONTEXTS AND IMPLICATIONS

Louis Kriesberg

My reflections, which are spurred by the analytical chapters in this volume, are of two kinds. First, I discuss the theoretical and empirical contexts within which the diverse analyses presented earlier may be usefully viewed. Then I consider the implications that these chapters have for conflict resolution theory, teaching, and practice.

CONTEXTS

The variety of the subjects examined in the preceding chapters reflects the vastness of the contemporary conflict resolution field. To discuss contexts that encompass them requires relying on basic conflict processes. I have chosen such processes related to three fundamental matters: (1) that conflicts are interlocked with each other, (2) that various kinds of inducements are used in conflicts, and (3) that how conflicts are waged and settled is related to conflict outcomes.

Every conflict is linked to many other conflicts (Simmel, 1955). This should be evident when we recognize that conflicts are about many different issues among a wide array of adversaries and are usually conducted without violence or even without inflicting great injury or threatening to do so.

Pushing the Boundaries: New Frontiers in Conflict Resolution and Collaboration
Research in Social Movements, Conflicts and Change, Volume 29, 267–279
Copyright © 2008 by Emerald Group Publishing Limited
All rights of reproduction in any form reserved
ISSN: 0163-786X/doi:10.1016/S0163-786X(08)29010-5

Disagreements between persons and groups within each adversary in a fight are inevitable, often about the goals or the means of struggle against an external enemy. Furthermore, each adversary generally has conflicts with several antagonists, conflicts that vary in salience and intensity. Often, as well, a conflict is nested within more extensive conflicts, as was the case when the Cold War overlaid regional wars.

The complexities of such conflict linkages often hamper de-escalation and conflict settlement endeavors and too often greatly contribute to escalating and prolonging destructive conflicts. This is particularly the case when the conflicts are superimposed upon each other or nested within each other, while cross-cutting conflicts tend to inhibit conflict escalation (Dahrendorf, 1959). Furthermore, internal and external developments shift the salience of these conflicts for each party in a fight, which then affects the trajectory of each conflict. At times and in some ways, therefore, changes in one conflict can exacerbate a related conflict, but may also interrupt and de-escalate another conflict (Kriesberg, 1980).

Several of the cases analyzed in this volume illustrate various ways the linkages among conflicts affect the course of each conflict. For example, Keles analyzes how the Croat-Muslim conflicts at the local and Bosnian levels affect each other. In the village of Dolina they seem to reinforce each other. However, in some other settings, perhaps in an urban area, there may be local resistance to the escalation-inducing efforts from the top.

Indeed, in the process of conflict de-escalation, settlement, and reconciliation some of the initial steps are often taken by particular persons and organizations from opposing sides, although they do not represent those sides in their entirety. Thus, Funk-Unrau analyzes the series of reconciliation steps taken by particular Canadian churches in relations with aboriginal communities. Boudreau and Polkinghorn's analysis of Onondaga County Sheriff John Dillon handing over the remains of a centuries old Indian woman to Lee Lyons, brother of Onondaga Indian Chief Oren Lyons, also illustrates a conflict-transforming event embedded within the context of a much broader conflict. In a sense, even the dialogue experiences examined by Pincock deal with dormant interpersonal conflicts that exist in a larger contentious setting.

Thinking about these cases in the context of the interlocking quality of conflicts raises several broad questions. For example, in what ways do actions in a microlevel conflict affect the larger conflict of which it is a part? In what ways does the conflict at the macro-level constrain or nullify the actions at the microlevel? How do changes in the parameters of a macro-conflict change relations at the microlevel and generate conflict escalation, or de-escalation? Thus, the breakup of Yugoslavia or the Soviet Union, or the secession of Bangladesh from Pakistan may shift the relative power of ethnic and religious groups within the component parts, generating violent conflicts (Roy, 1994).

These observations may seem far away from issues relating to leadership and collaborative governance, which are examined in Getha-Taylor's chapter. The distance may seem too great to leap across, but I will suggest how bridges might allow us to cross over the gap, and discover that the traffic crossing the bridges is generally advantageous. On one side, conflict resolution concepts and practices may contribute to understanding how collaborative leadership works and could be done better. On the other side of the bridge, knowledge about the practices of collaborative governance can contribute to designing stable and mutually beneficial conflict-management systems.

A few other connections are worth noting here. Leaders generally must relate inwardly to followers, constituents, subordinates, and also outwardly in representing the organization or unit in which they hold offices. Furthermore, the boundaries of any organization are permeable and in some sense incorporate nonmembers: groups fulfilling essential functions, such as funders and consumers. All these relationships have conflicting as well as cooperative aspects and potentialities. The practice of collaborative governance entails using many of the methods of conflict resolution. The analysis by Pace and Kew demonstrates the considerable overlap between democratic and conflict resolution procedures within nongovernmental civic organizations. To a significant degree, that may also be true for collaborative governance.

The choice of inducements used in conflicts is the second contextual matter that I discuss. It is a premise in the field of conflict resolution that conflicts can be waged with little or no violence nor even painful coercion. As Polkinghorn, La Chance, and La Chance indicate in their account of the development of the field, peace studies has contributed to this recognition. Many of the cases in this volume illuminate the important role of ideas, of persuasion, of collaborative engagement, and of mutual benefits in conducting and resolving conflicts. This is clearly the case in the mobilization of each side in a struggle and the way in which a fight is waged. For example, Keles examines the role of intellectuals and religious leaders in arousing Serbs' sense of grievance toward other groups.

Noncoercive inducements are also evident in struggles, among members of one side in a fight, about waging an external conflict. As Coy, Maney, and Woehrle demonstrate, references to religious beliefs used to justify making war may also be used by peace movement organizations to oppose war. Persuasive arguments directed at members of an opposing side are often made by using values and beliefs that are held in common. Such appeals directed at opponents also convey the idea that the adversaries share important values and beliefs, which may mitigate the intensity of a conflict and hasten its ending (Kriesberg, 2007). Leaders of the civil rights struggle in the United States during the 1950s and 1960s effectively made claims in the name of American ideals of equal opportunity for all Americans. Feminist leaders in the women's movement of the 1970s, among other appeals, made effective claims by referring to the value of equal opportunity and also of personal liberty, for men as well as women, to be free of rigid sex roles.

These appeals may be influential because they help reframe a conflict so that it is more amendable to transformation. The issues in contention may change and one side may become transformed, which is recognized by the opponent and a new relationship can emerge. The gradual transformation of the Cold War, the changes in Soviet leaders' thinking, and then the sudden ending of the Cold War in 1989 illustrate many ways in which conflict resolution principles operate, even when they are not self-consciously being followed. For example, this was the case for track-two undertakings, mutual security reassurances, and high level political and cultural exchanges during the Cold War (Evangelista, 1999; Kriesberg, 1992; Leffler, 2007).

Explicit recognition of earlier losses and hurts is helpful when conflicts begin to de-escalate or when adversaries move to overcome the legacies of their past. Apologies and expressions of regret are not easily made or accepted, particularly when those earlier injuries are highly asymmetrical. Funk-Unrau's analysis demonstrates that many steps may be needed to establish a more equitable relationship, requiring a series of interactions between members of the formerly antagonistic sides. Statements are made by some members of one camp, to which members of the other camp respond, resulting in new formulations, and this goes on with many iterations between various groups. Boudreau and Polkinghorn discuss such exchanges as epistemic encounters, as members of each side redefine themselves and the others. They also illustrate, by describing the exchanges between Sheriff Dillon and the Onondaga Indians, how words are more convincing when accompanied by actions that are consistent with sentiments that may otherwise not be credible. Importantly, the persuasive inducements are most effective when they are part of two-way communications or, in Buber's terms, when they fashion an I-thou rather than an I-other relationship.

Interestingly, none of the analytic chapters examine the use of violence or other forms of direct physical coercion. This is consistent with the general avoidance of the matter by workers in the conflict resolution field. Violence is generally decried by conflict resolvers, but relatively little attention is given to different kinds and degrees of violence and how it is combined with various kinds of nonviolent or noncoercive inducements. Yet, some degree of violence or threat of violence is pervasive in social life, and usually deemed legitimate by the perpetrators.

The final contextual matter to be discussed here is the processes by which conflicts are conducted and settled. As discussed in the chapter by Polkinghorn, LaChance, and LaChance, attention to the process of resolving conflicts has been an important theme in the field, particularly in the influential ADR component. This has included an emphasis on mediation conducted by outsiders acting in a neutral fashion. The realities of asymmetry in conflicts, the multiplicity of partisan groups, and the dynamics of contention in large-scale conflicts limit the relevance of such processes. Structural factors shape the course of a conflict and its outcome. Yet, the process has some influence.

Many workers in the field emphasize the processes in conflict de-escalation, settlement, and transformation. Quite interestingly, some of the chapters show how the characteristics of the agents in a change process affect the consequences of the change endeavors. Thus, as the chapters by Hemmer and by Pace and Kew demonstrate, the internal democratic nature of civil society organizations contributes to democratizing the larger society. That is, how conflicts are managed internally affects external relations. The use of elementary conflict resolution methods internally contributes to effective external collaboration; similarly, Getha-Taylor notes, collaborative leadership entails listening.

The chapters generally recognize that the de-escalation and transformation of a conflict is not a matter of a single event, but occurs over an extended period of time through interactions among the parties to the conflict (Lederach, 1997). At many levels, face-to-face encounters are important and have impact, as noted in Pincock's study of dialogue experiences.

The language used in interactions and appeals help define who the adversaries are and what methods each may justifiably use against the other. This is evident in Keles' analysis of the Serb-Muslim conflict in Bosnia and the reliance on ethno-nationalist terms that involve ascribed identities that are immutable. Demonizing the enemy justifies recourse to the most destructive methods to attack the subhuman or demonic evil doers. The resulting extreme conduct often becomes self-defeating and counterproductive.

In the current conflict between al Qaeda and the United States, extreme tactics have been used and justified by leading figures in al Qaeda and in the U.S. government. This is notably associated with the readiness to attack people who are generally viewed as noncombatants. For example, a senior al Qaeda operative, Ramzi bin al-Shibh, defended the 9/11 attacks, arguing: "They are legally legitimate, because they are committed against a country at war with us, and the people in that country are combatants" (Cullison, 2004). With such license provided by some interpretations of Islam, al Qaeda attacks in Iraq after the U.S. invasion there became widespread and included attacks on Muslim civilians. This has proved counterproductive and support for bin Laden and al Qaeda has plummeted. Former defenders of such violence, like Sayyid Imam al-Sharif, known as Dr. Fadl, argue that such killing is wrong and a failure and they now oppose (Wright, 2008). Leaders of the U.S. government, in response to the 9/11 attacks, declared war on terrorism, which legitimated extreme actions that also have been counterproductive in many ways (Mueller, 2006). The morality, effectiveness, and legality of various means of waging conflict are argued in many forums, within opposing sides and in other settings; the arguments help constrain some ways of fighting and in other circumstances contribute to the commission of what are later recognized as atrocities.

IMPLICATIONS

The findings and interpretations made in the analytic chapters have a great variety of implications in three areas of the contemporary conflict resolution field: (1) theory and research, (2) teaching and training, and (3) practice and consultation.

The findings in the preceding analytic chapters raise many questions and challenges for conflict resolution theory and research. The attention in many chapters to language in various aspects of waging and resolving conflicts should prompt more work about what affects the choice of words and what are the words' impacts upon those expressing them as well as upon their intended targets. Broad questions worth trying to answer include the following: To what extent is the choice of words shaped by actions, which are determined by various factors, and chosen to justify and explain these actions? Conversely, to what extent is the choice of words affected by prevailing kinds of discourse or elaborations by political leaders and public intellectuals, where that selection then affects the choice of actions? What are the likely responses by the recipients of various expressions of claims and justifications? What are the effects on target groups of various kinds of coercion when accompanied by different linguistic packaging?

Given the significance of language in internal mobilization and in efforts to convey persuasive information to members of opposing groups, more attention to the content of such efforts is warranted. It would be interesting to examine the content of appeals to shared values and beliefs related to national security or to ethno-national well-being, as Coy, Maney, and Woehrle do regarding religious appeals in their chapter. The possible self-limiting effects of such usage for making major changes in internal and external relations might be considered. On the other hand, trying to supersede major elementary shared values and beliefs may result in being disregarded and engaging in futile undertakings. The forms of rhetoric that convey inclusivity are particularly important in transforming and resolving conflicts (Vivian, 2009).

Another set of implications for theory and research suggested by several analytic chapters is the relationship between micro and macro levels of conflict. More attention should be given to the multitude of micro conflicts as they relate to a major, overarching conflict, and we should not expect that any single microlevel conflict will greatly impact the macro conflict in which it is embedded. Attention should also be given to the linkages between different conflict levels. These linkages include not only the persons who play in-between roles, which exist in all hierarchal organizations, but also persons who act as quasi mediators between antagonistic collectivities (Kriesberg, 1995).

Finally, the preceding chapters prompt me to stress the value of research. Theorizing about the interplay among different ways of conducting and resolving conflicts, which should be increased. Such work might examine the sequencing of different combinations of inducements by different parties in conflicts. Thus, attention should be given to various forms of violence different parties employ, or threaten to employ, in conjunction with various reassurances and cooperative undertakings they also provide. For example, the carefully limited "armed struggle" that the African National Congress conducted in South Africa was conducted alongside many nonviolent campaigns, reassurances, and expressions of shared identities that helped achieve a negotiated transformation of that country.

The analytic chapters also have implications for teaching and training in the field of conflict resolution. The chapters confirm the importance of experience in learning about conflict resolution. People learn how to practice and to teach the skills of conflict resolution by exercising the skills in simulations, in everyday interactions, and in collaboration with experienced conflict resolvers. Even the ideas of conflict resolution are better understood with such experience. People also learn from the experience of others; for instance, the stories related in these chapters exemplify the great variety of ways that conflicts become transformed and resolved and how practices can be instituted to prevent destructive escalations.

The analyses of episodes of destructive conflict escalations in the former Yugoslavia, of reconciliation in Canada and in Syracuse, and the analyses of societal transformation in Nigeria also provide insights about what might be done elsewhere. Since how a conflict is waged and transformed depends greatly on the conduct of the adversaries, the possible role conflict resolvers might play as consultants to one side deserves a great deal more attention. Lessons from various localities can be quite instructive, even recognizing the uniqueness of every conflict. Learning about peacemaking efforts from a country's past can provide people in that society new insights about what might be done currently in their country and in other countries. For example, Americans could better appreciate issues about reconciliation and recovery from civil wars, terrorism, and oppression by reexamining events in the South following the Civil War.

The field of conflict resolution should advance on two legs: theory and practice. At times, however, many workers in the field hop along on one leg. Indeed, joining the two together is difficult since the two areas of endeavor are worked to some degree by different people coming out of different traditions. Yet they depend on each other in many ways. As the chapter by Polkinghorn, LaChance, and LaChance shows, nearly all academic programs have both a theory course and an experiential-skills course. In actuality, however, I think the teaching of the two domains does not integrate them well. Often the theory is very general, with little specification of different kinds of conflicts, of the diverse roles of participants in conflicts, of various stages in the course of a conflict, and of other conflict dimensions. Teaching about the practice of conflict resolution often gives an idealized view of mediation and negotiation and is limited to interpersonal skills.

Broadening the teaching of practice to include consultation and policy making for persons in various roles may help to integrate theory and practice. Teaching might well draw more from research about actual practices in conducting and resolving conflicts, including what is done by practitioners who do not identify with or think they are using contemporary conflict resolution methods. In addition, the research about different levels of conflict and the relations between micro and macro conflicts and their resolution would help in integrating theory and practice.

Finally, I make some observations about the implications of the preceding chapters for the practice of conflict resolution. Several chapters examine how language is used in escalating and de-escalating conflicts, which is relevant for many areas of practice. Insights about the way words communicate inclusivity or exclusivity can be useful in communicating clearly and effectively. Such insights can help intermediaries be more effective with the advice they offer partisans and can help mediators in constructing formulas for settlement.

The forms of interaction discussed – for example in the chapter by Boudreau and Polkinghorn – also suggests ways that partisans can transform their relationship. The chapters relating to civil society organizations and the connections between small local fights and large national conflicts suggest strategies that may help build organizations and linkages that would foster democratization, recovery, and justice.

Societal and global developments and events shape changes in the conflict resolution field, particularly in the extent and forms of practice. Applications of conflict resolution ideas have expanded greatly in recent decades. This is attributable to the convergence of many factors. More and more people have been trained to do conflict resolution, as indicated by the growth of graduate degree-granting programs and also certificate programs in conjunction with professional degrees in law, international relations, and public administration. This growth reflects recognition of its utility in various aspects of social life. It also is due to an expansion of employment possibilities in governmental and nongovernmental organizations that are engaged in conflict resolution work. This is particularly the case in helping to settle civil wars and other large-scale conflicts, to recover from the disasters of war, and to sustain agreements that may be reached.

These developments are related to the remarkable decline in international and civil wars beginning around 1990. By many measures, the incidence of wars and the numbers killed in them have declined (Human Security Report Project, 2008). To some degree these declines are a result of the end of the Cold War in 1989, which contributed to settling the protracted wars in Central America, southern Africa, and elsewhere that the Cold War had perpetuated. The end of the Cold War also enabled the UN, the Organization for Security and Cooperation in Europe (OSCE), and other international organizations to more effectively intervene in highly conflicted situations and to help avert or end hostilities. This was notably the case in limiting and containing the conflicts in Eastern Europe and the former Soviet Union. Significantly, too, violent conflicts have more often been ended by negotiated agreements rather than by unilateral impositions.

Many other global developments contribute to the decline in wars and to the assistance of conflict resolution applications to those declines.

International norms supporting human rights have become stronger and more widespread and awareness of human rights violations has increased. The obligation to intervene and stop gross violations of human rights, under certain conditions, overcomes adherence to conventions of national sovereignty. In addition, technological and normative developments have helped foster an increase in the numbers of and activity levels of transnational nongovernmental organizations. For a variety of reasons they are playing a larger role in post-violent situations.

CONCLUSIONS

The field of conflict resolution has made immense progress during the last few decades. Workers in the field are conducting essential research, elaborating theory, building institutions, and applying its ideas in an increasing number of countries around the world. Most importantly, application of conflict resolution ideas have contributed to many peaceful accomplishments.

Despite these achievements, conflict resolvers face many challenges. Some of the challenges arise from the very growth of the field and others from new circumstances in the world. In these conclusions, I discuss these challenges and possible ways of meeting them, drawing on the analytical chapters and the implications I have noted earlier.

The increasing recognition of the value of a conflict resolution perspective results in more and more applications of it in new situations. Workers in the field, therefore for sometimes venture into tasks with which they have limited relevant experience or knowledge. The process of learning what to do by stumbling along and trying plausible but inappropriate strategies is likely to be unsatisfactory to everyone. Conflict resolvers facing such risks generally try to read and "ask around" to pick up relevant information. The internet and the extended networks it makes possible can be very helpful in exchanging information; this should be more institutionalized with workers in the field reporting their experience in using conflict resolution methods in new settings. Much research and theory-building about the consequences of specific kinds of actions in diverse circumstances would also be helpful. Indeed, to some degree this is happening, particularly relating to societal transitions away from authoritarian rule, the establishment of new forms of governance, and societal recovery from mass violence (Pouligny, Chesterman, & Schnabel, 2007).

Another set of issues relates to the funds that support conflict resolution work. Too often, assistance is provided only in immediate crises for short time periods. Recovering from destructive conflicts and building new relations and institutions that will sustain a new mutually acceptable accommodation takes a long time and also committed persons working diligently to accomplish those changes. Sometimes powerful external governments have the interest and the resources to make that possible. More often that is not the case and essential tasks are undertaken only in a limited way by international governmental organizations and by transnational nongovernmental organizations.

A significant development is that much conflict resolution, advocacy, and humanitarian work by nongovernmental organizations is increasingly funded by governments. Between 1995 and 2001, public financing of development NGOs doubled, and it is estimated that in Europe and in the United States, 50% of NGO activities are financed by public sources (Fischer, 2006). Such outsourcing by governments raises the possibility that NGOs implement state-determined policies. Some transnational NGOs decline to accept any government funding to remain, and to be seen as, independent. These NGOs raise money from private donors and foundations, which preserves varying levels of autonomy. Nevertheless, transnational NGOs generally are based around and the leadership generally drawn from economically developed Western countries. As the chapters by Pace and Kew and by Hemmer indicate, that may hamper some of the democracy-assisting work the NGO leadership seeks. Funding from a wider range of sources for locally-based NGOs would be beneficial.

Theory building, research, teaching, and practice should be more closely integrated with each other than is presently the case. Each of these areas of conflict resolution work would thereby be advanced. For example, assessments of the consequences of conflict resolution applications might well be done on a larger scale, including a greater variety of applications over longer time periods. In addition, more attention might well be given to the quality of and sustainability of conflict terminations as related to various processes in reaching an ending, and particular attention should be given to considering the role of asymmetries in conflicts that affect the ways they are ended. Integration of the various areas of conflict resolution work can be enhanced by conflict resolution teaching and training of conflict partisans as well as would-be intermediaries and of people in mid-careers as well as persons preparing to begin their careers.

Finally, I comment on a few recent global circumstances that pose new kinds of challenges for conflict resolution work. In recent years, religiosity and religious fundamentalism have become more salient among Christians, Hindus, Jews, and Muslims. Within some groups this has contributed to forming exclusive identities and claims of moral superiority; in some circumstances this is elaborated by denigrating others who are allegedly threatening their existence. Such formulations then can be used to justify resorting to extreme war-fighting methods, including attacking noncombatants. The hatreds and fears resulting from recourse to suicide bombings and other such tactics certainly makes applying conflict resolution approaches seem impossible. Nevertheless, they may be relevant among supporters of the perpetrators of such actions who are more pragmatic about the tactics, and have other values and interests inconsistent with committing such actions. Moreover, engaging in extreme violence often is carried too far and becomes counterproductive and discredited.

Another new development is the United States becoming the sole superpower. That opens up the possibility that the country's leaders believe that they cannot be checked and that their preferences are not to be questioned because of the superiority that comes with being the sole superpower. The international conduct of the U.S. government during the administration of President George W. Bush seems to have been affected by such illusions. The extraordinary ambitions about remaking countries, relying on military power, and acting unilaterally created conditions that in many regards were hostile to conflict resolution applications.

The evident failures of overreaching goals and reliance on military power and extreme violence can contribute to people in many countries turning toward methods of waging and transforming conflicts that are more in accord with the conflict resolution perspective. Indeed, there are many global changes that propel such movement in the long run. The changes include growing global interdependence and integration, strengthening norms protective of human rights, and expanding civil society organizations. Furthermore, increasing challenges such as those related to global warming, resource constraints, and inequalities require collaborative global problem-solving endeavors.

REFERENCES

Cullison, A. (2004). Inside Al-Qaeda's hard drive. *The Atlantic Monthly*, *68*, 55–70.

Dahrendorf, R. (1959). *Class and class conflict in industrial society*. Stanford, CA: Stanford University Press.

Evangelista, M. (1999). *Unarmed forces: The transnational movement to end the cold war*. Ithaca and London: Cornell University Press.

Fischer, M. (2006). *Civil society in conflict transformation: Ambivalence, potentials and challenges* (pp. 1–33). Berlin: Berghof Research Center for Constructive Conflict Management.

Human Security Report Project. (2008). Human security brief 2007. In: A. Mack (Ed.), Vancouver, Canada: Simon Fraser University.

Kriesberg, L. (1980). Interlocking conflicts in the Middle East. In: L. Kriesberg (Ed.), *Research in social movements, conflicts and change* (pp. 99–118). Greenwich, CT: JAI Press.

Kriesberg, L. (1992). *International conflict resolution: The U.S.-USSR and Middle East cases.* New Haven: Yale University Press.

Kriesberg, L. (1995). Varieties of mediating activities and of mediators. In: J. Bercovitch (Ed.), *Resolving international conflicts* (pp. 219–233). Boulder, CO: Lynne Rienner.

Kriesberg, L. (2007). *Constructive conflicts: From escalation to resolution* (3rd ed.). Lanham, MD: Rowman & Littlefield.

Lederach, J. P. (1997). *Building peace: Sustainable reconciliation in divided societies.* Washington, DC: United States Institute of Peace Press.

Leffler, M. P. (2007). *For the soul of mankind: The United States, the Soviet Union, and the Cold War.* New York: Hill and Wang.

Mueller, J. (2006). *Overblown: How politicians and the terrorism industry inflate national security threats and why we believe them.* New York: Free Press.

Pouligny, B., Chesterman, S., & Schnabel, A. (Eds). (2007). *After mass crime: Rebuilding states and communities.* Tokyo: United Nations University Press.

Roy, B. (1994). *Some trouble with cows.* Berkeley/Los Angeles/London: University of California Press.

Simmel, G. (1955). *Conflict and the web of intergroup affiliations.* New York: Free Press.

Vivian, B. J. (2009). Rhetorical arts of praise and blame in conflict transformation. In: W. D. Bruce & L. Kriesberg (Eds), *Conflict transformation and peacebuilding: Moving from violence to sustainable peace.* Oxford, UK: Routledge.

Wright, L. (2008). *The rebellion within: An Al Qaeda mastermind questions terrorism* (pp. 36–53). New York, NY: The New Yorker.

RESEARCH AND PRACTICE IN PEACE AND CONFLICT STUDIES: DIRECTIONS FOR THE NEXT DECADE

Robert A. Rubinstein

The papers in the present volume are impressive not only for their sophistication in research methods and theory development, but also for the variety of perspectives and range of topics that they cover. Because the Program on the Analysis and Resolution of Conflicts (PARC) is located in the Maxwell School of Syracuse University, an institution that simultaneously functions as a social science graduate school and a professional school for public administration and international affairs, this variety reflects the rich resources from which it draws its student and faculty associates. A volume that displays this variety is the most appropriate way to mark the PARC's 20th anniversary.

Yet, despite the diversity displayed by the papers, there are commonalities of perspective, compassion, and optimism about how conflicts ought to be approached and how they can be managed constructively. Perhaps this is not surprising, but it is nonetheless remarkable, since the authors participated in PARC at different times during the past 20 years, and some are current students at the program. While the relative importance of the topics in the mix of work done at PARC has changed over time, there have been several constant themes in that work. During its first 20 years, PARC

Pushing the Boundaries: New Frontiers in Conflict Resolution and Collaboration
Research in Social Movements, Conflicts and Change, Volume 29, 281–293
Copyright © 2008 by Emerald Group Publishing Limited
All rights of reproduction in any form reserved
ISSN: 0163-786X/doi:10.1016/S0163-786X(08)29011-7

associates consistently worked on scholarly research and applied projects that, among other things, were committed to:

(i) the mutual relevance of theory and practice;
(ii) understanding intractable conflicts and developing mechanisms for transforming these into conflicts which can be managed constructively;
(iii) mastering and improving the skills and techniques for assisting people in dispute settlement, through negotiation, mediation, facilitation, or consensus-building;
(iv) finding approaches that support social justice and the agencies, organizations, or social movements that strive to achieve it;
(v) the application of basic understandings of conflict dynamics and processes to specific social settings and policy arenas; and
(vi) the development of ways to demonstrate, if not formally evaluate, conflict management and dispute resolution interventions.

Each of these concerns is evident in the papers in this volume. PARC associates have always acknowledged that these diverse areas of investigation are not independent of each other but are mutually relevant, and that conflict management and dispute resolution and peace studies (the areas in which our work has its roots) is multi- and interdisciplinary in essential ways. It follows naturally that the papers in this volume, and others presented at the anniversary conference, can be sorted into more than one of these domains. For instance, the papers by Keles, Coy et al., and Hemmer deal with general societywide processes through which conflicts are expressed and experienced. But they also express the interplay of theory and practice, of the narrative construction of identity and conflict, and the need to evaluate conflict management efforts. Similarly, even though the main areas of investigation in Funk-Unrau's, Pincock's, and Getha-Taylor's papers revolve around the narrative construction of conflicts and of their management, their work also directs our attention toward issues of social justice, toward ways of evaluating conflict management efforts, and toward how either directly or indirectly each bears on societywide processes. The overlapping of concerns represented in these papers is yet another hallmark of the work that PARC associates have carried out during the past 20 years.

Perhaps it is counter-intuitive to suggest, but I have always believed that good, serious interdisciplinary work requires that those who engage in it have a strong background in a discipline, so that they will have a solid point of reference. In colloquial terms, "knowing where you come from makes it possible to explore new areas." All PARC faculty associates have a disciplinary background. Student associates have either come to PARC from their discipline-specific programs, or those who were pursuing the interdisciplinary social science Ph.D. were encouraged to complete a discipline-based master's degree. The authors of the papers in this volume share this characteristic: for example, Hemmer in political science, Keles in anthropology, and Woehrle in sociology.

Rather than looking back at what PARC associates have accomplished during the past two decades, in this brief paper I want to highlight some of the directions in which I think the field of peace and conflict studies will be developing in the coming decade. Some of these directions are resonant with and connected to some of the themes in the papers in this volume. Necessarily, my perspective on the general directions and the specific work that will be important to peace and conflict studies is contextualized by my disciplinary stance as an anthropologist. That said, however, I think the general directions and the specific implementations of them will require, as always, interdisciplinary work, and thus must engage all of those concerned about the development of peace and conflict studies and peace-building. I suggest that one of the advantages of developing these areas of work will be to bring us closer to finding ways to address conflicts that are effective and efficient *and* just. Although they overlap and are mutually supportive, for purposes of exposition I divide my reflections between areas of suggested research and professional practice.

RESEARCH THEMES FOR THE NEXT DECADE

In my view, during the coming decades, research in peace and conflict studies will be characterized by work on nonstate actors, identities, structural inequalities, and multilateral action. Our interdisciplinary research in these areas will be aimed at consolidating our understandings of these factors at all levels of society, from the individual to the macro. It will then: (i) develop understandings of how the dynamics of actions at each level affect and are affected by the other levels, and (ii) develop strategies as to how to promote constructive change in these dynamics, leading to the integration of theory with practice. I turn to some brief comments on each of these areas.

Nonstate Actors

In the next decades, it will become increasingly important for peace and conflict scholars to understand the dynamics of actors "below the level of the nation state"; that is, of citizens acting as individuals and in groups to effect change. Increasingly, citizens at a variety of levels of organization, from small voluntary associations through larger, more formally organized groupings, like nongovernmental organizations and activist organizations, are involved in defining the scope and nature of conflicts in the contemporary world.

As a result, it is especially important that peace and conflict scholars develop frameworks for understanding how local groups project political authority, and how they gain standing among large groups of people and articulate these understandings through the political process. Of course, the importance of nonstate actors has not escaped the attention of peace and conflict resolution scholars. Our literature reports, for instance, considerable work on track-two diplomacy and on dialogue groups intended to find common ground between those in conflict.

However, this attention has to a significant degree been linked to exporting to non-Western audiences the technical approaches developed in the West. These technical approaches include techniques like those of principled and joint problem-solving negotiation, guidelines for mediation efforts and problem-based workshops and dialogue groups (Furlong, 2005; Mitchell & Banks, 1996; Nolan-Haley, 2001). As Nader (1991, 1995) pointed out, many of these techniques are inappropriate for non-Western settings, and they treat conflict in the public sphere as unseemly, if not unacceptable. Colson (1995) too described the continuing contentiousness of disputes for which conflict resolution techniques are not entirely adequate.

Many nonstate actors work through social movements as a way to get the issues of concern to them into public awareness, to sharpen debate, and to achieve political and personal goals (McAdams, Tarrow, & Tilly, 2001; Tilly & Tarrow, 2006). During the next decades, peace and conflict studies will need to explore even more fully the way these groups work to sharpen or exacerbate conflicts, and how these groups might be transformed into partners for constructive conflict management (Kriesberg, 2006). It will be important that this work not be constrained by the boundaries of the current cannon of conflict resolution methodologies. Rather it should elaborate new modalities for working with groups in conflict. For instance, this work will need much better understandings of how local groups accumulate and project political authority, and draw from these accounts implications for conflict management interventions.

An added dimension that must be considered when looking at nonstate actors is that as local and global processes continue to collide, identity-based conflicts also intensify, as Castells (1997) makes clear. It has long been recognized that conflicts that are rooted in people's sense of identity can be among the most difficult to transform from destructive to constructive conflicts (Kriesberg, 2006; Kriesberg, Northrup, & Thorson, 1989). While the challenges posed by identity conflicts have led to the development of some very interesting intervention strategies (see, e.g., Rothman, 1997), there is still a strong need within peace and conflict studies to work out how to take account of issues of identity in conflict interventions. This issue is further complicated in that identity conflicts are often found together with structural inequalities, thus resulting in resource conflicts.

Structural Inequalities

Nearly 40 years ago, Galtung (1969) pointed out that some people and groups suffer "preventable harm or damage to persons... where there is no actor committing the violence or where it is not meaningful to search for the actor(s); such violence emerges from the unequal distribution of power and resources... [it is] built into the structure(s)" (Weigert, 1999, p. 431), what he called "structural violence." Despite Galtung's stature in the field of peace and conflict studies, the concept of structural violence has been slow to emerge as a major analytic category for the field. Weigert (1999, p. 439) suggests some reasons for this, including that being such a broad concept it is difficult to quantify and may seem overwhelmingly daunting, thus leading to inaction.

The structural inequalities from which structural violence results are often directed at groups, rather than individuals, although it is individuals who suffer as a result. It is therefore not surprising that as identity conflicts are emerging as an especially important area for peace and conflict studies, so too is work on structural violence and inequality. Recently, for instance, structural violence served as the organizing concept for peace-building work done by Farmer (2001) and his associates in Partners in Health, first in Haiti and now in many other locations around the globe.

Structural violence is also the organizing analytic concept for work done by PARC associates through a Research Roundtable on Structural Violence, Racial and Ethnic Disparities and Conflict. This work focuses on racial and ethic disparities and the conflicts that ensue in Syracuse (Lane, 2008; Lane et al., 2004, 2008), and PARC associates have taken this approach to investigate inequalities elsewhere (Levandowski, Torrone, Porter, Isler, & Thomas, 2007).

During the next decades, conflicts resulting from structural inequalities will increasingly be intertwined with identity-based conflicts. This potent mix will affect some traditional conflicts, including those that are often being reframed as being part of "the war on terror." As well, emergent social movements such as those resisting economic globalization will be animated by these dual forces (Nash, 2005).

Multilateral Action

Addressing the conflicts resulting from structural inequalities and their associated identity and resource conflicts requires the engagement of a variety of actors and institutions. Building coalitions to intervene to transform these conflicts will become increasingly important in the next decades. Whether these conflicts are in the United States or take place elsewhere, dealing with them will increasingly involve forming alliances among many actors to effect change. In the same way that peace and conflict studies earlier addressed the need to understand the relationships among individual conflict interveners, in the next decades the field will need to come to grips with the dynamics of effective multilateral action.

Domestically, developing coalitions to address conflicts requires the effective working together of individual citizens, community-based organizations, activist social movement organizations, and agencies from all levels of government. Work done by PARC associates has illuminated how, even domestically, actors at different levels of systemic organization understand the issues in different ways (Morrissey, 2006), thus leading to conflict. This necessarily complicates efforts to work in coalitions. In relation to the homeland security, Fosher (2008) described how organizational cultures and narrative understandings of the problem at hand cause conflicts and can frustrate joint action. As Getha-Taylor (this volume) suggests, part of what is necessary to transform potential conflicts into constructive collaboration are improvements in collaborative and leadership skills. This requires that peace and conflict studies scholars develop finer-grained understandings of the dynamics of domestic coalitions.

In the current political climate under the George W. Bush administration, the United States has tended to act in an essentially unilateral fashion, often opting for military intervention to carry out the "war on terror" (but on this framing, see Collins & Glover, 2002), as in Iraq and Afghanistan; thus, the prospects for multilateral action at the international level may seem dim indeed. It is nonetheless clear that as the international community seeks to make real the norm of the "responsibility to protect" people from structural and other harms, including food shortages, abrogation of human rights and genocide, multilateral action will be increasingly important (International Commission on Intervention and State Sovereignty, 2001).

As is the case domestically, international actors too bring different understandings of what is to be done and how it should be done (Rubinstein, Keller, & Scherger, 2008). Often these differences are encoded in narratives that give meaning and purpose to the work of organizations and individuals. It is now clear that effective international multilateral action requires harmonizing diverse understandings across national and institutional boundaries (Rubinstein, 2008, pp. 51–52). Discovering reliable ways to approach this will be an important task in the next decade for peace and conflict studies researchers.

PROFESSIONAL PRACTICE DIRECTIONS

Among the professional challenges during the next decades for those working in peace and conflict studies will be developing practices that accomplish several things: (i) improved evaluation of conflict management and dispute resolution efforts; (ii) tools for augmenting and revising the conflict management and dispute resolution skills base so that the techniques are situationally, socially, and culturally appropriate; and (iii) better tracing of and accounting for the overlapping networks of stakeholders involved in conflicts and disputes.

Improved Evaluation

One of the major challenges for peace and conflict professionals has been to demonstrate the effect of their practice. Considerably detailed testimonials from participants about their experiences, rather than systematic data collection, have served as the main mode of evaluating conflict management and dispute resolution interventions. As Funk-Unrau's (this volume) paper demonstrates, this is beginning to change, and there is an emerging literature on this topic (Çuhadar, 2004; Gürkaynak, Dayton, & Paffenholz, 2008; Zelizer & Rubinstein, in preparation).

Conflict management and dispute resolution efforts have real effects, yet exactly what those effects are and how they come about are still too little understood. Asking if track-two initiatives are effective, or if dialogue groups change attitudes, or if apologies work, or if reframing is effective in transforming conflicts, is to ask questions that are too broad for useful response. Rather, in each of these areas, and in regard to other interventions including mediation and negotiation, we must ask less global and more specific questions. For this reason, Funk-Unrau's (this volume) examination of public apology in the interaction between Canadian churches and aboriginal communities, Boudreau's and Polkinghorn's (this volume) careful study of reframing in the relations between the Onondaga and the Syracuse Sheriff's Department, and Pincock's (this volume) study of the effects of intergroup dialogues on racism are all important first steps toward adequate methodologies for the evaluation of conflict interventions.

In approaching this task, peace and conflict professionals should draw inspiration from the rich field of program evaluation as they seek to better document the results of their work. In doing so, they can opt for designs that draw on quantitative research designs or on well-established qualitative procedures (Cook & Campbell, 1979; Patton, 2001), or they can profitably find models for evaluation from sibling disciplines like public health (Øvretviet, 1993). However we proceed in this effort, evaluation will become increasingly important for the field.

Contextualizing Technical Skills

Perhaps one of the most widely acknowledged observations about the toolkit of peace and conflict management professionals is that they do not yet adequately take culture into account (Avruch, 1998; Dundes Renteln, 2004). Although conflict management and dispute resolution professionals have made great efforts to engage this area, for the most part the treatment of culture is still inadequate. It tends to make use of categories of analysis that suggest static, stereotyped, and globalizing views of culture that rely on dimensional analyses of cultural differences like those developed by Hofstede (1991). Advice about cross-cultural negotiation and leadership in multinational organizations rely on these characterizations of culture (Brett, 2001; House, Hanges, Javidan, Dorfman, & Gupta, 2004).

One result of using the dimensional approach for culturally contextualizing conflict interventions is that doing so obscures rather than clarifies the fundamental differences that may arise between interveners and their clients. Some time ago, I attended a mediation training program in Europe. As part of that training, participants were given a scenario in which they as professional mediators saw that a colleague and her partner were having difficulties. The trainers asked what action the mediator should take in this regard. The trainers stressed that despite the fact that the colleague had not sought help, the professional mediator should intervene, expressing what might be called a norm of intervention. This was very different from mediation trainings I have observed in the United States, where a norm of neutrality is often articulated. I am not suggesting that one stance is better or more effective than the other; but these are differences that link to deeper cultural understandings about social relations, and such differences are not captured by dimensional models of culture.

Similarly, in interventions undertaken by the international community, such as peace and stability operations, there is a possibility that the interveners' tools are culturally inappropriate (Rubinstein, 2008, p. 118). Hohe (2003), for instance, describes how in East Timor the international community sought to develop a justice system based on Western understandings of individual responsibility, guilt, and punishment which were quite at odds with those practiced by the local populations – differences which again are obscured by the dimensional analysis of culture. As peace and conflict practitioners move into the 21st century, they must fully take on the task of revising and reevaluating their skills toolkit so that interventions are situationally and culturally appropriate.

Engaging Stakeholders

It is generally acknowledged that enduring agreements, whether those that lead to the more constructive management of conflicts or to the settlement of disputes, require that all stakeholders be involved in reaching the agreement, and that the processes by which the agreements are reached be conducted in a way that makes false consensus unlikely. Conflict interveners have become quite adept at developing dispute resolution systems that involve opportunities for wide input. In spite of these efforts, it is my impression that conflict professionals have become very good at "rounding up the usual suspects," to paraphrase Captain Renault from the film *Casablanca*, rather than getting authentic engagement and buy-in from all sectors of a community.

By this, I mean that in public policy and international dispute interventions, people who are "marginal" to their societies are not well represented in conflict transformation processes. Poor people, people of color, indigenous and displaced persons, and women all are infrequent participants and their voices are heard only dimly, if at all, in the conflict management conversations (Bouta & Frerks, 2002; Brand, 2008). Given the rising importance of social movement and activist organizations, which involve non-elites in their struggle, it is necessary for peace and conflict professionals to find ways to make their efforts more inclusive than they are currently.

The issue of engagement and inclusion also applies to conflict interventions in the United States, and not only in relation to the redress of structural inequalities which animate domestic social movements. Despite the increasingly pluralistic nature of American society, the toolkit used by dispute resolution professionals still promotes interactions and interpretation patterns that privilege those preferred in some regional cultures and within some social classes (usually identified as "upper" class). The use of these tools and techniques has the perhaps unintended effect of biasing the dispute resolution processes, creating false consensus, and disenfranchisement (Nader, 1993). For the next decade, expanding models of practice to make them more inclusive must be a major focus for conflict management and dispute resolution professionals.

CONCLUSION

The academic field of peace and conflict studies coalesced at the intersection of the small academic field of conflict studies (Schelling, 1960) and two social movements, the peace movement and alternative dispute resolution movement (Barash & Webel, 2002; Menkel-Meadow, 2005). The characteristics and dynamics of an academic discipline are much different than those of a social movement. This is so because, among other reasons, academic disciplines create areas of expert knowledge, control of which is held by accredited members of the field. Social movements, in contrast, tend to be more open (they have a more "grassroots" character), and, rather than creating bounded knowledge, they struggle to define and achieve particular social goals. For both the peace studies and alternative dispute resolution movements, one goal was the achievement of a more just society.

What happens when the competing claims of disciplinary expert knowledge meet those strivings for social justice embodied in a social movement? The outcome of such an encounter depends, of course, on many factors and historical circumstances. For peace and conflict studies, the result has been an uneasy coexistence between the drive to increase technical expertise and the desire for social justice. Indeed, it seems to me that during much of the last two decades of the 20th century, peace and conflict studies have been dominated by a drive to increase expert control so as to define increasingly efficient ways to settle disputes (Bercovitch, 1991; Druckman & Harris,

1990; Kremenyuk, 1989), sometimes without sufficient attention being paid to the justice of the settlements (Colson, 1995; Lederach, Neufeldt, & Culbertson, 2007; Nader, 1995). This is a situation that needs to be redressed. Attending to each of the areas of research and practice that I have described in this paper will help begin this rebalancing. These are essential tasks for the next decade if peace and conflict studies are to be productive areas of scholarly work, making genuine contributions to creating a more just world.

REFERENCES

Avruch, K. (1998). *Culture and conflict resolution.* Washington, DC: United States Institute of Peace Press.

Barash, D. P., & Webel, C. (2002). *Peace and conflict studies.* Thousand Oaks, CA: Sage.

Bercovitch, J. (1991). International negotiations and conflict management: The importance of prenegotiation. *Jerusalem Journal of International Relations, 13,* 7.

Bouta, T., & Frerks, G. (2002). *Women's roles in conflict prevention, conflict resolution and post-conflict reconstruction.* The Hague: Netherlands Institute of International Relations.

Brand, C. (2008, March 6). Women's conference calls for greater female role in solving conflict and poverty. *Associated Press International News* (481 words).

Brett, J. M. (2001). *Negotiating globally: How to negotiate deals, resolve disputes, and make decisions across cultures.* San Francisco, CA: Jossey-Bass.

Castells, M. (1997). *The power of identity.* Oxford: Blackwell Publishers.

Collins, J., & Glover, R. (Eds). (2002). *Collateral language: A user's guide to America's new war.* New York, NY: New York University Press.

Colson, E. (1995). The contentiousness of disputes. In: P. Caplan (Ed.), *Understanding disputes: The politics of argument.* Oxford, UK: Berg Publishers.

Cook, T. M., & Campbell, D. T. (1979). *Quasi-experimentation: Design and analysis issues for field settings.* New York, NY: Houghton Mifflin.

Çuhadar, E. (2004). *Track two diplomacy in pre-negotiation: A comparative assessment of unofficial problem-solving initiatives on water and Jerusalem in the Israeli-Palestinian conflict.* Ph.D. dissertation, Syracuse University, Syracuse, NY.

Druckman, D., & Harris, R. (1990). Alternative models of responsiveness in international negotiation. *The Journal of Conflict Resolution, 34,* 234–251.

Dundes Renteln, A. (2004). *The cultural defense.* Oxford: Oxford University Press.

Farmer, P. (2001). *Infections and inequalities: The modern plagues.* Berkeley, CA: University of California Press.

Fosher, K. (2008). *Under construction: Making homeland security at the local level.* Chicago, IL: University of Chicago Press.

Furlong, G. T. (2005). *The conflict resolution toolbox: Models and maps for analyzing, diagnosing, and resolving conflict.* Mississauga, ON: Wiley.

Galtung, J. (1969). Violence, peace, and peace research. *Journal of Peace Research, 6,* 167–191.

Gürkaynak, E.Ç., Dayton, B., & Paffenholz, T. (2008). Evaluation in conflict resolution and peacebuilding. In: D. J. D. Sandole, S. Byrne, I. Sandole-Staroste & J. Senehi (Eds), *A handbook of conflict analysis and resolution* (in press). London, UK: Routledge.

Hofstede, G. (1991). *Culture and organizations, software of the mind: Intercultural cooperation and its importance for survival.* London, UK: McGraw Hill.

Hohe, T. (2003). Justice without judiciary in East Timor. *Conflict, Security and Development, 3*, 335–357.

House, R. J., Hanges, P. J., Javidan, M., Dorfman, P. W., & Gupta, V. (Eds). (2004). *Culture, leadership, and organizations: The GLOBE study of 62 societies.* Thousand Oaks, CA: Sage Publishers.

International Commission on Intervention and State Sovereignty. (2001). *The responsibility to protect: Report of the International Commission on Intervention and State Sovereignty.* International Development Research Centre, Ottawa, ON.

Kremenyuk, V. (1989). International negotiations need a scientific approach. *International Affairs, 6*, 99.

Kriesberg, L. (2006). *Constructive conflicts: From escalation to resolution* (3rd ed.). Lanham, MD: Rowman and Littlefield.

Kriesberg, L., Northrup, T. A., & Thorson, S. (Eds). (1989). *Intractable conflicts and their transformation.* Syracuse, NY: Syracuse, University Press.

Lane, S. D. (2008). *Why are our babies dying? Pregnancy, birth and death in America.* Boulder, CO: Paradigm Publishers.

Lane, S. D., Keefe, R. H., Rubinstein, R., Levandowski, B., Webster, N., Cibula, D., Boahene, A., Dele-Michael, O., Carter, D., Jones, T., Wojtowycz, M., & Brill, J. (2008). Structural violence, urban retail markets, and low birth weight. *Health and Place, 14*, 415–423.

Lane, S. D., Rubinstein, R., Keefe, R. H., Webster, N., Cibula, D., Rosenthall, A., & Dowdell, J. (2004). Structural violence and racial disparity in HIV transmission. *Journal of Health Care for the Poor and Underserved, 15*, 319–335.

Lederach, J. P., Neufeldt, R., & Culbertson, H. (2007). *Reflective peacebuilding: A learning, monitoring and evaluating toolkit.* Notre Dame, IN: University of Notre Dame and Catholic Relief Services.

Levandowski, B., Torrone, E., Porter, K., Isler, M. R. & Thomas, J. C. (2007). Breaking the cycle: Poverty, incarceration, and sexually transmitted infections in North Carolina. In: *Cutting edge theories and recent developments in conflict resolution: A conference celebrating 20 years of the program on the analysis and resolution of conflicts.* Syracuse, NY.

McAdams, D., Tarrow, S., & Tilly, C. (2001). *Dynamics of contention.* Cambridge, UK: Cambridge University Press.

Menkel-Meadow, C. (2005). Roots and inspirations: A brief history of the foundations of dispute resolution. In: M. L. Moffitt & R. C. Bordone (Eds), *The handbook of dispute resolution.* San Francisco, CA: Jossey-Bass.

Mitchell, C., & Banks, M. (1996). *Handbook of conflict resolution: The analytic problem-solving approach.* London, UK: Pinter Publishers.

Morrissey, S. (2006). *Life strategies: Motherhood, urban poverty, and the WIC program in Syracuse, New York.* Ph.D. dissertation, Syracuse University, Syracuse, NY.

Nader, L. (1991). Harmony models in the construction of law. In: K. Avruch, P. Black & J. Scimecca (Eds), *Conflict resolution: Cross-cultural perspectives.* New York, NY: Greenwood Press.

Nader, L. (1993). Controlling processes in the practice of law: Hierarchy and pacification in the movement to reform dispute ideology. *Ohio State Journal of Dispute Resolution, 9*, 1–25.

Nader, L. (1995). Civilization and its negotiators. In: P. Caplan (Ed.), *Understanding disputes. The politics of argument*. Oxford, UK: Berg Publishers.
Nash, J. (Ed.) (2005). *Social movements: An anthropological reader*. Malden, MA: Blackwell Publishing.
Nolan-Haley, J. M. (2001). *Alternative dispute resolution in a nutshell* (2nd ed.). St. Paul, MN: West Publishing.
Øvretviet, J. (1993). *Evaluating health interventions: An introduction to evaluation of health treatments, services, policies, and organizational interventions*. Berkshire, UK: Open University Press.
Patton, M. (2001). *Qualitative research and evaluation methods* (3rd ed.). Thousand Oaks, CA: Sage.
Rothman, J. (1997). *Resolving identity-based conflicts in nations, organizations and communities*. San Francisco, CA. Jossey-Bass.
Rubinstein, R. (2008). *Peacekeeping under fire: Culture and intervention*. Boulder, CO: Paradigm Publishers.
Rubinstein, R., Keller, D. M., & Scherger, M. E. (2008). Culture and interoperability in integrated missions. *International Peacekeeping*, *15*, 540–555.
Schelling, T. C. (1960). *The strategy of conflict*. Cambridge, MA: Harvard University Press.
Tilly, C., & Tarrow, S. (2006). *Contentious politics*. Boulder, CO: Paradigm Publishers.
Weigert, K. M. (1999). Structural violence. In: L. Kurtz (Ed.), *Encyclopedia of violence, peace and conflict* (Vol. 3, pp. 431–441). San Diego, CA: Academic Press.
Zelizer, C., & Rubinstein, R. (Eds) (in preparation). *Promoting peacebuilding: Reflections from the field*. Sterling, VA: Kumarian Press.

ABOUT THE AUTHORS

Thomas E. Boudreau graduated Phi Beta Kappa, summa cum laude from Boston College. He completed his PhD in the Social Science Program in 1985 at the Maxwell School of Citizen and Public Affairs at Syracuse University. While at the Maxwell School, Boudreau was the research assistant for Donald T. Campbell, the Schweitzer Chair of the Humanities at Syracuse University. He also worked as Project Director of the Crisis Management and United Nations Research Projects at the Carnegie Council in New York City. He taught at the School of International Service at American University and the University of Pennsylvania before coming back to the Maxwell School where he currently teaches in the Political Science Department. He is also a research fellow at the Institute for Resource and Security Studies in Cambridge, MA, where he has specialized in issues of global governance, global climate change, and nonproliferation. Boudreau has written two books: *Sheathing the Sword: The U.N. Secretary-General and the Prevention of International Conflict* and *Universitas: The Social Restructuring of Undergraduate Education in the United States*. He is currently working on a third book, *The Law of Nations: Legal Order in a Violent World*. He has a special interest in interdisciplinary inquiry, especially competing epistemologies and how they contribute to interpersonal, intergroup, and international conflict.

Patrick G. Coy is associate professor of political science and director of the Center for Applied Conflict Management at Kent State University. He has published on the Catholic worker movement, community mediation, international nonviolent accompaniment, and the U.S. peace movement in *Mediation Quarterly*, *Peace and Change*, *The Sociological Quarterly*, *Social Problems*, *Sociological Perspectives*, and the *American Behavioral Scientist*. He is the editor of *A Revolution of the Heart: Essays on the Catholic Worker*, numerous volumes of *Research in Social Movements, Conflicts and Change*, and coeditor of *Social Conflicts and Collective Identities*. He received the Distinguished Teaching Award of the College of Arts and Sciences at Kent State University in 2000, and was also recently named as one of the "101 Most Dangerous Academics in America" by right-wing "pundit" David Horowitz.

Rachel Fleishman is a PhD candidate in Public Administration at the Maxwell School of Citizenship and Public Affairs. Rachel is primarily interested in collaborative environmental management, citizen participation, and interorganizational networks. Her dissertation work focuses on the water quality outcomes of collaborative governance in the Chesapeake Bay watershed. Before starting at Maxwell, she earned a Bachelors degree in Chemistry from Vassar College and a Masters degree in Natural Resources from The Ohio State University. Most recently, she was awarded the 2007–2008 Budweiser Conservation Scholarship sponsored by the US Fish and Wildlife Foundation and Anheuser-Busch. She is also the author of a book chapter entitled "To Participate or Not Participate: Incentives and Obstacles for Collaboration," which is forthcoming in the Georgetown Press book *The Collaborative Manager*.

Neil Funk-Unrau is an Assistant Professor of Conflict Resolution Studies and currently also the Coordinator of the Conflict Resolution Studies Program at Menno Simons College at the University of Winnipeg in Winnipeg, Manitoba, Canada. He received a doctorate in social science from Syracuse University in 2001. His current research interests include the use of apology processes in legal and public settings, residential school abuse dispute resolution, and related issues of the development of Canadian aboriginal versus non-aboriginal relations. In addition to writing extensively on the use of public apology processes to respond to Canadian aboriginal issues, he has lectured on this topic in Canada, the United States, and Germany.

Catherine M. Gerard serves as Associate Director of Executive Education Programs and Co-Director of the Program on the Analysis and Resolution of Conflicts at Syracuse University's Maxwell School of Citizenship and Public Affairs. As Assistant Director for the New York State Governor's Office of Employee Relations, she led consulting and training devoted to statewide organizational effectiveness. She received her MA from the University of Toronto and MPA from the Rockefeller College of Public Affairs and Policy at SUNY Albany.

Heather Getha-Taylor is an assistant professor in the Department of Political Science at the University of South Carolina. Her research and teaching interests focus on public and nonprofit management, with special emphasis on personnel administration, executive leadership, and organizational behavior. She is the 2007 recipient of the Annual Dissertation Award from the National Association of Schools of Public Affairs and

Administration and the 2006 recipient of the Volcker Junior Scholar Research Award from the American Political Science Association. She received her BA in Communications from Augusta State University and her MPA from the University of Georgia. She received her PhD in Public Administration from the Maxwell School of Citizenship and Public Affairs at Syracuse University.

Bruce Hemmer is a PhD candidate in political science at the University of California, Irvine, where he is a fellow with the Center for the Study of Democracy and the Center for Citizen Peacebuilding. His article is based on a chapter of his dissertation, entitled "The Democratization of Peacebuilding: the Political Engagement of Peacebuilding NGOs in Democratizing Societies." He previously earned a MA in International Relations at Syracuse University and a Certificate of Achievement in Conflict Resolution at its Program on the Analysis and Resolution of Conflicts (PARC). He has several years of practical experience in peacebuilding and democratization in Bosnia and Herzegovina, Kosovo, and Ethiopia, with the Organization for Security and Cooperation in Europe and several peacebuilding NGOs, including Conflict Resolution Catalysts, Peaceworkers, and the Carter Center.

Fethi Keles is a PhD student in cultural anthropology at the Maxwell School of Syracuse University. He received his BA in Translation and Interpreting from Bogazici University in 1999, and his MA in History at Fatih University in Istanbul, Turkey. Funded by the Die Zeit Foundation, Fethi's dissertation research explores the resettlement experiences of Bosnian refugees in the United States. Identity formation in diaspora, questions of cultural belonging and exclusion, forced migration and its consequences, and anthropological studies in nationalism are among his areas of substantive focus. He is broadly interested in social theory, with a focus on the agency-structure nexus, theories of practice, and stages of immigrant incorporation. Fethi has published journal articles, commentaries, and encyclopedia entries on the conflict in former Yugoslavia, political anthropological theory, modernization theory, refugee resettlement in the United States, ethnic/forced migration and refugees in the twentieth century, and the relevance of critical anthropological thought to phenomena of global scope.

Darren Kew received his PhD in International Relations from Tufts University in 2002. He studies the connection between democratic institution building in Africa and the development of political cultures that support democracy, particularly in terms of the role of civil society groups in this development. He has worked with the Council on Foreign Relations' Center for Preventative Action to provide analysis and blueprints for preventing conflicts in several areas around the world, including Nigeria, Central Africa, and Kosovo. He has also been a consultant to the United Nations, USAID, the US State Department, and to a number of NGOs, including the Carter Center in a 1999 effort by former President Carter to mediate the Niger Delta conflicts. His research interests include civil society, conflict prevention, and transnational civil society development; conflict and democracy in Africa (especially Nigeria); and culture, religion, and conflict resolution.

Louis Kriesberg (PhD, 1953, University of Chicago) is Professor Emeritus of Sociology, Maxwell Professor Emeritus of Social Conflict Studies, and founding director of the Program on the Analysis and Resolution of Conflicts (1986–1994), all at Syracuse University. In addition to over 125 book chapters and articles, his published books include *Constructive Conflicts* (1998, 2003, 2007), *International Conflict Resolution* (1992), *Timing the De-Escalation of International Conflicts* (co-ed., 1991), *Intractable Conflicts and Their Transformation* (co-ed., 1989), *Social Conflicts* (1973, 1982), *Social Inequality* (1979), *Mothers in Poverty* (1970), *Social Processes in International Relations* (ed., 1968), and *Research in Social Movements, Conflicts and Change* (ed., Vols. 1–14, 1978–1992). He was President of the Society for the Study of Social Problems (1983–1984) and he lectures, consults, and provides training regarding conflict resolution, security issues, and peace studies. His current research focuses on alternative contemporary American foreign policies, the transformation of violent conflicts, and analyses of trends in the fields of peace and conflict resolution studies. Webpage: http://faculty.maxwell.syr.edu/lkriesbe

Haleigh La Chance is the Research Associate and Director of Special Projects at the Center for Conflict Resolution (CCR) at Salisbury University. She has been a researcher at CCR for three years and teaches in the Conflict Analysis and Dispute Resolution BA program. Her primary research is in the areas of international law, refugee movements, conflict analysis and dispute resolution in higher education, women's rights, social services, court alternative dispute resolution program assessment, international conflict intervention, and conflict process and dispute systems design model building. She earned a Masters degree in International Peace and Conflict Resolution at Arcadia University.

Robert La Chance is the Managing Director and Research Associate at the Center for Conflict Resolution (CCR) at Salisbury University. He has been a mediator and a researcher at CCR for six years and teaches in the Conflict Analysis and Dispute Resolution BA program. His primary research is in the areas of conflict analysis and dispute resolution in higher education, court alternative dispute resolution program evaluation, environmental disputes, international conflict intervention, and conflict process and dispute systems design model building. He received bachelor's degrees from Salisbury University in conflict analysis and dispute resolution and philosophy. He earned a Masters degree in International Peace and Conflict Resolution from Arcadia University.

Gregory M. Maney is an associate professor of sociology at Hofstra University. He received his PhD from the University of Wisconsin-Madison in 2001. His research examines social movements (e.g., strategies, discourses, and transnational dimensions) and ethnic group relations (e.g., dynamics of conflict and factors sustaining peace processes). Articles that he either sole authored or coauthored have appeared in several journals, including the *American Journal of Sociology*, *Journal of Peace Research*, *Social Problems*, and *Sociological Methods and Research*. Together with the Workplace Project, he received a grant from the Sociological Initiatives Foundation to conduct a study assessing the human rights effects of local government responses to day labor markets. Most recently, he received a grant from the American Sociological Association's Spivack Program in Applied Social Research and Policy to examine strategies for responding to NIMBY opposition to social services for immigrants.

Rosemary O'Leary is Distinguished Professor of Public Administration and Maxwell School Advisory Board Endowed Chair at Syracuse University. She is also Co-Director of the Program on the Analysis and Resolution of Conflicts and the Collaborative Governance Initiative. An elected member of the National Academy of Public Administration, she was a senior Fulbright scholar in Malaysia and in the Philippines. O'Leary is the author or editor of 6 books and more than 100 articles and book chapters. She has won 10 national research awards and 8 teaching awards. She is the only person to win three National Association of Schools of Public Affairs and Administration awards for Best Dissertation (1989), Excellence in Teaching (1996), and Distinguished Research (2004). From 2003 to 2005 O'Leary was a member of the NASA's Return to Flight Task Group assembled in response to the Columbia space shuttle accident. She has also served as a consultant to the US Department of the Interior, the US Environmental

Protection Agency, the Indiana Department of Environmental Management, the International City/County Management Association, the National Science Foundation, and the National Academy of Sciences. In the early 1980s, she worked as an environmental attorney and as an administrator for the State of Kansas.

Marie Pace joined USIP in August 2008 as a program officer for the Center for Mediation and Conflict Resolution. She has over 10 years of international experience conducting research and working in Africa, the Middle East, the South Caucasus, and South Asia. In Nigeria, Pace served as Peace and Development Advisor for UNDP from 2005 to 2007 when she led the development of conflict prevention strategies for UNDP-Nigeria. Subsequently as a consultant to the Carter Center, she provided on-the-ground political analysis during Nigeria's April 2007 general elections and in the post-election environment. This collaborative writing project combines her Nigeria experience with her interests in qualitative research and multitrack approaches to peace building. Her dissertation was a qualitative study of a citizen diplomacy effort working to create peace and reconciliation between Arabs and Jews in the Israeli-Palestinian conflict. At the Consensus Building Institute, she facilitated strategic planning exercises for U.N. country teams in Haiti, Niger, and Congo-Brazzaville. She is the Haiti case study author for the Reflecting on Peace Practices Project with Collaborative Development Associates. From 2000 to 2005, Pace taught courses on research methods and issues of development, conflict, and gender at the University of Connecticut, Clark University, the College of the Holy Cross, and the University of Massachusetts in Boston. Pace has researched citizen peacemaking efforts in the Israeli-Palestinian conflict and studied women's experiences as agents of social change in Sri Lanka. Before returning to graduate school, from 1995 to 1997 she was lead trainer for a USAID-funded NGO training and resource center in Armenia. As a consultant for a UNIFEM project in 2003, Pace returned to the region and trained women in Armenia, Georgia, and Azerbaijan on mainstreaming gender into ongoing peace building initiatives. Pace holds an M.A. in international studies from the University of Oregon and a Ph.D. in social science from Syracuse University, where she was an affiliate with the Program on the Analysis and Resolution of Conflict (PARC).

Heather Pincock is a PhD candidate in political science at the Maxwell School of Citizenship and Public Affairs, Syracuse University and an associate with the Maxwell School's Program on the Analysis and Resolution of Conflicts (PARC). Heather is currently a graduate research fellow at the Program on Negotiation (PON) at Harvard Law School.

Brian D. Polkinghorn is the University System of Maryland Wilson Elkins Professor and Distinguished Professor of Conflict Analysis and Dispute Resolution. Since 2000 he has been the Program Director in the Department of Conflict Analysis and Dispute Resolution and Executive Director of the Center for Conflict Resolution at Salisbury University. Prior to that (1994–2000) he was a founding member of the Department of Conflict Analysis and Resolution at Nova Southeastern University. He has worked in the conflict intervention field since 1985 as a mediator, arbitrator, facilitator, trainer, researcher, academic program administrator, dispute systems designer, and ombudsman. He has also practiced in over 30 countries primarily in the areas of environmental policy dispute intervention, labor-management, and civil society training, including work for focused humanitarian assistance groups. His primary research interests are in the areas of environmental disputes, graduate program developments in the English-speaking world, court program assessment, EEOC mediation program assessment, state agency partnering and mediation programs, dispute systems design, and conflict model building. He has published primarily in the areas of conflict processes, intervention strategies, and applied research findings. He is a graduate of the Institute for Conflict Analysis and Dispute Resolution (ICAR) at George Mason University and the Program on the Analysis and Resolution of Conflicts (PARC) at Syracuse University. He was also a visiting fellow with the Program on Negotiation (PON) at Harvard University, a US Environmental Protection Agency Fellow and a United States Presidential Fellow.

Robert A. Rubinstein is professor of anthropology and international relations at the Maxwell School of Syracuse University, where from 1994 to 2005 he directed the Program on the Analysis and Resolution of Conflicts. He earned his PhD in Anthropology from SUNY Binghamton, and a MSPH from the School of Public Health of the University of Illinois at Chicago. Rubinstein has published 100 journal articles and book chapters, and has authored or edited 7 books. His most recent book, published in 2008, is *Peacekeeping Under Fire: Culture and Intervention*. His work has been supported by numerous foundations, including the Ford Foundation, National Science Foundation, the John and Flora Hewlett Foundation, the United States Institute of Peace, and the Wenner-Gren Foundation for Anthropological Research. Among his several awards and honors, Rubinstein was the recipient in 2000 of the Edward Weisband

Distinguished Alumni Award for Public Service or Contributions to Public Affairs from Binghamton University. He is the current President of the Central New York Peace Studies Consortium and serves on the board of directors of the Ploughshares Fund.

Lynne M. Woehrle is an associate professor of sociology at Mount Mary College, Milwaukee, Wisconsin, where she coordinates the Peacebuilding Certificate. She holds an M.A. from the Institute for International Peace Studies at the University of Notre Dame (1988). She completed her PhD in Social Science at Syracuse University where she also earned an M.A. in Sociology and a Certificate in Women's Studies. She is coeditor of *Social Conflicts and Collective Identities*, (2000) and coauthor of *Contesting Patriotism: U.S. Peace Movement Discourses 1990–2005* (forthcoming). She has also written and published on the topics of women and war/peace, consensus and conflict in groups, and peace education. She has held leadership positions in many scholarly organizations in both sociology and peace studies. Over the years, she has also served on the boards of and volunteered for many community organizations. Locally she is actively involved with the Candlelight Coalition, Peace Action, the Hartung Park Community Association, Growing Power, and the Greater Milwaukee Human Rights Coalition. She has a long history of working for justice and studying the processes of social change.